THE TRIUMPH OF THE HUMAN SPIRIT™

THE ATLANTA PARALYMPIC EXPERIENCE

This book was made possible by:

GOLD SPONSOR

ORTHOTIC & PROSTHETIC ATHLETE ASSISTANCE FUND INC.

OTTO BOCK ORTHOPEDIC INDUSTRY, FLEX-FOOT® INC., HANGER PROSTHETICS & ORTHOTICS

SILVER SPONSOR

SUNRISE MEDICAL, INC.

BRONZE SPONSORS

GENERAL MOTORS MOBILITY PROGRAM FOR PERSONS WITH DISABILITIES

LIFT-U/DIV. OF HOGAN MFG., INC.

PATRONS

EASTMAN KODAK COMPANY
MARGARET A. STATON
MARTA

PUBLISHED BY

DTPG

Disability Today Publishing Group INC.

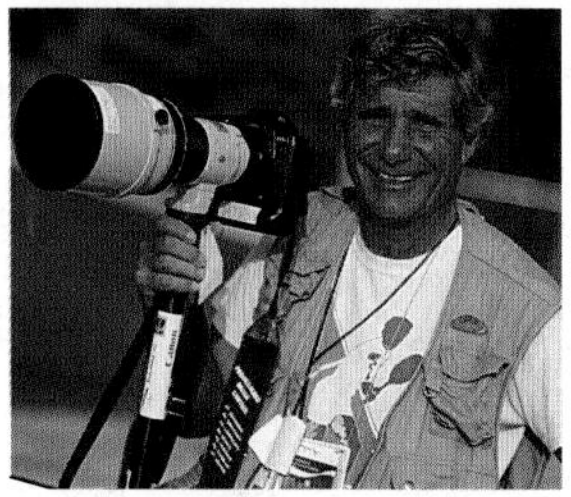

This is to salute the energy, passion and dedication of the team of photographers, writers and producers that brought this publication from concept to completion. Their commitment to the ideals of the Paralympic Movement is clearly evident in their work.

For our photographers, the story of the 1996 Paralympic Games had to be captured within the constrained time frame of ten days of competition. There were no second chances. Each assignment had to produce results, or a precious opportunity was lost. As you will sense over the following 200 pages, our inexhaustible photo team did not miss their mark.

Our photo team consisted of four individuals sharing in the common goal of upholding both the athleticism and the indomitable spirit of the Paralympic athlete. Official Paralympic Games photographer Chris Hamilton (top right) was a valuable contributor to the book's photo bank. Chris' commitment to Paralympic athletes reaches back to the 1992 Paralympics in Barcelona where his work for the Atlanta Paralympic Organizing Committee (APOC) began. The Atlanta resident's sports photography credits are countless. Notably for the Paralympic Movement, it was Chris' work upon which APOC's promotion, awareness and merchandising campaigns were built. Dan Galbraith (top left) also brought a wealth of experience to our team. The Milton, Ont. photographer specializes in corporate, sport and travel images as well as video production. Dan also covered the 1996 Olympic Games, the 1997 Winter Special Olympics as well as several Canada Games.

Bernard Gluckstein Q.C. (third from top) complemented the team with his expertise in panoramic photography and his passion for tennis coverage. The Toronto, Ont. personal injury attorney has over 35 years experience as a professional photographer. He has covered numerous international sporting events and also houses an impressive collection of travel and wildlife work from around the globe. Reginald Tiessen (second from top) rounded out the team with his artistic style of photography. With his experience in multi-media, the Windsor, Ont. teacher offered an added dimension to the remarkable group. Reginald also covered the 1992 Paralympics as well as the 1994 Winter Paralympics in Lillehammer.

Like the photographers, the authors were also circumscribed by the parameters of a ten day event. Hundreds of interviews, reports and observations were achieved through tireless pursuit of their subjects. Their research began nearly two years prior to the event, as they followed the development of the organizing committee and its many initiatives. Their chronicle of the 1996 Paralympic Games was completed as the Paralympic cauldron faded to black during the Closing Ceremony.

Kimberly Tiessen's (on right) reporting career began in news radio. Now working in print and television, the Toronto, Ont. resident was a co-writer and lead researcher of this commemorative publication. Prior to her work on the book, Kimberly served as managing editor of the Official Souvenir Program of the 1996 Paralympic Games, also produced by Disability Today Publishing Group, Inc. (DTPG). Moira Alfers (on left), a respected television producer for the Canadian Broadcasting Corporation (CBC), rounded out the book's editorial unit in Atlanta. With over six years experience in news gathering with the CBC, the Ottawa, Ont. native is also a columnist with the California-based *Inside Hockey Magazine*. Together, the duo returned from Atlanta with incredible stories of human achievement.

Once the book's text was complete and meticulously pored over by our editors, the onerous task of selecting 200 photos from a collection of over 10,000 for publication was at hand. That process preceded the publication's layout and design, both masterfully directed by Norm Lourenco of Toronto, Ont. As Art Director at DTPG, Norm's experience in the treatment of images of persons with a disability in print was invaluable to this project.

Disability Today Publishing Group, Inc.
627 Lyons Lane, Suite #203
Oakville, Ontario, Canada L6J 5Z7

Tel: 905.338.6894
Fax: 905.338.1836

Canadian Cataloguing in Publication Data

Triumph of the Human Spirit - The Atlanta Paralympic Experience
ISBN 0-9680667-2-0

Printed and bound in Canada

SPECIAL SALES

Triumph of the Human Spirit - The Atlanta Paralympic Experience, is available at special discounts for bulk purchases for sales promotions or premiums. For more information, contact Disability Today Publishing Group, Inc. at: 800.725.7136.

PUBLISHER & EDITOR:
Jeffrey A. Tiessen

ASSOCIATE EDITOR:
Brenda McCarthy

PRODUCTION ASSISTANTS:
Karen Penner, Laurene Hildebrandt

ART DIRECTION & DESIGN:
Norm Lourenco

SPONSORSHIP MARKETING:
Rachel Marionneaux, Carew & Marionneaux
Atlanta, GA

DJR Communications Group Inc.
Toronto, ON

Contents

THE TRIUMPH OF THE HUMAN SPIRIT

In 1992, I resided in what I believe was an ideal living environment. Although short-lived, I was part of a neighborhood comprised of 85 kingdoms. My 4,000 neighbors hailed from every corner of the world. Outside of our community we embraced our own political and religious convictions, our own philosophies and our own way of doing things. But inside, we banded together in the spirit of friendship and competition. We came together to represent our own nations, but to do it within the ideals of the Paralympic Games.

Fortunate enough to live in Paralympic Villages on three different continents as a three-time member of the Canadian Paralympic Team, I, like the athletes in Atlanta, have been afforded experiences of a lifetime. The affection that the partisan crowds have for their country's beloved athletes is always something to be beheld. The admiration they have for all athletes is moving. The appreciation they have for our athletic abilities is rewarding.

Now, as a publisher working in the business of social change for people with disabilities, the Paralympic Games take on even greater meaning. The Paralympic Games provide the vehicle to present the most dynamic and visible expression of the capabilities of people with disabilities that the world has ever seen. The Paralympic Games present an opportunity to change many myths and stereotypes about disabled persons that have been ingrained in our society and culture for many years. This international event reinforces the work of many where issues such as accessibility, employment, transportation and recreation for those with disabilities are concerned. These games can change society's perception of what it means to have a disability.

With the elevation of the status of the Paralympic athlete in our society, this athlete, not unlike the Olympic athlete, is being given tremendous potential to shape attitudes and promote awareness for a sport, a country and an issue. Society has begun to deem them ambassadors of their segment of the population. This summer, as the media focused on the accomplishments of these athletes, all persons with a disability benefitted from the awareness afforded to their triumphant spirit. The message was sent - having a disability does not preclude a full and active lifestyle; if one has the desire and the ability, much can be accomplished in life.

We at Disability Today Publishing Group are very proud to support the efforts of Paralympic athletes worldwide. *THE TRIUMPH OF THE HUMAN SPIRIT - The Official Commemorative Book of the 1996 Atlanta Paralympic Games* serves as the legacy publication for the Atlanta Paralympic Organizing Committee and a tribute to the dedicated athletes, coaches and officials who came from around the globe to be their best in Atlanta. Their pursuit of excellence inspires the human spirit in all of us.

Jeffrey A. Tiessen
President & Publisher, Disability Today Publishing Group, Inc.
Official Licensee of the 1996 Atlanta Paralympic Games

On behalf of the International Paralympic Committee (IPC), I wish to extend my sincere thanks to the City of Atlanta and the State of Georgia, for hosting the 1996 Summer Paralympic Games; and, to the American people, for exhibiting their enthusiasm and encouragement towards the success of this historic event. The final Summer Paralympic Games staged in this century provided an unparalleled archetype for Games in the next millennium.

The IPC is grateful to all members of the Atlanta Paralympic Organizing Committee who made an extraordinary effort to ensure that the best possible environment and opportunity were available for our athletes to excel. We express our profound thanks also to the thousands of volunteers involved, without whom the Xth Games of the Paralympiad would not have been possible. Their time, their work, and their enthusiastic interest in the Paralympic Movement is most sincerely appreciated.

To our athletes...in your quest for personal bests and medal performances, for yourself, your sport and your nation, you competed in the spirit of fair play, and you realized championship rewards from years of grueling and dedicated preparation. By producing over 200 world records in Atlanta, you became more than sport competitors, you were ambassadors; and, the IPC is proud to honour the essential role you played in setting the standard for future Paralympians.

Yours very truly,

Dr. Robert D. Steadward
President, International Paralympic Committee

The Triumph of the Human Spirit

In the beginning, there was a dream – a dream that inspired and motivated us to believe that we could contribute something lasting to a global movement seeking recognition and equality at the highest levels of sport.

In 1992, our dream became a mission – to help the International Paralympic Committee and the entire Paralympic Movement achieve its goals by conducting the most successful Paralympics in history and by leaving a legacy worthy of the aspirations of athletes with physical disabilities the world over.

At its moment of destiny, the 1996 Atlanta Paralympic Games lived up to our dream. Through the tireless devotion of thousands of volunteers, through the generosity of our family of corporate sponsors, donors and public agencies, through the professional and personal sacrifices of the staff of the organizing committee, and, most of all, through the brilliant performances of the world's elite Paralympic athletes, the 1996 Paralympics were a resounding *Triumph of the Human Spirit.*

No one touched by these Games will ever be the same. Although they are now a part of history, this magnificent volume recounts the moments of greatness and glory that will stand forever as the rich and rewarding legacy the Games and their heroes left behind.

From the spectacular Opening Ceremony – and the symbolically magnificent climb of the flame by Paralympian Mark Wellman – to the rocking ending of the Closing Ceremony, the 1996 Atlanta Paralympic Games made an indelible impression in the memories of millions.

To all those who turned this event from a moment of history to a date with destiny, we wish to express our deepest appreciation and heartfelt gratitude. The future of the International Paralympic Movement has been strengthened by what you did and why you gave of yourselves.

No matter where our lives take us, from this time forward we shall know that all things are possible – because we have beheld *The Triumph of the Human Spirit.*

Harald Hansen
Chairman, APOC

G. Andrew Fleming
President & Chief Executive Officer

On behalf of the sponsors, volunteers, members of the board of directors and staff of the Orthotic & Prosthetic Athlete Assistance Fund Inc. (dba. O&P Athletic Fund), I want to extend our sincere appreciation to the Atlanta Paralympic Organizing Committee for staging an exceptional event for the athletes of the Xth Paralympiad. The O&P Athletic Fund was proud to serve as the "Official Provider of O&P Services for the 1996 Atlanta Paralympic Games".

With the support of the entire O&P profession, the O&P Athletic Fund was able to provide on-site repairs for the athletes who wore orthotic or prosthetic devices. Our goal was to ensure that no athlete would miss out on his or her chance to compete for a medal because of a technical problem with a device. O&P professionals even came to the assistance of some Paralympic coaches and spectators. With more than 300 O&P repairs completed during the games, every athlete had a chance to make it to the starting line with the hope of earning a spot on the medal stand.

In addition to our logistical support, the O&P Athletic Fund launched an education and awareness campaign to help change attitudes about people who have disabilities and to recruit new athletes into the disabled sports arena. The 1996 Atlanta Paralympic Games and its associated outreach programs set the stage to continue disability awareness and make great strides in the disabled sports movement.

In order to continue the momentum created in Atlanta, the O&P Athletic Fund has now teamed up with Disabled Sports USA (DS/USA) to continue to promote sports opportunities for everybody. The O&P Initiative 2000 will build on the momentum achieved for disabled sports as a result of the O&P Athletic Fund's sponsorship of the games. O&P and DS/USA will continue educational and public relations initiatives and support programs for elite and recreational amputee and orthopedically impaired athletes. The O&P Athletic Fund is working to build stronger people through greater opportunities.

Being part of the first Paralympic Games staged entirely on American soil, the O&P Athletic Fund hopes the abilities of the athletes with disabilities opened the eyes of the more than 49 million Americans with disabilities and changed many hearts, minds and attitudes about people who have disabilities. The achievements of the Paralympic athletes in Atlanta have inspired others to strive to be their personal best and realize that there are no limits! We see the Paralympic Games as an important first step in an effort to make sports and recreational activities available to everyone.

Julie M. Gaydos, Executive Director
Orthotic & Prosthetic Athlete Assistance Fund Inc.

Breaking New Ground

A TRIBUTE TO CHAMPIONS

While billions of people around the world watched the Olympic cauldron fade to black to conclude the 1996 Centennial Olympic Games, over three thousand of the world's best athletes were still preparing for their trip to Atlanta. They too were coming to Atlanta to compete for gold and glory. But this time it would be Atlanta's Paralympic Games providing the international stage. This time it was *The Triumph of the Human Spirit* that would entertain and inspire.

Like the 1996 Olympics, Atlanta's Paralympic Games established a host of precedents. What the Atlanta Paralympic Games did better than any of the other Paralympic cities was to magnify the desire of these athletes to be received as serious competitors. Atlanta was the place to come to break records and rewrite the parameters of Paralympic competition. Atlanta was the place where the standards for fast and high and strong were redefined for elite athletes with a physical disability.

The records tumbled like never before. American Tony Volpentest ran an amazing 11.36-second 100 metres on a pair of prosthetic feet. Visually impaired German swimmer Yvonne Hopf shaved two seconds off the world record in the women's 100 metre freestyle event, finishing in just under one minute. In all, more than 200 world and Paralympic records fell during the ten days of competition – more than at any other Paralympic Games. The unprecedented pace of broken records was a result of better training for the athletes, a growing number of competitors, technological advances and more countries providing programs for athletes with a disability.

The Paralympics have grown alongside a disability movement that encompasses a wide variety of limitations – paralysis, visual impairment, amputation, cerebral palsy and others. The concept for the games began in England in 1948 to provide athletic therapy for persons in wheelchairs. Held at Stoke Mandeville Hospital in Aylesbury with just a few athletes, the events were more about enhancing the quality of life for people with spinal cord injuries than about competition. Twelve years later, the first Paralympic Games were held in Rome with 400 ath-

BERNARD GLUCKSTEIN

letes from 23 countries taking part. Athletes competed in archery, basketball, fencing, javelin, shotput and three swimming events.

Though the Paralympic Games began in Italy in 1960, the disabled sporting world traces the real start of the Paralympic Movement to Seoul, South Korea, in 1988, when the Paralympians' commitment and training earned them recognition as true athletes. The Paralympic Movement reached a number of benchmarks in Atlanta, said Canada's Dr. Robert Steadward, president of the International Paralympic Committee. These Paralympic Games had more television coverage than ever before. CBS carried four hours of paid coverage while SportSouth broadcast daily highlights. More than 40 countries bought the rights to televise the games abroad. Significant private sponsorship saw corporations pour over $39 million into the Paralympics. A spike in media attention brought more than 2,000 journalists from around the world to the Paralympics in Atlanta. These games also shattered attendance records for disabled sporting events in America. Moreover, these spectators were the first in the history of the Paralympic Games to pay for tickets. The Atlanta Paralympic Organizing Committee (APOC) attached a new value to the games by selling tickets to all events and both the Opening and Closing Ceremony. Over 700,000 tickets were sold.

Andrew Fleming, APOC president and chief executive officer, expressed that one of the most significant legacies of the Atlanta Paralympic Games will be one that is difficult to measure – the change in attitude toward people with disabilities among able-bodied people who attended the competitions. "People were moved by what they saw and what they were a part of," he enthused. When he remembers the 1996 Paralympic Games, Fleming said he'll remember the looks on the faces of people who watched the events for the first time and turned to him in amazement.

THE AMERICAN PARALYMPIC DREAM

On September 18, 1990, the world waited anxiously for the International Olympic Committee's announcement on the selection of the site for the 1996 Centennial Olympic Games. Juan Antonio Samaranch, president of the International Olympic Committee, made it official. "The City of At-lan-tuh." As the news sped across the airwaves, the incredible anticipation of the past months gave way to jubilation in the United States. The 1996 Olympic Games were coming to America.

But the fate of the 1996 Paralympic Games was yet to be determined. Until the announcement that the Olympic Games would be held in Atlanta in 1996, the American Paralympic Movement had given little attention to the possibility of hosting the Paralympics in the United States as well. The announcement garnered worldwide expectation that the 1996 Paralympic Games, like the Seoul Paralympics in 1988 and the soon-to-be-held Barcelona Paralympics in 1992, would be hosted in the same city and in many of the same venues as the Centennial Olympic Games.

The United States Olympic Committee empowered its own Committee on Sports for the Disabled (USOC-COSD) with readily pulling together a Paralympic Task Force, including representatives from each of the national disabled sports organizations (DSOs). In short time, the task force determined that the Atlanta Committee for the Olympic Games (ACOG) should also stage the Paralympics. A proposal from members of the task force and the president of the International Paralympic Committee (IPC) was made to senior ACOG executives requesting that ACOG create a division within its organization to assume full responsibility for the Paralympics. Also involved in the presentation were senior staff members of The Shepherd Center, a specialty hospital based in Atlanta, that would later become the Founding Sponsor of the 1996 Paralympic Games. The presentation group would later form the nucleus of the Atlanta Paralympic Organizing Committee (APOC).

In early January of 1992, ACOG made their decision not to assume the additional burden of staging the Paralympic Games, but instead to support a separate Paralympic organizing committee and to become that committee's first sponsor, furnishing it with critical contributions of value-in-kind goods and services (VIK) and sponsorship revenue. Within weeks of ACOG's pledge, the Atlanta Paralympic Organizing Committee was officially chartered as a nonprofit corporation. APOC's first major challenge would be to prepare and submit a bid to the IPC for Atlanta to be selected as host of the 1996 Paralympic Games. As an all-volunteer effort, the costs associated with this endeavor were supported by The Shepherd Center. The bid was favorably received by the IPC during the 1992 Winter Paralympics in Tignes, France and the Summer Paralympics were awarded to Atlanta on March 29, 1992.

Many of the members of the original task force stayed on to lead the Atlanta effort. Harald Hansen, chairman of the First Union National Bank of Georgia and a director of The Shepherd Center, was asked to chair APOC's Board of Directors. Andrew Fleming, selected by the USOC-COSD to chair the Paralympic Task Force, agreed to leave his position as director of sports and recreation programs with the Paralyzed Veterans of America (PVA) to serve as APOC's president and chief executive officer. Warren Quinley, a senior certified public accountant and Shepherd Center director agreed to assume one of the most sensitive and strategic APOC roles – that of chief financial officer. Michael Mushett, also of the task force and then executive director of the U.S. Cerebral Palsy Athletic Association, came to APOC as senior vice president in charge of Paralympic Games Operations. Barb Trader, a Shepherd Center staff member would serve as vice president of Youth & Education Programs.

BERNARD GLUCKSTEIN

FACING THE CHALLENGE

The mission statement adopted by APOC was simple in its wording, but daunting in its commitment. The committee embarked on a mission to conduct the most successful Paralympics in history and subsequently, leave a legacy for the Paralympic Movement. For all the individuals who came together to bring this mission to fruition, including the thousands of unfailing volunteers, these words provided a bonding force.

Upon its inception, three very significant and immediate challenges confronted the organizing committee. The first would be one of establishing the credibility of Paralympic competitors as elite athletes within the American conscience. Secondly, APOC would need to immediately begin to create an identity – for the athletes and for the Paralympic Movement – that the general populace, the media and potential sponsors would support. And the third, and possibly the greatest given the limited resources that would be available, would be that of heightening the visibility of the athletes to create broad public interest in the Paralympics whereby the value of an association with the event for corporate, government and individual supporters would be recognized.

APOC officially opened its operations in February, 1993 with a small staff of six. The committee began the mammoth assignment of staging the 1996 Paralympic Games by implementing their marketing plan, targeting major corporations that had already announced their Olympic sponsorships. The Coca-Cola Company was the first to respond with a commitment, becoming the first Official Worldwide Sponsor of the 1996 Paralympic Games. The visible support of Coca-Cola at a sponsorship level enjoyed only by a handful of sports properties significantly aided the credibility of the Paralympic Movement within the private sector, setting the standard for other Olympic sponsors. Shortly thereafter, the IBM Corporation, The Home Depot and Sunrise Medical, Inc. validated the credibility of a business association with the Paralympics with sponsorship agreements. By the end of 1994, several other sponsors were confirmed and negotiations were moving forward, albeit slowly, with further prospective sponsors and suppliers.

Astutely, APOC readily became aware that operating capital was – and would remain – a very scarce commodity. It was clear that other potential opportunities for support would be necessary. A strategy to cultivate vital philanthropic and government support was generated. In 1993, a $1 million grant from the Joseph B. Whitehead Foundation established the credibility of the philanthropic program in much the same way that Coca-Cola's early support launched the sponsorship program. APOC secured Dr. Jimmy Callaway, a nationally-recognized community relations professional, to lead its philanthropic initiative as vice president of governmental and philanthropic programs. That same year, APOC opened an office in Washington, D.C. in order to explore opportunities for federal funding for the games and related educational programs. Under the leadership of Sagamore Associates, the Washington office worked to match the requirements of the games and related programs with the missions of various federal agencies. The success of this program was instrumental to the success of the 1996 Paralympic Games, providing more than one third of the financial support for the event.

As APOC passed the "three years to go" mark, the marketing efforts for the event were being marshalled by seasoned executive Chuck Edwards, APOC's senior vice president of marketing services. Other key areas were also being organized and staffed. Kay Branch McKenzie, a respected public relations professional, was brought aboard as vice president of communications and creative services to direct the initiatives that would establish a visibility and awareness of the Paralympics that was critically important to the success of so many other aspects of the event. Annette Quinn, a highly-experienced corporate attorney, would round out the senior executive team to oversee the contractual and general corporate aspects of APOC.

With the business side of APOC up and running, attention was quickly turned to the staffing and planning of sports and venues operations. The operational planning involved determining the site of the Paralympic Village and competition venues, defining the technology platform, producing the entry system for the complex competition schedule, as well as the implementation of the volunteer recruitment strategy that would produce the 10,000 volunteers so lauded by athletes and spectators alike. An experienced team of individuals was crucial to the management of games operations. Xavier Gonzalez, an associate director of sports at the 1992 Paralympics in Barcelona was recruited to serve as APOC's vice president of sports. John Schwartz, a senior IBM retiree, was brought on as vice president of technology. Grant Peacock assumed the position of senior program director for venue operations while Fred Koch managed the competition planning. The assembling of the operational team was completed in 1995 with the addition of Joe Fredossa and Connie Israel. With extensive experience with the Goodwill Games, the duo joined APOC to manage logistics and support operations up to and throughout the games.

With "one year to go", the pivotal senior executive position of chief operating officer was created. David Simmons, who had supervised the highly successful Los Angeles venue during the 1994 World Soccer Cup, would manage the production of the games, affording the committee's president more time for resource acquisition, public relations and protocol.

STAYING THE COURSE

With the advent of 1996, the year of the games, APOC's marketing efforts shifted in priority from sponsorship generation to promotional support for ticket sales for the Opening Ceremony and athletic events. The ticket marketing program was driven by an extensive print and electronic media campaign crafted around a handful of Paralympians who were representative of the larger Paralympic experience. The push was to attain a sell-out for the Opening Ceremony which could fuel ticket sales to the sporting events throughout the ten days of competition.

The youth and education program was another effective vehicle for outreach to the community and a force for mobilizing family participation during the games. By the summer of 1996, APOC's Paralympic Day in the Schools initiative was presented to more than 300,000 school children.

As the Paralympics had never been televised in the United States, a mainstream broadcast network or cable operator that was willing to pay a rights fee or underwrite any costs of producing coverage of the games was difficult to secure. Instead, APOC purchased four hours of national broadcast time on the CBS network and ten hours on a regional cable network, with a rebroadcast arrangement with a national cable carrier. These costs were offset by revenue derived from the sale of commercial units on the national and regional coverage. A one-hour nightly international broadcast was carried in approximately 40 nations, with the costs being covered by the sale of rights to the international broadcasters. Additionally, a daily three-minute news feed was available via satellite for any broadcaster. It is estimated that a total audience of more than 50 million persons witnessed the 1996 Paralympic Games by way of these feeds.

THE DREAM FULFILLED

On August 6, 1996, several hundred dignitaries and APOC supporters gathered at the tomb of Dr. Martin Luther King, Jr. to light the Paralympic Torch from the eternal flame that to the world symbolizes equality for all people. The following day the President of the United States, Bill Clinton, welcomed the United States Paralympic Team, APOC executives, sponsors and hundreds of Paralympic supporters to a ceremony that would kick-off the 1996 NationsBank Paralympic Torch Relay. Over the next ten days, the Relay moved its way down the east coast, continuously building momentum for its jubilant arrival in Atlanta on August 15th. That evening, the entrance of the Paralympic Torch into Olympic Stadium culminated years of preparation with the most dramatic lighting of the Paralympic Cauldron ever witnessed. The Opening Ceremony, played to a sold-out arena, set the stage for a ten-day athletic competition that was unprecedented in its assault on the record books.

The 1996 Paralympic Games met its mission. On many levels, these Paralympic Games were the most successful games in Paralympic history. New ground was broken in the areas of funding, television and media coverage, ticket sales, and numbers and performance levels of the athletes. Herein, the 1996 Paralympic Games have left their legacy for the Paralympic Movement. Through heightened awareness of the Movement among persons not only in America but around the world, the powerful and far-reaching respect for the athletes and their performances will have its effects across many borders, boundaries and barriers.

Paralympic History

The late Sir Ludwig Guttmann

The development of sport for athletes with a disability has come a very long way in a relatively short period of time. It is remarkable to think that the Paralympic Games, the world's second largest sporting competition in 1996 – second only to the Olympic Games – had its humble beginnings less than 50 years ago in Stoke Mandeville Hospital in Aylesbury, England. The early beginnings of the Paralympic Games can be traced back to World War II and the efforts of one man, an English neurosurgeon named Sir Ludwig Guttmann. Known as the "Father of Sport for Disabled Persons", Sir Guttmann was a strong advocate of sports therapy to enhance the quality of life for people who were injured or wounded as a result of their involvement in the War.

Sir Guttmann organized the 1948 International Wheelchair Games to coincide with the 1948 London Olympics. It was his dream that a world-wide sports competition for people with disabilities be held every four years, as "the disabled men's and women's equivalent of the Olympic Games." It was twelve years later that his dream became a reality.

A deliberate attempt to connect the Olympics and Paralympics was not made again until 1960, when the first Paralympic Games were held in Rome, Italy, just a few weeks after the Rome Olympics. The competition involved 400 athletes from 23 countries. Only athletes in wheelchairs competed, but the Paralympic Movement was born and Sir Guttmann was saluted by Pope Paul XXIII who compared him to the founder of the modern Olympic Games by declaring, "You are the de Coubertin of the paralyzed."

Since Rome, the Paralympic Games have grown dramatically. The Paralympic and Olympic Games have shared the same city three times in the past (Tokyo 1968, Seoul 1988, Barcelona 1992) and now a fourth time in Atlanta. They have shared the same country on three other occasions (Germany 1972, Canada 1976, United States 1984).

The IInd Paralympiad, held in Tokyo in 1964, was supported by Japan's Royal Family. The organizing committee planned the event meticulously, including an independent Athlete Village for the first time. These were the first Paralympic Games to have a Paralympic flag, anthem and poster. The 1964 Paralympics also served as the impetus for the founding of the International Sports Organization for the Disabled (ISOD).

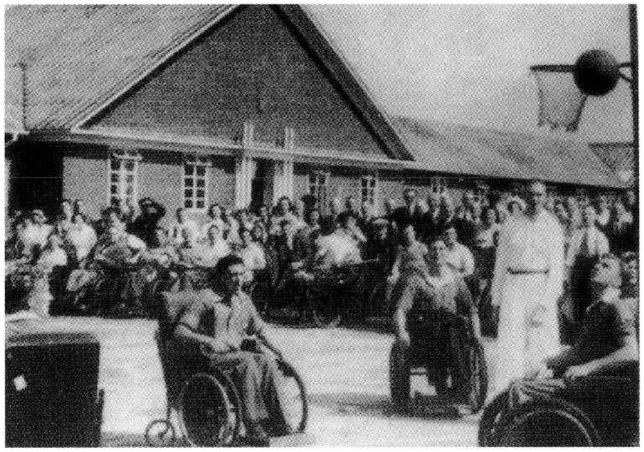

As the Paralympic Movement grew, other classes of athletes began to participate. The 1976 Paralympic Games in Toronto were the first to include amputees and athletes who are blind or have a visual impairment. Athletes with cerebral palsy first participated in the 1980 Paralympic Games in Arnhem, Holland. Accordingly, separate organizations for athletes with disabilities other than spinal cord injury were formed.

In 1982, the International Coordinating Committee of World Sport Organizations for the Disabled (ICC) was established to govern the Paralympics and represent the Paralympic ideals in dialogue with the International Olympic Committee (IOC). The 1984 Paralympic Games were the first to benefit from the centralized control of a single international body.

In succession, the 1988 Paralympic Games in Seoul, Korea and then the 1992 Paralympics in Barcelona, Spain were heralded as the most ambitious and successful events in Paralympic history. Each benefitted from the host Olympic Organizing Committee's involvement in staging the event. Each attracted record-setting numbers of athletes, participating nations, media coverage and fanfare. Barcelona boasts sell-out crowds at 46 events with a total ten day draw of 1.3 million spectators. In conjunction with the 1992 Paralympics, the ICC was replaced by a new governing

Above: 1988 Seoul Paralympic Games

Opposite page: 1992 Barcelona Paralympic Games

body, the International Paralympic Committee (IPC), which includes more than 120 member nations as well as the international federations that represent different disability groups. The Paralympic Movement continued its gains. The Paralympic Games are now considered the most revered and respected competitive event for elite athletes with physical disabilities.

In 1996, it was Atlanta's turn to forward the Movement. An unprecedented number of nations (104) and athletes (3,310) participated in the Paralympics in Atlanta. After the IPC's decision to award Atlanta the right to host the 1996 Paralympic Games, IPC president Dr. Robert Steadward said, "Atlanta's legacy of civil rights and its status as the Olympic city, coupled with the United States's commitment to a level playing field for all, will make the Xth Paralympiad a truly memorable event for the elite disabled athletes of the world."

The Atlanta Paralympic Organizing Committee also provided an unprecedented level of cultural, educational, merchandising and motivational programming in association with the event, forwarding the Paralympic Movement toward a greater world-wide acceptance of all people with a disability.

Sir Ludwig Guttmann died in 1980, but his vision of sport for athletes with disabilities continues on. Clearly, the value of sport for athletes with a disability extends far beyond the rehabilitative benefits out of which it was born.

Past Paralympic Games
DELEGATIONS AND PARTICIPANTS

PARALYMPIC GAMES		ATHLETES & SUPPORT STAFF	DELEGATIONS
1960	I Rome, Italy	400	23
1964	II Tokyo, Japan	390	22
1968	III Tel Aviv, Israel	1,100	29
1972	IV Heidelberg, Germany	1,400	44
1976	V Toronto, Canada	2,700	42
1980	VI Arnhem, Holland	2,560	42
1984	VII New York, USA	1,700	41
	VII Stoke Mandeville, England	2,300	45
1988	VIII Seoul, Korea	4,200	62
1992	IX Barcelona, Spain	4,158	83
1996	X Atlanta, USA	4,912	104

126
2

Celebration

OPENING CEREMONY

It was only 80 feet of rope from catwalk to cauldron, but Mark Wellman said his Paralympic flame-lighting climb was just as thrilling as his 1989 assault of a 3,570-foot sheer rockface called El Capitan. "This was more like a climbing stunt, but much more symbolic," said Wellman, a 36-year-old former Yosemite National Park ranger paralyzed from the waist down by a 50-foot fall from California's Seven Gables peak 14 years ago.

Pumped by the Paralympic effort, the climber said he did not even hear the roar of the capacity crowd below him. Lighting the torch like a "sign of victory," he took in the flood of support with a pump of his fist. He clearly embodied what the 1996 Paralympic Games were all about – *The Triumph of the Human Spirit.* That spirit filled the souls of every athlete, spectator, performer and dignitary in attendance at the Opening Ceremony of the 1996 Atlanta Parlaympic Games.

It was eight p.m. on the evening of August 15th when Teddy Pendergrass wheeled onto the stage and belted out the Star Spangled Banner to a packed Olympic Stadium. A paraplegic as a result of a 1982 automobile collision, Pendergrass performed a moving rendition of America's national anthem. It served as a mere glimpse of what was yet to come.

DANIEL GALBRAITH

REGINALD TIESSEN

REGINALD TIESSEN

DANIEL GALBRAITH

© CHRIS HAMILTON PHOTOGRAPHY, ATLANTA GA.

When a bald eagle, released from the top of the yet-to-be-lit cauldron, magnificently soared across the length of the stadium and slowly circled the flag pole where the red, white and blue colors of Old Glory gently danced in the breeze, the crowd simply watched in amazement. As the symbolic bird ultimately sought out the arm of its trainer 200 metres from its initial perch, all those in attendance knew they were to be part of a very special evening.

In short time, all eyes gazing skyward again, the Golden Knights were falling from the sky. The team of 14 U.S. Army parachuters targeted a child-formed

REGINALD TIESSEN

REGINALD TIESSEN

© CHRIS HAMILTON PHOTOGRAPHY, ATLANTA GA.

Paralympic star into which they would make their Stadium entrance. Dana Bowman was the focus of attention; his parachute was adorned with the Paralympic Starfire symbol. What's more, Bowman is a double leg amputee, the result of a parachuting accident in 1994. The crowd roared with admiration as he gracefully landed in the center of the stadium-floor star.

The excitement continued to build when thousands of children and young adults dressed in brilliant costumes flooded the stadium. The various raiment portrayed the distinctive cultures of the participating nations. The rambunctious youngsters were followed by the Parade of Nations. Each team proudly brandished their respective flags, patriotically representing their countries. When the huge American team entered the stadium, the partisan crowd went wild. The arrival of the 322 U.S. athletes, their coaches and staff, all dressed in red and white striped shirts, brought the stadium roar to new heights.

A flood of yellow followed as 5,000 Gospel singers poured into the aisles of the stadium stands and onto the field. The Queen of Soul, Aretha Franklin, took center stage launching into a powerful rendition of

REGINALD TIESSEN

"Oh Holy Day". The scene was breathtaking.

The show was designed to transcend its tiny budget with size and spirit. The high school students comprising the marching bands bought their own costumes. The dancers volunteered from local dance studios and some props were reused from the 1996

ABOVE: from left to right - APOC president Andrew Fleming, U.S. Vice President Al Gore, IPC president Dr. Robert Steadward

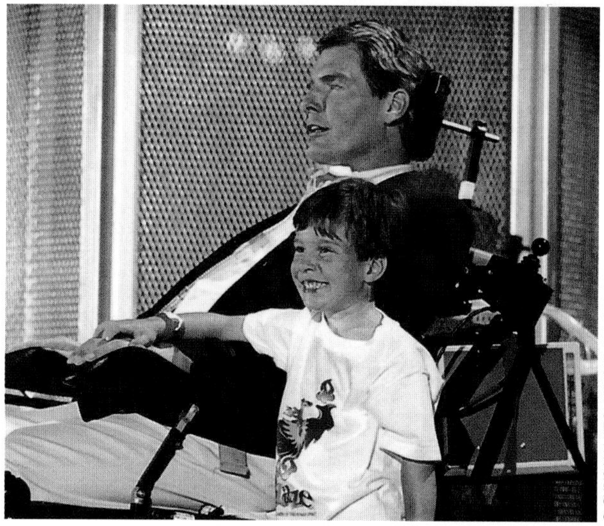

"Voice of Spirit" Christopher Reeve and son

© CHRIS HAMILTON PHOTOGRAPHY, ATLANTA GA.

Olympic Games ceremony. The cast for the evening's performances consisted of thousands of committed volunteers.

"To be surrounded by people who believe in you is one of life's most precious gifts," actor Christopher Reeve told the crowd of 64,588. "Look around you and see how many people believe in you," he said to the athletes. Reeve, paralyzed from a horse-riding injury in 1995, served as the "Voice of Spirit" for the ceremony, appearing on stage on several occasions. Reeve introduced each segment of the show in sentences that could only last about three seconds, giving his ventilator time to refill his lungs with air. He introduced video clips of Sir Ludwig Guttmann, founder of the Paralympic Games, U.S. Presidents John F. Kennedy and Franklin Roosevelt and civil rights leader Dr. Martin Luther King, Jr. to augment his message of equality and opportunity for all.

Dignitaries took to the podium to address the jubliant assembly. Atlanta Paralympic Organizing Committee president Andrew Fleming began: "May this celebration be everything we have hoped for. May it transcend this historic crossroads, and elevate the athletes and the Movement to a new level of prominence and respect." Fleming concluded with some powerful thoughts directed to those who remained unfamiliar with the mission of the Paralympic Games. "This is not about excuses. This is about victory. This is not about separation. This is about inclusion. This is about equality. It is about excellence. It is about indomitable will. It is about *The Triumph of the Human Spirit.*" The crowd responded with delight.

President of the International Paralympic Committee, Dr. Robert Steadward, was next to address the audience. Speaking directly to the athletes he said, "Now is the time for the best performances ever. The next ten days belong to you and your dreams. Our Paralympic Games are a gleam of splendor across what is sometimes a troubled story of our time. Sport alone cannot bring about a world of peace; but the unity of purpose, friendship and the spirit of fair play which accompanies any championship endeavor will help to plant the seed of hope. It will require the dedication of all of us to strive toward peace, globalization and solidarity for the people and nations of the world, and will be rewarded with a vision of the future that is unclouded, where dreams are fulfilled. Good luck to each and every athlete in your pursuit of excellence."

Darkness had set over the southern sky and the Paralympic torch was approaching Olympic Stadium. But first the Paralympic Games had to be officially declared open. U.S. Vice President Al Gore approached the podium. He elicited a huge response from his fellow Americans by congratulating Atlanta "for hosting by far the best Olympic Games in all of history." Gore added, "Atlanta has won the gold medal, and now Atlanta is going for double gold." He continued, "Athletes who are competing in Atlanta, have had to overcome great barriers, but managed to do so. True success comes from our spirit. We must strive for unity and respect. Most of us know in our minds, hearts and souls, through these athletes, disability does not discourage, disrespect or disqualify. I now declare the 1996 Summer Paralympic Games to be open!" The crowd roared and the trumpets sounded.

DANIEL GALBRAITH

The choir and Kirk Franklin and the Family broke into song - "Our Faith, Our Hope and Our Love".

At last, the final torch bearers entered the stadium. Aretha Franklin reappeared to sing "Climb Every Mountain." The crowd waited in anticipation as the torch made its way up the stairs toward the tower. It was handed to Mark Wellman, seated in his wheelchair, by Paralympian and Atlanta native, Al Mead. Wellman began to scale the tower to the cauldron. The flaming torch holstered to his legs, he pulled himself up by a bar that locked on the rope, then slid up while another lock held him in place – his own modification of a device used by window washers.

DANIEL GALBRAITH

REGINALD TIESSEN

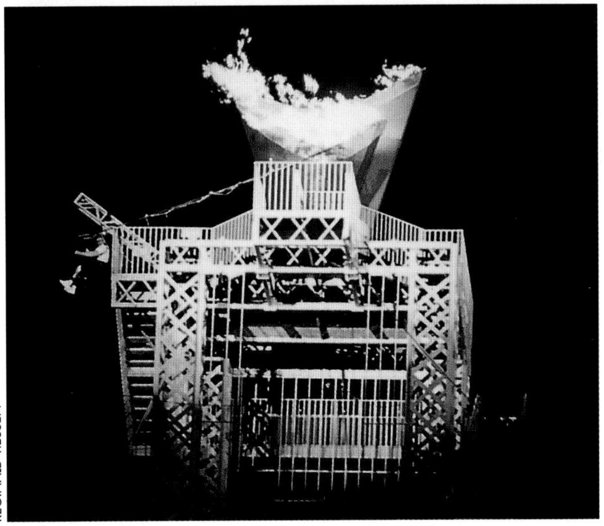

REGINALD TIESSEN

Apart from the symbolism, his climb was also risky. California outfitters had provided Wellman with a fire-protectant shield and jelly for his legs. But he wasn't prepared for the heat from the fuse's fireball, or from the lit cauldron itself, he said. He had practiced the difficult climb only once with fire – secretly, during the middle of the night, less than 24 hours earlier.

Wellman started his climb from the catwalk – 98 feet off the ground – to the top of the 184 foot cauldron tower. It was thrilling to see his arm extended triumphantly as the flame moved slowly toward its destination. With a boom, the cauldron was lit and the sky was decorated with fireworks. The 1996 Paralympic Games were underway. "The fireworks were tremendous," Wellman later joked, "I had the best seat in the house."

Before the ceremonial lighting of the cauldron, the evening had featured a star-studded entertainment extravaganza. Carly Simon was accompanied by a handful of children singers, several in wheelchairs, for a brilliant rendition of "Coming Around Again/Itsy Bitsy Spider." Simon was then joined by the popular duo of Daryl Hall and John Oates for a harmonious performance of several popular numbers. Liza Minelli then took over the stage wooing the party with fan favorites including the timeless hit tune "Caberet."

When the lights came up nearly four hours after Pendergrass opened the evening, a truly inspiring and educational show had been presented. The show envisioned the future, was mindful of the past and embraced the spirit of the present day. The Paralympic Movement took another step forward.

GEORGE PEARL

PARALYMPIC TORCH RELAY

Traveling an average of 100 miles a day, through four states and 1,000 hands, the NationsBank Paralympic Torch began its ten day journey in Washington, D.C. Its voyage was completed with a grand entrance into Olympic Stadium during the Opening Ceremony to light the Paralympic cauldron and officially begin the Xth Paralympiad.

The torch was lit from the Eternal Flame that burns at the tomb of Dr. Martin Luther King, Jr., the legendary civil rights leader. "Let this flame light the way to a new era of greater understanding between nations," said Coretta Scott King in a ceremony at the Martin Luther King, Jr. Center for Nonviolent Social Change in Atlanta, the site of the tomb of her slain husband.

"Our job is only half done," said Atlanta Mayor Bill Campbell. He explained

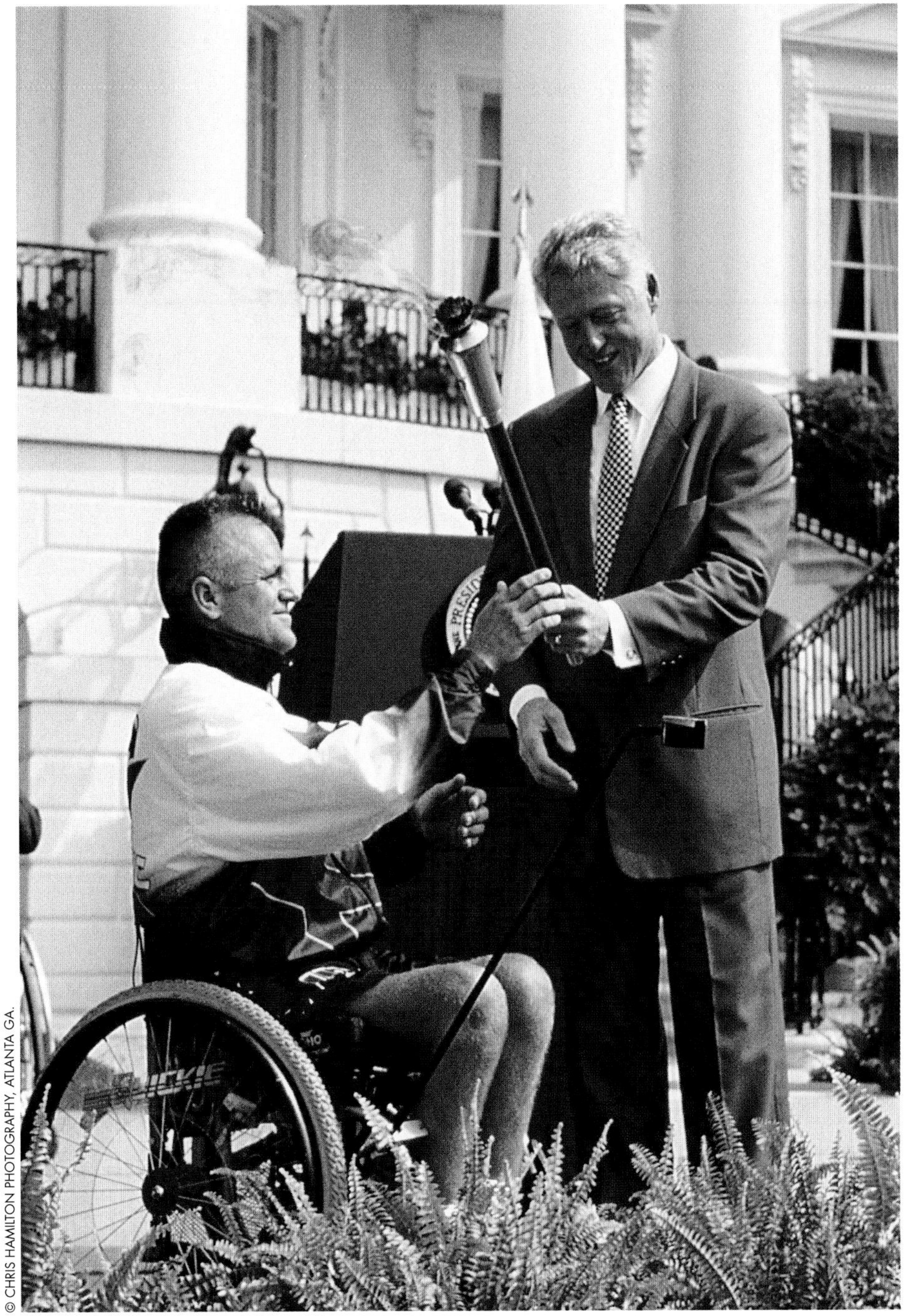

© CHRIS HAMILTON PHOTOGRAPHY, ATLANTA GA.

that the Paralympic Torch Relay would be the first step toward teaching people to "look beyond the disability to discover the true person."

The torch was transported to the nation's capitol where President Bill Clinton, from the White House, echoed the call for freedom concerning people with disabilities when he honored the departure of the torch and the largest Paralympic Torch Relay in history.

Operations for the NationsBank Paralympic Torch Relay were handled World T.E.A.M. Sports (The Exceptional Athlete Matters), an organization that promotes inclusionary opportunities for people with disabilities through sports. The torch traveled via runners, bicycles, wheelchairs, by horseback, kayak and even a water-skier. The tradition of the torch has always been very symbolic and reminds us of the ancient adage, "for we the old pass the torch, for you the young to hold it high."

REGINALD TIESSEN

CULTURAL PARALYMPIAD

After months of planning, the Cultural Paralympiad – the first-ever arts festival to celebrate the spirit of the Paralympic Games – was nearly a no-show. As the financial pressures of staging the Paralympics themselves mounted, APOC was forced to transfer the planning for the Paralympiad to interested groups in the Atlanta community. In short time, a number of Atlanta-based companies and arts organizations banded together to undertake the project. The Center for Puppetry Arts, Special Audiences, Very Special Arts Georgia, the Goethe-Institute Atlanta and the Georgia Council for the Arts spearheaded the planning for the unprecedented event. APOC welcomed the show of support. The new organizers assumed the responsibility of generating interest and funds for the exhibits and performances. The money raised by the arts organizations totalled more than $3 million dollars.

The Cultural Paralympiad was initiated to allow artists with disabilities the opportunity to present their talents while promoting their artistic integrity in association with the Paralympic Games – a world's stage for elite athletes with physical disabilities. Exhibits of visual arts and photographers were displayed while musical, theatrical and dance performances showcased those talents.

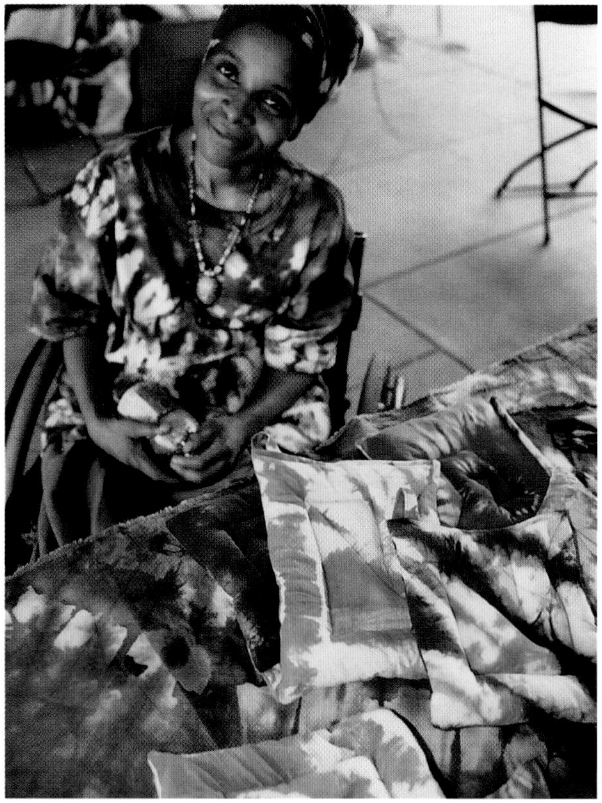
REGINALD TIESSEN

REGINALD TIESSEN

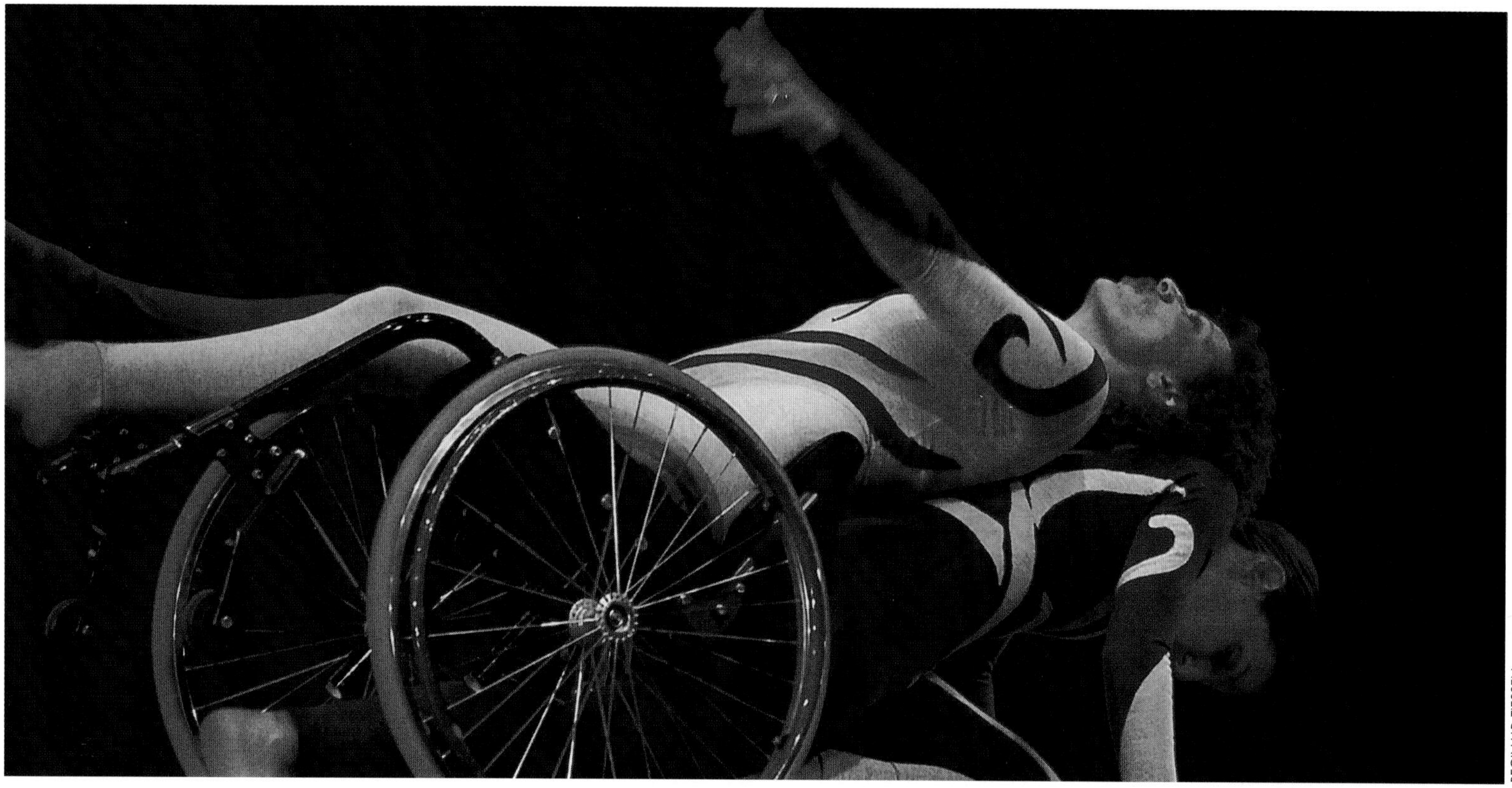
REGINALD TIESSEN

During the first few days of the Paralympiad, organizers were worried about attendance. The small audiences at performances such as *Storm Reading*, written and performed by Neil Marcus, an artist with Dystonia Musculorum Deformans, mostly consisted of people with disabilities and those who worked in the disability community. The same went for *Soundscapes*, an evening of improvisational music, including dialogue between a concert pianist and a wheelchair dancer. But in the end, the message of the Paralympiad got out. Two nights before Closing Ceremony, the well-publicized *Dancing Coast to Coast*, a performance by four elite wheelchair dance companies, attracted a capacity crowd. The artists sent a strong message to the able-bodied community: a disability might be a part of their lives, but it doesn't define it. Special Audiences Executive Director Deborah Lewis said that the festival came together perfectly, like it was meant to be. "To the people who believed in this project, it meant more than just saving the Paralympiad. It showed the artists that we believe in them and support them."

The Cultural Paralympiad featured 14 programs including a number of other high profile exhibits and performances. *The Very Special Arts Regional Festival* promoted understanding and acceptance of human differences. *The Miracle Worker* was the story of Helen Keller and her teacher Anne Sullivan. *Flight* premiered at the Cultural Paralympiad featuring the search for physical and spiritual flight throughout the ages. It was a technical show demonstrating the full accessibility of flight. *Portrait of Spirit: One Story at a Time*, was a compelling collection of photographs and text portraying the lives of 25 individuals with disabilities who occupy a middle ground: they were neither presented as heroes nor as victims of despair, but as people managing a disability as part of their everyday routines of life.

The Art Gallery Exhibit was a well-publicized event. David Sampson and Anthony Conway teamed up to make Paralympic history – not as athletes, but as the official artists of the Paralympic Games. Both artists created a number of pieces for the event, but the official creation was a collaborative effort featuring a wheelchair athlete in action. The original was purchased by one of the Paralympic corporate sponsors. Limited edition prints were a popular merchandise item at the venues.

Able-bodied artist Conway wanted an artistic challenge and knew the Paralympics could offer him that. "I wanted to create art pieces that focused on the ability of the athlete, not the disability," said Conway. As for Sampson, he makes reference to his cerebral palsy in describing how he got started as an artist by saying, "I think I got started making art, because I couldn't climb trees."

Like the Paralympic Games themselves, the Cultural Paralympiad showcased the abilities of people with disabilities. And like the Paralympic mascot Blaze which symbolized Atlanta's historical conquest over adversity, the Cultural Paralympiad too triumphed with grace and spirit.

REGINALD TIESSEN

WORLD CONGRESS ON DISABILITY

The Paralympic Games are not defined by athletic achievement only. The Paralympics are also about a movement: a movement that is informing the world about the capabilities of people with disabilities. Before the world's second largest sporting event of 1996 got underway, leaders in the world-wide disability movement convened in Atlanta at the Third Paralympic World Congress on Disability.

Over one thousand attendees representing more than 50 nations gathered to proactively address global problems facing people with disabilities.

At the heart of the Congress were three universal issues – human rights, economic opportunity and sporting opportunities – with a variety of sessions involving presentations and discussions associated with employment, technology, recreation, productivity, children, advocacy and disability policy. World leaders facilitated the development of action plans for change in each area.

To define a global human rights agenda inclusive of people with disabilities, the delegates overwhelmingly agreed to the formation of a world foundation for disability rights. "We want to send a historic message to the world," proclaimed Justin Dart, Congress Chair. Dart, known to many as the father of the disability rights movement in the U.S., continued, "We people with disabilities are going to be first class citizens of our communities, our nations and the world. We are not making a request. We are making a demand. We are making a promise." Dart described the Congress's human rights statement as a new standard of quality and inclusion where education, health services and employment are concerned. "This was not a gathering of 'photo-op' seekers or 'poster people'," he maintained.

Dart contracted polio in 1948 at the age of 18. "When I was young, I never knew anybody with a disability," Dart noted to the Congress. "I went to the movies where situations were solved in minutes by heroes on horseback. It's an illusion. It takes decades, even centuries, to make significant changes." Dart has recorded four decades of advocacy for human rights in the United States, Mexico, Japan, Canada, the Netherlands and Germany. He worked tirelessly for the passage of the Americans with Disabilities Act and only recently resigned as Chairman of the President's Committee on Employment of People with Disabilities in order to fervently advocate for the civil rights and empowerment of people with disabilities outside of America as well.

The Congress recognized the diverse economic needs of people with disabilities, particularly those in less industrialized countries, and insisted upon the development of programs that respect the needs, culture and aspirations of those who are currently under-served. In his keynote address, Joshua Malinga, President of the Pan African Federation of the Disabled and Mayor of Bulawayo, Zimbabwe, spoke of the conditions in Africa for people with disabilities. Speaking in a saddened tone he said, "In Africa, paraplegics will survive in the hospital, but die soon after their release from care. There are no support systems, no wheelchairs, nothing to help them get through the initial changes." Malinga added, "They are no longer productive in

African society, so death is inevitable." Like Dart, Malinga is also a survivor of polio and a wheelchair user. The 52-year-old was the only one of his father's 38 children (as an Ndebele headman, his father had six wives) who was not encouraged to go to school. Instead, he was in charge of looking after the family farm, left to drag himself around the property, keeping baboons and eagles away from livestock. It wasn't until his brother was hit by a car that the family discovered a rehabilitation center near their home. Malinga and his brother Samuel were admitted to the center and both began rehabilitation. There he was introduced to education. He calls it "an accident of fortune." In 1965 Malinga graduated from secondary school in Bulawayo. "I was the only disabled person from my country to get an education. When I finished high school, I decided that wasn't enough, I wanted a college education too." Malinga received his diploma in Business Studies from Bulawayo Technical College.

In 1970 Malinga spearheaded the formation of the National Council of Disabled Persons of Zimbabwe as a disability rights movement. His motto and message to the world is: "As disabled people we should know our rights, defend our rights and fight for our rights." Malinga said he was inspired by the common problems of people with disabilities world-wide. "Every country is fighting for the same things, we want to achieve standards, no matter what the country's conditions are," he offered. "But even though we share certain problems, disabled people in developing countries are not fighting for privileges, they're fighting for human rights, fighting to stay alive." Malinga asked delegates to consider that, and keep in mind that unity and partnership with disabled people in all countries will inspire change.

Defining the future of sports opportunities for people with disabilities, particularly greater linkages between Paralympic and Olympic Games, provided a cross section of sentiments at the Congress. President of the International Olympic Committee, Juan Antonio Samaranch, spoke of a closer relationship. "We are ready to increase help, to increase cooperation to your movement. There are no hidden agendas in our offer, we understand your mission and we want to assist you."

Henry Enns, President of the Canadian-based Disabled Persons International, told the Congress that full integration at the competitive level is unlikely between the two zenith events. He noted however, "integration at an administrative level – organizing one event – would send a clear message to the world that disabled athletes are valued in the same way that able-bodied athletes are." The end result, he explained, would be a city with total accessibility, enlightened public perception and ultimately, comprehensive disability legislation.

Fou Hwan Lai, Secretary General to Sports Organizations in the Republic of China offered opposition to Enns's vision of conglomeration during his own keynote presentation. Lai believes the Paralympic Movement is a step by step process and that Paralympians should stand on their own. "I cannot understand the reasoning behind this mission," he stated. "We are different than Olympic athletes, but that does not mean we are any less."

Lai questioned the motives of some delegates: "Why would delegates at a Paralympic Congress want to combine two totally different sporting events? If it is a question of recognition, we are well on our way. These Paralympic Games are being televised in America and sponsored by world-renowned companies. This is progress." Lai continued to point out, "Paralympians would get lost in the shuffle, and that's what we here at this Congress are trying to curb."

Making sport and recreational opportunities available to children with disabilities was also a major emphasis area at the Congress. The creation of a multi-agency global task force on sports opportunities for children was one of the most significant recommendations to emerge from the Congress. Carol Rasco, top domestic policy advisor to U.S. President Bill Clinton, and mother of a child with a disability, summarized its importance very succinctly. "As the Paralympics put the spotlight on these elite athletes, more mentors and heroes with disabilities will emerge. Young people, with and without disabilities, naturally look to popular sports figures for leadership and inspiration. But the very best way they can learn sportsmanship and courage is by practicing it in sports themselves. Children need heroes, but they should not live vicariously. They should feel that they have within themselves the capability to make their dreams real."

The Congress also offered a series of peripheral events and demonstrations as part of the four-day agenda. Ten scholarship students from different developing countries fortuitously earned a ticket to Atlanta to compile information from the sessions for newsletters and educational programs around the world. On the second day of the Congress, a collection of delegates took a field trip to a private Atlanta airport where they met an international crew of pilots with disabilities providing information, instruction and demonstrations. On hand to demonstrate his triumphs was skydiver Randy Haims, a ventilator-dependent quadriplegic.

Another Congress highlight was the Disability Film Festival. Independent filmmakers, including students, submitted work that portrayed people with disabilities in a positive manner for judging by film industry professionals. The film "When Billy broke his head...and other tales of wonder" took top honors. Directed by Billy Golfus and produced by David Simpson, the film provides a first-person account of the disabled community's emotional forging of a new civil rights movement. Abilities Expo, a sizable exhibition, displayed new technology, services and resources that many did not know existed.

The final words of Congress Chair, Justin Dart, energized the delegates, as he brought the Paralympic Congress to a close. "We are heartened by this effort, and feel that it is particularly significant because it was held in the context of the 1996 Paralympic Games, a graphic example of the abilities of people with disabilities. We look forward to Sydney 2000, and the opportunities the intervening years provide, to move forward on each action item in each mandate. Thank you, and Good Luck."

Spirit

TEAM SPIRIT

To meet the enormous personnel needs associated with hosting the 1996 Paralympic Games, the Atlanta Paralympic Organizing Committee (APOC) introduced TeamSpirit, a volunteer program designed to live on long after the conclusion of the event itself. The TeamSpirit program provided an opportunity for volunteers to be part of the thrills and emotions of the Paralympics. TeamSpirit volunteers would join athletes with disabilities from all over the world in the celebration of sport, harmony and the human spirit.

The well-trained volunteer staff had a critical mission of providing the best service possible during the Paralympic Games. But the TeamSpirit program had yet another goal. Committed to enriching the quality of life for all people with disabilities, volunteers promised to carry the spirit of the event into their homes, workplaces, neighborhoods and communities once their Paralympic tour of duty ended. In this way, the army of volunteers would continue to serve the interests of people with disabilities for years to come.

© CHRIS HAMILTON PHOTOGRAPHY, ATLANTA GA.

Volunteer training was extensive. Beginning early in 1996, over 10,000 ambitious recruits were formally

BERNARD GLUCKSTEIN

introduced to disability awareness, cultural awareness and customer service information to assist them on the job. The process included two training sessions plus venue orientation and familiarization with general policies and procedures.

Sibyl Langley, director of volunteer services for APOC, said she could not believe the volunteer interest they received upon the call for help. "Lines of people circled our building," she revealed.

"The athletes was the reason I volunteered," said Peggy Taylor. "I wanted to see how people have overcome their disabilities to become such great athletes. Plus, I love to be around positive people."

Margaret Kleiman, director of the Athlete Village, utilized over 600 volunteers within the residence area alone. Transportation and security services required an additional 1,700 faithfuls. "There is no way that we can ever express our gratitude for their extraordinary contributions to the Paralympic Games," Kleiman offered. "They were the most incredible group of people I have ever had the pleasure of working with. Their attitude, enthusiasm and commitment will never be forgotten," she concluded.

Many times, volunteers found themselves dealing with situations in which their training had not prepared them. For instance, as the last delegations arrived at the Village, staff became aware of a pillow shortage problem. One residence manager led a middle-of-the-night pillow making ensemble. Towels and toilet paper made for the impromtu materials available to them that night.

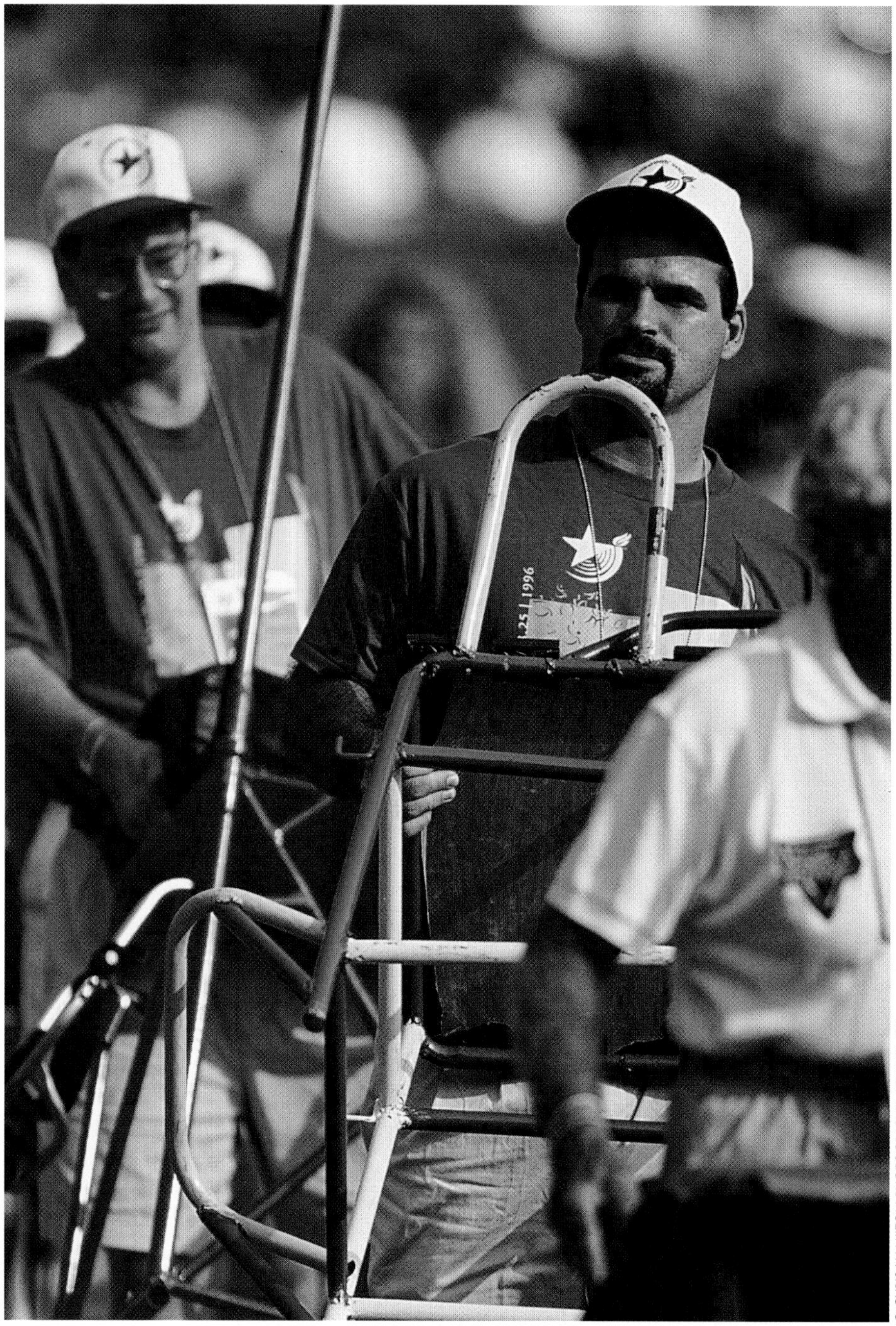

© CHRIS HAMILTON PHOTOGRAPHY, ATLANTA GA.

A Libyan athlete's luggage had been lost and his team searched for fresh clothes for him. Volunteer John Teevan contacted his office in Wisconsin requesting that Paralympic t-shirts that were designated for sale be sent to the Libyan athlete.

The repeated need for plumbers in the Athlete Village was not anticipated. Tony Gallippi did not go to school to become a plumber, but said he certainly learned one important thing about the trade while volunteering. "If the toilet does not

DANIEL GALBRAITH

flush, do not keep flushing it," he professed. "When the application said a 'learning experience,' little did I know," he laughed.

David Stewart, also a volunteer in the Village, received some unexpected additional sensitivity training when he broke both of his ankles while working out at a gym just days before his volunteer commitment to the Paralympic Games was to begin. Not to be deterred, he arrived in a wheelchair with two casts. "I don't know what it is like to have a disability, but I now have some insight," he explained. "In a few weeks these casts will come off and I'll start rehabilitation. I'll regain full movement, whereas the athletes don't have that expectation." Stewart went on to say, "My appreciation for their talents as athletes has grown immensely. I'm taking away a lot more than I put in."

Day after day, on buses, at competition venues and within the Village, a friendly face and a helping hand was ever-present for the athletes. During the Closing

REGINALD TIESSEN

20m
Leica

BERNARD GLUCKSTEIN

Ceremony, APOC president and CEO, Andrew Fleming, said it best, "From the bottom of my heart, I especially thank the thousands of volunteers who have given so much, in hundreds of thousands of acts of kindness, to make these Paralympic Games a success."

ENVOYS

Among the thousands of committed recruits, there was a very unique team of 200 volunteers that went even further than the extra mile to ensure the needs of the delegations were met. They were members of the IBM-Paralympic Envoy

Program. As part of this pioneer program, envoys served as liaisons between APOC and each delegations' Chef de Mission (Team Leader). During a six month training program, the envoy volunteers came together each Monday night to learn about all the operations of the Paralympic Games. They attended workshops on disabled sports, where they gained an understanding of the complete Paralympic competition program.

One objective of the envoy program was to enlist a team of individuals with the variety of bilingual skills needed to provide a match with each country. As it turned out, the recruit pool was shallow in some languages – mostly Russian – so some envoys were assigned to delegations for which they did not know the language. One of those volunteers was Betsy Melvin, who was assigned to Belarus three months before Paralympics began. She immediately commissioned a tutor to assist her in learning some basic Russian. She also bought books on the language and culture.

Like many volunteers, the envoys also found themselves in situations for which they were unprepared. They had to locate luggage, find keys for storage areas and help with the accreditation process upon arrival. One envoy found himself dealing with a very unnerving situation for an athlete. A Zambian competitor had arrived in Atlanta without her racing wheelchair. Romaine Washington quickly took matters into his own hands. A series of telephone calls resulted in a community group donating a competition wheelchair to the athlete to use not only during the competition, but to take back home to Zambia.

When APOC officials were recruiting envoys prior to the Paralympic Games, they described the experience to potential participants as a once-in-a-lifetime opportunity. That promised was fulfilled. And when you ask Betsy Melvin, the Russian envoy, if she speaks Russian now?, "ninmoga," she answers – "a little."

WELCOME GIFT OF QUILTS

In addition to warm smiles and southern hospitality, each nation that participated in an official welcoming ceremony upon their arrival at the Athlete Village received a work-of-art quilt created by volunteers.

Co-operating with the Georgia Quilt Project, the crafters consisted of both individual artisans and quilting clubs from small mountain communities and city neighborhoods. The country assignments were made randomly after the quilts were completed; the quilters had no idea which nation would receive their masterpiece.

The intent of the quilts was simple: something an entire delegation could keep as a memento of the 1996 Paralympic Games. Each stitch of each quilt was to represent friendship and understanding. The quilts served as the first gesture of friendship from their hosts. The welcome ceremony began with an exchange of official greetings between Village and delegation representatives, followed by a procession of volunteers carrying that nation's flag and the gift quilt.

JAPAN

BLAZE OF GLORY

Next to the athletes, BLAZE represented the best vehicle for awareness about the Games. BLAZE, a phoenix, was the colorful, official mascot of the 1996 Atlanta Paralympic Games. This mythical bird was said to have been burned by the rays of the sun, but rose from its own ashes, renewed. Symbolic of many aspects of the Paralympic Games, the phoenix has historically represented Atlanta's rising from the ashes after it was burned by the Union Army during the American Civil War.

BLAZE truly represented the philosophies of the Paralympic Games: triumph, strength, spirit, inclusion and performance. The fantastical bird embodied the character of the elite athlete who competes and accomplishes great things because of a burning desire from within.

"BLAZE symbolizes the Paralympic athlete's ability to overcome adversity and rise to greatness," said the mascot's designer Trevor Irvin. "I wanted to break people's perception of what a phoenix is supposed to look like." Importantly, his artistic endeavor parallels the Paralympic athlete's ability to change society's view of people with disabilities.

Noted children's author, Betsy Duffey, wrote the engaging story of BLAZE which captivated youth and adults alike. Weaving mythology and a search for inclusion into a metaphorical account, BLAZE's story closely linked the mascot to the principles of the Paralympic Games.

Prior to the event, a variety of BLAZE promotions and awareness events introduced thousands of people to the upcoming Paralympics in Atlanta. From the *BLAZEmobile* to *Santa BLAZE* delivering plush toys in his own likeness to Toys for Tots, to a presentation of a giant card signed by young faithfuls to the Governor of Georgia, the flamboyant bird was constantly campaigning for Paralympic followers. His efforts were immortalized through the Games' merchandising program which licensed his image to adorn a host of products from key tags to t-shirts.

LOOK OF THE GAMES

The *Look of the Games*, or visual theme of the event, decorated everything from street banners to kiosks to staff and volunteer uniforms. The graphic element was the *Ascending Flame*. The symbolic interpretations of the elegant flame were plen-

BERNARD GLUCKSTEIN

DANIEL GALBRAITH

DANIEL GALBRAITH

DANIEL GALBRAITH

DANIEL GALBRAITH

© CHRIS HAMILTON PHOTOGRAPHY, ATLANTA GA.

tiful. The fire represented the passion in the heart of each Paralympian while evoking the spirit and strength of the Paralympic Movement as a whole.

Historically, the fire suggests the legendary symbol of the re-birth of Atlanta – a phoenix rising from its own ashes. The fire also is reminiscent of the memorial flame at the tomb of Dr. Martin Luther King, Jr., forever burning as a glowing tribute to a dream of peace and equality for humanity.

"In the balance and flair of the flame's individual lines, we see the diversity of athletic aspirations and the richness of the Paralympic Movement attained through its distinctions," said Brad Copeland of Copeland Hirthler, creator of the *Paralympic Look.*

FANFARE

Overall attendance at the Paralympics was gratifying, but smaller than anticipated. Nonetheless, fans on hand were never short on spirit. When a technical difficulty during a medal ceremony at the cycling venue prevented the playing of an anthem, the crowd stood and sang the Star-Spangled Banner. The final count on attendance at the 1996 Paralympics was slightly more than 700,000 people.

These Paralympics were the first ever to sell tickets to the events. Prices ranged from $10-$25 for sporting events and up to $100 for the Opening and Closing Ceremonies. Although past Paralympics provided free admission to spectators, APOC officials believed in the value of the performances and the legitimacy that ticket purchases provided the event.

SPARX O'LYMPICS AT SHEPHERD CENTER

The day prior to the opening of the Xth Paralympiad, 28 American Paralympic athletes spent the morning in a gym full of kids, parents and media as participants in Shepherd Center's SPARX O'lympics. The athletes gave a brief demonstration of their sports before the kids tried them out for themselves. A spirited autograph session followed.

The SPARX O'lympics capped off an exciting summer for the children enrolled in the summer day camp at Shepherd Center, a program designed for 4-17 year old children with spina bifida. With the youngsters showing extreme interest in the Paralympic Games, camp organizers began including the Paralympics in daily activities. Camp-goers created banners that ultimately decorated the Paralympic Village. The youngsters wrote letters to their favorite athletes, inviting them to come visit the Shepherd Center when they were in Atlanta for the Games. They received an over-

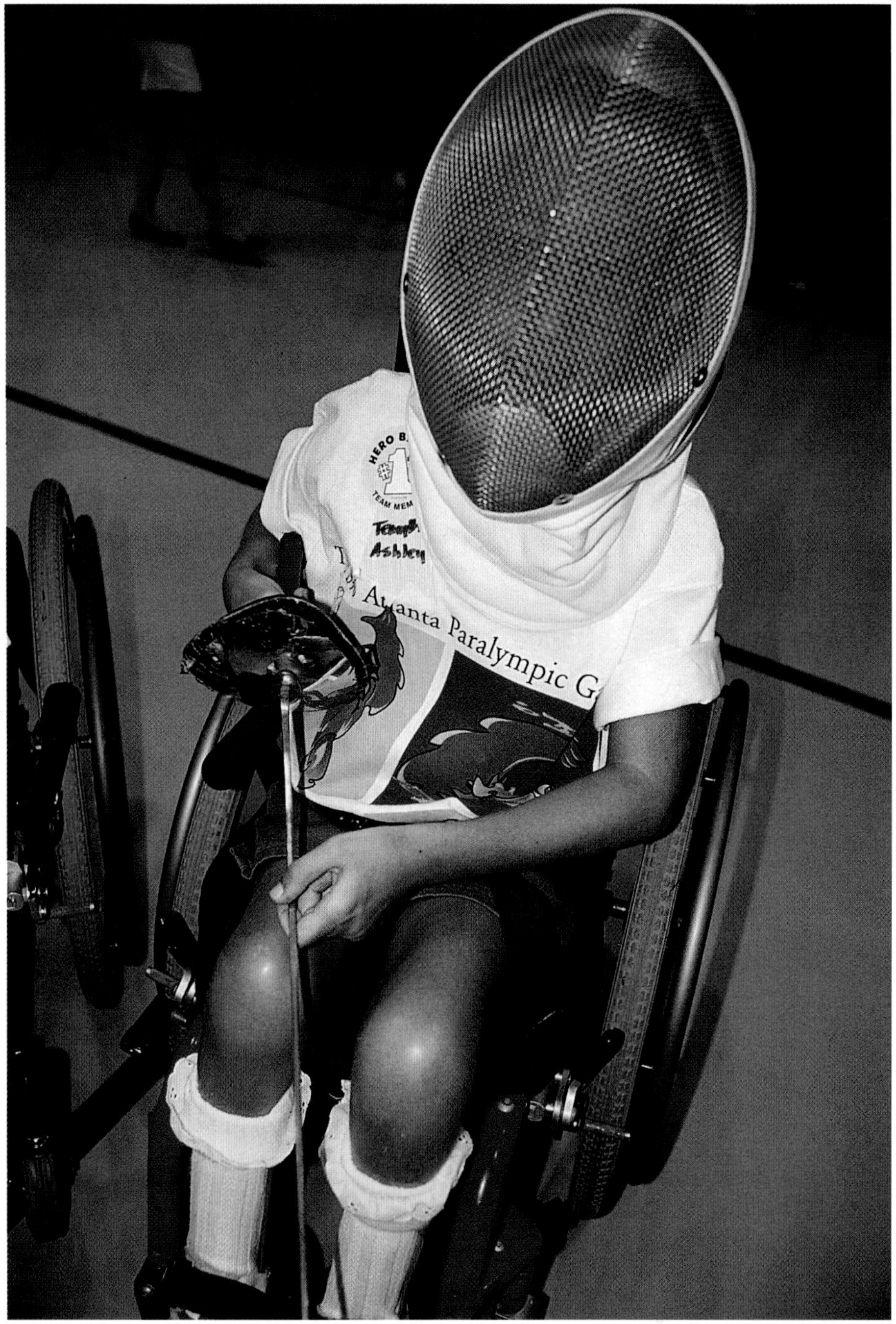

REGINALD TIESSEN

DANIEL GALBRAITH

whelming response in favor of the invite.

"I'm here to support the children," said Jeanie Waters, Paralympian and recent law school graduate. Kids are our number one resource for the future of these Games." Six-year-old Margaret Fredrick was inspired by the tennis demonstration. "I play tennis you know," she said as a matter of fact, "and someday I hope to play tennis at the Paralympics too."

Said a Paralympic fencer: "Disabled children are often overlooked and it takes a long time to get the word out that we can do anything we set our minds to. It's easier to show these kids what we can do in person. We're here to spread the word."

Ginny Posid, SPARX coordinator, explained that the SPARX O'lympics shows the kids that they can be active and feel great about themselves. "I wouldn't be surprised to see one of these kids competing at the Paralympics someday," she professed.

ATHLETE VILLAGE

The Paralympic's Athlete Village brimmed with activity day and night. The continuous support system for athletes, officials, family and friends kept Paralympic staff and volunteers in constant motion as well.

The International Zone provided a location where the Paralympic Family could socialize. The Club was designed as the location for entertainment and leisure providing live performances and movies each evening. A selection of recreational games was available as well.

The International Zone was also the hub of all commercial services, welcoming ceremonies, information services and chaplaincy counsel.

SHOWDOWN AT THE VILLAGE

The first thing an observer of a Showdown match in the Paralympic Village noticed was the jarring noise produced when a hard, plastic ball filled with beebees smacked off the wall of a wooden table. Game inventors Pat York and Joe Lewis hope the resounding thwack was loud enough to carry Showdown all the way to Sydney in the year 2000. Their goal is to have Showdown receive recognition as an official Paralympic sport one day.

The two Canadians came up with Showdown – a cross between table tennis and table hockey – while searching for a sport in the late 1970s that blind athletes could play without assistance from sighted persons. The object of Showdown is simple: Listen for the ball, then knock it into the opponent's goal.

Competitors need not be blind to play. A sighted person can compete fairly against a blind person. A

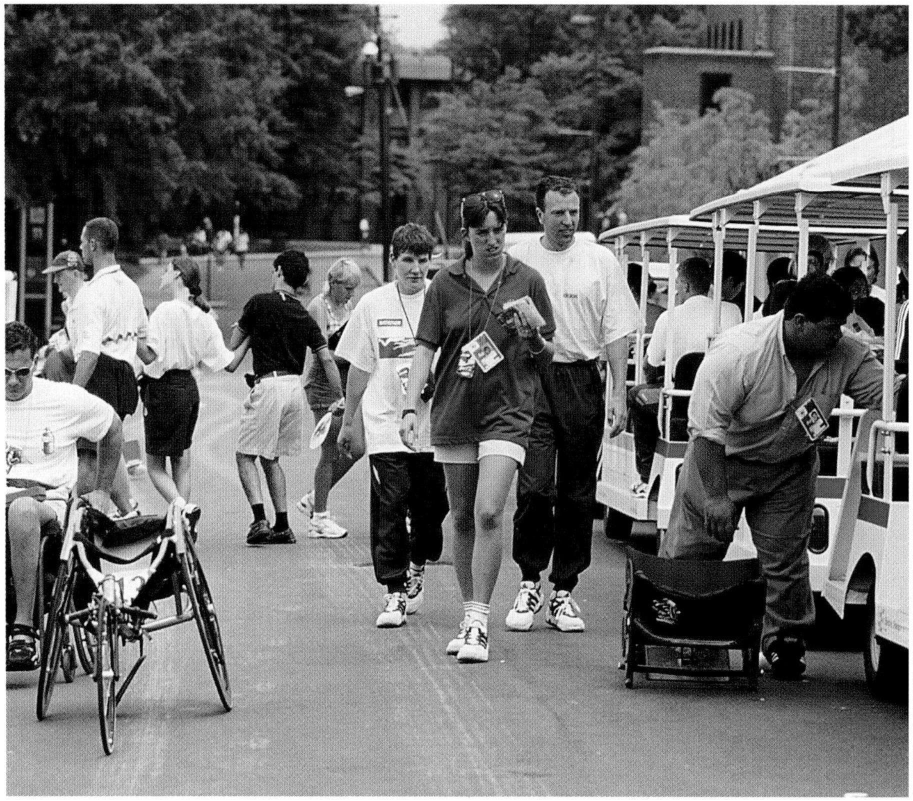

© CHRIS HAMILTON PHOTOGRAPHY, ATLANTA GA.

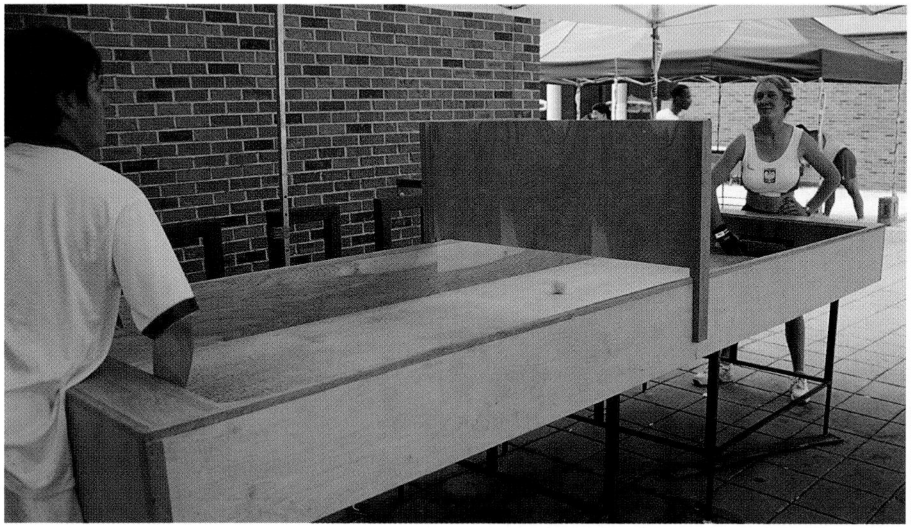

NORM LOURENCO

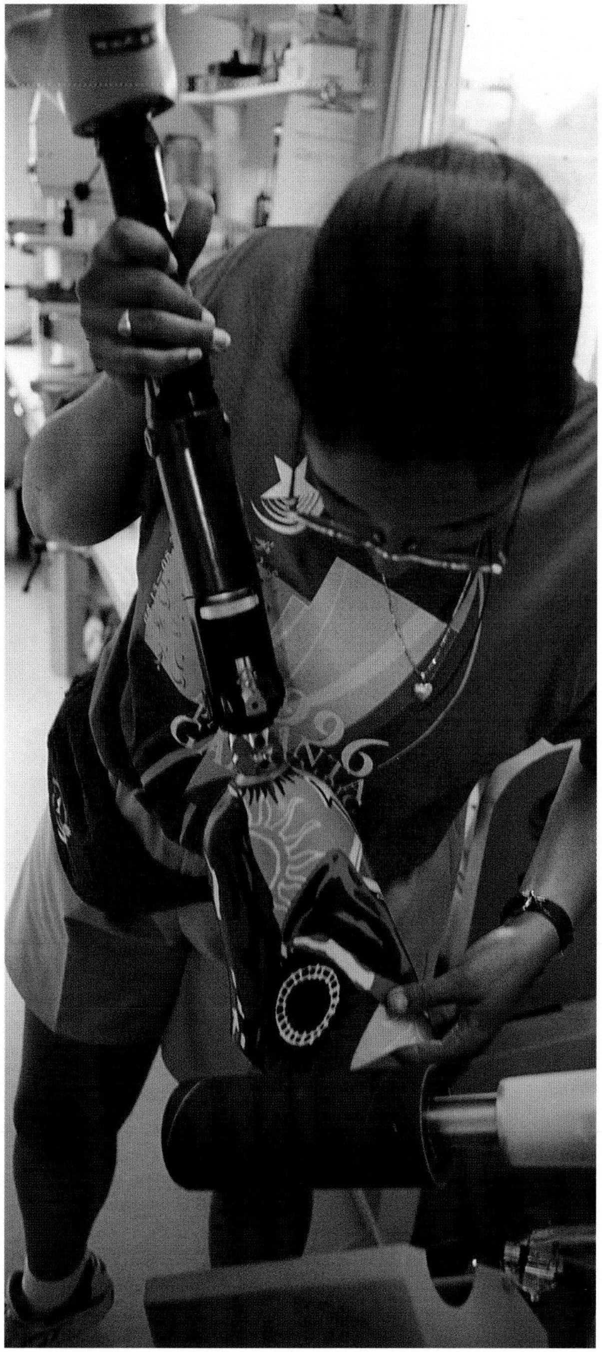
REGINALD TIESSEN

wooden screen divides the 4-by-12 foot table, preventing a sighted player from seeing the ball until it crosses into his or her end of the table. Cricket-like bats used to hit the ball add to the noise.

Showdown is currently played in Europe, Asia, Africa, Scandinavia and North America. To be accepted into the Paralympics, the game must have national championships in 18 countries on five continents. York says they're close, but not quite there yet. "That's why I'm in Atlanta, spreading the word," he promoted.

THE QUICK FIX FOR HIGH-TECH ATHLETES

During the 1992 Barcelona Paralympic Games, long jumper Al Mead found to his horror that he could not get his sports foot onto his prosthetic leg. Would he be a no-show for his event? Was disqualification a possibility? Would he simply watch while others went through the coveted medal ceremonies?

Fortunately, a prosthetic repair station came to his aid. "It required major surgery on the device right there," said Mead, recalling the experience with a shudder. "I had to put a different foot on the leg I was wearing before the long jump competition. But the foot I was wearing wouldn't come off. Basically, the repair station people sawed it off, got the athletic foot on, and I went on to win the silver medal. They saved me."

The Orthotic & Prosthetic Athlete Assistance Fund, Inc. (O&P Athletic Fund) was in Atlanta to assist amputee athletes should similar happenings occur. The O&P Athletic Fund was established by the O&P National Office to administer Paralympic-related activities for the professional field and administer funds collected from the field to support the O&P Paralympic Initiative. The O&P Athletic Fund was recognized as the "Official Provider of O&P Services for the 1996 Atlanta Paralympic Games," providing fixed, mobile and temporary repair stations during the event.

Approximately 70 O&P professionals donated a minimum of five days of their time to assist the amputee athletes competing at the Paralympics. Their goal was to ensure that no athlete would miss his or her competition because of a technical problem with a device. These volunteers recognized the devastation that a competitor who trained for years would experience if his or her medal hopes were

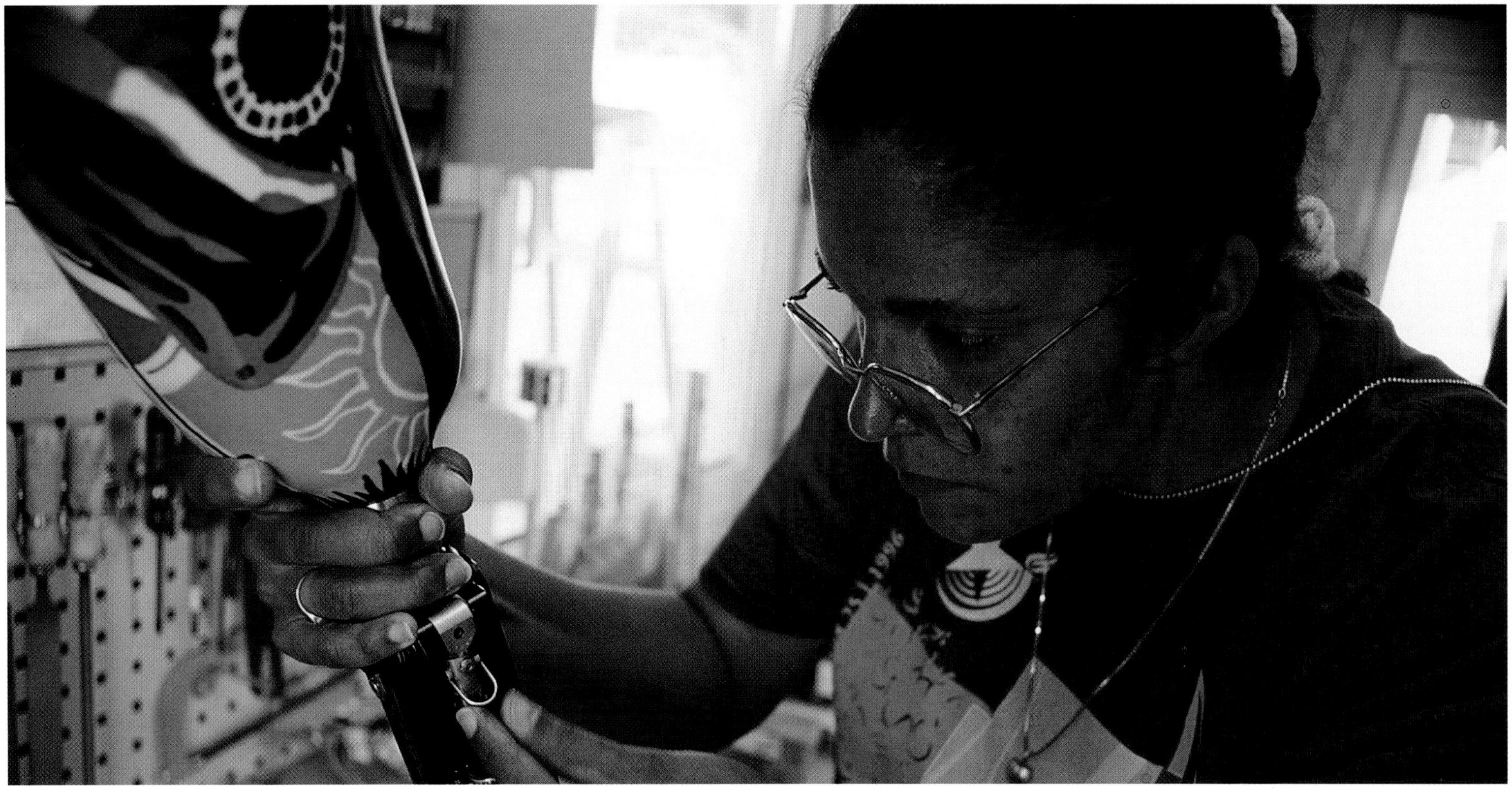

REGINALD TIESSEN

dashed by a mechanical problem. The O&P team handled close to 300 repairs before the competition came to an end. No one missed out on a chance to do his or her best.

The O&P Athletic Fund was created as a united effort to represent the entire field of orthotics and prosthetics. Because no one manufacturer or facility could have financed an effort of this magnitude, interested supporters signed on as contributors to the Fund.

As part of its sponsorship of the Paralympic Games, the O&P Athletic Fund also launched an education and awareness campaign to promote the notion that disabilities do not have to impede pride, achievement or personal growth. In the attempt to recruit "young blood" into the disabled sports arena, the O&P Athletic Fund sponsored two-part sports clinics around the country for two years prior to the

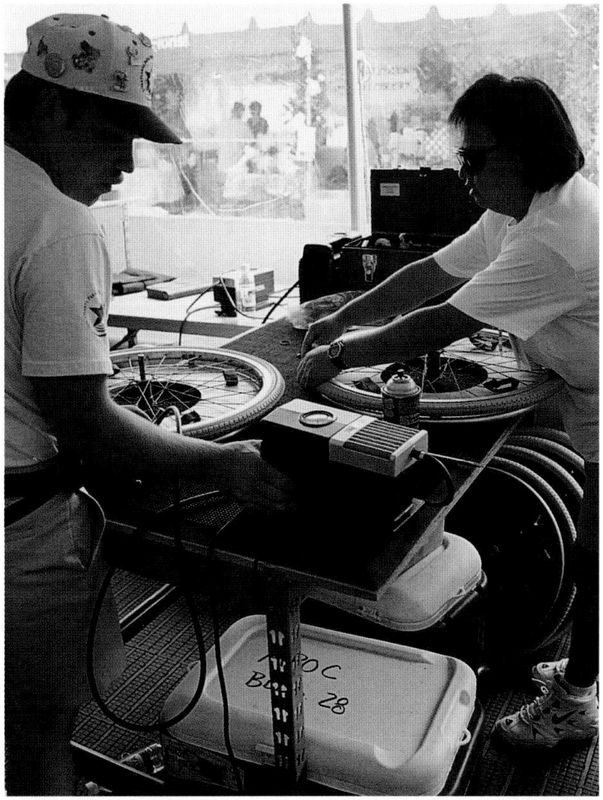

NORM LOURENCO

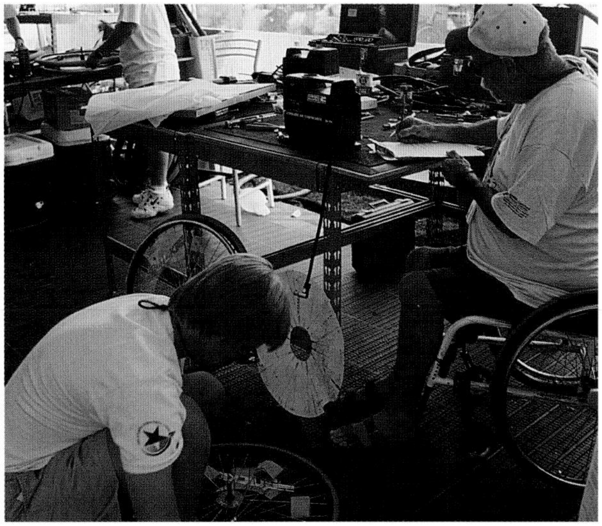

NORM LOURENCO

Paralympic Games. The clinics consisted of presentations by O&P practitioners with experience in designing and fitting athletic artificial limbs and orthopedic braces, and by physical therapists and trainers with disabled sports experience. It is believed that the clinics accounted for a 30 per cent increase in amputee athletes competing in national level events.

Paralympic athletes visited schools as part of the O&P campaign to change the hearts, minds and attitudes of children about disabilities. Paralympian Todd Schaffhauser regularly offers a spark of hope for hospitalized children with his own story. Schaffhauser lost his leg to cancer when he was only 15. After seeing the Terry Fox story about an amputee who lost his leg to cancer and subsequently vied to run across Canada to raise money for cancer research, Schaffhauser realized he too would run again. He captured the bronze medal in Atlanta in the 100-metre track event for single above-the-knee amputees.

Not unlike the amputee athlete, competitors using wheelchairs also required expert attention for their high-tech equipment. Wheelchairs often need repairs and without them, these athletes could also miss their competition and their opportunity to participate in the Paralympic Games.

Responding to the critical need to assist wheelchair athletes with mechanical problems, Sunrise Medical, an industry leader in the manufacturing of medical and home healthcare products and an Official Sponsor of the Atlanta Paralympic Games, teamed-up with the MED Group, a national network of independently-owned and operated home medical equipment providers, to offer comprehensive and quick response Wheelchair Repair Centers. The centers served athletes from all countries using any design or brand of chair.

With over 60 technicians on-site, 12 repair centers were set up at the wheelchair sports venues, as well as the Athlete Village, warm-up track and airport. Each repair center was stocked with parts from all major manufacturers. If the technicians did not have a specific component needed for a repair, welders and machinists were on-hand to modify or even create new parts.

One technician, Tony Esqueda, recalled helping an athlete from Equador whose wheelchair frame was held together with bailing wire. The seating upholstery was so torn that it consisted almost entirely of tape, he disclosed. "With the condition

BERNARD GLUCKSTEIN

the chair was in, the athlete wouldn't have had a chance to compete at his potential. Our team reacted immediately, re-welding the frame, adding new components and installing new upholstery. The athlete ended up with almost a new chair."

Performing over 3,500 repairs from changing tires to rebuilding wheels and welding cracked frames, the Wheelchair Repair Centers were ready to do whatever it took to have the athlete mechanically prepared for top competitive performance. In terms of service, coverage, flexibility and performance, the Sunrise MED Group Official Wheelchair Repair Centers set a benchmark for future Paralympic Games.

While no stories were reported of last-minute repairs that resulted in gold medals won, athletes from all nations truly appreciated the work that the Sunrise MED Group and O&P volunteers contributed. Many of the athletes could not say "thank you" in English, but the volunteers sensed their appreciation with the exchange of pins and smiles. The Danish swimmer who carried the flag for her country during the Opening Ceremony was an O&P repair station "patient" just hours before the start of the ceremony. It wasn't a medal she would have missed out on, but a once-in-a-lifetime opportunity nonetheless.

PIN-TRADING - THE UNIVERSAL LANGUAGE

The most universally understood English communication in the Athlete Village was "Pin?" and "Change?" Changing, or trading, pins was a way of life there.

A Korean athlete stepped into his residence hall elevator on the third floor. His eyes widened when he saw a plethora of pins around the neck of a volunteer. "Pin?" The deal was done before the elevator doors opened to the first floor. Just outside the lobby, the excited athlete tried again. "Pin?," he repeated as he offered another choice. A second deal was made. The language barrier had been transcended.

The addictive practise of pin-trading happened everywhere in the Village – in the residence halls, in the dining tent, in the courtyards and over the tram seats. Said one athlete, "It's a great way of meeting people and making friends."

Although delegations from every country participated in this mass mania, those from Mexico and South Africa, among a few others, seemed to have the system down to a calculated art-science. These professional traders were easily recognized. Under the weight of their booty, they moved about at a slightly slower pace than

NORM LOURENCO

their amateur counterparts.

Nearly everyone had that one special pin that others wanted. "Sorry, no trade," was heard as hopes for a coveted pin were dashed. A server at the dining tent wore a relatively rare Nelson Mandela pin. He obtained it by giving up an equally limited Olympic security pin. Paralympic Games Sponsor's pins were power pins. They were hard to find and were held tightly. When traded, they were often worth at least two in exchange.

Pin-trading embraced everything from obvious souvenir collection and gift giving to currency or compensation for favors rendered. Pins were given in gratitude for toilets plunged, directions given or friendly smiles.

Could a pin get a pin-handler anything he or she needed? Almost, but not quite. Acts of bribery were usually unsuccessful. "I'll give you a pin if you'll give me an extra towel or blanket," was offered to a residence hall manager who was quick to point out that people were not getting away with that tactic. "But," she added, "I was tempted if it was a really good pin."

As the Paralympic Games reached the halfway mark, the supply of tradable product was diminished. Other small objects began appearing in the marketplace: key chains, small stuffed animals, caps, shirts and postcards. South African athlete Rosabelle Riese donned her green team hat protectively, its brim covered with "keepers," including one pin designed with her own name emblazoned on it. "I'm very fussy about what I trade," Riese said as a volunteer was pushing postcards for pins. The volunteer was being innovative since she, like most volunteers, had no source for beginning a pin stockpile. Riese pulled out her traders for the volunteer to look over. "I've got a Korea. Let me see Egypt." A deal was struck. The pin was traded for two official Olympic postcards. "Nice doing business with you," offered the postcard purveyor. "Now I've got a start."

CORPORATE SPIRIT

The process of drumming up support and funding to initiate the planning and operations of the 1996 Paralympic Games was a monumental task. Andrew Fleming, president and CEO of the Atlanta Paralympic Organizing Committee (APOC), noted that at times it

NORM LOURENCO

REGINALD TIESSEN

was difficult to see "the forest for the trees." The feeling among Atlanta Paralympic organizers however, was that the disability movement had matured to a point where corporate sponsorship was possible and would serve not only to make the Paralympics economically independent, but to generate public awareness for the event as well. Additionally, it would begin to build a broader base of support for disabled sports in the United States and around the world long after the closing ceremony. They were correct. After only six months, corporate America began to come forward.

With the announcement that Atlanta would host the Olympic Games, board members at the Shepherd Center, a prominent Atlanta rehabilitation facility, strongly believed that Atlanta should continue the tradition of Seoul and Barcelona and host the Paralympics as well. Toward this goal the Center provided the "seed money" for a small staff and provided office space to those working to assemble the Paralympic bid which was presented to the International Paralympic Committee (IPC) in Tignes, France in 1992. In recognition of the Center's early commitment and continued support, APOC named the facility the Founding Sponsor of the 1996 Paralympic Games.

In the largest show of corporate support of the Paralympic Games ever, The Coca-Cola Company joined APOC and the IPC in late 1993 as the first worldwide sponsor of the Paralympics with a $1 million philanthropic grant from the company and a multi-million dollar sponsorship agreement to support Paralympic activities. "Coca-Cola's enthusiasm in sponsoring the 1996 Paralympic Games underscores the growing understanding, appreciation and sensitivity to disabled persons," said Dr. Robert Steadward, president of the IPC, in response to the sponsorship announcement. "Our support is more than a natural extension of the involvement of Coca-Cola with the Olympic movement worldwide," said Douglas Ivester, Coca-Cola president and CEO. "There is also an inspiring added dimension; it's gratifying to have a role in paying tribute to these athletes from so many different nations."

From a tiny office in the Shepherd Center, the small APOC staff would move into a donated section of IBM's former offices in midtown Atlanta. This eventually grew into a lease of two full floors encompassing the entire operations of the Paralympic Games, housing over 200 dedicated staff. IBM and Xerox, neither an official sponsor of the Paralympics at the time, provided the urgently needed computers, copiers and supplies to APOC.

IBM then added to its early support of the Paralympics by joining Coca-Cola as a Worldwide Sponsor. They would be joined by Motorola, another company that has made a commitment to the broader disabled community through the development of special products for special needs. "The athletes of the Paralympic Games represent the highest level of competitive perseverance in sports competition," said Merle L. Gilmore, president and general manager of Motorola's Land Mobile products sector and executive vice-president of Motorola, Inc.

BellSouth, the telecommunications power, was enlisted as an official sponsor in early 1994, helping to coordinate the complicated communications needs of the event. Shortly thereafter, Dick Chandler, chairman of Sunrise

Medical, Inc. announced that the world's largest manufacturer of home medical equipment (HME) would be the exclusive Paralympic sponsor within the HME industry. "The Paralympics provide positive role models for disabled people throughout the world, and Sunrise is proud to support their efforts," said Chandler. "Sunrise Medical wants to change perceptions about disabled people, shifting the focus to ability, not disability," he explained. "We want to open minds, which will then open doors in the workplace and other environments."

The Home Depot, the world's largest home improvement retailer, then came on board as did Eastman Kodak, Naya Spring Water, United Postal Service and Swatch. Bernard Marcus, chairman and CEO of The Home Depot, stated that their sponsorship reflected the company's commitment to being sensitive and responsive to all people. "The Paralympic Games provide positive role models and inspiration not only to those with physical disabilities, but everyone," offered Marcus. *The Paralympic Torch Relay* event was adopted by NationsBank, a Paralympic Supplier. Its path from Washington, D.C. to Atlanta covered much of the bank's eastcoast market.

Increasing the awareness in the Atlanta region that the world's greatest athletes were coming to Atlanta twice in 1996 was crucial to the success of the Paralympics. As the event had never before been televised in the United States, this was a daunting task. Through Turner Broadcasting, Inc.'s sponsorship and the enthusiastic advertising and editorial coverage from the Atlanta Journal-Constitution and WSB's television and radio stations, the Paralympic Games forged their own identity in an Olympic-dominated environment.

Numerous other corporate sponsors and suppliers supported the Paralympics. Delta Airlines supported the travel needs of APOC officials and assisted in transporting the wide variety of talent for the opening and closing ceremonies. Randstad, one of the world's largest temporary staffing agencies, stepped in to help staff the organizing committee and instituted a widespread disability employment initiative.

In total, 50 corporations contributed more than $60 million in cash, products and services to the staging of the Atlanta Paralympic Games. But it was not only major corporations that rallied behind this event. A multitude of individuals, not-for-profit associations, volunteer organizations, service providers, government agencies and smaller companies provided funds, products and services or both. APOC officials decided early on to seek support from a wide array of contributors. Sponsors and suppliers provided 45.6 per cent of total revenues; 3.9 per cent came from government; philanthropic and other donations generated 6.8 per cent. Ticket sales generated 3.5 per cent of the total revenue while entry fees and the coin and license tag programs combined to total 4.8 per cent. It was this strategic and timely support that enabled APOC to host a successful event.

Despite APOC's fundraising success, Fleming admitted that marketing the Paralympic Games was a difficult process. Some corporations were tapped out after their support of the Olympic Games. Many were simply unfamiliar with the magnitude of the Paralympic Games. But for those who recognized the value, the rewards are only beginning. Said Coca-Cola's Ivester, "The Coca-Cola Company is pleased to be the first worldwide sponsor of the Paralympics. We made that decision for two reasons: it's the right thing to do and it makes good business sense."

PARALYMPIC TRANSPORTATION SYSTEM

To bring athletes, coaches and other members of team delegations to training and competition venues, the Paralympic Transportation System made 56,000 trips during the event. More than 450,000 riders were transported, including 120,000 individuals in wheelchairs. To accommodate athletes and visitors in wheelchairs, transportation officials had seats removed from half the buses in the fleet so that wheelchair tie-down systems could be installed. This increased the capacity of each bus to transport 11 persons in wheelchairs per trip.

Many agencies worked together to make the Paralympic Transportation System a success. The Metropolitan Atlanta Rapid Transit Authority contributed staff to the system's operation and maintained all transit vehicles. The Federal Transit Administration arranged for the loan of 212 buses from ten U.S. cities. The Department of Defense provided 419 soldiers, sailors and Air Force personnel to drive the buses. Texaco donated the fuel.

The lift-equipped buses on loan from the transit systems all had front door lifts. All lifts were Lift-U models. Lift-U, a Division of Hogan Mfg., Inc. in California, is the prime wheelchair lift manufacturer for heavy-duty urban transit buses 30 feet and longer. Lift-U supplies lifts to all of the major bus manufacturers throughout the United States and Canada. To date, the company has produced over 27,000 lifts for public transportation vehicles. Hogan Mfg., Inc. is a privately owned company that has been in business as a steel fabricator since 1944 and has been in the wheelchair lift business since the 1980s.

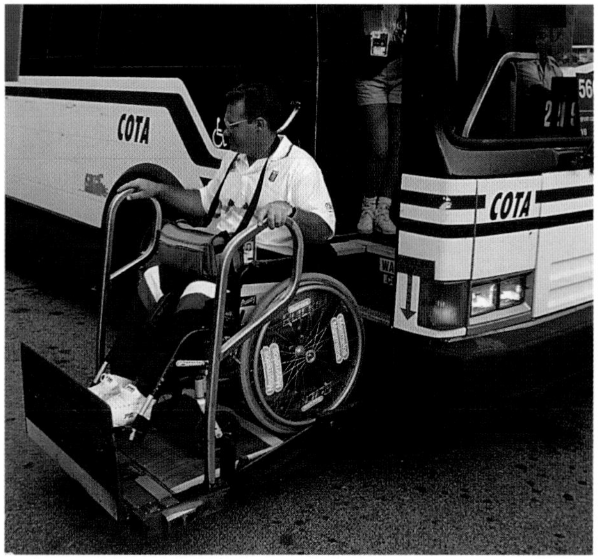

The lifts are designed and built with quality and reliability in mind using state-of-the-art lasers, robotics, machine centers, and electrostatic paint systems. Lift-U, selected as the lift of choice for the Paralympics, provided extra staff on site in the event that repairs to a lift were needed. Over the three weeks that the Paralympic Transportation System was in service, only 22 road calls were reported for lift failures while the units were deployed approximately 60,000 times.

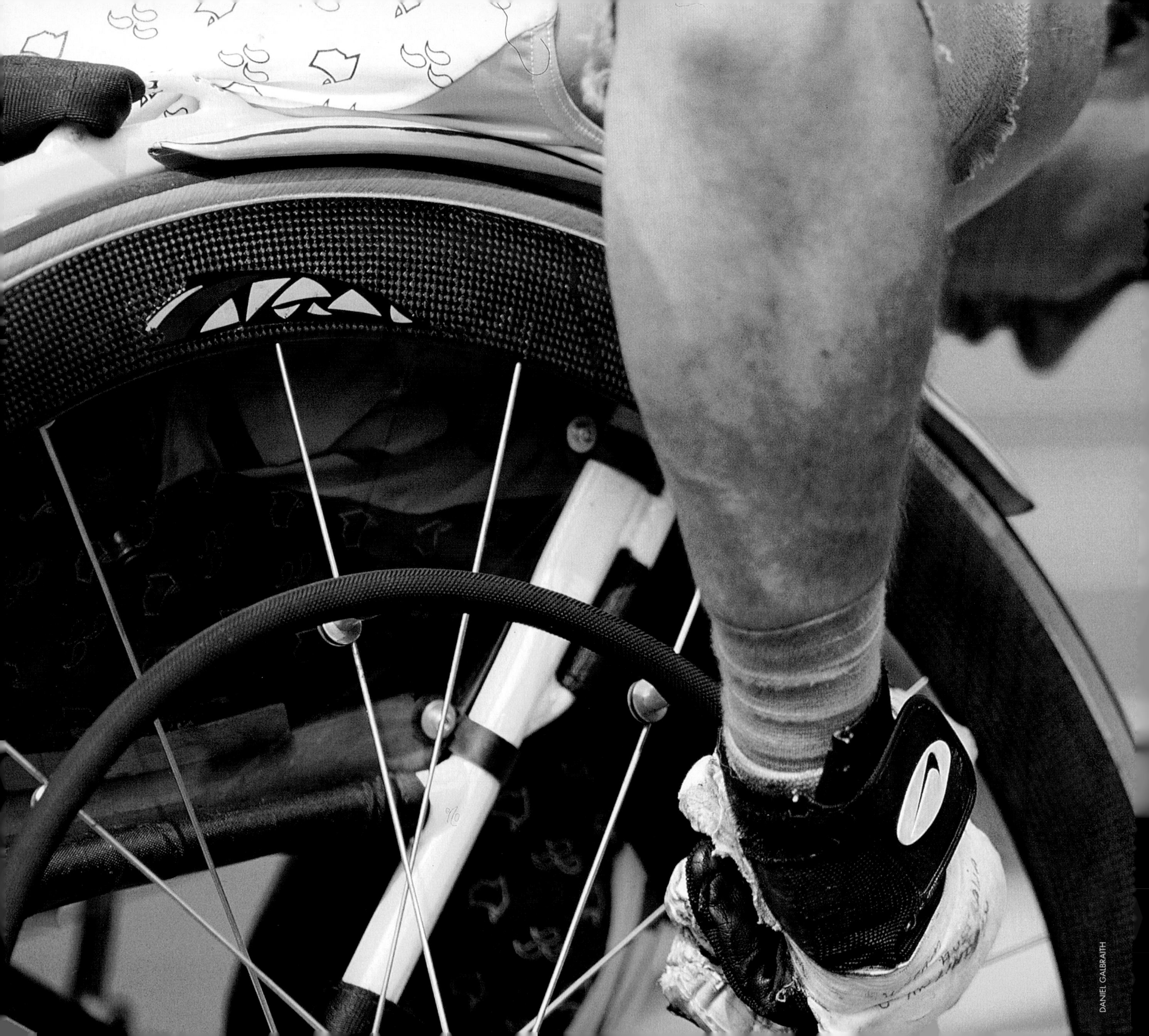
DANIEL GALBRAITH

Triumph

PURSUIT OF EXCELLENCE

With more than 3,310 athletes from an unprecedented 104 countries participating in the 1996 Paralympic Games in Atlanta, it was there that the best of the best met and competed against other athletes with similar disabilities from around the world. The fundamental philosophy guiding the Paralympic Movement is that athletes with a disability should have the opportunity to pursue their goals in sport on an international stage. Athletes who compete in the Paralympic Games have set their sights high. They have earned the privilege of representing their nation. They strive for personal best performances and dream of gold medal results. They trained hard, competed well and met strict qualifying standards. Each athlete came to Atlanta to pursue Paralympic excellence.

BERNARD GLUCKSTEIN

There were 17 full medal and two demonstration sports on the 1996 Paralympic Games program. Boccia, goalball and lawn bowls were the only full medal sports not included on the Olympic Games program. To be included on the program of events for the Paralympic Games, a sport must meet certain criteria. It must be played in 15 countries and on three continents to qualify as an event for men, and in ten countries and on three continents for women. Being included as a demonstration or exhibition sport at one Paralympic Games does not guarantee that the sport will be added as a full medal sport at the next Paralympic Games.

Athletes compete according to type of disability and/or functional level and only against others with similar abilities. In most instances, athletes compete within the following categories of disability: visually impaired and blind, amputee, cerebral palsy, quadriplegia and paraplegia (wheelchair), and les autres (athletes with a physical disability not defined by the above four). Some sports however, use a system which groups athletes from different disability categories together according to their functional ability level.

Minor modifications are sometimes made to the rules of individual sports in order to accommodate the abilities of the athletes.

DANIEL GALBRAITH

DANIEL GALBRAITH

REGINALD TIESSEN

REGINALD TIESSEN

Archery

Archery has been an event on the Paralympic program since the inception of the Games in 1960. Both ambulatory and wheelchair athletes participate in individual and team events under the Olympic FITA Round competition and scoring systems. Archers are grouped in classes according to disability. The competition is open to athletes with cerebral palsy, amputees and wheelchair users. The wheelchair competition has two open classes – one for paraplegic competitors and the other for athletes with quadriplegia.

Athletes shoot at a 122 centimetre face from a distance of 70 metres. Archers typically score from 1,000 to 2,500 points. Releases, compounds, recurve bows, strappings and body supports are allowed for quadriplegic athletes with severely limited upper limb motion.

REGINALD TIESSEN

POLAND'S DYNAMIC DUO
RYSZARD & MALGORZATA OLEJNIK

It seemed to be an unbearably hot August afternoon for a team meeting in the confined quarters of their dormitory. But it was evident that the humidity

REGINALD TIESSEN

Malgorzata Olejnik

that draped the room like a wet blanket would not impose on the small contingent of excited Paralympians representing Poland. Any attempt to assuage the heat ended in futility anyway.

Sitting center stage, and most decidedly holding court, were archers Ryszard and Malgorzata Olejnik. The duo has come to be the most popular athlete twosome to emerge out of their Eastern European homeland. Part of their popularity lies in their charm. Assuming the role of gracious hosts of the meeting, the Olejniks welcomed their teammates to the necessary formality. Acutely aware of the discomforting effects of the heat on their guests, they were quick to dole out water to their perspiring countrymen.

It was not long before the business on hand evolved into more unceremonious discourse. The Olejniks were soon regaling the small delegation with the story of how they met. "We first discovered each other at our workplace," began Malgorzata. "We fell in love and that was it. Really it was that quick. We both knew right away," she related with a smile.

In recounting to their fellow athletes the many things that the couple had in common with them, they amused with the most ironic discovery. "Really what are the odds?," exclaimed Ryszard. "That two people both love the same sport is not unusual, but for the sport to be archery?" He continued, "We began competing in the same meets. The great thing about archery is that you can participate in competitions for disabled and for able-bodied athletes."

REGINALD TIESSEN

When asked whom of the two is most proficient in their chosen sport, silence replaced the merriment of a moment ago. "I am," piped Ryszard. "I will agree," confessed Malgorzata, who then added, "but only because we have company and I wish to be polite." The laughter was restored. A second issue of contention within the couple bore itself out when Ryszard articulated his desire to compete in the Winter Olympics. "Downhill skiing! It's something that I really want to do," he enthused. "Why not? I ski all the time, I love it," he added in search for affirmation among his peers. "You have lost your mind," chided Malgorzata. "It's not enough that we have a beautiful life, a beautiful son. You need the extra challenge of broken limbs," she bantered.

Before the debate turned into a waging of war, the couple exchanged the look of a shared secret, turned to their audience and simultaneously shrugged their shoulders and smirked. The teasing had ended – for the moment. But the gleam in Ryszard's eye gave credence to the idea that the topic was far from buried.

REGINALD TIESSEN

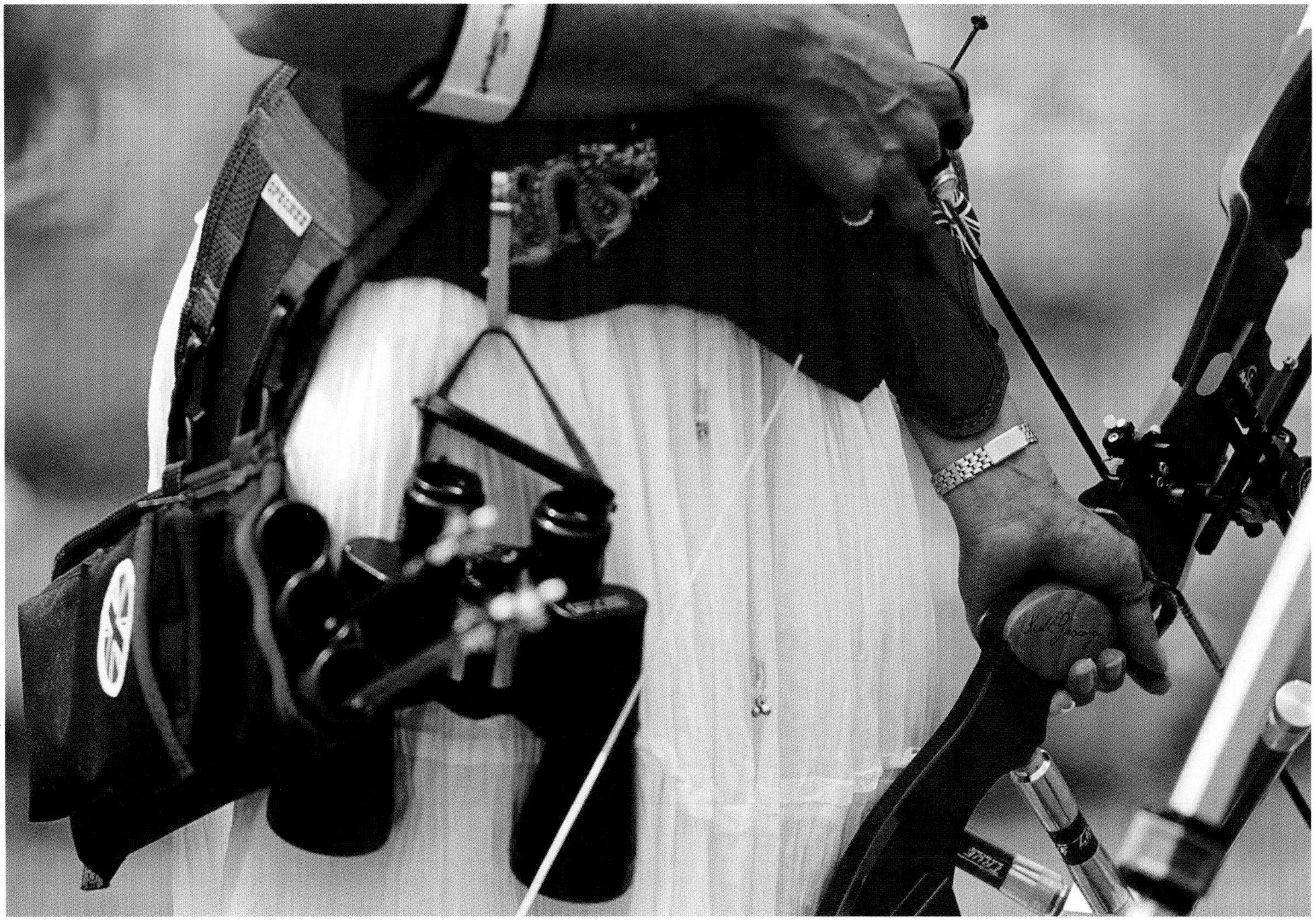

It was now time to focus on the sport that brought them together and to the pinnacle of competition for archers with a disability.

Their ranking in the sport is of little importance to them – they realize that they have made a long journey within a sport that requires discipline, a keen eye and a steady hand. They display these skills behind their bows, in front of their teammates and beside one another as they take aim on life.

BERNARD GLUCKSTEIN

REGINALD TIESSEN

Athletics

Athletics events are constantly re-defined to include as many athletes as possible. Athletics is open to all classes of athletes and includes track, throwing, jumping, pentathlon and the marathon. Although not all events are available to all disability categories, blind and visually impaired athletes, amputees, paraplegics, quadriplegics and athletes with cerebral palsy compete in most disciplines.

Competitive track and field events began in 1948 at the Stoke Mandeville Games in England and have been part of the Paralympic program since the first official Games in Rome in 1960. With 195 events and almost 900 competitors, the athletics competition was the largest sport at the 1996 Paralympic Games.

Athletes who are blind are allowed to use audible signals from fixed positions on the track or guide runners to assist them when they are competing. The guide, often

© CHRIS HAMILTON PHOTOGRAPHY, ATLANTA GA.

© CHRIS HAMILTON PHOTOGRAPHY, ATLANTA GA.

using a tether, can be even with or behind the athlete who they are piloting. A disqualification results if the guide finishes ahead of the runner. In the jumping events, a coach can give verbal cues to tell the athlete where the take-off mark is located.

Technological advances in prosthetic and wheelchair design have enabled athletes to enhance techniques and rapidly improve performances over the years. Composed of light-weight materials such as carbon fibre, athletes with lower limb prostheses continue to approach Olympic standards. Wheelchair racers now reach speeds in excess of 35 miles per hour on the road. In 1974, America's Bob Hall was the first wheelchair athlete to race the Boston Marathon taking 2 hours and 54 minutes to complete the course. In 1994, Heinz Frei of Switzerland covered Beantown's same 26 miles in 1 hour, 21 minutes and 23 seconds.

In wheelchair racing, there are strategies employed that are similar to bicycle or car racing. Being out in front has its advantages because the athlete can control the pace of the race and occupy the inside lane position. Any racer wishing to pass must use precious energy to swing wide. Staying behind another wheelchair racer also has its advantages – drafting off of the racer in front conserves energy.

Wheelchair racing began in 1952 at Stoke Mandeville as a means of competition for injured World War II veterans. The tarmac connecting the hospital to the medical helicopter pad was 60 metres long, so for years that was the distance at which wheelchair races were held. Bob Hall changed that forever, when he decided to try the mile. Soon after, distance racing became a competitive event.

New ground for athletes with a disability continues

Opposite page: Tony Volpentest

DANIEL GALBRAITH

to be broken. The 1996 Paralympic Games marked the first time that athletes with a mental disability were included in athletics with competitions in the 200 metre and long jump events for both men and women.

MARRIAGE OF MAN AND MACHINE
TONY VOLPENTEST

When no one else can beat him, Tony Volpentest strives to beat himself. That is exactly what happened on a much anticipated summer's evening in Georgia. Volpentest cut through the humid air to eclipse his own world record of 11.63 seconds in the 100 metre event for below-the-knee amputees. His winning time of 11.36 was only about one and a half seconds behind the world record set by Canada's Donovan Bailey at the Olympics two weeks earlier.

The 23-year-old was born without hands or feet,

DANIEL GALBRAITH

REGINALD TIESSEN

DANIEL GALBRAITH

but has reached his potential to be an outstanding athlete through the aid of high-tech prostheses. The Washington state resident has always strived to be the best in whatever he does. "Winning is never boring," he says. "But when you get out in front it is hard to continue to push yourself to go faster."

Volpentest's interest in sports started as a little boy. His dad taught him how to shoot a basketball when he was only three years old. His older brothers always included him, encouraging his participation in neighborhood games. When Volpentest was a sophomore in college, his friends pushed him to join the track team. "I did it for the camaraderie and friendship," explains Volpentest. He ended up earning a varsity letter in track, which inspired him to enter his first amputee competition. "I've never asked for special privileges; I believe a disability is all in the mind," he professes.

Volpentest began his athletic career using conventional prosthetic devices. It was only after he discovered a revolutionary spring mechanized foot that he began to fully reach his potential. The latest lightweight prosthetic componentry consists of an energy return system which enables him to train more like an able-bodied athlete. "My mechanics have changed 100 per cent throughout the years. By the year 2000, I hope to run every race under 11 seconds."

Aside from a three-hour a day training regimen, Volpentest reveals that he is also fueled by the enthusiasm of the crowd. "I try to draw as much energy as I can out of the crowds. When I know there are people out there who have come to see me run, that really energizes me for the race."

The class of his sport, Volpentest, through example and by his own volition, consistently champions the athleticism and ability within his field. Refering to his numerous media appearances prior to the Atlanta Paralympic Games, Volpentest suggests that athletes with a disability are finally being recognized as world class competitors. "That can only be a step in the right

REGINALD TIESSEN

direction for the Paralympic Movement," he offers, believing the best is yet to come for the Paralympics. Does that concern him at all as the reigning champion? Without hesitation he answers, "Like my coach always says, 'no matter how fast or strong you are, there is always someone out there who is bigger, faster or stronger.' I say bring 'em on."

TRUE GRIT
VASCO DA FONSECO

The sun was beating down hot and relentless on his back. The stage had been perfectly set. The event was the 100 metre, and Vasco Da Fonseco and his fellow competitors were pumped for the big race. Like prize fighters before their big bout, these athletes were already focusing on the accolades that would ensue with a win. The top finishers would advance to the final.

The Paralympics' 100 metre track event for below-the-knee amputees, like its Olympic counterpart, is historically regarded as one of the sports world's crowning events. "The fastest leg amputee in the world" would be determined.

But that afternoon, one of the eight men was not relishing the kudos that a victory would ensure. He was still trying to get over the enormity of having advanced this far. Da Fonseco was one of only two

Vasco Da Fonseco

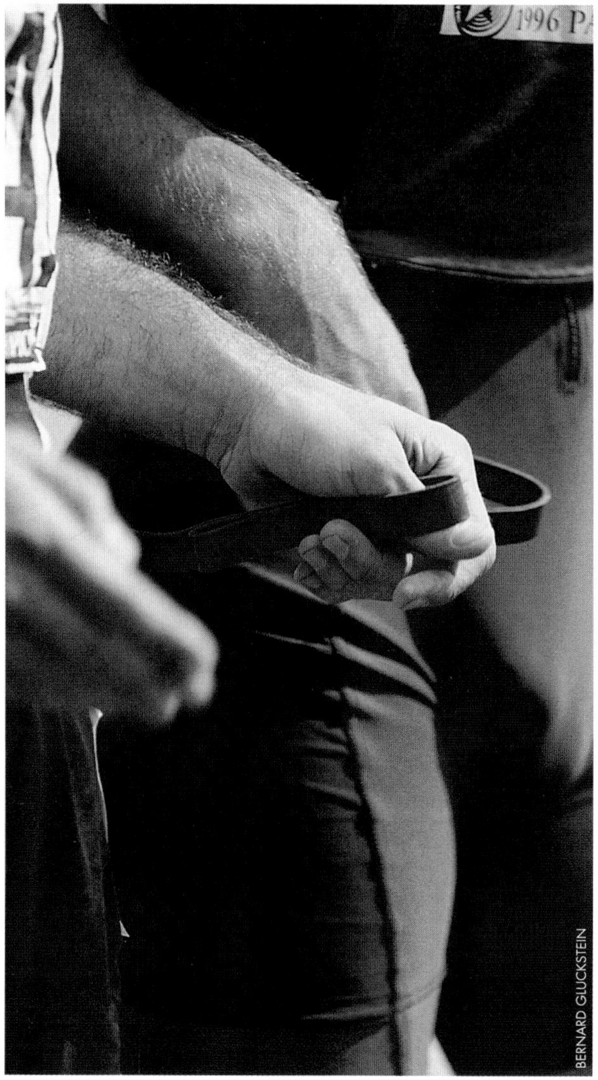

BERNARD GLUCKSTEIN

athletes in Atlanta representing the country of Angola in this nation's first foray into the Paralympic Games.

As the runners took their places at the start line with great deliberation, the minutes seeming to drag on unmercifully, Da Fonseco did the unthinkable. He had stared down adversity before, but this time, albeit briefly, he let his guard down. It was while he primed for take-off that the incident occurred. Da Fonseco lifted his gaze from the end of the track and turned it instead to the athletes surrounding him, revealing the awe that was overwhelming him. At first glance it did seem like a mismatch. The other competitors were sporting state-of-the-art prosthetic equipment and fashioning contemporary uniforms.

The moment had finally arrived. The starter's gun blasted and the runners exploded from their starting stances like shots from a cannon. Da Fonseco was just hitting his stride when he felt his fabricated leg buckle beneath him. The leather strap on his prosthetic leg had given way to the extreme pressure. He tumbled. The race was halted.

After a valiant effort by both volunteers and race officials to repair the strap, the limb was secured only by gaffer tape. Showing a grit and determination far beyond his 24 years, Da Fonseco opted to test his limb again. "I'm happy that I finished the race, but I'm sad that I couldn't represent my country the way it should have been represented," he explained afterward.

"I really wasn't intimidated because I know Angola does not have the money to spend like other countries do," summed Da Fonseco. "I was just trying to get out and show that I could run technically. I was just trying to get that across. I wasn't necessarily trying to beat the other guys." Having said that, when presented with the query of what would have happened had his strap not broken, the shy runner replied with a smile, "I would have finished first."

Da Fonseco is a young man who wears his patriotism proudly. There is not a trace of bitterness as he explains how he lost his leg. "I lost it while serving my country during the wars in Angola," remembers Da Fonseco. "I stepped on a land mine. I had been involved in soccer and athletics before the accident, but I gave them up to defend my country. I realized that losing my leg was not the end of the

world. I had to move on."

Moving on involves practicing the skill of his chosen craft – sewing – during the day and training for the sport he loves at night. Vasco Da Fonseco is one of those rare individuals who, unknowingly, gives far more than he or she recieves. What was expected to be a learning experience for him in Atlanta, instead became an education in spirit and hope for those fortunate enough to witness it.

REGINALD TIESSEN

© CHRIS HAMILTON PHOTOGRAPHY, ATLANTA GA.

PRIDE, HUMILITY & DISCIPLINE

BIN HOU

BE RD GLUCKSTE

It was a scene made for a movie. A young, nervous 23-year-old athlete staring up at his adversary – a fibreglass high jump bar hoisted over six feet from the ground. It was his third and final attempt at the height. He was jumping alone, having left behind the rest of his competition at a lower height. The gold medal was already his but the world record was not. He attained the mental advantage then dropped his crutches as unneeded things. On his one leg, he accelerated toward the launch point. His audience clapped and chanted, then at the moment of take-off instantly held its collective breath. The athlete powered straight up completing a forward flip over the bar. It did not budge. He was victorious.

It was the jump that was experienced throughout Atlanta. Front page news. Bin

Hou, a paper plant worker from northern China had shattered a world record with his 1.92 metre leap in the high jump event. No one was more surprised than the man himself, whose shy disposition was in sharp contrast with the media glare surrounding him and his accomplishment. "I'm not used to this kind of attention," explained Hou through an interpreter. "I'm happy I accomplished what I did, but I just came here to do my best, not necessarily to beat a record," he offered with a downward glance.

What later unfolded however, would not have made for a feel-good movie ending. His jump was incorrectly announced as a world record. It was not so. There are complexities in the business of the Paralympics that relate to the multiple records within events which is attributable to the classification system. The 1996 Paralympic Games served as the first competition in which those high jumpers with an amputation above the knee were in the same competitive category as those amputated below the knee. High jumpers with the more severe amputation can actually have an advantage, because they have less leg – and no prosthesis – to propel over the bar. And there existed Canadian record holder Arnold Boldt's mark of 1.98 metres for above-the-knee amputees. Hou was six centimetres shy of the long-standing target.

Bin Hou

DANIEL GALBRAITH

Still it is hard to imagine how anyone – no matter how humble – would not take pride in this personal achievement. "I am proud," said Hou, "it's just that the other athletes are very good as well. They should get the attention too." Hou takes an almost methodical approach to his sport, taking nothing for granted, training beyond the point of endurance, and expecting nothing less than excellence from himself.

It was at age nine that Hou, on a family outing, went to meet some relatives at the train station. A tragic slip from the platform resulted in Hou being swept underneath the train. The accident left him an above-the-knee amputee. "At first it was very difficult for me to adjust," remembered Hou, "because I was very young and I didn't understand what was happening to me. All I knew was that I only had one leg, while all my friends had two." After a lengthy rehabilitation that included learning to walk on a prosthetic leg, Hou learned to accept his disability with strength and determination. "Once you get used to the idea, it's not that difficult," he explained. "It's a question of discipline."

BERNARD GLUCKSTEIN

DANIEL GALBRAITH

BERNARD GLUCKSTEIN

SOLDIERING AFIELD
MOSTAFA GUHDIJA

So many Paralympic athletes have overcome personal barriers through great determination. Their stories inspire others to believe that anything is possible. Some athletes seem to have a way of always finding their way into the limelight while others, albeit equally deserving, never seem to surface under the spotlight. This account is a tribute to all those whose determination remains unsung.

Try to imagine waiting for what you think is a break in shelling so that you can return to streets blanketed by rubble to resume training for your sport. Bosnia's Mostafa Guhdija does not have to imagine; it is his reality.

"Everything has been destroyed in the ongoing war in the former Yugoslavia and nothing is left for the residents to live in, let alone train in," laments Guhdija. He describes early morning as the safest time of the day to practice javelin and shot put in the streets. "Soldiers are trying to get some sleep before a long day of fighting, so early morning seems to be quiet," he reports. "But you never know, I'm always aware of what's going on around me and any noise usually sends me into hiding."

Mostafa Guhdija

© CHRIS HAMILTON PHOTOGRAPHY, ATLANTA GA.

REGINALD TIESSEN

REGINALD TIESSEN

Guhdija was a commander in the engineering unit for the Bosnian army. His job was to disarm trip and land mines on the battle field, a task Guhdija knew was dangerous, but understood had to be done. On his second day he eliminated ninety-nine mines but was ordered to do one more before the day's work was done. That one, a step mine, went off. Guhdija's heel was blown off. The rest of his foot was filled with shrapnel. He administered first-aid before searching out a medical center a distant 16 kilometres away. There, the medical supplies were scarce, but the situation worsened when the enemy surrounded the center obstructing the admittance of medical personnel and supplies.

After 15 days of inadequate care, gangrene took hold. Guhdija's foot rapidly decayed. "There was no food in the hospital," Guhdija recalls. "I begged the doctor to cut bark from the trees outside and boil it in water for soup."

The gangrene was spreading up his leg and Guhdija knew something had to be done or he would die. He asked the doctor to amputate his leg, but the doctor refused. "The doctor told me he didn't have the proper instruments to do the amputation. He didn't have

DANIEL GALBRAITH

BERNARD GLUCKSTEIN

REGINALD TIESSEN

any anesthetic to numb the area or any antibiotics to fight infection. I knew the leg had to come off, so I did it myself. I remember holding the saw in my hand and singing my favorite song to calm me down. After the amputation I used my cigarette lighter to cauterize the severed tissue."

Six months after the amputation, Guhdija was released from care and allowed to return to Sarejavo. "I may be able to walk and live an active life, but I will never recover from the psychological damage of war," he says.

The 48-year-old is now the president of the Republic Association of Amputees for Bosnia Herzegovina. Guhdija is trying to introduce proper prosthetic devices to the country's thousands of amputee victims of war.

It was through the association that Guhdija became aware of sports for athletes with a disability. He wanted to participate to show the world that Bosnia is still

BERNARD GLUCKSTEIN

REGINALD TIESSEN

strong and the people still cling to the hope of peace. "I came to Atlanta for my country; I talk to other athletes and tell them about my beautiful home. I want to go back and spread the word of unity and friendship to the children. I want to show them pictures and teach them that people can live in peace."

Guhdija did not expect that he would return from Atlanta with a medal from his competitions. "I know the differences between me and the other athletes. While some have excellent living and training conditions, my country is at terrible war. I just wanted to witness the way life should be."

Guhdija did not place well in his shot put event, but progressed to the semi-final in his javelin event as the second seed overall. An infection in his residual limb nearly forced him out of that competition. But Guhdija endured, ultimately finishing fourth in the competition.

For a man who has been shot six times, amputated his own leg and refers to his war torn country as beautiful, he exemplifies the power of the human spirit. One can easily see from a soldier like Guhdija that it is easy to destroy buildings, but it is not easy to destroy man's spirit.

THE PARALYMPICS' FASTEST MAN
AJIBOLA ADEOYE

"I thank God for giving me the strength and courage to get here." That is what the fastest man in the world of sport for athletes with a disability had to say immediately after capturing track and field's coveted 100 metre gold medal. Ajibola Adeoye won convincingly in a time of 11.1 seconds in the classification for single arm amputees, but was just shy of his own world mark of 10.72 seconds recorded at the 1992 Paralympics in Barcelona.

The mild mannered Nigerian was beaming as he ran his victory lap around Centennial Olympic Stadium. It was the final day of competition at the Xth Paralympic Games, a fitting end to ten days of eye-opening competition for the uninitiated spectator. "The organizing committee saved the best for last," vaunted Adeoye.

Adeoye's 100 metre performances make for the most frequently compared Paralympic and Olympic results. According to some, Adeoye could, if he had both arms, have possibly run a time that would have put him on the medal podium in Olympic competition. Adeoye says that is encouraging, but he would

© CHRIS HAMILTON PHOTOGRAPHY, ATLANTA GA.

Ajibola Adeoye

DANIEL GALBRAITH

not trade his Paralympic experience for anything. "It is because of my disability that I am here. It is a great feeling to know I could compete in the Olympics, but I am grateful to compete in the Paralympics."

Adeoye lost his arm as a young boy after he toppled down a flight of stairs. His left arm got caught in the wrought-iron railing, breaking the bone in several places. Adeoye knows that with modern medicine his arm could have been secured in a cast and saved, but he does not begrudge his homeland for its medical shortcom-

REGINALD TIESSEN

ings. "Nigeria is a developing country, and was not advanced medically, so the doctor said my arm had to be amputated." Adeoye would rather look for the good that came from his injury. "It changed my life when I lost my arm, but you have to live with what God gives you; He obviously wanted it to be this way. Everyone has a purpose in life and I'm beginning to understand what mine is." Adeoye works for a sports council in Nigeria to advance sports for both disabled and able-bodied people in his country.

Earlier in the competition, Adeoye injured his hamstring muscle in the 200 metre track event. On the morning of his 100 metre final, he considered pulling out of his most important race to avoid more serious or permanent injury to his leg. "My leg was hurting me, but I knew what I had to do. After all the obstacles I've overcome in my life, I could overcome this one too."

When the gun sounded, Adeoye took off out of the starting blocks like a bullet. He had begun his victory lap before some of his competitors had crossed the finish line. "When you finish the race first, the rush of joy is unbelievable, but when you turn around and see the scoreboard showing you've broke the world record, it's like living in a dream," he described. Adeoye missed living that dream in Atlanta but was more than satisfied with his gold medal performance. "I did it. I overcame the obstacles and accomplished what I set out to do. It is over and I'm proud to be Nigerian."

Adeoye says, if he could turn back time and Nigeria

DANIEL GALBRAITH

POWERADE
582

had the means, he would definitely choose a cast to save his arm. "But then again, I wouldn't have the incredible memories of competing in the Paralympics. I would probably never know the feelings I'm experiencing right now, and I would never know how it feels to be called the fastest amputee in the world. Maybe tomorrow my answer would be different, but today, I'm glad I don't have to make that choice."

MARATHON MAN
HEINZ FREI

The name Heinz Frei is not only synonymous with wheelchair racing, it also exhorts the highest level of athleticism and dedication. This 37-year-old Swiss champion has been at the forefront of wheelchair sport since his induction many years ago.

Not surprisingly, Frei has become a mentor to many younger athletes following in his trail. With nine Paralympic gold medals, seven World Championship victories, and countless marathon titles to boast of upon his arrival in Atlanta, Frei has become a symbol of excellence.

The position of role model is one that Frei takes very seriously. "I try to work hard for the younger guys," explained Frei. "Not just in Switzerland, but everywhere. That way young people will know that there is this venue for them. They will want to strive for this goal, and that will help them and the Paralympic Games."

Frei is not just paying lip service to the Paralympic Movement. In addition to his cartography job, he also maps out time to conduct presidential duties for a local wheelchair sports club and spearheads the technical committee on wheelchair sports in Switzerland.

Already a hero in his homeland, Frei takes every advantage of that status by including public speaking engagements at local schools as part of his schedule. "We are very lucky in Switzerland," explained Frei, "as far as integration among persons with and without disabilities is concerned. I think it's nearly perfect," he exulted. Frei believes that, "the Paralympics is the venue to help it be the same elsewhere."

Previous page: Heinz Frei

DANIEL GALBRAITH

When he is not competing, Frei can inevitably be found talking with other athletes, offering compassion and expertise whenever needed. It is this down-to-earth quality that has afforded him so much respect among his peers.

Dedication to sports and striving to be the best is nothing new for this Paralympian. It was while competing in a mountain marathon 18 years ago that Frei lost his balance and plunged six metres before coming to rest on the moun-

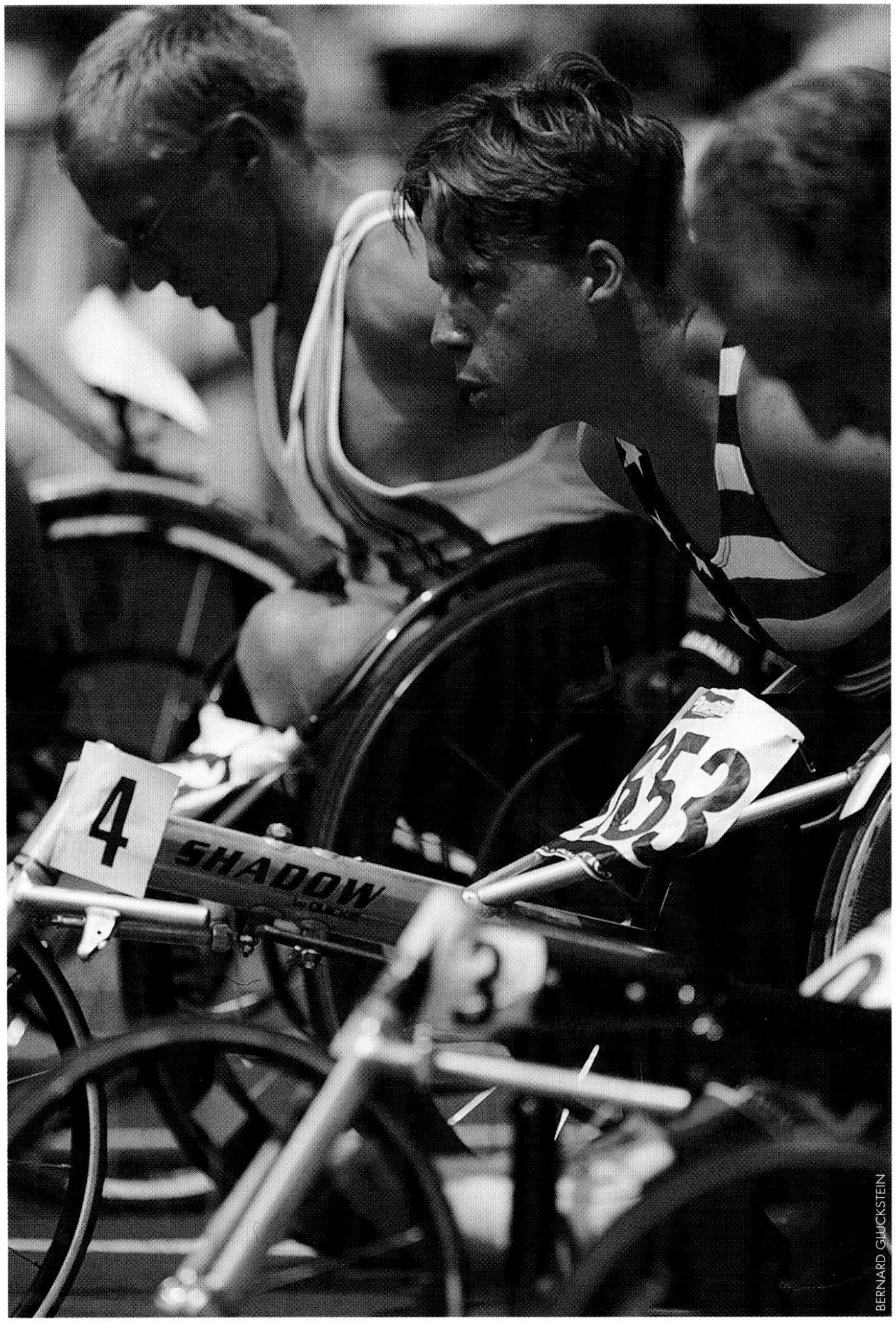

BERNARD GLUCKSTEIN

tain's side. The ensuing result was a broken back.

"At first it was really hard to think about sports, or the future," remembers Frei. "Before it happened I knew my body really well. I didn't know what I would be able to do in a wheelchair. I was at home for a full year, studying. Then I thought I should do a little bit for myself, to be able to empower myself. It was then that I took up wheelchair sports. I find that I'm mentally stronger now than I was before the injury."

It is that strength that constantly pushes Frei to excel. Case in point, Frei was slotted to compete in the 400 metre event in Atlanta but decided to pull himself out and compete instead in the marathon. "I'm sure it would have been easier for me to win gold in the 400 metre," explained Frei, "but the marathon is more of a challenge for me. It's more difficult. It's important to me to keep pushing myself." Frei certainly recognizes a challenge when he sees one. He finished in third position.

A strong sense of family helps to keep this athlete focused. Married with two young children, Frei tries to spend as much time at home now as possible. Nonetheless, visions of Sydney are already swirling in his head. "I will be 42 years old in the year 2000," he revealled with a smile, "but, if I have good results, why not?" For such an ambassador, why not indeed.

DANIEL GALBRAITH

Basketball

Wheelchair basketball players set picks, run fast breaks and shoot with incredible accuracy from three-point range. Played in wheelchairs by competitors with paraplegia, amputees, athletes with polio and with cerebral palsy, the Paralympic basketball program is virtually the same as that played in the Olympic Games. Games last 40 minutes and are played on regulation courts with regulation-height baskets and a three-point line.

Slight modifications to the rules allow players two pushes of the wheelchair to every dribble of the ball. More than two pushes is considered a traveling violation. A technical foul results if a player touches his or her feet to the ground.

To ensure fairness in the ability levels of opposing teams, each player is classified according to his or her disability within a point system ranging from one to 4.5. The higher the classification, the less severe the athlete's disability. For International Wheelchair Basketball Federation competition, the points for each player on the court during play cannot exceed 14.0 when totalled for each team.

Wheelchair basketball has been on the Paralympic competition schedule since the first set of games in Rome in 1960. With its beginnings in 1946 in Veterans Administration Hospitals in California and Massachusetts, the Paralympic Games were a fitting celebration of the 50th anniversary of the game of wheelchair basketball.

© CHRIS HAMILTON PHOTOGRAPHY, ATLANTA

CANADA

DANIEL GALBRAITH

WITH GLOWING HEARTS
CHANTAL BENOIT

One of the most poignant moments during the 1996 Paralympic Games followed the crowning of the Canadian women's wheelchair basketball team as tournament champions. Minutes after the first blush of celebration, Canada's team captain Chantal Benoit hoisted herself ten feet above court level to cut down the net for her teammates in traditional fashion. It was a gesture that perfectly encapsulated a game that was frought with nail-biting, on-edge excitement.

The Canadians successfully shouldered the weight of being deemed "tournament favorites" throughout the event, but found themselves facing an intimidating adversary in Team Holland for the gold medal show-down. It was victory for the Canucks – but a narrow one. Up until the last five minutes of play, it was either team's game. But from deep within, the Canadians found the will to turn the game around in their favor. They harnessed the momentum. They knew it. The crowd felt it.

"We had the desire," declared Benoit. "Our coach said to us at half time, 'we came here to win – and we will win.'" The tactics of coach Tim Frick were to be

Previous page: Chantal Benoit

applauded. He was fundamental in the unifying of his team. His effectiveness lies in his belief that a team that can gel as a unit off the court, can not lose on the court.

"That is one reason why the women's wheelchair basketball program is so strong in Canada," said Benoit. "We are not just a basketball team, we are a family. What makes this team a unit is the love we have for one another. When we get on the court, we don't complain; we understand where people come from."

Where Benoit comes from is a small town just twenty miles outside of Montreal. There, she eats, breathes and sleeps sports. At the age of eighteen, she learned she had bone cancer as she neared the national level in the sport of diving. One year later she had her leg amputated. But with that anguish came a new passion – wheelchair basketball. "After I

DANIEL GALBRAITH

DANIEL GALBRAITH

lost my leg, I started looking for a new sport," explained Benoit. "I needed that in my life. Sport gives me the opportunity to be the best I can be technically, physically and emotionally. Wheelchair basketball is a sport that gives me all of that. It's so intense and aggressive ... each day that I go to the court, I learn something new."

An added ingredient in the team's winning formula was the outreach of sup-

DANIEL GALBRAITH

port from family and friends at home in Canada and courtside in Atlanta. "We had our family in the stands, and we received dozens of fax messages from Canada every day," beamed Benoit. "The walls in our residence were wallpapered with well wishes. When you experience that each day, it empowers you."

Benoit embodies her team's character, mental and physical prowess and fervent desire to win. They play with pride each and every time out. And for

them there was no prouder moment in Atlanta than that that held Canada's signature Maple Leaf overhead, flanked by the flags of the silver and bronze medal-winning nations, swaying to the sounds of the anthem of the true north.

Boccia

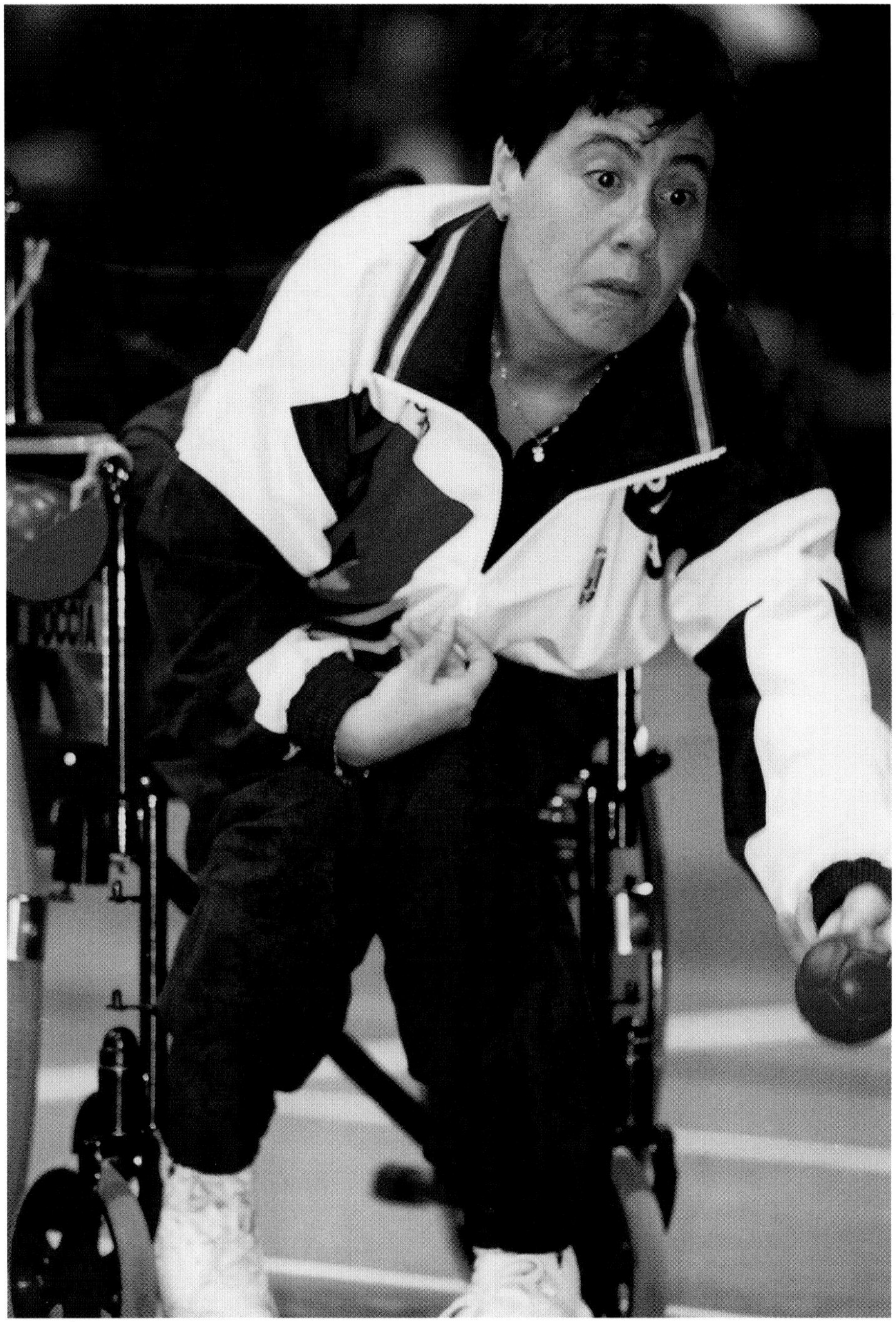

REGINALD TIESSEN

Passed down from Greek ball-tossing games, this ancient game is said to have been refined by the Italians in 16th century Florence. Successfully adapted for people with disabilities, this game of precision is played by athletes with cerebral palsy. The athlete attempts to place leather balls as close to a small white ball as possible by throwing them down a long, narrow playing field. Points are awarded according to placement nearest the white ball, also known as 'the jack'. There are team and individual competitions. The 1992 Paralympic Games in Barcelona marked the first time boccia was included in the program of events.

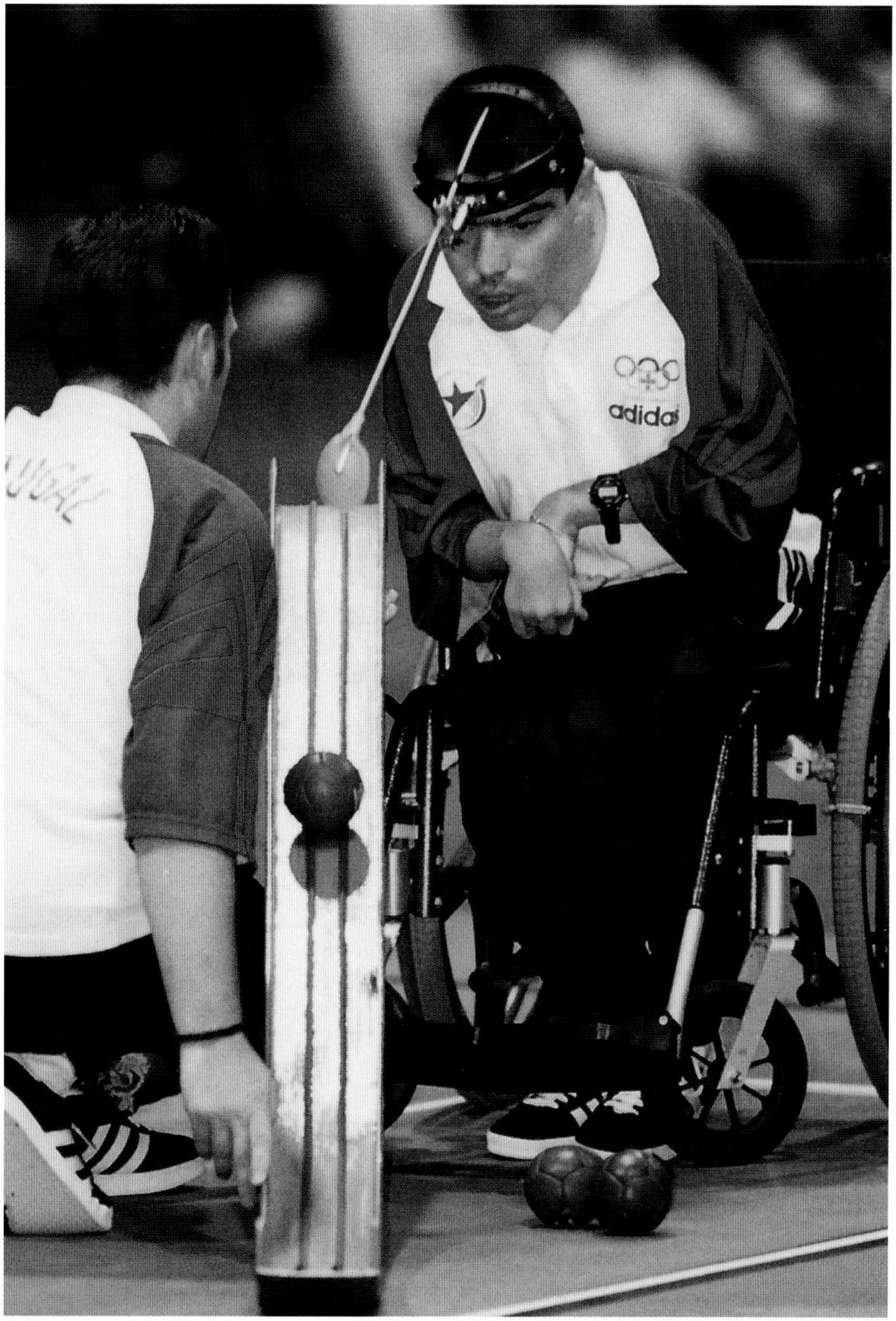

REGINALD TIESSEN

MASTER OF THE JACK
JOSE CARLOS MACEDO

At seven years old, Jose Carlos Macedo was like any other active young boy growing up in Portugal. It was after a play fight with a childhood friend that his life would become forever altered. A blow to the head resulted in severe brain trauma.

"At first I didn't even notice it," recalls Macedo, "but then I started to get sick. They thought at first it was just a concussion, but when I was getting worse instead of better the doctors realized it was much more serious." Although Macedo, because of his age, did not realize what was happening, he knew that things he could do easily before had become almost impossible. After a lengthy rehabilitation process that Macedo concedes "did not work", he decided instead to turn his focus on something he could master – the game of boccia.

"I found that I had the ability to play this game," enthuses Macedo. "Not only could I play it, but I could play it very well. I love this game very much, I think I would enjoy it even if I didn't play so well. Well, maybe not *as* much," he muses.

But athletic success has not always come easy for the young man with the easy laugh. His teammates

Jose Carlos Macedo

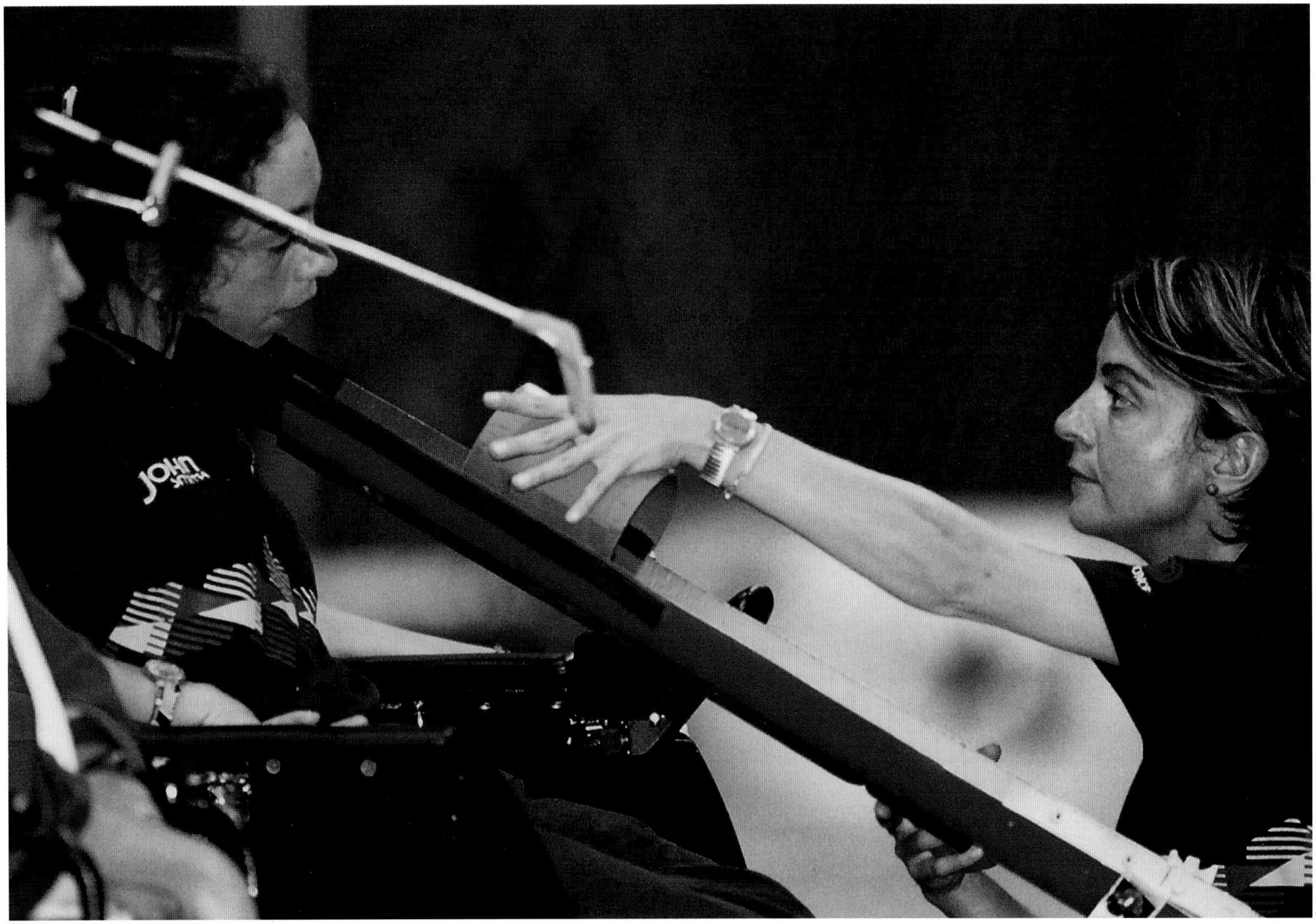

REGINALD TIESSEN

in Atlanta had dubbed him *the bridesmaid* – “always there for the first dance but gone by the time the music was off,” they teased affectionately.

In an effort to springboard his competitiveness into a chance at a spot on Portugal’s Paralympic Team, Macedo entered every boccia competition possible. All the major European events saw his shadow, at least until the final round, at which point he consistently succumbed to defeat. “I lost them all,” remembers

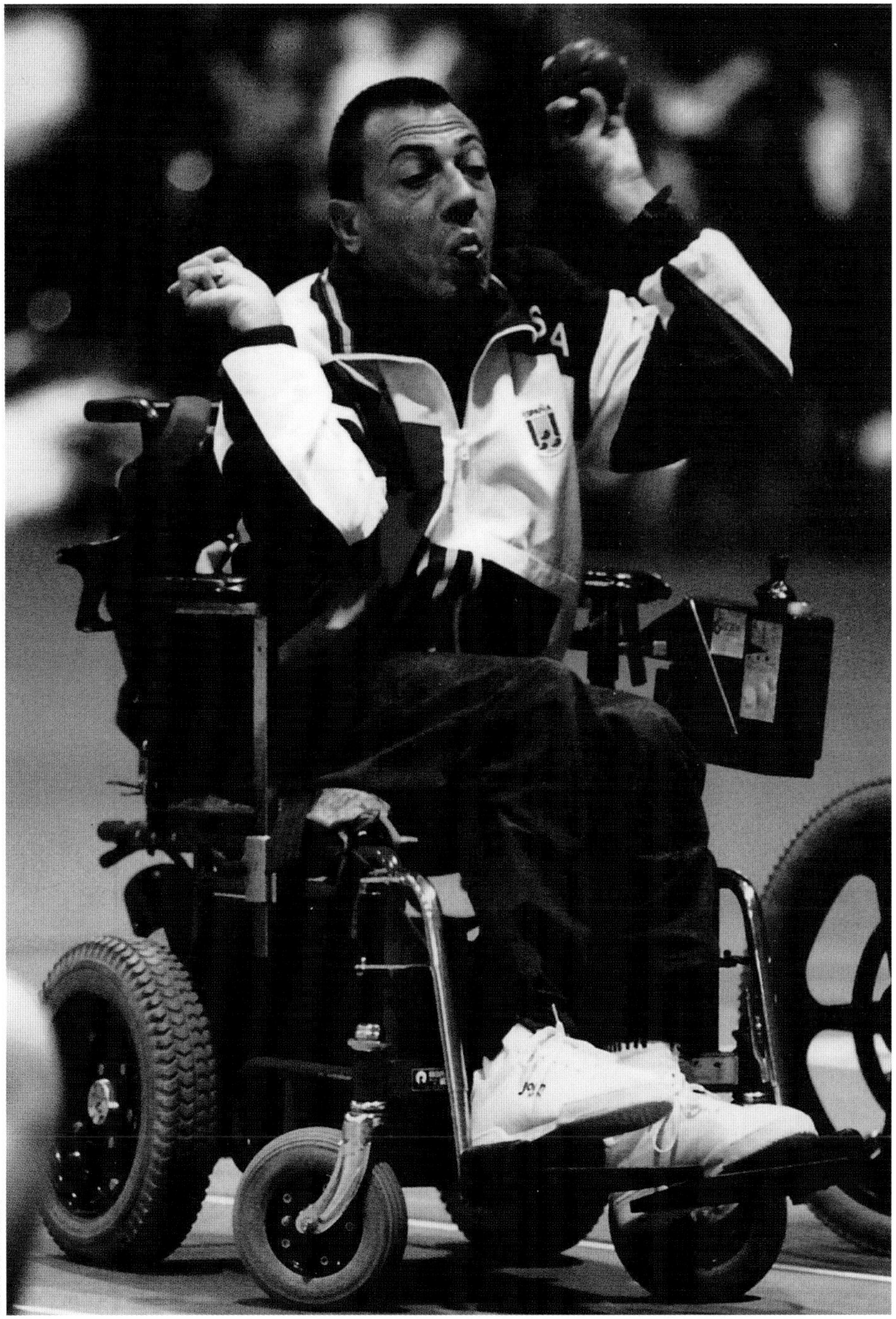

REGINALD TIESSEN

Macedo with a smile. "It seemed the more I tried to do, the worse I got. I wanted so much to play in Atlanta."

Although the road to Atlanta was paved with some disappointments, the reward far outweighed any past injustices. Nothing short of top honors was what Macedo accomplished in Georgia. The gold medal in his category left him harboring no ill will toward his teammates' taunts.

He expected nothing less than a ticker tape parade when he returned to the small village that he calls home. "People there have been very supportive of me," says Macedo. "There will be many anxious people awaiting my return. We will all celebrate together."

Jose Carlos Macedo went to Atlanta with the dream of winning it all. Four years of finishing just short in international play had taught him to be optimistic but cautious. A natural aptitude in the sport in which he excels, and the ability to appreciate the positive in everything he sees, made his victory a sweet one for the Portugese.

Cycling

Technology and old-fashioned competitiveness combined for crowd-pleasing shows in the Paralympic cycling competition on the road and at the Velodrome. Cycling has long been a popular sport for athletes with a disability, but was only added to the Paralympic program in 1988 in Seoul, Korea.

Competition rules are the same as those of the International Amateur Cycling Federation, but allow for modifications to the cycles for reasons of safety and accommodation according to disability classification. Three categories of athletes participate in cycling. Athletes with cerebral palsy compete in bicycle and tricycle events. Visually impaired and blind competitors cycle in tandems, forming a team with a sighted guide or "pilot" for the road and track events. Two tandems racing side by side, shoulder to shoulder, at speeds in excess of 30 miles per hour, provided some of the most compelling drama that the 1996 Paralympic Games had to offer.

Amputees compete in individual road and omnimium events. From carbon fibre legs to electronic shifting units, many of these competitors use specially constructed cycles and prosthetic devices offering a variety of styles and strategies that accommodate for their missing limbs.

NORM LOURENCO

NORM LOURENCO

TAKES TWO TO TANDEM

PATRIZIA SPADACCINI AND CLAUDIO COSTA

The Paralympic Games bring people together in a way that is both inspiring and enlightening. Nowhere was this more evident than in the case of Patrizia Spadaccini and Claudio Costa, who together make up one of Italy's most celebrated duos.

Upon first meeting the cycling pair, each athlete couldn't appear more different from the other. Spadaccini's boldness and vivacity seem in direct opposition to Costa's more reserved manner. But the dedication and respect that the twosome demonstrate toward one another is equally apparent.

Spadaccini and Costa compete on a tandem cycle in road and track events for blind competitors. Spadaccini is the sighted cyclist. On foot, she breezes about the venue, hand in hand with Costa, like a starlet in Monaco.

"I knew we would win gold," Spadaccini admitted. "The course felt good for both of us, and you know, we deserved it," she said with a confidence that has been nourished by the accolades and media hype surrounding her own solo career. An accomplished cyclist in her own right, she gave up competing on the Italian Women's Cycling Tour in order to ride with Costa in Atlanta.

"I was looking for something," she revealed of her decision to take up tandem cycling. "It seemed a little crazy, but you know, so am I." Crazy? Maybe, but this duo forms an impenetrable weave that

REGINALD TIESSEN

appears seamless. Costa and Spadaccini have been riding together since 1995. "I just took a chance on her," remembered Costa. "I went to the Italian Federation for Cycling and asked her if she wanted to try it." His timing couldn't have been better; Spadaccini was looking for something more from the sport in which she excelled.

"I know that I can play a role in changing things," maintained Spadaccini. "My name is already known in Italy, so I can use that to bring more attention to sports for disabled athletes. People are not yet aware of the intensity of the Paralympic Games or the talent of these athletes. Claudio is one of the best cyclists I've ever seen, sighted or not."

There is, however, one point of dissention between the two. "I want to drive," protested Costa. "She won't let me." Exasperated, Spadaccini reminded him that

NORM LOURENCO

REGINALD TIESSEN

he can't see the road. Costa remained unfazed. A chafed Spadaccini recalled an incident where they lost a race because of Costa's lack of trust in her driving. Working with a partner is as new a sensation for Costa as it is for Spadaccini. Before commiting to tandem cycling, Costa competed in athletics at the Paralympic level. He turned his body towards Spadaccini putting his hand on hers, "I trust you Patrizia."

The warmth and compassion that the two openly share toward each other gives the impression of a married couple. Not so. Costa has been married for six years to Christina, who was present for her husband's gold medal victories. Spadaccini is unmarried but – with the passion of an Italian actress – emoted, 'I have a great love'.

The bond that these two have created comes from constant contact. Living 300 kilometres apart makes it impossible for them to train together on a regular basis. Instead, they talk almost daily.

"We are always in touch," explained Spadaccini. "If we are having any kind of problem we speak about it. Not just sport, anything. He is very open-minded. We would never be able to compete at this level if we didn't have a very strong friendship. We care very much for each other."

It is their skill and competitiveness that has catapulted this pair into the upper sphere of their sport, but it is the considerateness and respect that this duo shows one another that puts them in front of the pack.

NORM LOURENCO

Equestrian

For the first time in Paralympic history, equestrian events were part of the program. Although new to the competition calendar, equestrian was a full medal sport. Modern competitive dressage for riders with physical disabilities began in the 1970s in Scandinavia and England.

Unlike Olympic equestrian athletes, Paralympians compete only in dressage, a series of ballet-like movements performed during the walk, trot and canter gaits. Riders are judged on their horsemanship skills – how well the horse responds to his or her commands.

Also unlike Olympic riders, Paralympians are not judged on their posture or how they hold their hands. Open to all disability categories, many competitors do not have complete use of their legs and therefore use their hands to stay balanced on the horse.

Riders are divided into four classes of disability, or "grades", that range from high levels of paralysis to those who are blind or visually impaired. Riders develop creative ways to communicate with their horses if they are unable to give signals with their legs, which is standard for dressage. For example, the rider may use a dressage whip or other aid in place of a leg. Equestrians who are blind or have a visual impairment rely on the voices of "callers" to guide them around the 20-by -40 foot dressage ring. These "living letters" stand in place of the pillared letters that sighted riders navigate by and call them out as the athlete approaches. Riders are also allowed to use adaptive equipment such as deep-seated saddles to assist them to stay on the horse. They may not however, strap themselves to the saddle.

One of the toughest challenges facing the Paralympic riders in Atlanta was having to perform on borrowed horses, which they mounted for the first time only one week before the competition began. Once the horse became familiar with its rider, it then was trained to respond to the movements that athlete used as commands. The teams that gelled proficiently generally finished in the medals.

NORM LOURENCO

NORM LOURENCO

SIGHTS SET HIGH
MIRJAM AMSING

One thing becomes apparent when you first meet Mirjam Amsing – she is a mass of contradictions. At once shy and retiring, she is also tenacious and exacting. While boasting a smile that could light up even the dourest of faces, she also possesses a steely countenance that rests under a blue-eyed facade.

But there can be no misinterpretation of the way Amsing feels about her sport. Her passion for equestrian events is all-encompassing. "When I was eight, my parents bought me a pony," recalls the Dutch competitor. "It was difficult at first, but other sports posed greater hurdles for me because of my physical disability." Amsing is legally blind. "A horse made sense, I live on a farm."

For a sighted person to climb up on an animal twice their size can be intimidating enough, but for someone who must rely on the good nature of their steed, it can be a daunting task. "I was never nervous," explained Amsing, "I have never been an anxious person and I have a fondness for animals that makes it impossible for me to fear them."

She began her competitive career in able-bodied equestrian events, but felt that there, she would

Opposite page: Mirjam Amsing

NORM LOURENCO

never attain international status. The Paralympics became her stage upon which she could challenge the world.

Paradoxically, Amsing admitted to riding more confidently in regular events than she did in the Paralympic competition. "Because we were on borrowed horses, it was very difficult," described Amsing. "The time is too short to create a bond with the horse."

Not one to shy away from taking action in the face of percieved inadequacy, Amsing, in the middle of one of her tests, directed her 'borrowed horse' out of the arena. "I stopped it," reflected Amsing, "it was impossible to ride further. I had a very bad horse. This was just something I couldn't accept."

What some may perceive as intolerance in Amsing, is in actuality a plea for progress. "I understand that all the riders are at the same disadvantage," she offered. "I just hope that in Sydney (Australia) they realize that because of the faith we put in these animals, allowing us to ride our own horses will only benefit the riders and the Paralympic Games."

Some of Amsing's immense fortitude comes from having the support of her family squarely behind her. Growing up on a farm in a small village in Holland, Amsing was not allowed to be merely a token hand in the family business. "I don't know what it is like to see, so for me people have never treated me differently; it was not like I lost something I once had. I never, ever thought 'oh, I can't do that because I'm blind'."

© CHRIS HAMILTON PHOTOGRAPHY, ATLANTA GA.

NORM LOURENCO

Life for this vivacious athlete is a constant whirlwind of activity. She has cut back her hours on the farm to allow for a university education in marketing, and still demands from herself an exacting schedule which will allow her to excel in the equestrian arena. No doubt about it, this young woman has her sights set on the future.

Fencing

Fencing is a sport that demands quickness, agility and discipline. This sport features amputees, athletes with cerebral palsy and competitors who use wheelchairs. All athletes compete in wheelchairs in one of only two categories. Wheelchairs are fastened to the floor to prevent tipping and to allow freedom of movement of the fencer's upper body only.

With the exception of the seated position, wheelchair fencing remains essentially the same sport as that for able-bodied fencers. Three blades – foil, epee and sabre – are the weapons used and combatants are connected electronically to a signal box that records touches. Because wheelchair fencers rely only on leaning backward and forward to evade an opponent, the focus is on complex lightning-like blade movement and skilled hand-eye coordination.

Fencing for athletes with a disability was introduced by Sir Ludwig Guttmann in 1953 with the first international competition taking place two years later. Fencing has been part of the Paralympic program since its inception in 1960.

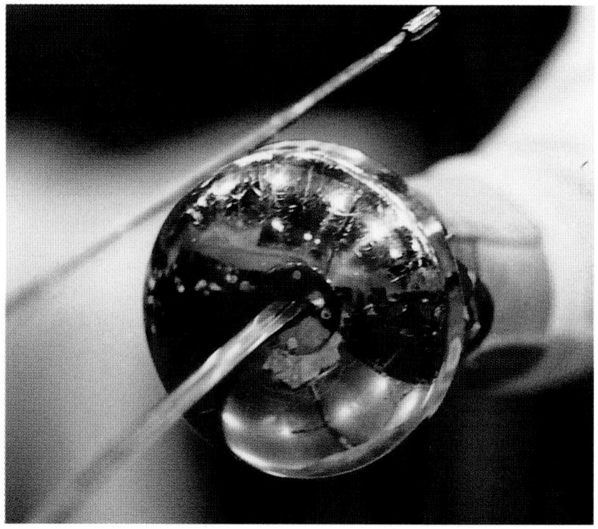

DANIEL GALBRAITH

NORM LOURENCO

NORM LOURENCO

EN GARDE!
PAL SZEKERES

Long considered the game of gentlemen, the sport of fencing comes from a distinguished past, from a time when any issue of honor was solved with a pair of leather gloves and an epee. Although still demanding the same quickness and precision, the sport has taken on a more civilized tone. No longer is the intent

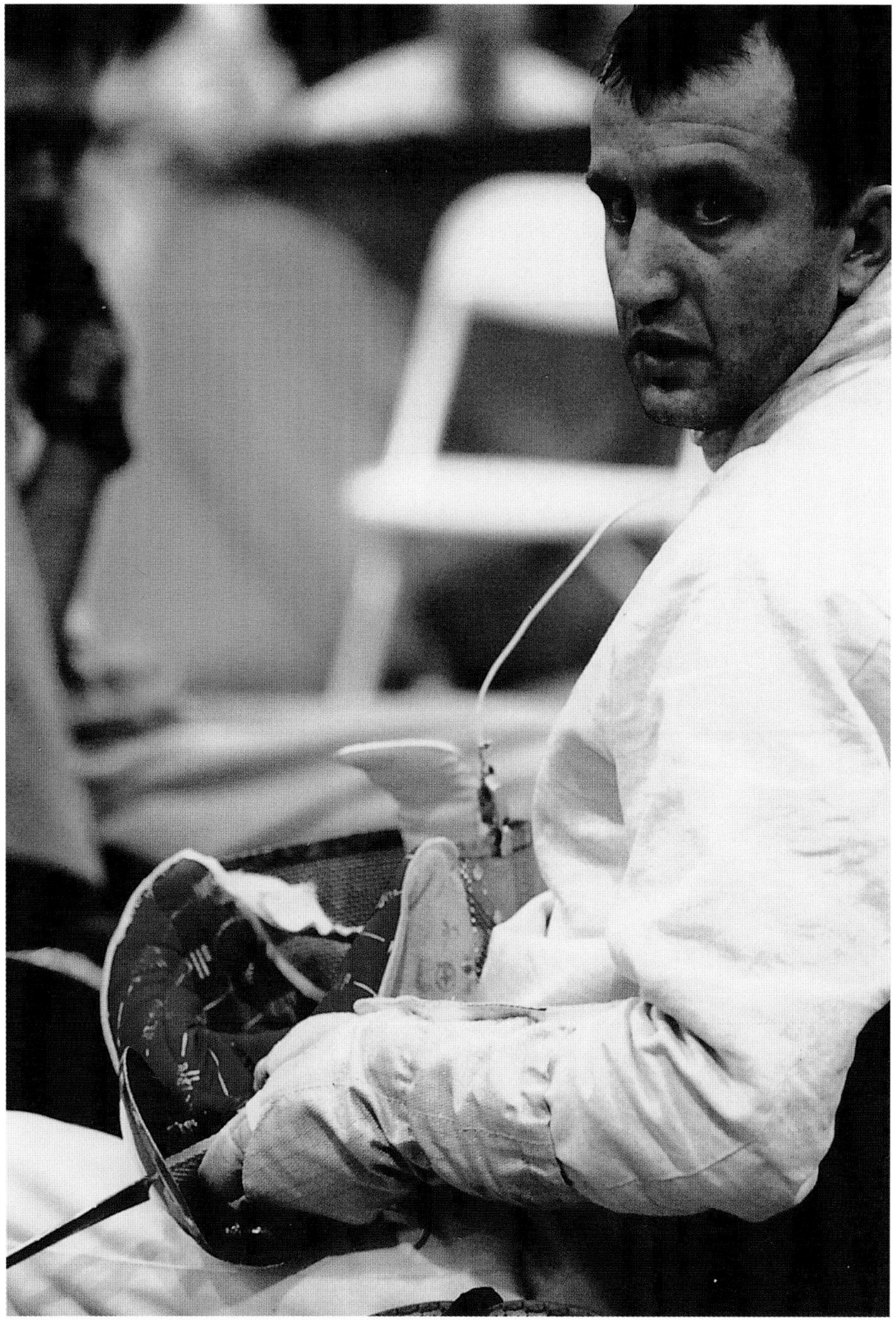
NORM LOURENCO

to seriously injure an opponent a motivating force.

It was in the serene environment of Atlanta's fencing venue one afternoon that a reaction occurred reminiscent of days gone by. A young Hungarian man had just won the gold in the Individual Epee. Without warning, a shriek from the typically sedate crowd caused spectators to gasp in horror as they witnessed a lovely young woman hurdling her way through the onlookers to the competitors' field of play. With unabashed joy, she sealed the victory with a kiss. "Aaaah," was heard throughout the arena as news traveled into the stands – "newlyweds".

For Pal and Aniko Szekeres, it was a gesture that perfectly capped their immense devotion toward one another. Their relationship had survived the tribulations and uncertainties associated with the sudden onset of a disability. More than that, it had flourished because of it.

The couple had met through their mutual passion for fencing. Pal was near the top of his field in the men's category, competing internationally in able-bodied events. It was on the way back from a fencing competition in Germany that the bus on which he and his teammates were traveling lost control. "I

Pal Szekeres

PAYS
CARTON
NOM
SCORE
Piste 1
HABIB
KUW

was just changing seats to play cards," recalled Szekeres, "when all of a sudden the driver slammed on the breaks. The bus jumped and I was thrown out the window. My spinal cord was severed at the seventh vertebrae. Everybody else on the bus was fine. I ended up in a wheelchair."

The transition from able-bodied athlete to disabled athlete was a difficult one for Szekeres. "The first thing I thought was 'my God, my life is over'," remembered Szekeres. "I wanted to commit suicide. I wasn't even thinking of Aniko or our relationship together. I thought she wouldn't want me in a chair." Szekeres continued, "Then slowly things started to change. One day I saw a bunch of guys in wheelchairs and they had women around. I started realizing that being disabled didn't mean being a prisoner. Aniko never stopped loving or supporting me. I was the one who couldn't accept the disability."

Szekeres says that once he was able to deal with what was happening, things improved very quickly. "I left the hospital and went straight to my first disabled fencing competition and I haven't looked back since."

Now all Szekeres wants to do is to give back to the woman and the country to which he owes so much. "In Hungary I have always been considered a sportsman," said Szekeres. "They have never put the disibility first. Now part of my job – with my status – is to show what can be accomplished from the chair."

Part of Szekeres' journey of retribution includes studying physical therapy with the intent of becoming a fencing coach. For now though, he is somewhat preoccupied. Not on the gold medal that hangs from his neck, nor on the trials that have seen him arrive at this point. He is focused instead on the young woman who has never left his side and who is now receiving his full attention. Atlanta was not only a chance to achieve the highest rewards in his chosen sport. There was a second agenda. To truly encapsulate what this sport and this journey has meant to this couple they chose to add special significance to it by making the Atlanta 1996 Paralympic Games the site of their honeymoon.

REGINALD TIESSEN

DANIEL GALBRAITH

A variant of the game of soccer, football is played by teams fielding seven athletes with cerebral palsy. The game is played under Federation Internationale de Football Association rules with only slight modifications to accommodate the athlete's disability. For example, the standard over-head, two-arm throw-in can be performed with one arm. The field and the goal nets are smaller in size and the penalty kick is closer to the goal line than a conventional soccer field.

The Netherlands came to Atlanta as the defending European and Paralympic champions, capturing the gold medal in all international competitions held since 1986. There were no surprises in Atlanta, with the Netherlands defeating Russia in the gold medal game to continue their dominance.

Football
SOCCER

BERNARD GLUCKSTEIN

RUSSIAN STRIKER
ALEXEI CHEMANINE

One day Alexei Chemanine will understand the magnitude of what he has accomplished at such a tender age. But while in Atlanta, his only weighty concern was what to do, and where to go, without getting into too much trouble in his first venture outside of his country and away from the influence of his parents.

Alexei was not only the youngest player on Russia's football team, he also held the distinction of being the youngest player among the eight teams vieing for international top honors. When questioned about his inexperience and how that could have prevented him from being selected for the Russian squad, Alexei's blue-eyed gaze took on a dimension that is common among his age group and fellow sportsmen – confidence. "What do you mean, 'not make the team'," asked the bewildered striker. "I wasn't surprised at all; I happen to be a very good player."

Alexei Chemanine

What Alexei has yet to fully understand or appreciate is what his predecessors had to endure to get him to this point. It was not all that long ago that Alexei's homeland had an abominable reputation where their relations with persons with disabilities were concerned. Preferring to take a 'see no evil, hear no evil' stance, the country that was the Soviet Union simply did not acknowledge the existence of disabled persons at all. As Alexei's translator explained, "it used to be forbidden in Russia to admit you were not perfect." To realize the hardship that was the Soviet Union is to understand the great strides that the new regime has made in participating in only their second Paralympic Games. The nation's inaugural appearance at the 1992 Paralympic Games in Barcelona denoted monumental social change for not only Russian athletes with a disability, but perhaps the greater community of disabled persons as well.

Nonetheless, Alexei personifies the average teenager. His main interests include buying the latest CDs and trying to impress members of the opposite sex. But life for the young athlete is not as easy as it sounds. "People treat me like anyone else, until they learn I have cerebral palsy," revealed Alexei. "It is not easy to go to college, or to get a job if you have a disability, but I'm hoping that will change by the time I get there."

DANIEL GALBRAITH

DANIEL GALBRAITH

Goalball

Goalball officials are happy to have spectators at their games – as long as they keep quiet. As word of the unique sport spread among event-goers in Atlanta, officials had greater difficulty in keeping law and order off the court throughout games that demand total silence during competition.

Played by blind and visually impaired athletes, goalball involves a ball equipped with a bell inside to help players to locate it. The ball, roughly the size of a bas-

NORM LOURENCO

BERNARD GLUCKSTEIN

ketball for men and a volleyball for women, is hurled down the court at the opposing team's net which runs the width of the court floor at each end. Visual impairments range among competitors, so each player wears a blindfold made from light-resistant cloth, tape and modified ski goggles to equal the visual acuity of the athletes.

The ball is thrown along the ground at speeds of up to 40 miles per hour, with the hope of finding a hole in the opposition's three-person line. Defenders, equipped with knee and elbow pads and padded pants, typically sprawl out horizontally, parallel to the goal, absorbing shots with their bodies to prevent a score. Goalballers require complete silence to concentrate on the sound and thus, location, of the incoming ball. Raised tape markings on the floor provide the tactile feedback orientation.

Invented in 1946 by Austria's Hanz Lorenzen and Germany's Sett Reindle, goalball first became a Paralympic sport in 1988 in Seoul, Korea.

CODE OF SILENCE
TEAM DENMARK

Sasanne Noyen has been a member of Denmark's women's goalball team since 1993. A year prior to her selection to her nation's team, the 25-year-old was attending university in a small Danish town when introduced to the sport. "There are not many sports available for blind people," Noyen emphasized, "so when I heard about goalball, I saw it as a great way to stay in shape and release stress."

BERNARD GLUCKSTEIN

She began playing recreational goalball once a week. Then she found out about a competitive league. Goalball is now serious business for her. "I now work out at least twice a week in the gym practicing concentration exercises and mobility skills," related Noyen. A game with a lengthy learning process, Noyen describes goalball to be tremendously challenging and at times very frustrating. "It's much harder for players who are totally blind to pick up the game," she asserted. "Players who are partially sighted can at least take off their goggles and see the technical details of the game." But during a match all is even with players wearing light-resistant goggles, to prevent any visual advantage on the court.

Noyen plays all three of the game's positions. Using her versatility to her advantage, she said, "I get more playing time ... whenever the team needs a substitute, I'm up for the challenge anywhere on the court." Denmark's team did not win a trip to the medal podium in Atlanta, but the players agreed that the experience was well worth the journey. "We're a relatively new team and we'll keep practicing and working together," explained Noyen. "It takes time to build up trust and gel as a team. I'm confident we'll be ready for the 2000 Paralympic Games," she promised. Not only is she convinced that her country's future in the sport is bright, but Noyen is seeing gold in the future – gold at the 2000 Paralympic Games in Sydney.

BERNARD GLUCKSTEIN

Judo

THE SPORT OF WARRIORS

Judo developed during the 16th century from the Martial Art of Jujitsu as one of many forms of empty handed fighting by the Samurai Warriors. Twentieth century Japanese educator Jigoro Kano refined the combat activity by eliminating the dangerous elements to achieve a true form of physical education and sport. Dr. Kano was an Oxford scholar and the first Asian appointed to the International Olympic Committee. Judo became a full medal Olympic sport at the 1972 Munich Games.

The Paralympic judo competition in Atlanta was an open competition for blind and visually impaired athletes only. During a match, points are scored based on the type of moves used by opponents. Competitors are brought together on a 16-by-16 metre mat called a "tatami". Using strength and agility to score points, competitors rely on traditional judo techniques like throwing, pinning, choking and applying an "arm bar." Balance, touch, sensitivity and instinct are key to success in the sport.

The competition was divided over seven open-class weight categories. In the event of a tie, the judges' decision determines the winner. Based on "kinsa" (small advantages), judges use red and white flags to reflect the most significant attack, the number of attacks and aggressiveness.

The competition follows the International Judo Federation rules with only slight modifications. For example, the texture of the mat is different in Paralympic competition to indicate the limits of the competition area for competitors.

Judo, one of the newest Paralympic sports, having been introduced at the 1988 Seoul Games, was also one of the few sports without women competitors.

REGINALD TIESSEN

BERNARD GLUCKSTEIN

The competition in Atlanta represented the introduction of lawn bowls to the Paralympic calendar. As a precision sport, lawn bowls is similar to boccia in that the goal for competitors is to position balls, called woods or bowls, as close as possible to the smaller target ball, known within the sport as 'the jack'. The object is to roll as many bowls as possible nearest the jack. Unlike Paralympic boccia, which is played by athletes with cerebral palsy only, lawn bowls is open to amputees, wheelchair athletes and blind and visually impaired athletes. The latter utilize sighted guides or "directors" in preparing to make their shots.

Lawn bowls, historically known as "bowling on the green," is played primarily in Europe with its greatest popularity in England and Ireland. It is also commonly played in Canada, South Africa, Australia and New Zealand. An average game lasts three and a half hours.

The field of play for lawn bowls is called the green which measures, at minimum, 37 metres square and is surrounded by a 30-centimetre wide ditch. The green is divided into six alleys and matches can be played by either individuals (singles) or by teams of two to four players (pairs, triples and fours).

BERNARD GLUCKSTEIN

GENTLEMEN OF THE GREEN
BILLY BEHAN & PETER HORNE

At 57 years old, Billy Behan's career seems to be just getting started – that is, his lawn bowls career. Thirteen years ago Behan was a semi-professional cricket player in Ireland, but an on-the-job fall from a beam to the concrete floor six metres below significantly changed not only the engineer's athletic course, but his entire life's direction as well. "After I fell, I realized life as I knew it, was over," Behan recalled.

He spent one year at Stoke Mandeville Hospital in Aylesbury, England where Sir Ludwig Guttmann, the father of the Paralympic Games, practiced medicine. Behan broke his back and uses a wheelchair for mobil-

Lawn Bowls

ity. "I have been married for 33 years, I have two great kids ... after such a tragedy you learn quickly that life is a gift and is worth fighting for," he offered. Behan admits his recovery was gruelling but said that dealing with his injury was not as hard as people imagined. "I just wanted to get on with life. There was nothing I could do to change what had happened, I had to accept it and move forward."

Two years after his injury, Behan witnessed several events at the 1984 Paralympic competition at Stoke Mandeville. Having been a serious sportsman with an eye for the ball all of his life, he thought he would give the sport of lawn bowls a chance.

Fellow competitor Peter Horne of New Zealand also gave the sport a chance, but for different reasons. The 43-year-old Horne, well respected in the sport, was kicked off his boyhood rugby and soccer teams because the parents of the other children were worried he would hurt them. But that didn't shy the double arm, double leg amputee away from sports at all. "My family encouraged me to remain active in sports," he explained. "They refused to pity me or treat me differently than my siblings. They taught me I was capable of doing anything I set my mind to."

Horne's attitude toward his sport and his disability has offered him international respect. New Zealand's

Peter Horne & Billy Behan

BERNARD GLUCKSTEIN

long-standing lawn bowls champion, Horne won gold at the 1988 Paralympic Games in Korea.

Lawn bowls is one of the few sports that provide the opportunity for competitors with and without disabilities to compete against each other without any rule changes. Both Behan and Horne agree that not all able-bodied competitors take them seriously at first. But after they emerge victoriously, "it's a different story," they chuckled.

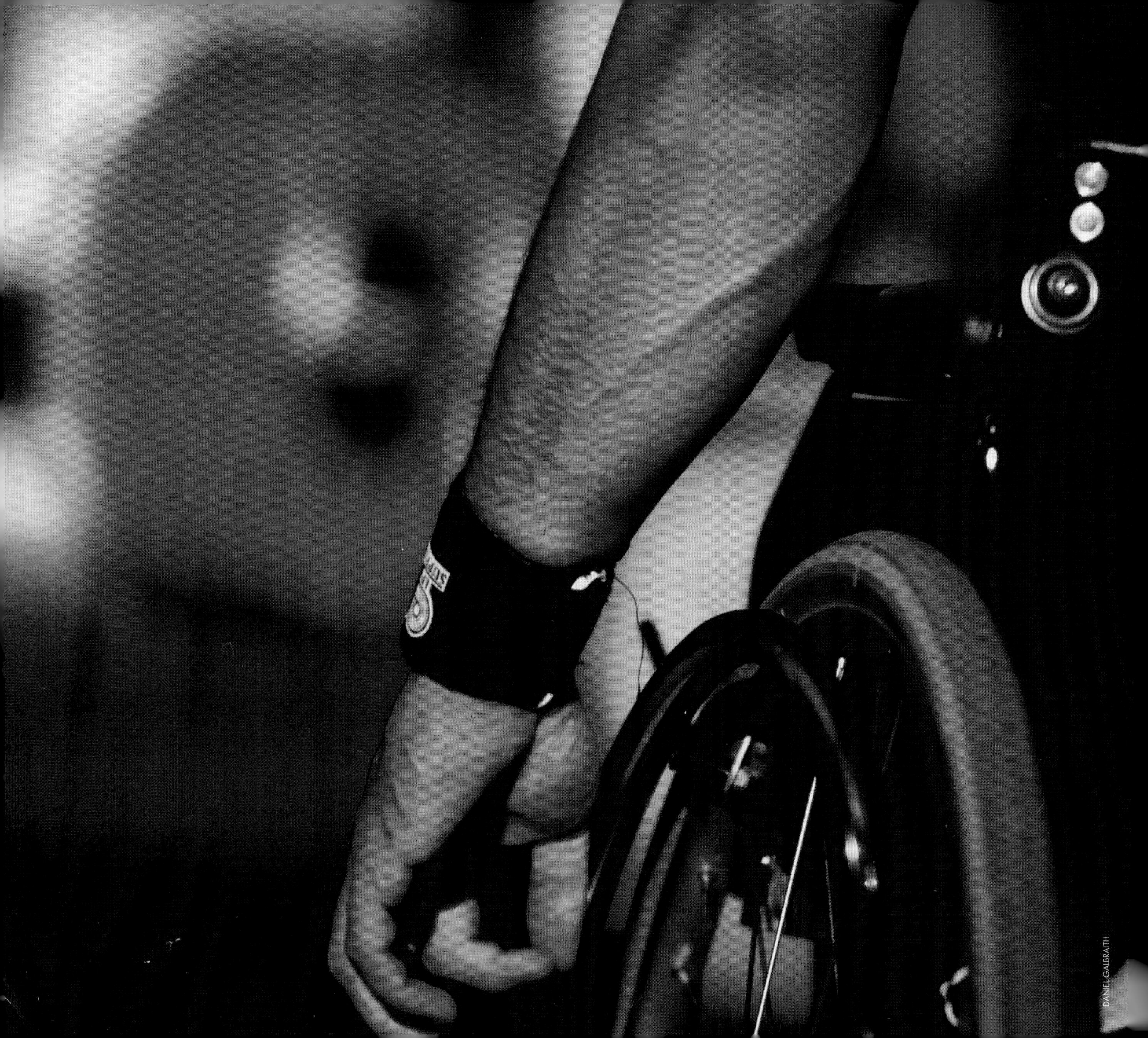

DANIEL GALBRAITH

Paralympic powerlifting took center stage in Atlanta. Spotlights, music blasting and frenzied crowds provided this sport with the most inspired competition venue hands down. Powerlifting established itself as a genuine spectator sport.

Powerlifting is an open-class event with ten categories based on an adjusted body weight. This sport is open to all competitors who meet the minimal disability qualifications as described for the amputee, wheelchair, les autres and cerebral palsy athlete classes. In the interest of fairness, additions to body weight are made for amputees. Another exception, to accommodate athletes with cerebral palsy, allows these athletes to lift with flexed legs supported by an approved wedge.

The traditional sport of weightlifting develops quick strength through jerk and snatch and clean movements. In powerlifting, maximum strength is expressed through the bench press only. Powerlifting was one of the earliest sports on the Paralympic program with its introduction in 1964 in Tokyo. Men's events only are on the schedule.

Powerlifting

A CROWD FAVORITE
AHMED AHMED

When Egyptian powerlifter Ahmed Ahmed entered the competition area, the crowd roared with excitement. Many of the spectators were there to see him. Ahmed was a world record holder when he arrived in Atlanta and left with the same title after breaking his own mark four times in one afternoon.

The 33-year-old was born with polio and became involved in disabled sports 11 years ago. "I was working out in the gym on a regular basis to stay in shape," Ahmed described through a translator. "I didn't know it would turn into something this big." Able-bodied men who worked out with Ahmed started challenging him to friendly weightlifting competitions. "I kept beating them and decided to take my talents a step further. I entered competitions for disabled athletes in Egypt, and here I am."

Ahmed took home a silver medal from his first Paralympic Games in Seoul, Korea in 1988. "After Seoul, I knew this is what I wanted to pursue, but I also knew I wouldn't settle for anything but gold," revealed the enthusiastic athlete. Ahmed lived that dream for four years as he prepared for the 1992 Barcelona Games. There he accomplished his mission, winning gold and establishing new world and

DANIEL GALBRAITH

Ahmed Ahmed

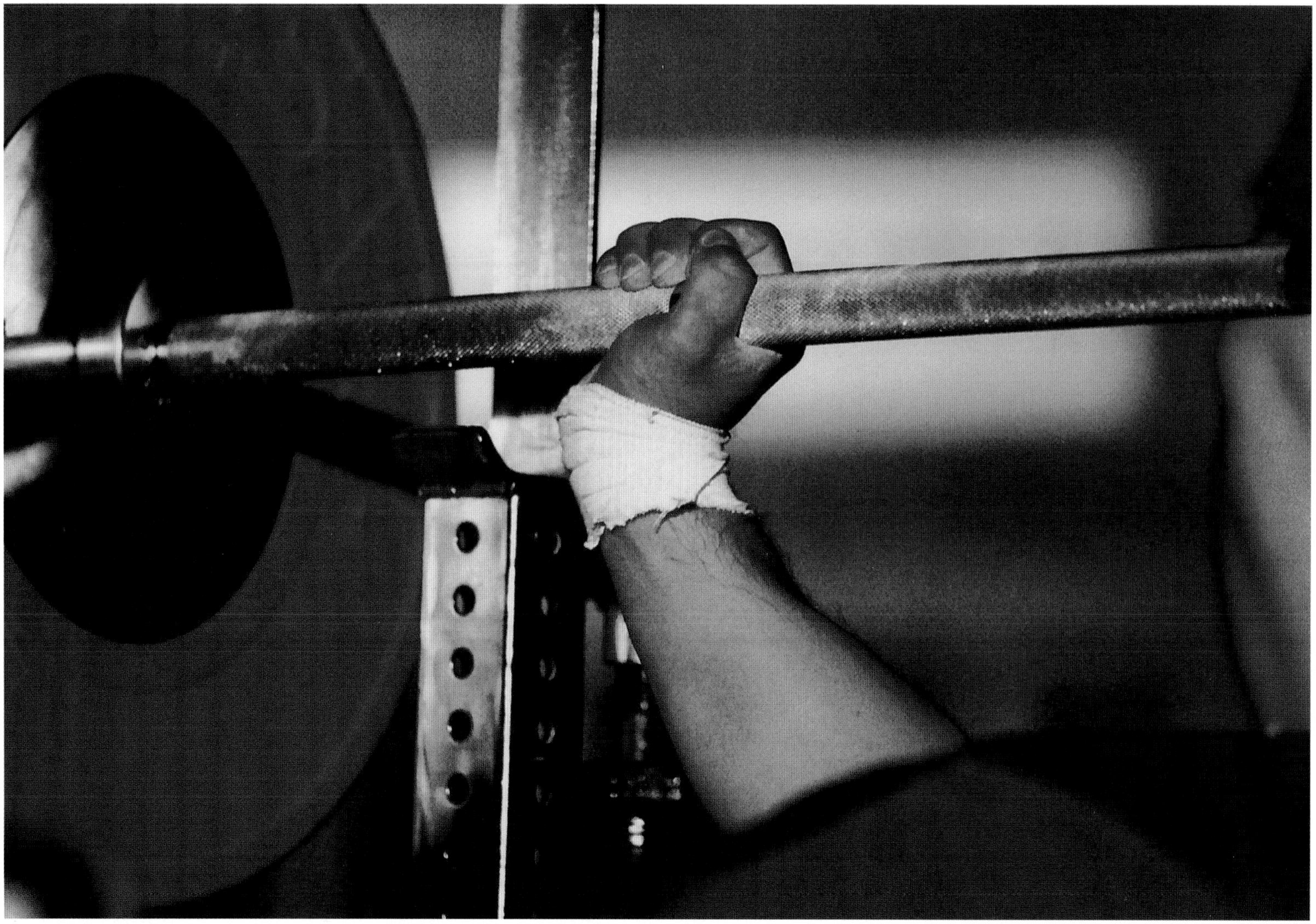

DANIEL GALBRAITH

Paralympic records. "I was confident I had the ability to break the records, so I trained everyday with that in mind," he said as a matter of fact.

The Egyptian government recognizes disabled sports as world class events and as such fully funds the Paralympic and Olympic Teams alike. Ahmed also spoke highly of a new government-funded center where people with disabilities can live, rehabilitate, train and go to school. Ahmed said the only problem with the com-

DANIEL GALBRAITH

munity-like center is the reality outside of its walls. “Once you step outside, it’s almost impossible to get around,” he described. “Egypt is very old, and nothing was ever built for disabled people. Now that there are laws requiring contractors to include accessibility in their plans, things will start to improve, but it will take time before we notice the differences.”

Ahmed says the 1988 Paralympic Games in Seoul brought about a new percep-

DANIEL GALBRAITH

tion about disabled people at home in Egypt. "People are beginning to understand that people with disabilities can live an active life and contribute to society," he asserted. "More athletes are becoming aware of disabled sports because the Egyptian media is taking an interest in the Paralympic Movement."

Before departing for the U.S., the Paralympic athletes from Egypt publicly announced that the team would return from Atlanta with 26 medals. That vow made headlines across the country, particularily in light of the fact that Egypt's Olympians returned from the Centennial Games with none. "Our promise was not to criticize the Olympians, but to prove the ability of people with disabilities," Ahmed explained.

Upon making good on their pledge, news of their accomplishment also made headlines in their homeland. Their nation's President responded by sending word to the athletes that he would greet them at the airport upon their return to congratulate the team on its success and welcome them all home. "That meant a lot to us, because we have worked hard to get here. The recognition from our President of our accomplishments in Atlanta will help advance our movement proving we too are capable of making our country proud," Ahmed affirmed.

REGINALD TIESSEN

Shooting

Shooting has a long history as a sporting activity. Like many sports, target shooting began as an activity designed to prepare combatants for war. By turning these activities into games or contests, shooting took on elements of recreation and competition making practice more desirable. Target shooting activities with bows, crossbows or early firearms are part of the cultural history of many peoples. Records of early target contests are found in ancient Greece, China, Bhutan and among the Islamic peoples.

Shooting events for athletes with physical disabilities began in 1977 in England and first became a Paralympic sport in 1980. Shooting is one of the few sports in which men and women compete against one another for medals. Of the 15 Paralympic shooting events, seven are mixed events open to men and women equally.

The shooting competition includes air rifle and pistol, and .22 calibre rifle and pistol events. Competition is open to amputee and wheelchair athletes, utilizing a classification system to ensure an equitable match. Competitors shoot from a variation of conventional international shooting positions – prone, standing and kneeling – adapted for athletes with disabilities. All events have specific time limits for a prescribed number of shots which vary according to the type of event.

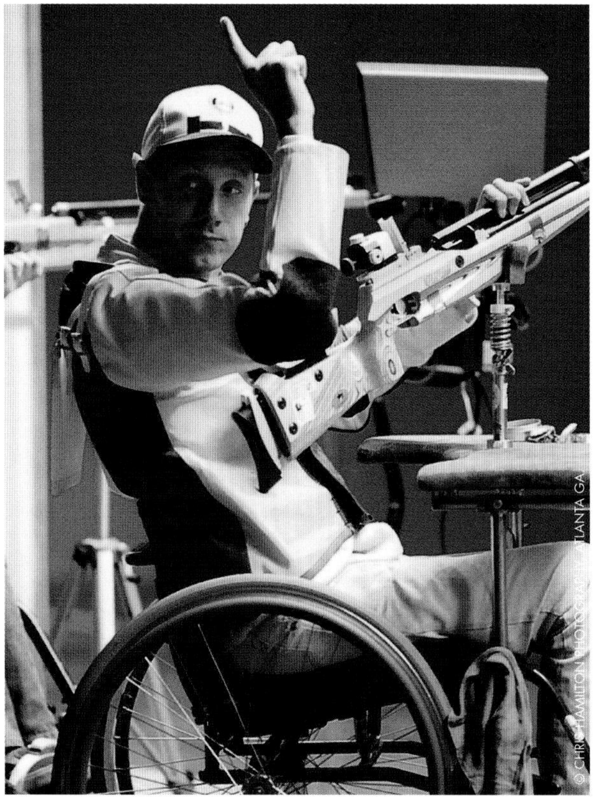

Opposite page: Rosabelle Riese

ARMED TO SUCCEED

ROSABELLE RIESE

Rosabelle Riese is a woman armed with a mission to succeed. The 41-year-old South African capped her Paralympic comeback in Atlanta with a bronze medal performance in the 10 metre air pistol competition. She began competing in the sport of shooting in 1984, at Stoke Mandeville in England. Riese is also South Africa's top table tennis player and a provincial lawn bowls champion in her disability category. Neither the national table tennis team nor the lawn bowls unit qualified to compete at the 1996 Paralympic Games. Riese was not phased; she simply concentrated on her shooting.

Riese contracted polio in 1956. She has feeling in her legs, but uses a wheelchair for ease of mobility. Despite her easy going approach to life, she does not let anything stand in the way of her success. She quit her job as a receptionist at one of the biggest companies in her province. "My employer wasn't giving me the time off I needed to train," she recalled. "It was a huge decision, but I didn't want anything to interfere with my dream, so I quit." Riese admitted she experienced anxiety when she left her position, concerned about her financial situation, but planned to worry about the consequences when she returned from Atlanta.

Riese, the only female shooter with a disability in South Africa, educated herself by reading books on the sport. Training seven days a week, she relies on a very supportive family. "When I get home I intend to spend much more time with them," she offered with a smile. They however, may have their doubts as she is planning to continue to play lawn bowls and table tennis as well. She has reservations about telling them about her future athletic designs. "I think I scared off my ex-husband when I told him I wanted to take up shooting," laughed Riese.

Riese reported that Paralympic athletes have gained much awareness among fellow South Africans as well as significant financial support from the country's corporate community. Riese believes that the interest stems largely from a proliferation of media coverage for Paralympic athletes in South Africa. "We've come a long way in our country; the Paralympic Team has received more recognition than the Olympians," she exulted.

REGINALD TIESSEN

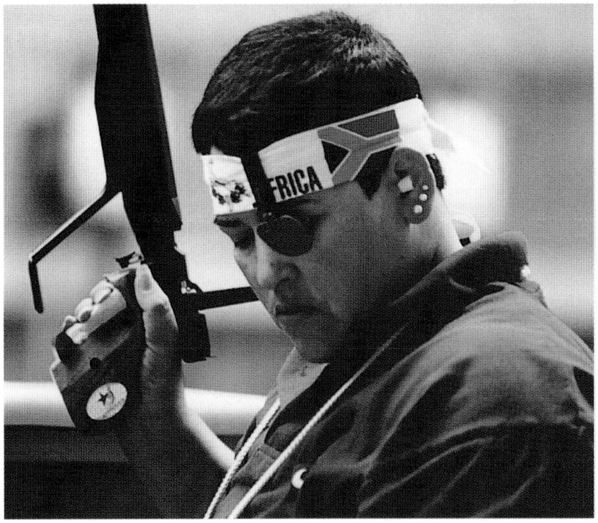

REGINALD TIESSEN

Riese said it was wonderful to compete internationally again. The political situations in South Africa in the 1980s resulted in her country being banned from all international sporting events. After the apartheid ended in the early 1990s, athletes were invited back. South Africa returned to Paralympic competition in 1992 in Barcelona. Riese did not vie for a place on that team as she was in the midst of starting a family.

DANIEL GALBRAITH

Swimming

Swimming records fell fast and furiously throughout the competition in Atlanta. The final count totalled 107 new world records and 113 new Paralympic marks – the most in Paralympic Games history. The sport of swimming is long in Paralympic tradition, dating back to the first official games in Rome in 1960.

The swimming events are open to all athletes. Events are divided into two groups: blind and visually impaired athletes as one group and athletes with all other physical disabilities (wheelchair, amputee and cerebral palsy) as the second. The blind and visually impaired category has three divisions, while the "functional" category has ten. Within the functional category, swimmers with different types of disabilities compete against one another under specific classification criteria. The competition in Atlanta also included – for the first time – events for athletes with a mental disability.

The swimming events are limited to four official styles: freestyle, backstroke, breaststroke and butterfly. International swimming rules are followed with only a few exceptions. In some instances, athletes are allowed to start a race from the pool deck or in the water. In the events for swimmers who are blind, coaches are allowed to warn the athletes when they are approaching the end of a length of the pool by tapping them on the head with a padded pole or "bopper".

Swimming is among the top sports on the

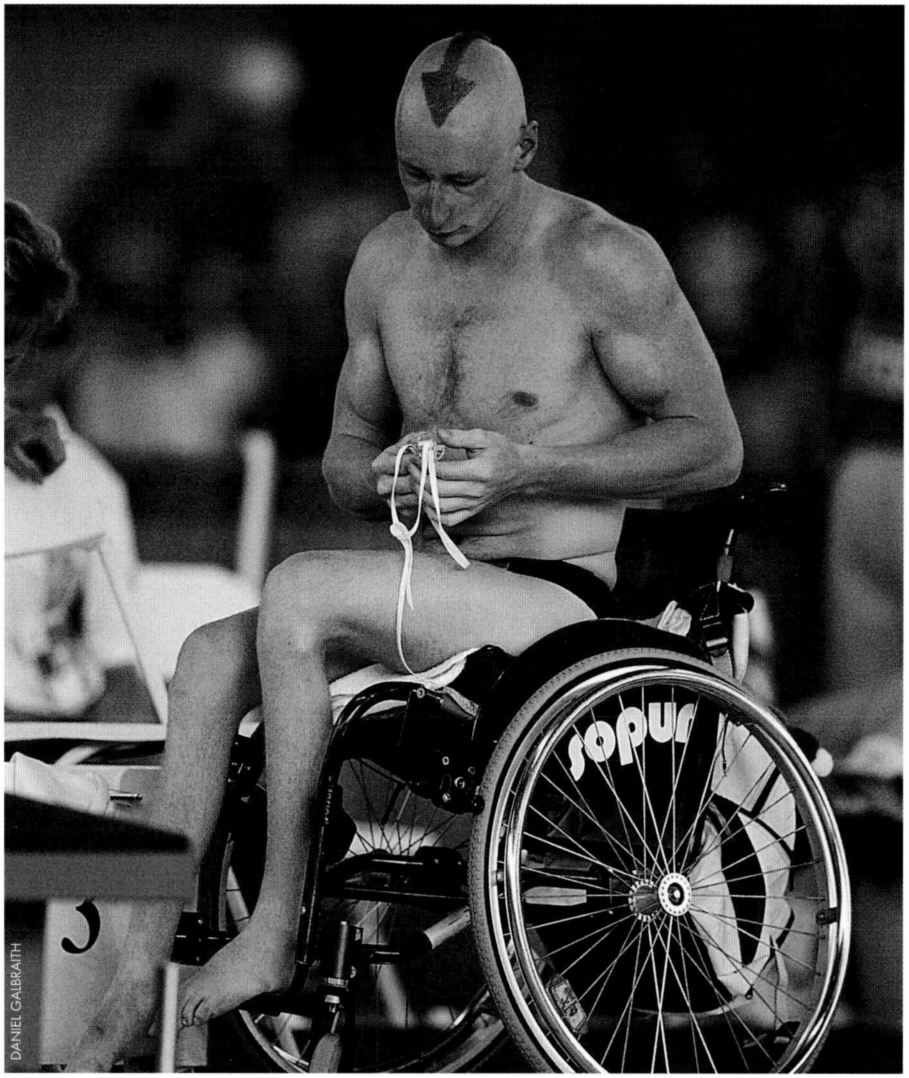
DANIEL GALBRAITH

Paralympic program in terms of number of competitors and spectator appeal. In several events, the world records of blind and visually impaired swimmers closely match those of their able-bodied peers.

LIFE IN THE FAST LANE
BRENDAN BURKETT

With so many different events in the sport of swimming, it is not uncommon for top swimmers to earn their way to the medal podium more than once during the competition. But for those who do, their road to a combination of gold, silver or bronze was not the one most easily traveled.

Australian athlete Brendan Burkett knows that very well. The 32-year-old bio-mechanical engineer captured both gold and silver at the Georgia Tech Aquatic Center. Extensive daily training – regular two-hour, twice-a-day sessions – was his key ingredient to success. "All of the hard work and long days keep paying off for me," exclaimed Burkett. The trip to Atlanta made for Burkett's third time to the Paralympics. "It doesn't matter how many medals I have won, winning gets sweeter every time. Each time I'm on the podium, I know I've overcome another obstacle."

© CHRIS HAMILTON PHOTOGRAPHY, ATLANTA GA.

Brendan Burkett

DANIEL GALBRAITH

Ten years ago Burkett lost a leg as a result of a collision between a car and the motorcycle on which he was traveling. His life at the time consisted of a good job, a carefree attitude and plenty of time for sports. But he admits that his injury left him with little hope. "In the beginning I was rather bitter; rehab was something I didn't want to devote time to." Burkett continued, "But after awhile it finally hit me, I couldn't turn back time, I had to learn to live with it." Three months after Burkett's amputation, he checked out of rehab and hit his own road to recovery. "I wanted to get on with life. I wanted to find a job, and my mates wanted me back on the teams I previously played on."

Burkett was an avid swimmer and rugby player before his injury and notices little difference in competing in disabled sports. "To me, it's just another competition. I love competing in sports, so it's not any less challenging racing against

5
SPEEDO

DANIEL GALBRAITH

DANIEL GALBRAITH

disabled athletes." But he did run across stumbling blocks when it came to employment. "I went for an interview at an engineering firm, and it was apparent that they were interested in hiring me. I was still walking with a cane at the time. After my final interview the employer asked me how I hurt my foot. I told him I lost my leg in an accident. We shook hands and I left. I never heard from him again."

Burkett attributed his inability to gain employment to the proverbial fear of the unknown. He noticed employers to be cautious about hiring someone with a disability, so he decided to try a different approach. "Instead of walking in with my cane, waiting for the employer to ask me what happened, I decided to tell them I had a disability right away so we didn't have to waste any time. It worked on the first try. Burkett doesn't resent those who turned him away, but hopes that one day they too will understand that people with disabilities are capable of leading productive and active lives.

Looking ahead excites Burkett. He hopes to compete in his fourth Paralympic Games at home, in Sydney. "It gave me chills during the Closing Ceremony, when the flag was passed to Australia as the host of the 2000 Paralympic Games," he beamed. "We have so much culture in Australia – the natives, the world famous wildlife – we'll kick butt with Opening and Closing Ceremonies!" No doubt mate.

Table Tennis

Except for two minor modifications for wheelchair athletes, Paralympic table tennis events are played identically to conventional table tennis matches. Wheelchair athletes may grip the table to maintain balance so long as the table is not moved and, at service, the ball must clear the end of the table only (not the sides).

Table tennis is open to all but blind and visually impaired athletes and is organized on the basis of direct elimination. A ten-class functional classification system is used to match abilities of athletes with varying disabilities and takes two forms: standing and wheelchair events. Table tennis has been on the Paralympic slate since the inception of the games in 1960.

NORM LOURENCO

© CHRIS HAMILTON PHOTOGRAPHY, ATLANTA GA.

BERNARD GLUCKSTEIN

BERNARD GLUCKSTEIN

Tennis

Armed with precise down-the-line, cross-court, drop and overhead shot-making skills, elite-level wheelchair tennis players must also employ quick maneouvering techniques to be competitive. The Paralympic tennis tournament is an open competition eligible to only those athletes with a mobility related disability. Players must compete in a wheelchair.

The game is played in the same manner as traditional tennis except the ball is allowed to bounce twice before the return hit. Events are provided for both men and women in singles and doubles tournaments.

Wheelchair tennis started as a demonstration sport at the 1988 Seoul Paralympic Games gaining full medal status at the 1992 Paralympics in Barcelona.

SERVING UP AWARENESS
JOHAN HAGLUND

Johan Haglund is taking his athletic career in stride. He doesn't expect miracles. He is just taking it day by day until he accomplishes his goals. The 26-year-old Swedish athlete was seeded 16th in the world of wheelchair tennis in 1996. His new goal is to be ranked 8th. He was only introduced to the sport in 1991 and admits he has come a long way in a short time. "I didn't come to Atlanta expecting to win gold even though I dreamed about it," he disclosed.

Haglund was born with a rare disease called osteogenesisimperfecta, more commonly known as brittle bone syndrome. He acquired his first wheelchair at the age of four and by the time he reached age twelve, he had broken his legs 30 times. "Knock on wood," he said, "I haven't broken a bone since."

Haglund's fortuitous wheelchair tennis career, which has included travel around the world, recently got even better when his boss called him into his office. Expecting the worst, Haglund was offered a deal he could not refuse. He works for a mobile communications company in Sweden which pro-

BERNARD GLUCKSTEIN

SHADOW
by QUICKIE

posed to be his official sponsor. He now receives the necessary time off to train and play in tournaments. "I am giving back," he submitted. "I have introduced them to disabled sports, so it has been educational for them as well."

Haglund is also trying to change the image of people with disabilities in his community. He does so by practicing against able-bodied tennis players who, he revealed, at first don't take him seriously. "When I first meet them before practice, you can tell they humor me, but that soon changes after we start our match." Haglund says it is good practice for him to play against able-bodied players, and it also gives him the opportunity to show young adults that people with disabilities are able to live active lives.

Retired professional tennis player Bjorn Borg recognizes Swedish wheelchair tennis players as exceptional athletes, and helps to change the perception of disabled sports. Each year, Borg holds exhibition tournaments in Sweden and invites wheelchair tennis players to hold their own exhibition before the professional players compete. Haglund remembers the time when Borg was challenged by one of the country's top ranked wheelchair tennis players. Borg

BERNARD GLUCKSTEIN

BERNARD GLUCKSTEIN

accepted, but there was a catch. Borg had to play in a wheelchair. Borg wanted to show his fans just how challenging wheelchair tennis is to play. He wheeled onto the court, racket in hand and played in front of a sell-out crowd. The fans loved it. But Borg may not have enjoyed it so much. He did not score one point.

Haglund believes people's perceptions of disabled athletes will change quickly with celebrities like Borg throwing support behind wheelchair tennis. "He's a big star in Sweden, people look up to him," Haglund enthused. "If he accepts us into the sports world, then the fans will follow his lead."

REGINALD TIESSEN

Volleyball

Volleyball has become a popular sport around the world in both Olympic and Paralympic competition. Both standing and sitting volleyball are played at the Paralympic Games, allowing competition for paraplegic, amputee and cerebral palsy athletes. The

players' demonstration of quick reflexes and good ball-handling skills make it an exciting sport to watch.

The rules in Paralympic volleyball are very similar to Olympic and Federation Internationale de Volleyball rules. The most significant changes are found in sitting volleyball, where the lower net height and smaller court size are the most obvious differences. The sitting players are also allowed to block the serve, but must keep their buttocks on the floor.

In both sitting and standing volleyball, a classification system assigns a point value to each player. By assigning this point value, fairness of teams is controlled by allowing only a certain total point value for each team to be on the court at any one time.

Volleyball became an official part of the Paralympic program in 1976 in Toronto. Sitting volleyball's roots trace back to the Netherlands where the first sports club for athletes with a disability was founded in 1953 in the form of sitting ball. By 1956 sitting ball had evolved into sitting volleyball, which has now become a very popular sport around the world with more than 38 member countries in the International Volleyball Organization for the Disabled. The International Paralympic Committee is looking to introduce women's volleyball at the 2000 Games in Sydney.

REGINALD TIESSEN

ALL FOR ONE AND ONE FOR ALL
ISRAELI STANDING VOLLEYBALL TEAM

What started out as a rehabilitation activity, is now world-class competition for members of Israel's standing volleyball team. And while some of the veteran players on the team still like to consider the game a pastime, their talents brought them to Atlanta to compete for the world's top honors in the sport. In fact, their accomplishments on the volleyball court have awarded them a ticket to numerous tournaments around the world over the last two decades.

Hagia Zamir, veteran player and coach, said it is an honor to be part of the Israeli Paralympic Team. "We competed in our first volleyball competition in 1973 in Austria, the first unofficial European Championship," he recalled. There the team placed third. But between 1976 and 1984, the Israeli standing volleyball team reigned as the world and Paralympic champions.

Zamir attributes the team's success to his country's government. In 1974, the Israeli administration financed a support center in Telaviv which is operated by the Israeli Army's Disabled Association. The government financially supports war victims and their families throughout the course of their lifetime. "There are so many people wounded during military service," Zamir explained, "that we needed a place to go."

So many citizens were hurt during the years of war in Israel that the center became well known and very reputable. Zamir described how many of the men were athletic before their injuries and wanted to continue in sports while rehabilitating. "We played volleyball. The sport kept growing over the years, so we began organizing tournaments," he related. Their volleyball team in Atlanta consisted of ten players, five of whom were war victims.

Zamir said their nation's winning ways ended in 1988, after the Seoul Paralympic Games. One player interrupted jokingly, "Ever since I joined the team we've been losing." The room echoed with laughter as his teammates nodded their heads and agreed. A laughing Zamir continued, "I didn't want to say that, but it is true. He put a curse on us."

Zamir intends to step aside as a player and encourage younger athletes to carry

© CHRIS HAMILTON PHOTOGRAPHY, ATLANTA GA.

the team upon their return from Atlanta. He will take on full coaching responsibilities. He also wishes to spread the word about disabled sports in his Middle Eastern country. "Reporters never appear at our events," he lamented. "Even Olympians get little coverage because media attention is always focused on the political situations in Israel," he added.

What is the public perception of people with disabilities in Israel? "Great, if you are a war victim," stated Zamir. "Citizens are proud of those who fight for their country. They respect us for doing what's right for Israel. However, they tend to shun others with disabilities from injuries or by birth."

To enter the Israeli dormitory within the already tightly secured Athlete Village, a visitor had to be escorted by undercover security guards, pass through a metal detector, an interview and a security check – all a product of Israel's unforgotten past. In 1972, eleven Israeli Olympians were gunned down by terrorists during the Munich Olympic Games. Zamir proclaimed, "It's a way of life for us. We don't take chances anymore."

The Israeli standing volleyball team placed sixth in Atlanta, but that did not discourage them. "Our goal is to be back on the medal podium in Sydney," professed Zamir. "We will also work to receive the media coverage we deserve in Israel," he added. "The team is a proud family."

Rugby

DEMONSTRATION SPORT

The name had to change from murderball to rugby to be considered for the Paralympic program, but the original name still aptly describes this high-contact wheelchair sport. Played for the first time as a Paralympic demonstration sport in Atlanta, rugby readily earned official inclusion in the 2000 Sydney Paralympics.

Wheelchair rugby is a hybrid of basketball and football played with a volleyball. Invented by Canadians in the late 1970s, rugby is played by athletes who are quadriplegics and is often referred to as "quad rugby". Rugby was the only quadriplegic team sport on the Paralympic slate.

Play begins at one end of the court like basketball as a four-person team moves the ball downcourt, passing forward and backward. Competing in reinforced chairs with guard rails that bear the nicks and scratches of combat, players are free to smash into one another as they try to block and score a point by carrying the ball over the eight metre strip of boundary line inside the key. Players carry, dribble or pass the ball while moving toward the opponent's goal area. The team with the greatest point total at game's end is declared the winner. Each player is classified according to their disability on a point system. Each team is allowed no more than a total of eight points on the court during play.

In addition to providing some of the most intense and dramatic competition at the Paralympic Games, rugby quickly is dispelling any notions of disabled athletes as reticent or fragile.

NORM LOURENCO

SWE
NZL
ESP
9
8

Yachting

DEMONSTRATION SPORT

Atlanta represented the first time that yachting was held at the Paralympic Games. Athletes competed in three-person keelboats. The 23-foot Sonars, with open cockpits, sailed in a fleet-race format. A scoring system which assigns points based on level of disability allowed athletes from different disability groups to compete together in this demonstration sport.

Getting a good start is a significant factor in yacht racing. The start is a mass start, which means that prior to the starting gun, all 15 yachts were vying for position at the starting line. The sailors also had to time their yacht's position with the starting signal. If a yacht crossed the starting line too soon, the crew had to turn around and re-start.

Positioning remains a strategic key for the yachts throughout the race as the sailors constantly fight for clear air. If a yacht is blocking the wind from reaching another yacht's sails the wind power is taken from the blocked yacht and the front yacht has the clear air.

The sailors maneouver their yachts to the designated course marks by coordinating both steering and sail trim with the wind direction and strength. The points of sail (the direction that the yacht is headed relative to the wind direction) change as the sailors round one mark and head to the next, trimming their sails to take full advantage of the wind.

NORM LOURENCO

REGINALD TIESSEN

Legacy

CLOSING CEREMONY

A burst of color from the City of Atlanta Fire Department. An F-18 fighter jet flyby. Flag bearers, the Star Spangled Banner, military pomp and the trendy sounds of the Macarena – somehow it all came together to close the Xth Paralympiad.

Taking advantage of true southern spirit in the grand fashion of a Mardi Gras, spectators at the Closing Ceremony of the 1996 Paralympic Games were treated to a colorful procession of people and props. A pageantry of art and music provided an electric atmosphere for Blaze, the mystical mascot of the Paralympic Games. The phoenix marshalled the sea of dancers in what may have been the world's largest Macarena ensemble in history.

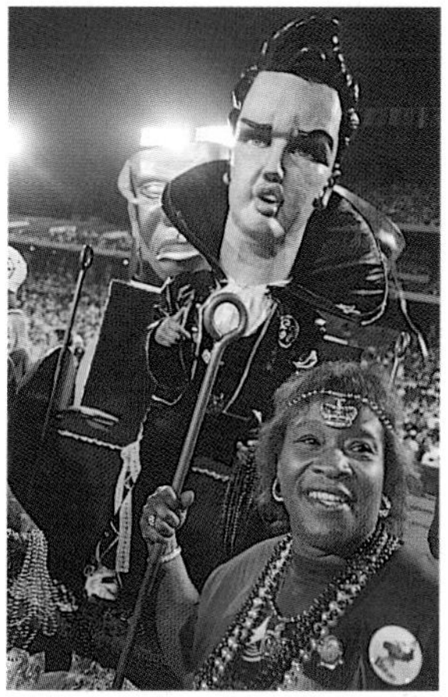
REGINALD TIESSEN

But the demands of tradition and protocol were not lost within the jubliant send-off. Atlanta's last party of the summer was honored with expressions of gratitude for the spirit and the triumph that prevailed over all else during the ten days of competition. Dignitaries spoke of courage, of justice, of equality for all citizens, with an acknowledgement that Atlanta as a city is still working toward achieving equal opportunity for all.

U.S. Attorney General, Janet Reno, praised the efforts of the Paralympic Games, saying in part, "Nations throughout the world are seeking to bolster the independence, freedom and dignity of people with disabilities. I salute all those people across the globe who are working tirelessly in this struggle to open doors and to open minds."

With no less eloquence, the Mayor of Atlanta, Bill Campbell, praised the athletes. "We will never forget your athletic power and grace – the rush of the wheelchairs, the teamwork of the tandems. We will never forget your courage, your determination, your heart. But the greatest gift you have given us is the gift of truth. The truth that the difference between disabled and able-bodied athletes is measured in seconds."

Hometown hero and two-time Paralympian Al Mead was selected to ceremoniously extinguish the cauldron with a stirring rendition of the song "What a Mighty Spirit". The cauldron of the Xth Paralympiad was darkened, but the flame which embodied the *Mind, Body and Spirit* of the Paralympic Movement burned strong in all those who experienced its message.

The torch was passed to the Sydney Paralympic Organizing Committee and the crowd was treated to a preview of what's to come at the next set of Paralympic Games in the year 2000. Australia appeared ready and waiting; their enthusiasm was palpable. The flush of excitement set the stage for Atlanta to play out its final hour as world's host. Under the lively leadership of Master of Ceremonies, Casey Kasem, rock and roll music icon Chubby Checker got the party started! While the house jubliantly jived to the 'The Twist', the World of Wheels car club paraded their classic American autos onto the field to the delight of the spectators. Next on the lively stage was Bo Diddley, treating fans to a selection of some of his most popular numbers. Hundreds of dancers then filled the stadium, introducing show-goers to the finer points of the hand jive. The Four Tops kept toes tapping during the next segment of the nostalgia-filled evening. Jerry Lee Lewis then took his turn on stage, further inducing the frenzied crowd.

DANIEL GALBRAITH

The evening was then harnessed with a recording of Aretha Franklin's rendition of 'Climb Every Mountain' supporting a spectacular fireworks display overhead. Pride and admiration were the lasting sentiments when a review of the most memorable images of the past ten days of competition acknowledged *The Triumph of the Human Spirit* one last time. With an emotional good-bye, Atlanta said "farewell." With the enthusiasm that comes with a look into the future, Australia said, "see y'all in Sydney, mate!"

DANIEL GALBRAITH

Mayor Bill Campbell

THE GIFT OF TRUTH - *Closing Ceremony Address*

Bill Campbell, Mayor of Atlanta

This summer, Atlanta welcomed the world not once, but twice. Once again, our streets were filled with the shades and sounds of five continents. Once again, we were humbled by the gift bestowed upon us. And my heart filled with the same pride and humility as when we welcomed our Olympic visitors – even more so, because this time we revisited a dream. This time, the struggle for equality came home to Atlanta.

Long before the Paralympic flame found its way to our city, the fate of Atlanta and the fate of the Paralympic Movement were linked through history. We have come a long way, we have overcome obstacles. We share the same dream. And this summer, we made the dream come true. So many people gave so much. The International Paralympic Committee ́provided the vision and guidance for the Games. The Atlanta Paralympic Organizing Committee made it all a reality. Countless dedicated volunteers worked around the clock. The supportive spectators cheered endlessly. But in the end, it all came down to the athletes, and you put on a show for the people of Atlanta and the world!

We will never forget your courage, your determination, your heart, but the greatest gift you have given us is the gift of truth. The truth that the difference between disabled and able-bodied athletes is measured in seconds. The truth that beyond the disability is just another person. The truth that as a city we are still working toward achieving equal opportunity for all our citizens, especially disabled people. Like a mirror, the Paralympics helped us see ourselves more clearly. We thank you for the gift of truth, and the opportunity to learn as a community.

I know that we have been forever changed, and I hope that when you leave, you will always carry a piece of Atlanta in your heart.

A GREAT CELEBRATION - *Closing Ceremony Address*

G. Andrew Fleming, President/CEO, Atlanta Paralympic Organizing Committee

The most important thing I have to say tonight is thank you. Thank you to our sponsors and supporters – who through their generosity, literally have made these Paralympic Games possible. Thank you to our board of directors and staff, whose dedication and tireless devotion over the past several years have been at the very core of this effort. And especially, thank you to the thousands of volunteers who have given so much – in hundreds of thousands of acts of kindness – to make this event a success. Please know that you will always have our gratitude and our affection. Finally, thank you to the athletes who have competed here, and who now take their rightful place in history beside many other great champions in sport.

It has been our privilege and our honor to have hosted you. When we first met ten days ago in the Opening Ceremony, we promised that the Games of the Xth Paralympiad would be a great celebration of life, a great celebration of achievement, a great celebration of our common humanity. In short, a great celebration of *The Triumph of the Human Spirit.*

We have seen *The Triumph of the Human Spirit* revealed in so many ways these past ten days. First and foremost, by our athletes. Over and over again, they have met the challenge of world-class performance. And in so doing, revealed their incredible commitment to excellence and re-defined what it truly means to be a champion.

We have also seen it in our artists, performers, lecturers and other individuals with disabilities who have presented their works and their ideas as part of our cultural and scientific programs. Together with the athletes, they have made the important and powerful statement that people with disabilities can perform at the very highest levels of human endeavour, and ought to be given more opportunities to do so.

We have also seen *The Triumph of the Human Spirit* in the thousands of peo-

G. Andrew Fleming

REGINALD TIESSEN

ple who have given so much to make these Paralympic Games the success we all hoped it would be. In the final analysis, I believe this event will long be remembered by everyone who in any way took part, as a tremendous and positive reaffirmation of our common humanity, and of the power of the human spirit to meet the greatest of life's challenges.

THE SPIRIT OF EMPOWERMENT - *Closing Ceremony Address*
Janet Reno, U.S. Attorney General

I am thrilled to be here to salute the accomplishments of such an extraordinary group of athletes from all over the world. You have demonstrated the very best of human dedication and achievement.

The Paralympics reflect an ever-widening spirit of inclusiveness around the globe. This event has shattered stereotypes about what people with disabilities can and cannot do. They have demonstrated what people with disabilities can achieve when they are empowered to participate fully in society.

This spirit of empowerment is the driving force behind the Americans with Disabilities Act, which I am privileged to enforce. This civil rights law stands on the shoulders of Dr. Martin Luther King, Jr., whose ties to this city are so deep. Through the years, the disability rights movement has been energized by Dr. King's vision of a society that comes to embrace those who have been shut out.

Look beyond Atlanta – doors are opening all across America, to workplaces, to stores, to restaurants and to city halls. All that this nation has to offer is becoming more accessible every day. It's happening because America has committed itself to assuring that all of its people have the opportunity to realize their potential.

What is happening here isn't just happening in Atlanta and all across America. It is happening in nations throughout the world seeking to bolster the independence, freedom and dignity of people with disabilities. I salute all those people across the globe who are working tirelessly in this struggle to open doors and to open minds. And I salute the athletes of these Paralympic Games for empowering people everywhere to dream and to excel.

DANIEL GALBRAITH

THE PROMISE OF THE HUMAN SPIRIT - *Closing Ceremony Address*

Dr. Robert D. Steadward, President, International Paralympic Committee

On behalf of the International Paralympic Committee and our athletes, I wish to express our sincere gratitude to the people of Atlanta and the United States of America for hosting the Xth Summer Paralympic Games. You have been outstanding. I cannot thank you enough for opening up your hearts in welcoming our athletes and the entire Paralympic Family from all corners of the world. This warm reception has made possible the dreams of thousands of athletes who came to record the best-ever performances.

Atlanta, throughout these 1996 Summer Paralympic Games you have unfailingly lived up to your world-wide reputation for gracious southern hospitality. You have lived up to the legacy of Dr. Martin Luther King, Jr., who this day, would have been so very proud of your contribution to the true spirit of both Paralympism and Volunteerism itself: the unselfish dedication of thousands to the ultimate betterment of life for every man, woman and child in our entire global village. Furthermore, you also have left the world a legacy of tolerance, understanding, good-will, hope and unity.

You have lived up to both your motto, *The Triumph of the Human Spirit* and our's of *Mind, Body and Spirit*, by promoting and embracing the spirit of the City of Atlanta which I see as one of magic, generosity and intense civic pride.

You have lived up to your promise of exceptional volunteers, all of whom possessed a passion for our Paralympics and our athletes. For almost six years you have lived the dream. You can not only be justifiably proud of your contributions, but you will be left with memories that will last forever. You have lived up to your promise of world-class sport facilities which have provided our athletes with the perfect environment for unequalled athletic achievements. You have lived up to your promise of unparalleled media and television coverage.

More world records were established during the past two weeks than ever before, and these extraordinary accomplishments occurred because more of our athletes

REGINALD TIESSEN

are being provided with improved training, coaching and equipment, thereby exhibiting greater skill and speed than ever before.

Paralympians, you have all achieved heights thought to be possible only in your dreams. We congratulate each and every one of you, not only for providing us with the excitement and thrill of elite competition, but for your demonstration of the true meaning of Paralympism.

History will record that the City of Atlanta reinforced for all of us an optimism for aspiring Paralympic athletes from all over the world to compete in future Paralympic Games. I declare the Games of the Xth Paralympiad closed, until our athletes gather again in Sydney, Australia, in the year 2000, to celebrate with us the Games of the XIth Paralympiad and welcome in the twenty-first century.

DANIEL GALBRAITH

MEDIA ATTENTION

If there was one moment that defined the press operations of the Atlanta Paralympics, it may well have been at one of the daily briefings held by the Deutscher Behinderten-Sportverbande (German Paralympic Team) for the large German media contingent, second in size only to the ensemble of news gatherers from the United States. Never timid about probing around the corners or asking the provocative question, an APOC press officer was bluntly asked to describe the relationship between APOC and ACOG, the Olympic organizing committee, and the problems in transition between the two events.

The press officer responded by explaining that although the transition may have been difficult, it did not matter, for the Paralympic organizers simply followed the example of the Paralympic athletes. "We will take any situation, no matter how difficult," he said, "and we will deal with it. We will take any problem or barrier that confronts us and we will work to solve it. As our athletes show us every day, there is nothing we cannot do." Unexpectedly, the press officer was presented with a strong round of applause. The German media understood that, as with everything else in the Atlanta Paralympics, the communications effort was predicated upon inclusion.

The close association with the Olympic Games was a twin-edged sword providing both unique opportunities and tremendous obstacles to the media efforts of the Paralympic Games. The foremost challenge was the myopic focus of major media outlets on the tremendous international popularity of the Olympics. After the rigorous and time-consuming demands of covering the Olympics were met, there was little, if anything, left to give. "Yet the time will come," said Steve Goldberg, APOC Press Chief, "when the Paralympics are on every editorial schedule and assignment calendar. As it was in Atlanta, much of the media effort will continue to be an educative process."

Prior to the beginning of the APOC communications effort, the vast majority of the mainstream media, especially those in the United States, had been only vaguely aware of the Paralympics if they knew anything at all. But they came to the

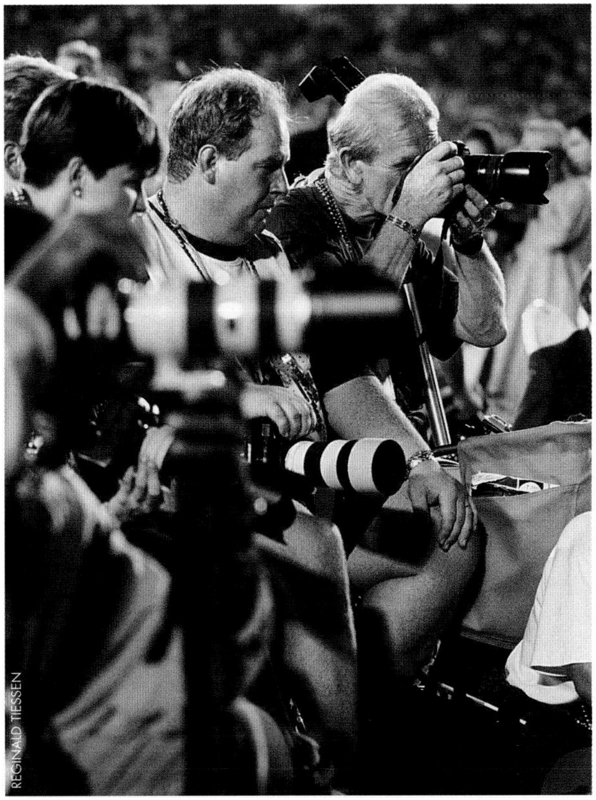

REGINALD TIESSEN

Paralympics in record numbers. Writers, photographers, television, documentary film and radio crews came from North and South America, Europe and Asia. There was at least one credentialed member of the media for every two athletes at the Paralympic Games.

Despite an initial international distribution of more than 3,000 applications for media credentials, it seemed that only after the priority of the Centennial Olympic Games had passed, much of the media world suddenly awoke to the fact that the Paralympic Games were taking place and that they should cover them. In all, 2,088 applications were approved.

For the first time, the Paralympics were televised in the United States with four hours of weekend coverage on the CBS television network, and a one-hour highlight show each night on cable television's SportSouth and the Prime Network. SportSouth turned to two former Paralympians to supply the kind of on-air authenticity to Paralympic broadcasts that only former participants can deliver. The duo represented the effort to focus on athlete excellence rather than human interest stories.

Nightly program feeds also went back to Australia, England and Germany. An unprecedented number of more than twenty countries paid for the right to televise competition from the Paralympic Games. Locally, the *Atlanta Journal-Constitution* established a special Paralympic section providing daily coverage of every sport. Local television stations also featured taped highlights and live news shots from Paralympic venues daily.

"A new environment has been created for the Paralympics which has firmly established the elite level and value of the event to both the media and the public," explained Goldberg. "While the Paralympics will always require diligence, determination and extra effort to be successful, no longer should these Games catch the media by surprise."

GAMES PATRONS

The National Organization Patrons (NOPs) and National Publication Patrons (NPPs) were welcomed as Paralympic partners to serve as a strong link between the Paralympics and the disability community. The NOPs were a powerful partner in APOC's federal government awareness agenda. Both the NOPs and the NPPs provided potent vehicles for the Paralympics to run advertisements, editorials, and articles in publications specifically targeting the disability community. The Atlanta Paralympic Organizing Committee signed 36 NOPs and seven NPPs.

CONSUMER AWARENESS CAMPAIGN

In what may have been one of the most provocative commercial presentations ever to hit U.S. airwaves, the Atlanta Paralympic Organizing Committee (APOC) initiated a national consumer media campaign with a series of television, radio, print and billboard advertisements/public service announcements that began airing in 1995.

Capturing the inspirational essence of the Paralympic Movement, the 1996 Paralympic Games' media campaign was designed to heighten awareness, traditionally low in the U.S. The campaign actively featured elite American athletes with physical disabilities with incredible competitive records.

Posing the provocative question: WHAT'S YOUR EXCUSE? was the theme for the Paralympic media campaign. As part of a series of print ads, one Paralympic athlete rhetorically asked: WHAT'S CHANGED MOST IN MY LIFE SINCE I LOST MY LEG? The answer: I RUN MORE. WHAT'S YOUR EXCUSE? In a second ad, another Paralympian, wheeling her way to the finish line said: IT TOOK ME TWO YEARS TO STOP FEELING SORRY FOR MYSELF. IT WILL TAKE YOU 16.1 SECONDS. WHAT'S YOUR EXCUSE? Featured in a third ad, another Paralympic runner said: I HAD A SEEING EYE DOG ONCE. HE COULDN'T KEEP UP. WHAT'S YOUR EXCUSE? For television, dynamic Paralympic athletes in action raised the same question: WHAT'S YOUR EXCUSE? For radio, a soul-stirring original song was created.

"Americans today are more conscious of fitness, health and self-initiative than ever before, and who could better serve as ultimate role models for this positive preoccupation than the extraordinary men and women who have trained and excelled as Paralympic athletes," said Andrew Fleming, APOC president and chief executive officer. "We believe the 1996 Paralympic Games' national media campaign stunningly captured the spirit of the Paralympic Movement and the enormous energy and drive these athletes embody."

The creative concept for the campaign was developed by Atlanta advertising executive Joey Reiman, president of Bright House. "The creative challenge presented by APOC was to convey the remarkable energy and enthusiasm of some of the world's most accomplished athletes, world-class athletes who have prevailed despite awesome odds," Reiman said. We wanted to communicate this positive message in a way that motivates and inspires and makes us all recognize our own potential waiting to be tapped."

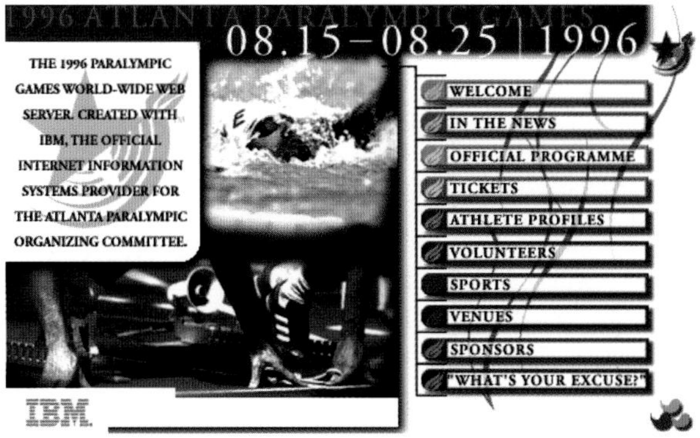

PARALYMPICS ON THE NET

The APOC Internet Program, in conjunction with IBM, provided an internet homepage to better inform the public about the Paralympics. As part of IBM's Paralympic sponsorship, the corporation provided the Paralympics with an internet address and the programming for the page. The Paralympic homepage provided excellent information for the web searching world and received an average of 120,000 hits per day during the event.

PARALYMPIC YOUTH PROGRAMS

Education is a key to many of life's doors of opportunity. While reading, writing and arithmetic are the staples of any education, today's complex society presses for attention to more than just the basics. Following the announcement that Atlanta would play host to the 1996 Paralympic Games came an education initiative that changed the way thousands of youngsters across North America think about disability. Recognizing that very few schools include units about disability in their curriculum, the Atlanta Paralympic Organizing Committee (APOC) officials saw the staging of the Paralympic Games in the United States to be an exceptional vehicle for bringing disability awareness into America's schools.

With limited funding from a federal grant, more than a dozen successful projects were implemented to create an awareness and identity for the Paralympics across the U.S. and Canada. The mission was to excite students about the Paralympic Games and make a significant and lasting impact on community awareness of persons with a disability and Paralympic ideals.

As part of the *Youth Initiative*, a curriculum was developed that provided teachers with resource material, including videos, to promote a better understanding of people with disabilities. Two units were produced – one at a kindergarten to fifth grade level and the second for students from sixth to twelfth grades. Some in-class exercises included having students put one hand behind their backs and trying to tie their shoes or shutting their eyes and walking around the classroom. Teachers took students on a tour through their schools and asked what could be changed to better accommodate a person in a wheelchair or a person who is blind. The older students engaged in discussions about issues that pertain to persons with a disability such as attitudes, stereotypes, etc.

Every school in the state of Georgia received a copy of the curriculum and was encouraged to implement it. The units were available for purchase to schools outside of Georgia. The curriculum was adopted by the

Canadian Paralympic Committee, modified slightly, and with the help of corporate funding, sent to every elementary school in Canada.

Paralympic Day in the Schools, which augmented the curriculum, brought Paralympic athletes to classrooms and gymnasiums to demonstrate such disability-specific events as goalball, wheelchair basketball and sitting volleyball. Wayne recalls how one young student's life changed after a Paralympic Day in her school. "The girl used a power wheelchair and rarely ever spoke," explained APOC's Linda Wayne. "She got into one of the sports chairs and loved it so much, she wouldn't get out. She used it for the entire day. When we asked her for the chair back at the end of the day, she said she would get out of the chair on one condition: she wanted to tell the teachers, students and her friends why she was in a wheelchair." Wayne said she sat in front of about 400 people and told them she tried to commit suicide by taking an overdose of drugs. She said the drugs paralyzed part of her body and she didn't have the balance she once had and that's why she uses a wheelchair. She then told her fellow students the importance of saying no to drugs. After she was finished she put herself in her old power chair and went home. The following day, the girl's mother telephoned program officials and said she had never seen her daughter so excited. The same day her mother purchased a new sports chair and the girl hasn't been out of it since, described Wayne.

Other *Youth Initiative* activities included a *4-H project* giving students a chance to serve as a Paralympic volunteer, a *banner project* which invited youths to make welcoming banners to hang in the Athlete Village and a *high school media project* which encouraged students to write features in school papers, neighborhood newspapers, and produce in-house videos to highlight the Paralympic Games and earn the privilege of working in the Paralympic Media Center during the competition. APOC also collaborated with *Odyssey of the Mind*, a worldwide invention contest involving students at four levels of education: elementary, middle, high school and college. The 1996 inventions had to be geared toward improving existing products to make life easier for people with disabilities. Wayne said some of the inventions were incredible. "One group invented a cane with a scanner and headphones for blind people. The mechanism allows visually impaired people to enter a grocery store and scan the items while listening to product names and prices in the headphones."

The National Forensic League's *"Lincoln-Douglas Debates"* incorporated the Paralympics into their topic list and featured the issue in *Rostrum Magazine*, the League's publication. The competition topic for debate was whether individuals with disabilities ought to be afforded the same athletic competition opportunities as able-bodied athletes.

APOC enjoyed unprecedented success in educating students about elite athletes with a physical disability. In providing the opportunity for North America's youth to learn about Paralympic athletes and others with a disability, the *Youth Initiative* provided a legacy for APOC, for Atlanta, for the athletes competing for gold, silver and bronze, for others with a disability, and for all those who experienced APOC's *Paralympic Youth Programs.*

THE PARALYMPIC EXPERIENCE

Athletes at every venue were signing autographs both before and after competitions. And many of their admirers were participants in the *Paralympic Experience*, a special program designed to bring young people to the Paralympic Games and thus, expose them to sports for people with disabilities.

About 75,000 complimentary tickets were distributed to youth groups from 900 different organizations: schools, churches, Girl Scouts, Boy Scouts, Boys and Girls Clubs and so forth. These young spectators came from a total of 16 states. And while the majority were from the metropolitan Atlanta area, all parts of the state of Georgia were represented.

Some tickets were distributed through parks and recreation departments in various cities in an effort to encourage inclusion of sports for people with disabilities in their programs.

BERNARD GLUCKSTEIN

REGINALD TIESSEN

LICENSING & MERCHANDISING

For the first time in the history of the Paralympic Games, a complete licensing and merchandising program accompanied the Paralympiad. Under the management of Battle Enterprises, over fifty officially licensed manufacturers produced a variety of products from t-shirts, caps and glassware to trading pins, toys and publications. Another first was the wide availability of Paralympic merchandise inside and outside the venues. Numerous concession stands, coupled with a variety of retail outlets, made Paralympic merchandise "hot ticket" items in and around Atlanta.

SEE YOU IN SYDNEY

The Australian public embraced the success of their Paralympians at the 1992 Paralympic Games in Barcelona with a ticker-tape parade through the streets of Sydney. The 1996 Atlanta Paralympic Games lifted these athletes to even greater heights as Sydney prepares to set new standards for the Paralympic Games in the year 2000. The event is expected to attract 5,000 athletes from 125 countries. Over 1,500 media representatives from around the world are expected to converge on the Paralympic Games to deliver the widest coverage ever of the event.

The organizing and staging of the Sydney 2000 Paralympic Games is the responsibility of the Sydney Paralympic Organizing Committee (SPOC), which has a close working relationship with the organizing committee for the Sydney Olympic Games. Together, they are managing issues related to sports, venues, transportation, security, accommodation, cultural programs and marketing for the Paralympic Games. With the Federal and New South Wales governments each committing $25 million to the Paralympics, SPOC plans to meet their $110 million budget through key sponsorship commitments, fundraising and ticket sales.

DANIEL GALBRAITH

DANIEL GALBRAITH

DANIEL GALBRAITH

Official Results

The first Paralympic Games were held in Rome, Italy in 1960 and involved 400 athletes from 23 countries. Only athletes in wheelchairs were invited to compete. Nearly ten times that number competed in Atlanta. The 1996 Paralympic Games welcomed 3,310 athletes from 104 nations. The number of nations participating in the Paralympic Games has grown most dramatically over this last quadrennial. In 1992, Barcelona hosted only 83 countries at the IX Paralympiad.

PARTICIPATING NATIONS

FINAL STANDINGS

Country		Gold	Silver	Bronze	Total
USA	United States	46	46	65	157
AUS	Australia	42	37	27	106
GER	Germany	40	58	51	149
GBR	Great Britain	39	42	41	122
ESP	Spain	39	31	36	106
FRA	France	35	29	31	95
CAN	Canada	24	21	24	65
NED	Netherlands	17	11	17	45
CHN	People's Rep. of China	16	13	10	39
JPN	Japan	14	10	13	37
POL	Poland	13	14	8	35
KOR	Korea*	13	2	15	30
SWE	Sweden	12	14	10	36
ITA	Italy	11	20	15	46
RSA	South Africia	10	8	10	28
RUS	Russian Federation*	9	7	11	27
SUI	Switzerland	9	6	6	21
NOR	Norway	9	7	4	20
NZL	New Zealand	9	6	3	18
IRI	Iran	9	5	3	7
EGY	Egypt	8	11	11	30
BEL	Belgium	8	10	7	25
CUB	Cuba	8	3	0	11
DEN	Denmark	7	17	17	41
AUT	Austria	6	6	10	22
POR	Portugal	6	4	4	14
HUN	Hungary	5	2	3	10
FIN	Finland	4	5	4	13
BLS	Belarus*	3	3	7	13
MEX	Mexico	3	5	4	12
LTU	Lithuania	3	2	6	11
EST	Estonia	3	4	2	9
NGR	Nigeria	3	2	3	8
BRA	Brazil	2	6	13	21
SVK	Slovakia*	2	4	5	11
CZE	Czech Republic	2	7	1	10

Country		Gold	Silver	Bronze	Total
ARG	Argentina	2	5	2	9
ALG	Algeria	2	2	3	7
YUG	Yugoslavia*	2	2	0	4
CIV	Cote D'Ivoire*	2	0	0	2
PAN	Panama	2	0	0	2
IRL	Ireland	1	3	6	10
UKR	Ukraine*	1	4	2	7
GRE	Greece	1	1	3	5
KUW	Kuwait	1	1	1	3
TPE	Chinese Taipei*	1	0	2	3
KEN	Kenya	1	1	0	2
DOM	Dominican Republic	1	0	0	1
PER	Peru	1	0	0	1
ISR	Israel	0	4	5	9
SLO	Slovenia	0	2	3	5
TUN	Tunisia	0	2	0	2
BUL	Bulgaria	0	1	1	2
MLD	Moldova*	0	0	2	2
THA	Thailand	0	0	2	2
JOR	Jordan*	0	1	0	1
JAM	Jamacia	0	0	1	1
URA	Uraguay	0	0	1	1
AFG	Afghanistan*	0	0	0	0
ANG	Angola*	0	0	0	0
AZE	Azerbaijan*	0	0	0	0
BRN	Bahrain	0	0	0	0
BER	Bermuda*	0	0	0	0
BIH	Bosnia & Herzegovina*	0	0	0	0
BUR	Burkina Faso	0	0	0	0
CHI	Chile	0	0	0	0
COL	Colombia	0	0	0	0
CRO	Croatia	0	0	0	0
CYP	Cyprus	0	0	0	0
ECU	Ecuador	0	0	0	0
FAR	Faroe Island	0	0	0	0
FIJ	Fiji*	0	0	0	0

Country		Gold	Silver	Bronze	Total
HON	Honduras*	0	0	0	0
HKG	Hong Kong	0	0	0	0
ISL	Iceland	0	0	0	0
IND	India	0	0	0	0
INA	Indonesia	0	0	0	0
KAZ	Kazakhstan*	0	0	0	0
KGZ	Kyrghyzstan*	0	0	0	0
LAT	Latvia	0	0	0	0
LBA	Libya	0	0	0	0
LUX	Luxembourg	0	0	0	0
MAC	Macau	0	0	0	0
MKD	Macedonia*	0	0	0	0
MAS	Malaysia	0	0	0	0
MRI	Mauritius*	0	0	0	0
MAR	Morocco	0	0	0	0
NIG	Niger*	0	0	0	0
OMA	Oman	0	0	0	0
PAK	Pakistan	0	0	0	0
PUR	Puerto Rico	0	0	0	0
QAT	Qatar*	0	0	0	0
ROM	Romania*	0	0	0	0
KSA	Saudi Arabia*	0	0	0	0
SLE	Sierra Leone	0	0	0	0
SIN	Singapore	0	0	0	0
SRI	Sri Lanka*	0	0	0	0
SYR	Syria	0	0	0	0
UGA	Uganda*	0	0	0	0
UAE	United Arab Emirates	0	0	0	0
VEN	Venezuela	0	0	0	0
ZAM	Zambia*	0	0	0	0
ZIM	Zimbabwe*	0	0	0	0

* DID NOT PARTICIPATE IN
1992 PARALYMPIC GAMES IN BARCELONA

CLASSIFICATION

Why are there more than 10 Paralympic Records in the 100 metre track event? Just what is a T51? And why can't a T51 compete against a T10? The answer to all of these questions lies in one word: classification. Classification is one of the keys to competitiveness at the Paralympic Games. Before the first race is run or the first jump is attempted, all Paralympic athletes must be given a specific classification. The classification process evaluates athletes by disability and functional ability. It strives to place athletes in any given sport on an equal plane at the start of the event.

Visually Impaired Classes
Athletics

T10 No light perception; unable to recognize hand shapes

T11 F11 2/60 and/or visual field of less than five degrees*

T12 F12 2/60-6/60 and visual field of more than five degrees and less than twenty degrees*

Amputee Classes

T42 Single above-the-knee; combined lower and upper limb amputations; minimum disability

T43 Double below-the-knee; combined lower and upper limb amputations; normal function in throwing arm

T44 Single below-the-knee; combined lower and upper limb amputations; moderate reduced function in one or both limbs

T45 Double above-the-elbow; double below-the-elbow

T46 Single above-the-elbow; single below-the-elbow; upper limb function in throwing arm

F40 Double above-the-knee; combined lower and upper limb amputations; severe problems when walking

F41 Standing athletes with no more than seventy points in the lower limbs**

F42 Single above-the-knee; combined lower and upper limb amputation; normal function in throwing arm

F43 Double below-the-knee; combined lower and upper limb amputations; normal function in throwing arm

F44 Single below-the-knee; combined lower and upper limb amputations; normal function in throwing arm

F45 Double above-the-elbow; double below-the-elbow

F46 Single above-the-elbow; single below-the-elbow; upper limb function in throwing arm

Cerebral Palsy Classes

T30 Severe to moderate involvement; uses one or two arms to push wheelchair; control is poor; affects both arms and legs

T31 Severe to moderate involvement; foot propelled wheelchair push; affects both arms and legs

F30 Limited control of movements; some throwing motion

T32 F32 Full upper strength in upper extremity; propels wheelchair independently; affects both arms and legs; or same side arm and leg

T33 F33 Good functional strength with minimal limitation or control problems in upper limbs and trunk; affects lower legs

T34 F34 May use assistive devices; slight loss of balance; affects lower legs or both legs and one arm

T35 F35 Walks or runs without assistive devices; balance and fine motor control problems

T36 F36 Good functional ability in dominant side of body; affects arm and leg on same side of body

T37 F37 Minimal involvement; could be present in lower legs, arm and leg on same side of body, one leg, or demonstrate problems with balance

Wheelchair Classes

T50 Uses palms to push wheelchair; may have shoulder weakness

T51 Pushing power comes from elbow extension

T52 Normal upper limb function; no active trunk

T53 Backwards movement of trunk; uses trunk to steer; double above-the-knee amputations

F50 No grip with non-throwing arm; may have shoulder weakness

F51 Difficulty gripping with non-throwing arm

F52 Nearly normal grip with non-throwing arm

F53 No sitting balance

F54 Fair to good sitting balance

F55 Good balance and movements backwards and forwards; good trunk rotation

F56 Good movements backwards and forwards; usually to one side (side to side movements)

F57 Standard muscle chart of all limbs must not exceed seventy points**

Functional Classes

S1 Unable to catch water; restricted range of motion; no trunk control; leg drag; assisted water start

S2 Unable to catch water; restricted range of motion; no trunk control; slight leg propulsion; unassisted water start

S3 Wrist control limited; limited arm propulsion; minimal trunk control; hips below water; water start

S4 Wrist control; arms not fully fluent; minimal trunk control; hips below water; better body position

S5 Full propulsion in catch phase; limited arm movement; trunk function; leg propulsion; sit or stand starts

S6 Catch phase present; arm movement efficient; trunk control; leg propulsion; push start, sit or stand

S7 Good hands; good arms; good trunk; hips level; stand or sit dive start

S8 Hand propulsion; arm cycle good; trunk good; hips and legs level; use of start blocks

S9 Full hand propulsion; full arm propulsion; full trunk control; propulsive kick; dive start from blocks

S10 Full hand and arm propulsion; full trunk control; strong leg kick; dive start and propulsion in turns

Visually Impaired Classes
Cycling, Goalball, Judo & Swimming

B1 No light perception, unable to recognize hand shapes

B2 Visual acuity of 2/60 with less than 5 degrees field of vision

B3 Visual acuity of 2/60-6/60 and field of vision from 5-20 degrees

* Normal field of vision is approximately 120-180 degrees

** The extent of the disability is represented by an evaluation which tests function and strength of the muscle groups. Function and muscle strength are represented by point values for each class (i.e. less than 70 points equals an F41 or F57 athlete)

ARCHERY

Team MEN Standing

Gold	AHN, Tae	KOR
	CHO, Hyeon	
	LEE, Hack	
Silver	JONSKI, S.	POL
	LEZANSKI, Tomasz	
	OLEJNIK, Ryszard	
Bronze	ISHIDA, Mitoya	JPN
	NISHII, Kenichi	
	SATO, Masao	

Team MEN W1 / W2

Gold	NORTMANN, H.	GER
	OEHME, Mario	
	WOLF, Udo	
Silver	GABELLI, G.	ITA
	MAI, Marco	
	MALOVINI, L.	
Bronze	LEE, Ouk	KOR
	OH, Doo	
	YOU, In	

Individual MEN Standing

Gold	OLEJNIK, Ryszard	POL
Silver	GARCIA, Jean F.	FRA
Bronze	AHN, Tae	KOR

Individual MEN W1

Gold	RANTAVOURI, Martti	FIN
Silver	MACCAFERRI, Kurt	SUI
Bronze	MINAMI, Koichi	JPN

Individual MEN W2

Gold	LEE, Ouk	KOR
Silver	WALSTRA, Jacob	NED
Bronze	WOLF, Udo	GER

Team WOMEN Open

Gold	FANTATO, Paola	ITA
	LAZZARONI, R.	
	TRUCCOLO, Sandra	
Silver	YONEZAWA, Masako	JPN
	MATSUEDA, S.	
	SUZUKI, Hifumi	
Bronze	CHAPMAN, Anita	GBR
	SMITH, Kathleen	
	GALE, Rebecca	

Individual WOMEN Standing

Gold	OLEJNIK, Malgorzata	POL
Silver	CHAPMAN, Anita	GBR
Bronze	HYBOIS, Marie F.	FRA

Individual WOMEN W2

Gold	SUZUKI, Hifumi	JPN
Silver	TRUCCOLO, Sandra	ITA
Bronze	FANTATO, Paola	ITA

ATHLETICS

100m MEN T10

Gold	REQUENA, Julio	ESP	11.66 NPR
Silver	RODRIGUEZ, Jose	SPAIN	11.70
Bronze	CURTIS, Andrew	GBR	11.73

100m MEN T11

Gold	PRIETO, Juan	ESP	11.38
Silver	PYCH, Miroslaw	POL	11.39
Bronze	NUNEZ, Jorge	ESP	11.51

100m MEN T12

Gold	MANGANARO, Aldo	ITA	11.01 NPR
Silver	CABALLERO, Enrique	CUB	11.38
Bronze	COURT, Leroi	AUS	11.48

100m MEN T32

Gold	JONES, Lachlan	AUS	19.90 NWR
Silver	RADMORE, Joseph	CAN	21.59
Bronze	WILLIAMS, Paul	GBR	21.86

100m MEN T33

Gold	DAVIS, William	USA	16.46
Silver	KRANTZ, Gunnar	SWE	16.52
Bronze	LARSON, David	USA	16.86

100m MEN T34

Gold	NESTOR, Suarez	ARG	14.34
Silver	ROMAGUERA, Jaime	AUS	14.96
Bronze	HUGHES, Paul	GBR	15.23

100m MEN T35

Gold	KIM, Du	KOR	13.22
Silver	GOMEZ, Fernando	ESP	13.23
Bronze	REGISTER IV, Freeman	USA	13.31

100m MEN T36

Gold	ALLEK, Mohamed	ALG	12.03 NWR
Silver	HABER, Peter	GER	12.45
Bronze	MAHMOUD, Ahmed	EGY	12.65

100m MEN T37

Gold	PAYTON, Stephen	GBR	11.90
Silver	SCOTT, Lincoln	USA	12.29
Bronze	AMADOR, Douglas	BRA	12.65

100m MEN T42

Gold	CHRISTEN, Lucas	SUI	13.55
Silver	GREGORI, Paul	FRA	14.05
Bronze	SCHAFFHAUSER, Todd	USA	14.60

100m MEN T43, 44

Gold	VOLPENTEST, Anthony	USA	11.36 NWR
Silver	FULLER, Neil	AUS	11.97
Bronze	THOMAS, Bradley	AUS	12.02

100m MEN T45, 46

Gold	AJIBOLA, Adeoye	NGR	11.11
Silver	SVERRISSON, Geir	ISL	11.23
Bronze	FELSER, Klaus	AUT	11.28

100m MEN T51

Gold	NITZ, Paul	USA	17.62 NWR
Silver	BEAUDOIN, Andre	CAN	17.80
Bronze	BERGERON, Dean	CAN	17.83

100m MEN T52

Gold	LINDSAY, John	AUS	15.22
Silver	UNE, Yasuhiro	JPN	15.37
Bronze	PARRY, Matthew	USA	15.41

100m MEN T53

Gold	HOLDING, David	GBR	14.45 NWR
Silver	ERIKSSON, Hakan	SWE	14.60
Bronze	ISSORAT, Claude	FRA	14.79

200m MEN T10

Gold	REQUENA, Julio	ESP	23.80 NPR
Silver	CURTIS, Andrew	GBR	23.89
Bronze	LLERENA, Jorge	URA	24.28

200m MEN T11

Gold	MOYA, Omar	CUB	22.89 NWR
Silver	PRIETO, Juan	ESP	23.10
Bronze	GEFFERS, Holger	GER	23.10

200m MEN T12

Gold	JIMENEZ, Robert	DOM	22.57
Silver	MANGANARO, Aldo	ITA	22.74
Bronze	LEWIS III, Arthur	USA	23.13

200m MEN T36

Gold	ALLEK, Mohamed	ALG	24.32 NWR
Silver	HABER, Peter	GER	25.30
Bronze	MAHMOUD, Ahmed	EGY	25.50

200m MEN T37

Gold	PAYTON, Stephen	GBR	24.34
Silver	AMADOR, Douglas	BRA	25.18
Bronze	THRUPP, Darren	AUS	25.52

200m MEN T34, 35

Gold	REGISTER IV, Freeman	USA	26.96
Silver	GOMEZ, Fernando	ESP	27.04
Bronze	KIM, Du	KOR	27.26

200m MEN T42

Gold	CHRISTEN, Lukas	SUI	27.62
Silver	GREGORI, Paul	FRA	30.16
Bronze	OVERESCH, Lothar	GER	30.79

200m MEN T43, 44

Gold	VOLPENTEST, Anthony	USA	23.28
Silver	FULLER, Neil	AUS	24.72
Bronze	STOLL, Patrick	SUI	25.86

200m MEN T45, 46

Gold	AJIBOLA, Adeoye	NGR	21.89
Silver	SVERRISSON, Geir	ISL	22.24
Bronze	LOUW, Daniel	RSA	22.76

200m MEN T51

Gold	BERGERON, Dean	CAN	31.44
Silver	MEREDITH, Shawn	USA	31.83
Bronze	RAMAGE, Bradley	USA	31.90

200m MEN T52

Gold	UNE, Yasuhiro	JPN	26.90 NWR
Silver	LINDSAY, John	AUS	27.38
Bronze	PETERSEN, Wolfgang	GER	27.72

200m MEN T53

Gold	ISSORAT, Claude	FRA	26.07
Silver	ERIKSSON, Hakan	SWE	26.21
Bronze	HOLDING, David	GBR	26.52

200m MEN MH

Gold	BOURNE, Nigel	GBR	22.20 NWR
Silver	CLAWSON, Tico	USA	22.24
Bronze	COLAINE, Kenneth	GBR	22.65

400m MEN T10

Gold	DOMINGOS R. GAME	POR	52.92
Silver	TOVAR, J.	ESP	52.99
Bronze	DACONCEICAO LOPES	POR	53.64

400m MEN T11

Gold	MOYA, Omar	CUB	50.02
Silver	SANCHEZ, Sergio	ESP	51.40
Bronze	GEFFERS, Ingo	GER	52.67

400m MEN T12

Gold	ZALDIVAR, Ambrosio	CUB	50.72
Silver	BOUDJELTIA, Youcef	ALG	51.09
Bronze	MANGANARO, Aldo	ITA	52.11

400m MEN T36

Gold	MAHMOUD, Ahmed	EGY	56.15 NPR
Silver	RAHMOUNI, Lamouri	FRA	56.83
Bronze	CHEUNG, Yiu Cheung	HKG	57.37

400m MEN T37

Gold	PAYTON, Stephen	GBR	54.23 NWR
Silver	PRINGLE, Malcolm	RSA	55.34
Bronze	GONZALEZ, Jose	ESP	56.83

400m MEN T32, 33

Gold	LARSON, David	USA	54.60 NWR
Silver	KRANTZ, Gunnar	SWE	55.78
Bronze	DAVIS, William	USA	55.97

400m MEN T34, 35

Gold	KIM, Du	KOR	1:00.25 NWR
Silver	GOMEZ, Fernando	ESP	1:02.15
Bronze	COLLINS, Richard	GBR	1:02.91

400m MEN T42, 46

Gold	KONE OUMAR, B.	CIV	50.23
Silver	SVERRISSON, Geir	ISL	50.25
Bronze	GERGES, Patrice	FRA	50.62

400m MEN T50

Gold	DE VIDI, Alvise	ITA	1:22.16
Silver	JOHANSSON, Tim	SWE	1:22.40
Bronze	FORNI, Giuseppe	SUI	1:22.56

400m MEN T51

Gold	MEREDITH, Shawn	USA	1:01.90
Silver	BERGERON, Dean	CAN	1:01.93
Bronze	BEAUDOIN, Andre	CAN	1:02.50

400m MEN T52

Gold	SIGG, Winfried	GER	52.43
Silver	PILZ, Markus	GER	52.61
Bronze	LINDSAY, John	AUS	52.93

400m MEN T53

Gold	ISSORAT, Claude	FRA	48.67
Silver	ADAMS, Jeffery	CAN	48.95
Bronze	MURALT, Jeferey	NZL	49.08

800m MEN T10

Gold	DOMINGOS R. GAME	POR	2:05.48
Silver	DE ALMEIDA COELHO	POR	2:06.02
Bronze	DELGADO, Pedro	ESP	2:06.40

800m MEN T11

Gold	SANCHEZ, Jose	ESP	1:59.90
Silver	SAURA, Jose	ESP	2:00.94
Bronze	DELGADO, Ruben	ESP	2:01.57

800m MEN T37

Gold	PRINGLE, Malcolm	RSA	2:06.78 NWR
Silver	NETHERCOTT, John	GBR	2:11.13
Bronze	KOOY, Manfred	NED	2:12.25

800m MEN T34, 35, 36

Gold	PARKER, Joseph	USA	2:09.67 NWR
Silver	WROBEL, Andrzej	POL	2:10.79
Bronze	BELLELE, Faouzi	ALG	2:12.00

800m MEN T50

Gold	DE VIDI, Alvise	ITA	2:46.34
Silver	BLATTMAN, Fabian	AUS	2:46.67
Bronze	DODSON, Barton	USA	2:47.63

800m MEN T51

Gold	MEREDITH, Shawn	USA	2:09.57
Silver	BERGERON, Dean	CAN	2:09.91
Bronze	VERTERLUND, Per	SWE	2:11.45

800m MEN T52

Gold	ORENS, Steve	BEL	1:41.71 NWR
Silver	FREI, Heinz	SUI	1:41.76
Bronze	QUESSY, Marc	CAN	1:42.13

800m MEN T53

Gold	ADAMS, Jeffrey	CAN	1:38.34 NPR
Silver	HOLLONBECK, Scot	USA	1:38.43
Bronze	BADID, Mustapha	FRA	1:38.55

800m MEN T44, 45, 46

Gold	KONE OUMAR, B.	CIV	1:55.45 NWR
Silver	EVANS, David	AUS	1:55.81
Bronze	ZERGOUNE, Bachir	ALG	1:57.05

1,500m MEN T10

Gold	DE ALMEIDA COELHO	POR	4:08.52 NPR
Silver	MATTHEWS, Robert	GBR	4:12.48
Bronze	WILLIS, Henry	USA	4:19.25

1,500m MEN T11

Gold	SANCHEZ, Jose	ESP	4:01.19
Silver	CARLAVILLA, Cesar	ESP	4:03.61
Bronze	LEONAVICIUS, Saulius	LTU	4:04.44

1,500m MEN T12

Gold	GOMEZ, Said	PAN	3:57.53 NWR
Silver	MCGREGOR, Stuart	CAN	4:03.70
Bronze	CARAYON, Christophe	FRA	4:07.93

1,500m MEN T34, 35, 36, 37

Gold	WROBEL, Andrzej	POL	4:24.82
Silver	PRINGLE, Malcolm	RSA	4:25.61
Bronze	BELLELE, Faouzi	ALG	4:26.78

1,500m MEN T50

Gold	BLATTMAN, Fabian	AUS	5:09.41 NPR
Silver	DE VIDI, Alvise	ITA	5:09.80
Bronze	JOHANSSON, Tim	SWE	5:41.73

1,500m MEN T51

Gold	VESTERLUND, Per	SWE	4:00.86
Silver	BERGERON, Dean	CAN	4:01.02
Bronze	GEREIN, Clayton	CAN	4:03.23

1,500m MEN T52, 53

Gold	FREI, Heinz	SUI	3:05.52
Silver	HOLLONBECK, Scot	USA	3:05.76
Bronze	COUPRIE, Philippe	FRA	3:05.76

1,500m MEN T44, 45, 46

Gold	EVANS, David	AUS	3:59.68
Silver	WU, Yanjian	CHN	4:00.10
Bronze	LACROIZ, Emmanuel	FRA	4:01.07

5,000m MEN T10

Gold	DE ALMEIDA COELHO	POR	16:04.28 NPR
Silver	GUERRERO, Alejandro	MEX	16:07.55
Bronze	WILLIS, Henry	USA	16:08.77

5,000m MEN T11

Gold	THATCHER, Noel	GBR	15:24.66
Silver	BARTKENAS, Kestutis	LTU	15:25.99
Bronze	KIKOLSKI, Waldemar	POL	15:33.56

5,000m MEN T12

Gold	GOMEZ, Said	PAN	15:01.49 NPR
Silver	GONZALEZ, Diosmany	CUB	15:54.74
Bronze	POMYKALOV, Ildar	RUS	16:16.93

5,000m MEN T34, 35, 36, 37

Gold	PARKER, Joseph	USA	16:34.36 NWR
Silver	BELLELE, Faouzi	ALG	16:49.35
Bronze	GOVAERTS, Benny	BEL	17:33.42

5,000m MEN T45, 46

Gold	CONDE, Javier	ESP	15:02.00
Silver	WU, Yanjian	CHN	15:15.44
Bronze	LACROIX, Emmanuel	FRA	15:28.97

5,000m MEN T51

Gold	GEREIN, Clayton	CAN	13:39.04 NPR
Silver	SMITH, Gregory	AUS	13:39.90
Bronze	COTTINI, Patrick	USA	13:40.44

5,000m MEN T52, 53

Gold	MENDOZA, Saul	MEX	10.46.83
Silver	ORENS, Steve	BEL	10:46.92
Bronze	NIETLISPACH, Franz	SUI	10:47.05

10,000m MEN T10

Gold	GUERRERO, Alejandro	MEX	10:46.83 NPR
Silver	WILLIS, Henry	USA	35:38.65
Bronze	AMARAL FERREIRA, C.	POR	35:41.51

10,000m MEN T11

Gold	THATCHER, Noel	GBR	32:20.27 NWR
Silver	KIKOLSKI, Waldemar	POL	33:00.78
Bronze	BARTKENAS, Kestutis	LTU	33:12.78

10,000m MEN T12

Gold	GONZALEZ, Diosmany	CUB	33:34.42
Silver	FARNELL, Mark	GBR	34:20.57
Bronze	TCHOUMAK, Nikolai	MLD	34:36.85

10,000m MEN T52, 53

Gold	FREI, Heinz	SUI	21:58.31
Silver	ORENS, Steve	BEL	21:58.40
Bronze	KLUNNGERN, P.	THA	21:58.49

Marathon MEN T10

Gold	YANAGAWA, Harumi	JPN	2:54:56
Silver	DURANTE, Carlo	ITA	2:57:32
Bronze	LEDEZMA, Nicolas	MEX	3:00:13

Marathon MEN T11

Gold	KIKOLSKI, Waldemar	POL	2:39:57
Silver	CHMURZYNSKI, Thomasz	POL	2:46:01
Bronze	PEREZ, Francisco	ESP	2:48:24

Marathon MEN T12

Gold	SLUKA, Anton	SVK	2:43:23
Silver	FARNELL, Mark	GBR	2:56:46
Bronze	ONOFRE DA COSTA, J.	POR	2:58:04

Marathon MEN T50

Gold	KOEBERLE, Heinrich	GER	2:52:11
Silver	DODSON, Barton	USA	3:11:26
Bronze	JOHANSSON, Tim	SWE	3:39:41

Marathon MEN T51

Gold	MCMAHON, Brent	CAN	2:09:08
Silver	GEREIN, Clayton	CAN	2:09:08
Bronze	COTTINI, Patrick	USA	2:10.31

Marathon MEN T52, 53

Gold	NIETLISPACH, Franz	SUI	1:29:44 NPR
Silver	MUROZUKA, Kazuya	JPN	1:31:56
Bronze	FREI, Heinz	SUI	1:32:42

Marathon MEN T42, 43, 44

Gold	CONDE, Javier	ESP	2:35:15 NWR
Silver	LARRINGA, Joseba	ESP	2:47:23
Bronze	BROWN, Mark	GBR	2:59:33

4 x 100 MEN T10, 11, 12

Gold	PRIETO, Juan	ESP	42.36
	SANCHEZ-GUIJ		
	NUNEZ, Jorge		
	REQUENA, J.		
Silver	GEFFERS, H.	GER	43.00
	TRIPPEN-HILG		
	GEFFERS, Ingo		
	FRANZKA, Gerd		
Bronze	LEWIS III, A.	USA	43.65
	CAMPBELL, M.		
	ASBURY, Andre		
	HAYNES, W.		

4 x 100 MEN T34, 35, 36, 37

Gold	N/A	HKG	50.46 NWR
Silver	BLANKENSHIP	USA	50.94
	REGISTER IV		
	TERCEY, Jason		
	SCOTT, L.		
Bronze	ROBERTSON, G.	GBR	52.18
	COLLINS, R.		
	NEWTON, M.		
	PAYTON, S.		

4 x 100m MEN T42, 43, 44, 45, 46

Gold	MATTHEWS, T.	AUS	45.40 NWR
	FULLER, N.		
	THOMAS, B.		
	EVANS, D.		
Silver	N/A	AUT	46.55
Bronze	COLLIER, D.	USA	49.72
	OEHLER, D.		
	BOURGEOIS, T.		
	BULOW, M.		

4 x 100m MEN T52, 53

Gold	N/A	GER	56.05

4 x 400m MEN T10, 11, 12

Gold	PRIETO, Juan	ESP	3:28.65
	SNACHEZ, S.		
	SANCHEZ-GUIJ		
	SANCHEZ, Jose		
Silver	GEFFERS, Ingo	GER	3:33.61
	FRANZKA, Gerd		
	GEFFERS, H.		
	VALIDIS, T.		
Bronze	MUNRO, Edward	USA	3:53.36
	HOGANS, K.		
	HAYNES, W.		
	MALLINCKRODT		

4 x 400 MEN T52, 53

Gold	ISSORAT, C.	FRA	3:14.45 NWR
	COUPRIE, P.		
	TOLLIE, C.		
	BADID, M.		
Silver	BOGLI, Daniel	SUI	3:16.46
	MULLER, Guido		
	FREI, Heinz		
	NIETLISPACH, F.		
Bronze	MATHIESON, C.	CAN	3:21.63
	QUESSY, Marc		
	MARQUIS, Carl		
	ADAMS, J.		

Shot Put MEN F10

Gold	FIDALGO, Alfonso	ESP	13.30 NWR
Silver	DENISSEVITCH, N.	BLS	12.27
Bronze	MARTINEZ, Andres	ESP	12.08

Shot Put MEN F11

Gold	LISHCHYNSKY, Vasyl	UKR	13.66 NPR
Silver	MAYR, Karl	AUT	13.62
Bronze	KHODAKOV, Serguei	RUS	13.54

Shot Put MEN F12

Gold	SUN, Haitao	CHN	15.66 NWR
Silver	SHORT, Russell	AUS	14.94
Bronze	URBONAS, Rolandas	LTU	14.02

Shot Put MEN F35

Gold	NOORDUIN, Willem	NED	13.74 NPR
Silver	HERMANS, Alex	BEL	13.73
Bronze	DUBIN, Wolfgang	AUT	11.82

Shot Put MEN F35

Gold	VAN DER MERWE, Gert	RSA	12.65
Silver	IZLAKAR, Franjo	SLO	11.68
Bronze	CHURCHILL, Kenneth	GBR	10.98

Shot Put MEN F32, 33

Gold	MACDONALD, Hamish	AUS	10.45 NWR
Silver	MUELLER, Andreas	GER	9.25
Bronze	WEST, Daniel	GBR	8.80

Shot Put MEN F34, 35, 36, 37

Gold	SHAW, James	CAN	11.55
Silver	JANECEK, Miroslav	CZE	11.36
Bronze	KOLEK, Roma	CZE	11.21

Shot Put MEN F42

Gold	DAUBRESSE, Thierry	BEL	11.79
Silver	ECKERT, Detlef	GER	11.68
Bronze	BEYER, Horst	GER	11.46

Shot Put MEN F46

Gold	DABROWSKI, Jerzy	POL	14.50 NPR
Silver	REBISZ, Tomasz	POL	13.84
Bronze	LIU, Hongru	CHN	13.35

Shot Put MEN F43, 44

Gold	HALAGAHU, Lutovico	FRA	14.23 NPR
Silver	FRISCHMANN, Joerg	GER	14.21
Bronze	ISON, Asa	USA	13.83

Shot Put MEN F51

Gold	MODABBERRAZ, Ghader	IRI	7.17 NWR
Silver	HEIR, Douglas	USA	7.05
Bronze	MERRILL, Hal	CAN	6.75

Shot Put MEN F52

Gold	MARTIN, Peter	NZL	7.69 NWR
Silver	LIMA, Josias	BRA	7.11
Bronze	MAXIMO, Mauro	MEX	6.56

Shot Put MEN F53

Gold	WALLRODT, Bruce	AUS	9.12 NWR
Silver	NOURAFSHAN, Mokhtar	IRI	8.77
Bronze	DEETS, Jerry	USA	8.22

Shot Put MEN F54

Gold	ASTRADA, Arnold	USA	10.90
Silver	DUDLEY, David	GBR	10.24
Bronze	ANARGYROY, Stefanos	GRE	9.55

Shot Put MEN F55

Gold	KONSTANTANGAS, D.	GRE	9.78
Silver	SADEGHI MEHRYAR, M.	IRI	9.77
Bronze	GIDDY, Terence	AUS	9.44

Shot Put MEN F56

Gold	LOUWRENS, Michael	RSA	12.86 NWR
Silver	HUMPHRIES, STEYN	RSA	12.05
Bronze	NALIN, Maurizio	ITA	12.05

Shot Put MEN F57

Gold	LOMBAARD, Stephanus	RSA	14.28 NWR
Silver	ELBEHIRY, Hany	EGY	13.06
Bronze	EL KHATIB, Shaaban	EGY	12.30

Shot Put MEN F41

Gold	ABD ELGAWAD, Ahmed	EGY	13.91 NPR
Silver	ELSAFI, Ashraf	EGY	13.06
Bronze	LEBRERO, Juan	ESP	12.20

Discus MEN F10

Gold	FIDALGO, Alfonso	ESP	40.12 NPR
Silver	TURTELTAUBE, S.	GER	35.96
Bronze	DENISSEVITCH, N.	BLS	35.14

Discus MEN F11

Gold	KHODAKOV, Serguei	RUS	43.10 NWR
Silver	LISHCHYNSKY, Vasyl	UKR	39.60
Bronze	SAKELAROV, Gueorgi	BUL	38.56

Discus MEN F12

Gold	SUN, Haitao	CHN	47.56 NWR
Silver	SHORT, Russell	AUS	42.56
Bronze	DELESALLE, Jason	CAN	42.36

Discus MEN F35

Gold	BARGHCHI, Hossein	IRI	35.92 NWR
Silver	KUBALA, Milan	CZE	34.76
Bronze	NOORDUIN, Willem	NED	32.86

Discus MEN F36

Gold	BURROUGHS, Damien	AUS	38.40 NWR
Silver	BEN DHIFALLAH, A.	TUN	37.90
Bronze	SANTOS, Anderson	BRA	37.46

Discus MEN F34, 35, 36, 37

Gold	SHAW, James	CAN	41.24 NWR
Silver	JOHNSON, Denton	USA	27.00
Bronze	WILLIAMS, Paul	GBR	26.78

Discus MEN F42

Gold	DE KEERSMAEKER, Gino	BEL	43.26 NWR
Silver	BEYER, Horst	GER	42.12
Bronze	EDEN, John	AUS	41.14

Discus MEN F46

Gold	DABROWSKI, Jerzy	POL	45.20
Silver	REBISZ, Tomasz	POL	45.08
Bronze	ABOU ELATA, Ayman	EGY	40.84

Discus MEN F43, 44

Gold	BROWN, Shawn	USA	53.08 NWR
Silver	LI, Xiuqing	CHN	43.48
Bronze	KULLA, Klaus	GER	42.96

Discus MEN F51

Gold	MODABBERRAZ, Ghader	IRI	16.48 NPR
Silver	BASCIONI, Horacio	ARG	14.54
Bronze	HEIR, Douglas	USA	13.88

Discus MEN F52

Gold	LOREH JOKAR, A.	IRI	20.34 NWR
Silver	GHARBAWI, Imad	JOR	17.14
Bronze	DIAZ DE LEON, G.	USA	17.06

Discus MEN F53

Gold	LABUSCHANGNE, L.	RSA	28.04 NPR
Silver	NOURAFSHAN, Mokhtar	IRI	27.12
Bronze	MENDEZ, Francisco	ESP	24.56

Discus MEN F54

Gold	MARTIN, Jacques	CAN	33.24
Silver	FENN, Marc	USA	30.82
Bronze	O'GRADY, Sean	IRL	28.24

Discus MEN F55

Gold	HUMPHRIES, Steyn	RSA	36.06
Silver	SADEGHI MEHRYAR, M.	IRI	35.52
Bronze	BAKER, Kevan	GBR	34.40

Discus MEN F56

Gold	HUGHES, Larry	USA	41.34 NPR
Silver	NALIN, Maurizio	ITA	40.70
Bronze	ABDEL LATIF, H.	EGY	40.68

Discus MEN F57

Gold	GAWAD, Mohamed	EGY	50.66 NWR
Silver	ELBEHIRY, Hany	EGY	49.42
Bronze	LOMBAARD, Stephanus	RSA	47.96

Discus MEN F41

Gold	DAHY, Ahmed	EGY	51.12 NWR
Silver	WOLF, Nachman	ISR	45.54
Bronze	ABDELGAWAD, Ahmed	EGY	43.94

Club MEN F50

Gold	MILLER, Stephen	GBR	25.84 NWR
Silver	RICHARDSON, James	GBR	22.75
Bronze	LITTLE, Aaron	USA	20.65

Javelin MEN F10

Gold	OZAKI, Mineho	JPN	42.60
Silver	GIRNIUS, Vytautas	LTU	42.46
Bronze	RUFFALO, Richard	USA	39.20

Javelin MEN F11

Gold	PYCH, Miroslaw	POL	58.48 NWR
Silver	HEGEHOLZ, Siegmund	GER	48.84
Bronze	WHITELEY, Mark	GBR	43.52

Javelin MEN F12

Gold	SUN, Haitao	CHN	51.50 NPR
Silver	GAGNE, Fra	CAN	48.88
Bronze	VALIDIS, Thomas	GER	48.54

Javelin MEN F35

Gold	AL-MUTAIRI, Fahed	KUW	31.74 NPR
Silver	GARDNER, Keith	GBR	29.12
Bronze	CHOI, Yeon	KOR	28.50

Javelin MEN F36

Gold	CHURCHILL, Kenneth	GBR	45.54 NWR
Silver	JONKER, Jacobus	RSA	43.80
Bronze	JANSE VAN VUUREN, J.	RSA	41.24

Javelin MEN F34, 35, 36, 37

Gold	HARVEY, Brian	AUS	34.70 NPR
Silver	WILLIAMS, Paul	GBR	34.42
Bronze	SHAW, James	CAN	32.54

Javelin MEN F42

Gold	PEREZ, Guillermo	CUB	49.70 NWR
Silver	MATHIASEN, Jakob	DEN	43.38
Bronze	SIMONAZZI, Roberto	GER	42.00

Javelin MEN F46

Gold	SCHIEDEK, Joerg	GER	53.58 NPR
Silver	TUIPOLOTO, Patita	FRA	52.50
Bronze	REBISZ, Tomasz	POL	49.70

Javelin MEN F43, 44

Gold	HA, Silao	CHN	53.54 NWR
Silver	HALAGAHU, Lutovico	FRA	50.00
Bronze	MIMBERG, Dirk	GER	49.72

Javelin MEN F51

Gold	MODABBERRAZ, Ghader	IRI	15.68 NWR
Silver	MACCALMAN, David	NZL	14.78
Bronze	HEIR, Douglas	USA	13.86

Javelin MEN F52

Gold	PAZ, Adrian	MEX	16.72 NWR
Silver	MARTIN, Peter	NZL	15.80
Bronze	LOREH JOKAR, A.	IRI	15.08

Javelin MEN F53

Gold	NOURAFSHAN, Mokhtar	IRI	25.78 NPR
Silver	SUANAVAARA, Rauno	FIN	24.42
Bronze	WALLRODT, Bruce	AUS	23.68

Javelin MEN F54

Gold	SALEVA, Mikael	FIN	29.32 NPR
Silver	MARTIN, Jacques	CAN	27.22
Bronze	ROSKAR, Janez	SLO	25.88

Javelin MEN F55

Gold	DANKO, Stefan	CZE	26.00
Silver	BALK, Robert	USA	25.28
Bronze	AL-OTAIBI, Mashal	KUW	24.80

Javelin MEN F56

Gold	MIRZAEI JABERI, M.	IRI	40.42 NPR
Silver	POHLMANN, Rostislav	CZE	37.98
Bronze	HUMPHRIES, Steyn	RSA	30.96

Javelin MEN F57

Gold	LOMBAARD, Stephanus	RSA	51.06 NWR
Silver	MOHAMMAD, Ali	KUW	41.42
Bronze	HASSAN, Mohamed	EGY	41.28

Javelin MEN F41

Gold	MOORI, Christopher	KEN	44.44
Silver	DAHY, Ahmed	EGY	41.20
Bronze	ABD ELGAWAD, Ahmed	EGY	40.48

High Jump MEN F10, 11

Gold	CHEPEL, Oleg	BLS	1.85
Silver	VELEZ, Alejo	ESP	1.82
Bronze	YOSHIHARA, Shigeo	JPN	1.73

High Jump MEN F42, 43, 44

Gold	HOU, Bin	CHN	1.92 NWR
Silver	EARLE, Alan	GBR	1.79
Bronze	KERN, Juergen	GER	1.79

Long Jump MEN F10

Gold	RODRIGUEZ, Jose	ESP	6.67 NWR
Silver	SEVOSTIANOV, Serguei	RUS	6.21
Bronze	WANG, Sen	CHN	5.96

Long Jump MEN F11

Gold	BOZZOLO, Stephane	FRA	6.74 NPR
Silver	ESMERALDA, Moises	ESP	6.61
Bronze	VIEDMA, Juan	ESP	6.59

Long Jump MEN F12

Gold	CABALLERO, Enrique	CUB	7.17 NPR
Silver	FORTOUYNOV, Igor	BLS	7.02
Bronze	VAN RAEFELGHEM, Kurt	BEL	6.83

Long Jump MEN F34, 35, 36, 37

Gold	THRUPP, Darren	AUS	5.74
Silver	HABER, Peter	GER	5.60
Bronze	AMADOR, Douglas	BRA	5.42

Long Jump MEN F42

Gold	CHRISTEN, Lukas	SUI	5.20 NWR
Silver	BELITZ, Gunther	GER	4.55
Bronze	SIEGL, Andreas	AUT	4.32

Long Jump MEN F44

Gold	KOLLY, Urs	SUI	5.20 NWR
Silver	STOLL, Patrick	SUI	5.75
Bronze	THOMAS, Bradley	AUS	5.74

Long Jump MEN F45, 46

Gold	ALVAREZ, Ruben	ESP	6.75 NWR
Silver	AJIBOLA, Adeoye	NGR	6.64
Bronze	TOPTSIS, Georgios	GRE	6.36

Long Jump MEN MH

Gold	BOURNE, Nigel	GBR	6.81 NPR
Silver	BEN BAHRI, Wissem	TUN	6.42
Bronze	GADSON, Wardell	USA	6.24

Triple Jump MEN F10

Gold	RODRIGUEZ, Jose	ESP	12.93
Silver	WANG, Sen	CHN	12.06
Bronze	JUOKOVSKI, Victor	BLS	11.56

Triple Jump MEN F11

Gold	VIEDMA, Juan	ESP	14.10 NPR
Silver	HUANG, Wentao	CHN	14.03
Bronze	HORBENKO, Ihor	UKR	13.90

Triple Jump MEN F12

Gold	CABALLERO, Enrique	CUB	14.87 NPR
Silver	FORTOUNOV, Igor	BLS	14.30
Bronze	STRIEGEL, Ulrich	GER	13.29

Triple Jump MEN F45, 46

Gold	ZHAO, Xueen	CHN	13.39 NWR
Silver	BOEHL, Florian	GER	13.28
Bronze	ALVAREZ, Ruben	ESP	13.24

Pentathlon MEN P10

Gold	SEVOSTIANOV, Serguei	RUS	2,597 NWR
Silver	HAUCKE, Rayk	GER	2,135
Bronze	JOUKOVSKI, Victor	BLS	2,051

Pentathlon MEN P11

Gold	PYCH, Miroslaw	POL	3,118
Silver	BOZZOLO, Stephane	FRA	2,826
Bronze	GODRI, Frantisek	SVK	2,738

Pentathlon MEN P12

Gold	DELESALLE, Jason	CAN	3,050 NPR
Silver	VAN RAEFELGHEM, Kurt	BEL	3,040
Bronze	FORTOUNOV, Igor	BLS	2,896

Pentathlon MEN P53, 54, 55, 56, 57

Gold	NALIN, Maurizio	ITA	5,130
Silver	BALK, Robert	USA	4,947
Bronze	DEETS, Jerry	USA	4,792

Pentathlon MEN P42

Gold	BEYER, Horst	GER	4,316 NWR
Silver	MCGREGOR, Kerrod	AUS	4,097
Bronze	MATHIASEN, Jakob	DEN	3,826

Pentathlon MEN P44

Gold	KOLLY, Urs	SUI	4,947 NWR
Silver	BOURGEOIS, Thomas	USA	4,761
Bronze	COLLIER, Douglas	USA	4,693

100m WOMEN T10

Gold	SANTAMARTA, Puri	ESP	12.59
Silver	SANTOS, Adria	BRA	12.92
Bronze	DIAZ, Raquel	ESP	12.99

100m WOMEN T11

Gold	MENDOZA, Beatriz	ESP	13.02
Silver	BRUNOTTE, Clair	GER	13.19
Bronze	ALVES, Maria Jose	BRA	13.38

100m WOMEN T32, 33

Gold	ARAI, Moriko	JPN	19.89 NWR
Silver	MASTANDREA, Linda	USA	20.02
Bronze	O'NEIL, Sheila	USA	21.80

100m WOMEN T34, 35

Gold	INNES, Caroline	GBR	15.78
Silver	ALVAREZ, Maria	ESP	16.11
Bronze	TEUBNER, Cornelia	GER	16.54

100m WOMEN T36, 37

Gold	WEBB, Katrina	AUS	14.79
Silver	FOERDER, Isabelle	GER	15.08
Bronze	QUINN, Alison	AUS	15.31

100m WOMEN T42, 43, 44, 45, 46

Gold	OJASTU, Annely	EST	12.78
Silver	SACHSE, Jessica	GER	12.86
Bronze	WINTERS, Amy	AUS	12.89

100m WOMEN T52

Gold	SHANNON, Leann	USA	16.62 NWR
Silver	GREY, Tanni	GBR	17.18
Bronze	BOUGONJE, Colette	CAN	18.35

100m WOMEN T53

Gold	PETITCLERC, Chantal	CAN	16.70 NWR
Silver	BECERRA, Cheri	USA	16.74
Bronze	JARVIS, Nicola	GBR	17.93

200m WOMEN T10

Gold	SANTAMARTA, Puri	ESP	25.45 NWR
Silver	SANTOS, Adria	BRA	26.15
Bronze	LIGORIO, Maria	ITA	26.23

200m WOMEN T11

Gold	MENDOZA, Beatriz	ESP	26.32 NWR
Silver	BRUNOTTE, Claire	GER	26.80
Bronze	ALVES, Maria Jose	BRA	26.87

200m WOMEN T32, 33

Gold	MASTANDREA, Linda	USA	35.30 NWR
Silver	ARAI, Noriko	JPN	37.18
Bronze	RICE, Mary	IRL	39.96

200m WOMEN T34, 35, 36, 37

Gold	WEBB, Katrina	AUS	30.70
Silver	FOERDER, Isabelle	GER	31.14
Bronze	MARTINEZ, Alicia	ESP	31.73

200m WOMEN T42, 43, 44, 45, 46

Gold	WINTERS, Amy	AUS	25.97 NWR
Silver	OJASTU, Annely	EST	26.26
Bronze	LEONTIOUK, Irina	BLS	26.34

200m WOMEN T51

Gold	SMITH, Cristeen	NZL	41.11 NPR
Silver	TORRRES, Leticia	MEX	42.08
Bronze	GREUTER, Ursina	SUI	42.73

200m WOMEN T52

Gold	SHANNON, Leann	USA	29.76
Silver	GREY, Tanni	GBR	30.38
Bronze	BOURGONJE, Colette	CAN	33.18

200m WOMEN T53

Gold	PETITCLERC, Chantal	CAN	29.41
Silver	BECERRA, Cheri	USA	29.64
Bronze	JARVIS, Nicola	GBR	31.27

200m WOMEN MH

Gold	RACKHAM, Sharon	AUS	26.79 NWR
Silver	MELESKO, Tracey	CAN	26.79 NWR
Bronze	LLORENS, Lisa	AUS	27.32

400m WOMEN T10

Gold	SANTAMARTA, Puri	ESP	58.16
Silver	SANTOS, Adria	BRA	59.97
Bronze	LIGORIO, Maria	ITA	1:00.11

400m WOMEN T11

Gold	BATALOVA, Rima	RUS	59.39 NPR
Silver	ORTEGA, Maria	ESP	1:02.94
Bronze	JDANOVA, Elena	RUS	1:03.06

400m WOMEN T51

Gold	GREUTER, Ursina	SUI	1:21.99 NWR
Silver	WATERS, Jean	USA	1:22.29
Bronze	TORRES, Leticia	MEX	1:22.55

400m WOMEN T52

Gold	SHANNON, Leann	USA	57.55
Silver	GREY, Tanni	GBR	58.09
Bronze	VOGEL, Joelle	FRA	1:03.52

400m WOMEN T53

Gold	SAUVAGE, Luise	AUS	54.96 NPR
Silver	PETITCLERC, Chantal	CAN	56.83
Bronze	BECERRA, Cheri	USA	57.15

800m WOMEN T10, 11

Gold	BATALOVA, Rima	RUS	2:15.65 NWR
Silver	MEIER, Claudia	GER	2:21.77
Bronze	MARKEVICIENE, Sigita	LTU	2:22.17

800m WOMEN T51

Gold	TANAKA, Teruyo	JPN	2:43.17 NWR
Silver	SMITH, Cristeen	NZL	2:43.28
Bronze	GREUTER, Ursina	SUI	2:43.85

800m WOMEN T52

Gold	GREY, Tanni	GBR	1:55.12 NWR
Silver	SHANNON, Leann	USA	1:55.89
Bronze	WALTERS, Ann	USA	2:02.41

800m WOMEN T53

Gold	SAUVAGE, Louise	AUS	1:52.80 NPR
Silver	PETITCLERC, Chantal	CAN	1:53.30
Bronze	BECERRA, Cheri	USA	1:53.41

1,500m WOMEN T10, 11

Gold	BATALOVA, Rima	RUS	4:51.17
Silver	MEIER, Claudia	GER	4:51.98
Bronze	MARKEVICIENE, Sigita	LTU	5:00.85

1,500m WOMEN T52, 53

Gold	SAUVAGE, Louise	AUS	3:30.45 NWR
Silver	PETTITCLERC, Chantal	CAN	3:30.63
Bronze	DRISCOLL, Jean	USA	3:30.83

3,000m WOMEN T10, 11

Gold	BATALOVA, Rima	RUS	10:35.67 NPR
Silver	MEIER, Claudia	GER	10:37.39
Bronze	MENGHELLI, Samanta	ITA	11:00.00

5,000m WOMEN T52, 53

Gold	SAUVAGE, Louise	AUS	12:40.71 NWR
Silver	DRISCOLL, Jean	USA	12:40.80
Bronze	HATANAKA, Kazu	JPN	12:41.49

10,000m WOMEN T52, 53

Gold	DRISCOLL, Jean	USA	24:21:64 NWR
Silver	HATANAKA, Kazu	JPN	24:31.88
Bronze	ANGGRENY, Lily	GER	25:23.01

Marathon WOMEN T52, 53

Gold	DRISCOLL, Jean	USA	1:52:54
Silver	HATANAKA, Kazu	JPN	1:52:56
Bronze	SODOMA, Deanna	USA	1:57:16

Shot Put WOMEN F12

Gold	SIVAKOVA, Tamara	BLS	12.51 NPR
Silver	RUNYAN, Marla	USA	11.40
Bronze	LYNCH, Bridie	IRL	10.72

Shot Put WOMEN F10, 11

Gold	XU, Hongyan	CHN	12.12 NWR
Silver	WILLIS-ROBERTS, Jodi	AUS	11.46
Bronze	LJUBISIC, Ljiljana	CAN	10.99

Shot Put WOMEN F32, 33

Gold	POHL, Birgit	GER	8.36 NWR
Silver	LAWTON, Janice	GBR	6.12
Bronze	RICE, Sharon	IRL	5.01

Shot Put WOMEN F42, 43, 44

Gold	WU, Hongping	CHN	11.06 NWR
Silver	JAENICKE, Britta	GER	10.98
Bronze	BARRETT, Jennifer	USA	10.88

Shot Put WOMEN F53, 54

Gold	BUGGENHAGEN, M.	GER	8.39 NWR
Silver	SCHWANGER, Laura	USA	8.29
Bronze	WILLING, Martina	GER	7.51

Shot Put WOMEN F55, 56, 57

Gold	OMAR, Mervat	EGY	7.83 NPR
Silver	ABDIN, Zakia	EGY	7.54
Bronze	ELKOUMY, Sohir	EGY	7.49

Shot Put WOMEN F41

Gold	BAUMGARTE, Malda	LTU	9.07 NWR
Silver	ROSALES, Catalina	MEX	8.86
Bronze	BARRETT-CONDRON, G.	IRL	8.07

Discus WOMEN F12

Gold	LYNCH, Bridie	IRL	37.14
Silver	KNIGHT, Courtney	CAN	36.98
Bronze	SIVAKOVA, Tamara	BLS	35.48

Discus WOMEN F10, 11

Gold	BELISER, Liiudys	CUB	45.06 NWR
Silver	XU, Hongyan	CHN	41.32
Bronze	LJUBISIC, Ljiljana	CAN	37.20

Discus WOMEN F34, 35

Gold	HYMAN, Ellen	USA	19.62 NWR
Silver	RODRIGUEZ, Maria	ARG	18.80
Bronze	HODGING, Kris	CAN	18.38

Discus WOMEN F42, 43, 44

Gold	BARRETT, Jennifer	USA	38.92 NWR
Silver	WU, Hongping	CHN	37.56
Bronze	JAENICKE, Britta	GER	32.28

Discus WOMEN F53, 54

Gold	BUGGENHAGEN, M.	GER	23.67
Silver	SCHWANGER, Laura	USA	21.40
Bronze	WILLING, Martina	GER	20.92

Discus WOMEN F55, 56, 57

Gold	FELEIFAL, Karima	EGY	26.34 NWR
Silver	OMAR, Mervat	EGY	24.92
Bronze	GUIMARAES, Suely	BRA	24.54

Discus WOMEN F41

Gold	BAUMGARTE, Malda	LTU	30.80 NWR
Silver	CASTRO, Araceli	MEX	25.82
Bronze	ROSALES, Catalina	MEX	25.68

Javelin WOMEN F10, 11

Gold	VAN BRUSSEL, M.	BEL	32.04 NPR
Silver	BELISER, Liiudys	CUB	31.92
Bronze	SKOROBOGATAIA, I.	BLS	27.74

Javelin WOMEN F42, 43, 44

Gold	SCHERNEY, Andrea	AUT	31.98 NWR
Silver	MEZINOVA, Tatiana	RUS	30.60
Bronze	KLETSKOVA, Natalia	RUS	30.28

Javelin WOMEN F55, 56, 57

Gold	ABDIN, Zakia	EGY	23.40 NWR
Silver	NAKHUMICHA, Mary	KEN	19.82
Bronze	GRANT, Sylvia	JAM	18.98

Long Jump WOMEN F10, 11

Gold	AMO, Magdalena	ESP	5.22 NPR
Silver	LAZARO, Rosalia	ESP	5.22 NPR
Bronze	ORTIZ, Purificacion	ESP	5.07

Long Jump WOMEN F34, 35, 36, 37

Gold	GRIGALIUNIENE, A.	LTU	4.49 NWR
Silver	WEBB, Katrina	AUS	4.46
Bronze	STORCH, Carmen	GER	3.92

Long Jump WOMEN F42, 43, 44, 45, 46

Gold	LEONTIOUK, Irina	BLS	5.70 NWR
Silver	OJASTU, Annely	EST	5.37
Bronze	BASFORD, Alice	GBR	4.35

Long Jump WOMEN MH

Gold	LLORENS, Lisa	AUS	4.95 NWR
Silver	MELESKO, Tracey	CAN	4.80
Bronze	JUHKAM, Malle	EST	4.76

Pentathlon WOMEN F10, 11, 12

Gold	RUNYAN, Marla	USA	3,661 NWR
Silver	TCHOURKINA, Olga	RUS	2,830
Bronze	SILM, Helena	EST	2,713

BASKETBALL

WOMEN

Gold	KREMPIEN, J.	CAN
	ABBOTT, Marni	
	OHAMA, Kendra	
	STEVENS, Lisa	
	DEL COLLIE, Renee	
	BENOIT, Chantal	
	SMITHIES, Marney	
	PETTINICCHI, S.	
	ERGUSON, Tracey	
	RADKE, Lori	
	KUTROWSKI, Linda	
	KRYWA, Kelly	
Silver	JANSEN, Jenniqje	NED
	DE ZEEU, Jaapie	
	IBRAHIMI, A.	
	BROERSE, Yolanda	
	TIGGELMAN, I.	
	VAN DER LAAN, G.	
	MOS, Jozina	
	VAN LEEUWEN, M.	
	BUURMAN, Jorien	
	VAN VEGGEL, J.	
	BENNEKER, Erna	
	VAN LEEUW, E.	
Bronze	STUMP, Jana	USA
	DANSKIN, Jamie	
	NUNEZ, Ruth	
	HERBST, Sharon	
	FONTAINE, Pamela	
	MARIN, Kimberly	
	TYREE-GROSS, R.	
	HAGEL, Susan	
	JARVIS, Ronda	
	STRAN, Margaret	
	TOZER, Tiana	
	JOHNSON, Josie	

MEN

Gold	OLIVER, Richard	AUS
	SACHS, Troy	
	GOULD, David	
	BLYTHE, Robert	
	COX, Benjamin	
	ANDREWS, Troy	
	MORRIS, Nicholas	
	HEWSON, Gerard	
	ELWIN, Stuart	
	SELBY, David	
	MALONEY, Timothy	
	CECCONATO, Orfeo	
Silver	CAINE, Stevan	GBR
	WOOLLARD, A.	
	PEEL, Garry	
	CHEANEY, Mark	
	MUNN, Simon	
	GORDON, Calum	
	SMITH, Nigel	
	JOHNSON, Daniel	
	TARKENTER, M.	
	JAYARATNE, J.	
	PRICE, Colin	
	BRAMLEY, David	
Bronze	SNOW, Randy	USA
	JUETTE, Mel	
	SHEPHERD, Mark	
	GILL, Chuck	
	KAZEE, Tim	
	MILLER, Jimbo	
	COLTON, Reggie	
	SHEWMAKE, Craig	
	SCHLAPPI, Mike	
	KNIGHT, Rob	
	JOHNSON, T.	
	WALLER, Darryl	

BOCCIA

Pairs C1 W

Gold	MACEDO, Jose	POR
	COSTA, Armando	
Silver	CARLE, Joyce	GBR
	EDGE, Zoe	
Bronze	BIGNALL, Kris	AUS
	HUYHN, Tu	

Team C1, C2

Gold	GOMEZ, Miguel	ESP
	CID, Antonio	
	RODRIGUEZ, Maria	
	FRAILE, Jesus	
Silver	SILVA, Pedro	POR
	ALVES, Joao	
	MARQUES, Antonio	
	FERREIRA, F.	
Bronze	JUNG, Yoo	KOR
	YOU, Won	
	KIM, Hae	
	KIM, Joon	

Individual C1 W

Gold	MACEDO, Jose	POR
Silver	MARTIN, Yolanda	ESP
Bronze	DRIESEN, Paul	BEL

Individual C1

Gold	KIM, Hae	KOR
Silver	JORGENSEN, Henrik	DEN
Bronze	THOMPSON, Steven	USA

Individual C2

Gold	RODRIGUEZ, Maria	ESP
Silver	LEAHY, Thomas	IRL
Bronze	FRAILE, Jesus	ESP

CYCLING

Tandem Kilo MEN Open

Gold	GINTRAND, Thierry	FRA	1:06.858
	SENMARTIN, Patrice		
Silver	GUEZO, Eric	FRA	1:07.092
	MIGNON, Vincent		
Bronze	BOTTI, Paolo	ITA	1:07.474
	GALLI, Giancarlo		

Tandem Kilo WOMEN Open

Gold	SMITH, Sandra	AUS	1:13.473
	POOLE, Teresa		
Silver	RANZ, Elfriede	GER	1:16.612
	EGNER, Ursula		
Bronze	LAROUCHE, Guylaine	CAN	1:18.346
	COURNOYER, Julie		

Tandem Kilo MIXED Open

Gold	SPADACCINI, Patrizia	ITA	1:11.467
	COSTA, Claudio		
Silver	EVANS, Scott	USA	1:12.094
	DUNNE, Cara		
Bronze	ROSENBERG, Michael	USA	1:12.915
	FERNANDES, Pamela		

Tandem Ind Pursuit MEN Open

Gold	SCHOOTS, Pascal	NED	4:37.598
	MULDER, Jan		
Silver	HOLLANDS, Eddy	AUS	4:38.901
	CLOHESSY, Paul		
Bronze	ROUCHOVZE, Guy	FRA	4:37.497
	DECHAMP, Herve		

Tandem Ind Pursuit WOMEN Open

Gold	SMITH, Sandra	AUS	3:54.563
	POOLE, Teresa		
Silver	LAROUCHE, Guylaine	CAN	4:01.323
	COURNOYER, Julie		
Bronze	TRETCHIOK, Tiffany	USA	4:01327
	HAFT, Julia		

Tandem Ind Pursuit MIXED Open

Gold	SPADACCINI, Patrizia	ITA	3:43.534
	COSTA, Claudio		
Silver	HOPPER, Michael	USA	3:48.860
	URSCHEL, Kathleen		
Bronze	LARA, Francisco	ESP	3:47.057
	PEREZ, Belen		

200m Sprint Tandem MEN Open

Gold	BOTTI, Paolo	ITA
	GALLI, Giancarlo	
Silver	TAKAC, Pavel	SVK
	JAMBOR, Miroslav	
Bronze	GUEZO, Eric	FRA
	MIGNON, Vincent	

200m Sprint Tandem MIXED Open

Gold	GOLDING, Kerry	AUS
	MODRA, Kieran	
Silver	AGNESE, Manuela	ITA
	ZANOTTI, Damiano	
Bronze	EVANS, Scott	USA
	DUNNE, Cara	

Omnium MIXED LC1

Gold	EIBECK, Wolfgang	AUT	5
Silver	GRAY, Matthew	AUS	10
Bronze	JOENSBERG, Aage	NOR	11

Omniun MIXED LC2

Gold	SELINGER, Dory	USA	3
Silver	LAKE, Paul	AUS	7
Bronze	CERIA, Partick	FRA	9

Omniun MIXED LC3

Gold	PEREX, Miguel	ESP	9
Silver	PATRICK, Rex	USA	9
Bronze	ZETTLER, Norbert	AUT	10

1500m Tricycle T.T. MIXED Div. 2

Gold	CULOT, Guy	BEL	2:47.00
Silver	HILLERS, Andreas	GER	2:51.00
Bronze	OGAWA, Mutsuhiko	JPN	2:56.00

50/60km Tandem Road WOMEN Open

Gold	LAROUCHE, Guylaine	CAN	1:30:49.00
	COURNOYER, Julie		
Silver	TRETSCHIOK, Tiffany	USA	1:30:50.00
	HAFT, Julia		
Bronze	CORRAL, Rosario	ESP	1:30:54.00
	CHAVES, Maria		

20km Bicycle Road MIXED Div 3

Gold	NICHOLSON, Daniel	USA	34:58.00
Silver	KIM, Jong	KOR	35:00.00
Bronze	LONGHI, Gary	CAN	36:20.00

20km Bicycle Road MIXED Div 4

Gold	HOMAN, Peter	AUS	31:05.00
Silver	SCOTT, Christopher	AUS	32:41.00
Bronze	SCHULTZ, Lawrence	USA	33:36.00

100/120km Tandem Road MEN Open

Gold	BERTRAND, Jean	FRA	2:26:35.00
	MIQUARD, Franck		
Silver	CAMPEDELLI, Pasquale	ITA	2:26:35.00
	GALLI, Giancarlo		
Bronze	BOESCH, Martin	GER	2:26:35.00
	HOEFLE, Frank		

65/75km Bicycle Road MIXED LC1

Gold	MERCIER, David	FRA	1:48:09.00
Silver	MAHLER, Wolfgang	GER	1:48:22.00
Bronze	JOENSBERG, Aage	NOR	1:48:48.00

55/65km Bicycle Road MIXED LC2

Gold	CERIA, Patrick	FRA	1:44:00.00
Silver	SIMOVEC, Lubomir	CZE	1:45:09.00
Bronze	BONNEAU, Patrice	CAN	1:45:15.00

45/55km Bicycle Road MIXED LC3

Gold	RAOUL, Luc	FRA	1:46:16.00
Silver	SCHWARZENBACH, Beat	SUI	1:46:16.00
Bronze	ZETTLER, Norbert	AUT	1:46:16.00

5000m Tricycle T.T MIXED Div 2

Gold	OGAWA, Mutsuhiko	JPN	10:15.00
Silver	CULOT, Guy	BEL	10:24.00
Bronze	HUNTLEY, Corey	USA	11:32.00

60/70km Tandem Road MIXED Open

Gold	CLOUTIER, Alexandre	CAN	1:31:42.00
	COURNOYER, Julie		
Silver	LARA, Francisco	ESP	1:31:42.00
	PEREZ, Belen		
Bronze	SANTIAGO, Jose	ESP	1:31:50.00
	PADRONES, Elena		

5000m Bicycle T.T MIXED Div 3

Gold	LONGHI, Gary	CAN	8:24.14
Silver	NICHOLSON, Daniel	USA	8:25.34
Bronze	MAEDA, Shojiro	JPN	8:29.31

500m Bicycle T.T MIXED Div 4

Gold	SCOTT, Christopher	AUS	7:13.76
Silver	HOMAN, Peter	AUS	7:56.06
Bronze	SCHULTZ, Lawrence	USA	7:56.57

EQUESTRIAN

Kur Canter Grade III

Gold	ORE, Anne Cecilie	NOR	74.19
Silver	AGUILLAUME, Frederic	FRA	69.81
Bronze	SALMON, Joan	IRL	69.67

Kur Canter Grade IV

Gold	JACKSON, Joanna	GBR	73.37
Silver	JENSEN, Charlotte	DEN	69.70
Bronze	SORENSEN, Britta	DEN	68.93

Kur Trot Grade I

Gold	DREISZIS, Birgit	GER	78.44
Silver	ANDERSEN, Brita	DEN	75.19
Bronze	TUBBS, Dianne	GBR	71.30

Kur Trot Grade II

Gold	SWEIGART, Vicki	USA	72.07
Silver	TRABERT, Angelika	GER	72.00
Bronze	DUNHAM, Anne	GBR	66.26

Dressage Grade I

Gold	ANDERSEN, Brita	DEN	70.67
Silver	TUBBS, Dianne	GBR	61.33
Bronze	RYDH, Sara	SWE	60.00

Dressage Grade II

Gold	SWEIGART, Vicki	USA	65.79
Silver	TRABERT, Angelika	GER	62.98
Bronze	MCDEVITT, Lauren	USA	58.77

Dressage Grade III

Gold	ORE, Anne Cecilie	NOR	67.22
Silver	STONE, Elizabeth	GBR	67.04
Bronze	STOKKEL, Joop	NED	65.93

Dressage Grade IV

Gold	JACKSON, Joanna	GBR	67.92
Silver	STRAUGHAN, Patricia	GBR	63.89
Bronze	SORENSEN, Britta	DEN	63.19

Team Open

Gold		GBR	65.43
Silver		DEN	63.79
Bronze		FRA	60.68

FENCING

Team Epee MEN A & B

Gold	CHEUNG, W.	HKG
	CHUI, Man	
	KWONG, Wai	
	TAI, Yan Yun	
Silver	CECCANTI, S.	ITA
	PELLEGRINI, A.	
	MARI, Gerardo	
	LERRE, Ernesto	
Bronze	CITERNE, Robert	FRA
	LACHAUD, C.	
	ROSIER, Jean	
	BELLANCE, Arthur	

Team Foil MEN A & B

Gold	CHAN, Kam Loi	HKG
	CHAN, Sze Kit	
	CHEUNG, W.	
	KWONG, Wai	
Silver	CITERNE, Robert	FRA
	DURAND, Pascal	
	PACAULT, Yvon	
	ROSIER, Jean	
Bronze	CECCANTI, S.	ITA
	ALFIERI, G.	
	SERAFINI, A.	
	PELLEGRINI, A.	

Team Sabre MEN A & B

Gold	DURAND, Pascal	FRA
	MORE, Cyril	
	LACHAUD, C.	
	PACAULT, Yvon	
Silver	CHAN, Kam Loi	HKG
	CHAN, Sze Kit	
	CHUI, Man Fai	
	TAI, Yan Yun	
Bronze	BARTMANN, Uwe	GER
	KEMPF, Wolfgang	
	LIPINSKI, W.	
	MILLER, M.	

Individual Epee MEN A

Gold	CHEUNG, Wai Leung	HKG
Silver	PELLEGRINI, Alberto	ITA
Bronze	LIPINSKI, Wilfried	GER

Individual Epee MEN B

Gold	ROSIER, Jean	FRA
Silver	CECCANTI, Soriano	ITA
Bronze	PARK, Tae Hoon	KOR

Individual Foil MEN A

Gold	CHEUNG, Wai Leung	HKG
Silver	PELLEGRINI, Alberto	ITA
Bronze	CHAN, Kam Loi	HKG

Individual Foil MEN B

Gold	SZEKERES, Pal	HUN
Silver	ROSIER, Jean	FRA
Bronze	DURAND, Pascal	FRA

Individual Sabre MEN A

Gold	PACAULT, Yvon	FRA
Silver	LIPINSKI, Wilfried	GER
Bronze	TAI, Yan Yun	HKG

Individual Sabre MEN B

Gold	SZEKERES, Pal	HUN
Silver	MARI, Gerardo	ITA
Bronze	DURAND, Pascal	FRA

Team Epee WOMEN A & B

Gold	BELGODE, Sophie	FRA
	BOURGAIN, J.	
	PICOT, Patricia	
	VAN DE CAPPELLE	
Silver	HERTRICH, Monika	GER
	JACOB, Jutta	
	SCHWARZ, Silke	
	AWEVER-KRANZ, E.	
Bronze	HASSEN-BEY, G.	ESP
	BAZALO, F.	
	PEREZ, Christina	

Team Foil WOMEN A & B

Gold	BELGODE, Sophie	FRA
	BOURGAIN, J.	
	PICOT, Patricia	
	VAN DE CAPPELLE	
Silver	PRESUTTO, Laura	ITA
	VETTRAINO, R.	
	BERTINI, M.	
Bronze	HERTRICH, Monika	GER
	JACOB, Jutta	
	SCHWARZ, Silke	
	WEBER-KRANZ, E.	

Individual Epee WOMEN A

Gold	SCHWARZ, Silke	GER
Silver	POLASIK, Jadwiga	POL
Bronze	BELGODERE-PARALITICI	FRA

Individual Epee WOMEN B

Gold	BERTINI, Mariella	ITA
Silver	VETTRAINO, Rosalba	ITA
Bronze	WEBER-KRANZ, Esther	GER

Individual Foil WOMEN A

Gold	BOURGAIN, Josette	FRA
Silver	BELGODERE-PARALITICI	FRA
Bronze	PICOT, Patricia	FRA

Individual Foil WOMEN B

Gold	VAN DE CAPPELLE, M.	FRA
Silver	PALFI, Judit	HUN
Bronze	WEBER-KRANZ, Esther	GER

FOOTBALL

Gold	DE JONG, Arno	NED
	GLIMMERVEEN, R.	
	DONNERS, Olaf	
	ENSER, Percy	
	HENNINK, Dirk	
	GUNTLISBERGEN	
	KARSSEN, Olaf	
	DENGERINK, Carlo	
	HEERSINK, Paul	
	DE VRIES, Jacob	
	VAN BREEMEN, R.	
Silver	SILATCHEV, A.	RUS
	LOJETCHNIKOV, A.	
	KORENKOV, N.	
	SIZOV, Pavel	
	GUERASSIMOV, G.	
	MOROZOV, Victor	
	CHEMANINE, A.	
	FATIAKHDINOV, M.	
	KHRIACHTHEV, S.	
	NIKACHINE, S.	
Bronze	PELETEIRO, Jorge	ESP
	TAIBO, Juan	
	ARZALLUS, Aitzol	
	RUFO, Manuel	
	JIMENEZ, David	
	LOPEZ, Santiago	
	HURTADO, Jose	
	GALILEA, Julian	
	PARDO, Borja	
	VAZQUEZ, Juan	
	VISTACION, J.	

GOALBALL

MEN

Gold	KAUPPILA, Marko	FIN
	KINNUNEN, Asko	
	KIVINEN, Jorma	
	KALLUNKI, Jani	
	MAKINEN, Artu	
	OIKARAINEN, Juha	
Silver	HOULE, Eric	CAN
	CHEPAULT, J.	
	CARON, Mario	
	CHRISTY, Jeff	
	GAUNT, Robert	
	KOZAK, Dean	
Bronze	GONZALEZ, H.	ESP
	MUNOZ, Francicco	
	ABENIA, Roberto	
	MENDOZA, Jordi	
	SARDINA, F.	
	FERNANDEZ, R.	

WOMEN

Gold	BETHKE, Martina	GER
	DIETZ, Cornelia	
	DEMMELHUBER, G.	
	EWERT, Edda	
	BETTINGER, C.	
	KRAUSE, C.	
Silver	HANSKI, Merja	FIN
	PELKONEN, Tarja	
	PEKKALA, Mari	
	KEITEL, Iiris	
	PIIROINEN, M.	
Bronze	DAVIS-SPARKS, I.	USA
	EGENSTEINER-ASB	
	GORDON, Sheryl	
	OSTROWSKI, M.	
	ESPOSITO, M.	
	ARMBRUSTER, J.	

JUDO

Up to 60 kg

Gold	LEE, Ching-Chung	TPE
Silver	KANKI, Nobuhiro	JPN
Bronze	KIM, Il	KOR
	MITCHOURINE, V.	RUS

Up to 65 kg

Gold	FUJIMOTO, Satoshi	JPN
Silver	GAZEMAGOMEDOVA, A.	RUS
Bronze	MOREL, Cyril	FRA
	LOPEZ, Marlon	USA

Up to 71 kg

Gold	USHIKUBO, Takio	JPN
Silver	ROLLO, Gerald	FRA
Bronze	CUI, Baoji	CHN
	MOORE, Stephen	USA

Up to 78 kg

Gold	JACKSON, Simon	GBR
Silver	RAMIREZ, Fabian	ARG
Bronze	SANTANA, Eugenio	ESP
	STOSKUS, Jonas	LTU

Up to 86 kg			
Gold	DA SILVA, Antonio	BRA	
Silver	BOEDO, Francisco	ESP	
Bronze	ROSE, Ian	GBR	
	AN, You	KOR	
Up to 95 kg			
Gold	CLARKE, Anthony	AUS	
Silver	MEN, Runming	CHN	
Bronze	POWELL, Terence	GBR	
	MASTRO, James	USA	
Over 95 kg			
Gold	HANL, Walter	AUT	
Silver	SZOTT, Kevin	USA	
Bronze	CENSIER, Eric	FRA	
	TAKAGAKI, Osamu	JPN	

LAWN BOWLS

MEN LB2		
Gold	CURRAN, William	GBR
Silver	NIEMANN, Willem	RSA
Bronze	LIM, Chul	KOR
MEN LB6		
Gold	MCDONALD, Lance	CAN
Silver	PHILLIPS, Ronald	RSA
Bronze	BARANES, Itzhak	ISR
MEN LB3/4/5		
Gold	SHAW, Samuel	GBR
Silver	HEDDLE, David	GBR
Bronze	CHIU, Lun	HKG
MEN LB7/8		
Gold	LYNE, Alan	GBR
Silver	WRIGHT, George	GBR
Bronze	BRENTON, Keith	GBR
WOMEN LB2		
Gold	MOORE, Vera	GBR
Silver	TYLER, Penny	GBR
Bronze	HARRIMAN, Margaret	RSA
WOMEN LB6		
Gold	BULLER, Deidre	RSA
Silver	BERKELEY, Vivian	CAN
Bronze	CAREMLI, Tami	ISR
WOMEN LB3/4/5		
Gold	CHEER, Irene	GBR
Silver	CLARK, June	AUS
Bronze	CAHILL, Pauline	AUS
WOMEN LB7/8		
Gold	CREAN, Rose	GBR
Silver	TANG, Lai	HKG
Bronze	ELIAS, Mary	GBR

POWERLIFTING

Up to 48 kg			
Gold	KWAK, Jung	KOR	165.0 NWR
Silver	OBARETIN, Anthony	NGR	160.0
Bronze	PEDDLE, Anthony	GBR	160.0
Up to 52 kg			
Gold	JUNG, Keum	KOR	177.5 NWR
Silver	WANG, Jian	CHN	162.5
Bronze	SULOLA, Johnson	NGR	150.0
Up to 56 kg			
Gold	AHMED, Ahmed	EGY	177.5 NWR
Silver	KARIMIPOUR, Ferydon	IRI	170.0
Bronze	YOON, Sang	KOR	165.0
Up to 60 kg			
Gold	EMOGHAVWE, Monday	NGR	195.0 NWR
Silver	MATHNA, Metwaly	EGY	177.5
Bronze	AKBARI, Allahbakhsh	IRI	177.5
Up to 67.5 kg			
Gold	ZHANG, Haidong	CHN	195.0 NWR
Silver	MOHAMED, Emadeldin	EGY	187.5
Bronze	ZEYNAL SIAVOSHANI	IRI	185.0
Up to 75 kg			
Gold	FORNALCZYK, Ryszard	POL	207.5 NWR
Silver	PARK, Jong	KOR	205.0
Bronze	FARAG, Abd Elmonem	EGY	197.5
Up to 82.5 kg			
Gold	VOGEL, Bernd	GER	205.0 NPR
Silver	HAMED, Mostafa	EGY	200.0
Bronze	ZHOU, Jaihua	CHN	190.0
Up to 90 kg			
Gold	TOMASZEWSKI, Ryszard	POL	220.0
Silver	MCNICHOLL, Brian	AUS	202.5
Bronze	GYLAND, Frank	NOR	200.0
Up to 100 kg			
Gold	LUO, Zhiqiang	CHN	232.5 NWR
Silver	BAKR, Sherif	EGY	222.5
Bronze	AKUTAEKWE, Patrick	NGR	220.0
100 kg and Over			
Gold	BROWNFIELD, Kim	USA	237.5 NWR
Silver	HALLMANN, Leszek	POL	225.0
Bronze	COOPER, Pernell	USA	225.0

RUGBY

Gold	CHUNN, Clifton	USA
	CROUCH, Charles	
	GOULD, David	
	UPDEGROVE, B.	
	CERUTI, David	
	SOARES, Joseph	
	RENJE, William	
Silver	HICKLING, Garett	CAN
	BELANGER, Dany	
	SEMENIUK, Allan	
	LIZOTTE, Raymond	
	MCPHATE, Brian	
	TWEED, David	
	STUBEL, Daryl	
	KRANABETTER, K.	
Bronze	SHARMAN, Grant	NZL
	PALMER, Curtis	
	MCMURRAY, Gary	
	TAYLOR, Sholto	
	DICKIE, Robert	
	TINKER, Geremy	
	GUTHRIE, Stephen	
	LEEFE, Paul	

SHOOTING

Free Rifle 3x40 MEN SH1			
Gold	NEUMAIER, Josef	GER	1,238.3 NWR
Silver	SHEZIRI, Doron	ISR	1,237.0
Bronze	SAMUELSSON, Bjorn	SWE	1,229.9
Air Rifle Standing MIXED SH2			
Gold	JOHANSSON, Thomas	SWE	703.2 NWR
Silver	MANGANO, Santo	ITA	700.8
Bronze	HELSINGER, Lotta	SWE	698.9
Air Rifle Standing MEN SH1			
Gold	HAN, Tae	KOR	687.8 NPR
Silver	PINTER, Franc	SLO	686.1
Bronze	FALKE, Franz	GER	683.1
Air Rifle Prone MIXED SH1			
Gold	BOKHARAEI, E.	IRI	705.8 NPR
Silver	MECHULA, Kazimierz	DEN	704.7
Bronze	JACOBSSON, Jonas	SWE	704.7
Air Rifle Standing WOMEN SH1			
Gold	COATES, Deanna	GBR	491.3 NPR
Silver	ZHANG, Nan	CHN	490.5
Bronze	KIM, Im	KOR	489.1
Air Rifle Prone MIXED SH2			
Gold	JOHANSSON, Thomas	SWE	705.8 =WR
Silver	HELSINGER, Lotta	SWE	703.5
Bronze	MANGANO, Santo	ITA	700.9
Air Rifle 3x20 WOMEN SH1			
Gold	KIM, Im	KOR	690.1 NPR
Silver	COATES, Deanna	GBR	689.7
Bronze	BROGLE, Sabine	GER	686.4
Air Rifle 3x40 MEN SH1			
Gold	JACOBSSON, Jonas	SWE	1,289.7 NPR
Silver	NEUMAIER, Josef	GER	1,282.2
Bronze	BERINGER, Alfred	GER	1,280.9
Air Pistol MEN SH1			
Gold	LEBEDINSKI, Andrei	RUS	662.2 NPR
Silver	AUFSCHNAITER, Hubert	AUT	659.6
Bronze	MARTELLA, Antonio	ITA	659.0
Air Rifle 3x40 MIXED SH2			
Gold	JOHANSSON, Thomas	SWE	1,302.2 NPR
Silver	HELSINGER, Lotta	SWE	1,301.8
Bronze	MANGANO, Santo	ITA	1,298.4
Air Pistol WOMEN SH1			
Gold	ALEKSOV, Ruzica	YUG	456.9 NPR
Silver	OVERBYE, Lone	DEN	454.3
Bronze	RIESE, Rosabelle	RSA	448.2
Standard Rifle 3x20 WOMEN SH1			
Gold	KIM, Im	KOR	661.8 NWR
Silver	AMIEL, Michele	FRA	653.0
Bronze	BROGLE, Sabine	GER	651.6
Sport Pistol MIXED SH1			
Gold	LEBEDINSKI, Andrei	RUS	682.3 NWR
Silver	NOMARHAS, James	AUS	660.7
Bronze	HARTMANN, Roland	GER	657.3
Free Pistol .22 MIXED SH1			
Gold	SORIANO, Francisco	ESP	620.9 NPR
Silver	ALEKSOV, Ruzica	YUG	617.1
Bronze	LEBEDINSKI, Andrei	RUS	613.9
English Match MIXED SH1			
Gold	JACOBSSON, Jonas	SWE	691.4 NWR
Silver	SHEZIRI, Doron	ISR	691.0
Bronze	DE PELLEGRIN, Oscar	ITA	690.7

SWIMMING

150m Indiv. Medley MEN SM3			
Gold	EDSTROM, Petter	SWE	3:30.54
Silver	ANDRADE, Genezi	BRA	3:34.32
Bronze	SANDVIK, Stig Morten	NOR	3:38.23
150m Indiv. Medley MEN SM4			
Gold	TORRES, Javier	ESP	2:38.64 NWR
Silver	SLECZKA, Krysztof	POL	2:43.17
Bronze	PETERSSON, John	DEN	2:53.88
150m Indiv. Medley WOMEN SM4			
Gold	ESPENHAYN, Kay	GER	3:00.39
Silver	MCELENY, Margaret	GBR	3:04.24
Bronze	NARITA, Mayumi	JPN	3:08.63
200m Indiv. Medley MEN SM5			
Gold	PAWLOWSKI, Arkadiusz	POL	3:13.90 NWR
Silver	PINARD, Pascal	FRA	3:19.17
Bronze	ANDERSEN, Peter	DEN	3:19.32
200m Indiv. Medley WOMEN SM5			
Gold	HESS, Beatrice	FRA	3:35.94 NWR
Silver	NEWSTEAD, Jennifer	NZL	3:39.08
Bronze	ENGELHARDT, Katalin	HUN	4:14.83
200m Indiv. Medley MEN SM6			
Gold	KALE, Duane	NZL	2:58.80 NWR
Silver	XHROUET, Sebastian	BEL	3:00.41
Bronze	GRIMM, Thomas	GER	3:06.26
200m Indiv. Medley WOMEN SM6			
Gold	NESHEIM, Eva	NOR	3:24.87 NWR
Silver	GOTZE, Maria	GER	3:41.84
Bronze	LOISEAU, Ludivine	FRA	3:42.35
200m Indiv. Medley MEN SM7			
Gold	LINDMANN, Eric	FRA	2:52.05
Silver	AHLSTAD, Simon	SWE	2:52.80
Bronze	SOARES, Gledson	BRA	2:54.10
200m Indiv. Medley WOMEN SM7			
Gold	HAKONARD, Kristin	ISL	3:15.16 NWR
Silver	OKUPNIAK, Malgorzata	POL	3:23.66
Bronze	GUERCHOUCHE, Hadda	FRA	3:26.78
200m Indiv. Medley MEN SM8			
Gold	TERBLANCHE, J.	RSA	2:40.83 NWR
Silver	KIMMIG, Holger	GER	2:44.04
Bronze	LONG, Giles	GBR	2:45.80
200m Indiv. Medley WOMEN SM8			
Gold	COOPER, Priya	AUS	3:05.32 NWR
Silver	VAN AMELSVOORT, S.	NED	3:11.30
Bronze	VIVES, Silvia	ESP	3:12.65
200m Indiv. Medley MEN SM9			
Gold	BJORNSTAD, Helge	NOR	2:30.55 NWR
Silver	STURKENBOON, Rutger	NED	2:30.96
Bronze	EIRIKSSON, Olafur	ISL	2:32.89
200m Indiv. Medley WOMEN SM9			
Gold	JENNINGS, Emily	GBR	2:49.60
Silver	LUNCHER, Joyce	USA	2:49.62
Bronze	STENGER, Ricka	DEN	2:53.00

200m Indiv. Medley MEN SM10

Gold	DE GROOT, Alwin	NED	2:21.12
Silver	ENGELSMAN, Jurjen	NED	2:21.12
Bronze	LOEFFLER, Stefan	GER	2:26.94

200m Indiv. Medley WOMEN SM10

Gold	BAILEY, Sarah	GBR	2:38.38 NWR
Silver	DASHWOOD, Gemma	AUS	2:38.93
Bronze	HENGST, Claudia	GER	2:42.60

100m Butterfly WOMEN B1

Gold	CROSS, Tracey	AUS	1:27.53
Silver	FINGERROOS, E.	FIN	1:28.83
Bronze	BURTON, Janice	GBR	1:35.25

50m Butterfly WOMEN S7

Gold	NESHEIM, Eva	NOR	41.55 NWR
Silver	PROKEINOVA, Margita	SVK	41.64
Bronze	OKUPNIAK, Malgorzata	POL	41.96

100m Butterfly MEN S8

Gold	LONG, Giles	GBR	1:09.80 NPR
Silver	BRONDUM, Emil	DEN	1:10.24
Bronze	TERBLANCHE, J.	RSA	1:11.99

100m Butterfly WOMEN S8

Gold	VAN AMELSVOORT, S.	NED	1:25.71
Silver	VIVES, Silvia	ESP	1:28.55
Bronze	COOPER, Priya	AUS	1:30.42

100m Butterfly MEN S9

Gold	EIRIKSSON, Olafur	ISL	1:05.02
Silver	KAPURA, Alexey	RUS	1:06.88
Bronze	HALEY, Andrew	CAN	1:06.90

100m Butterfly WOMEN S9

Gold	LUNCHER, Joyce	USA	1:14.40 NWR
Silver	CARLTON, Melissa	AUS	1:16.21
Bronze	TOZZINI, Marina	ITA	1:19.63

100m Butterfly MEN S10

Gold	CUNDY, Jody	GBR	1:02.44 NWR
Silver	DE GROOT, Alwin	NED	1:03.02
Bronze	BROCKENSHIRE, Scott	AUS	1:04.59

100m Butterfly WOMEN S10

Gold	DASHWOOD, Gemma	AUS	1:08.88 NWR
Silver	YOUNG, Judith	AUS	1:12.64
Bronze	BERNARDO, Ana	ESP	1:13.55

400m Freestyle MEN S7

Gold	LINDMANN, Eric	FRA	5:04.86
Silver	XHROUET, Sebastian	BEL	5:08.45
Bronze	DELPY, Frederic	FRA	5:09.49

400m Freestyle WOMEN S7

Gold	BORNEMANN, Rebeccah	CAN	5:59.82
Silver	WOLFE, Julie	USA	6:00.55
Bronze	RIERA, Mireia	ESP	6:03.11

400m Freestyle MEN S8

Gold	WENING, Jason	USA	4:49.87 NWR
Silver	KIMMIG, Holger	GER	4:52.04
Bronze	BRONDUM, Emil	DEN	4:53.85

400m Freestyle WOMEN S8

Gold	COOPER, Priya	AUS	5:11.47 NWR
Silver	REUVEKAMP, Petra	NED	5:55.08
Bronze	FALZON, Janelle	AUS	5:57.28

400m Freestyle MEN S9

Gold	TORNERO, Enrique	ESP	4:34.04 NWR
Silver	ALICEA III, Luis	USA	4:39.78
Bronze	HALEY, Andrew	CAN	4:39.94

400m Freestyle WOMEN S9

Gold	CARLTON, Melissa	AUS	5:01.22
Silver	TOZZINI, Marina	ITA	5:01.96
Bronze	BELLAVIA, Sabrina	BEL	5:05.25

400m Freestyle MEN S10

Gold	DE GROOT, Alwin	NED	4:26.55 NWR
Silver	LOEFFLER, Stefan	GER	4:30.72
Bronze	WOODS, Marc	GBR	4:31.87

400m Freestyle WOMEN S10

Gold	DASHWOOD, Gemma	AUS	4:40.94 NWR
Silver	BAILEY, Sarah	GBR	4:50.98
Bronze	HENGST, Claudia	GER	4:54.34

100m Breaststroke MEN B1

Gold	BUNDGAARD, Christian	DEN	1:13.84
Silver	KELLY, Daniel	USA	1:19.79
Bronze	LAGSANAPRIM, Panom	THA	1:21.76

100m Breaststroke MEN B2

Gold	BUGARIN, Kingsley	AUS	1:10.81 NWR
Silver	ARRIBAS, Jose	ESP	1:15.36
Bronze	KRYLOV, Vitali	RUS	1:17.92

100m Breaststroke WOMEN B2

Gold	VAN PUYVELDE, Carine	BEL	1:31.00
Silver	BARRETT, Elaine	GBR	1:31.84
Bronze	ZORN, Trischa	USA	1:32.27

100m Breaststroke MEN B3

Gold	PEDERSEN, Noel	NOR	1:08.18
Silver	NIELSEN, Ivan	DEN	1:12.84
Bronze	LENTINK, Jurgen	NED	1:16.09

100m Breaststroke WOMEN B3

Gold	ROSS, Marie Claire	CAN	1:20.45 NWR
Silver	HENKE, Daniela	GER	1:24.37
Bronze	SCOTT, Elizabeth	USA	1:26.48

100m Freestyle MEN S2

Gold	ANDERSON, James	GBR	2:41.94 NWR
Silver	MCGREGOR, Alan	GBR	2:44.18
Bronze	PEREIRA, Adriano	BRA	2:54.50

100m Freestyle WOMEN S2

Gold	BASUALDO, Betiana	ARG	3:09.00 NWR
Silver	PEREZLINDO, A.	ARG	3:11.02
Bronze	CARRACELAS, Sara	ESP	3:17.28

400m Freestyle MEN B2

Gold	HARDY, Jeffrey	AUS	4:33.85
Silver	SEGARRA, Francisco	ESP	4:35.36
Bronze	VUGARIN, Kingsley	AUS	4:35.52

400m Freestyle WOMEN B2

Gold	EASTER, Melanie	GBR	5:11.32
Silver	ZORN, Trischa	USA	5:17.57
Bronze	FERNANDEZ, Maria	ESP	5:17.97

400m Freestyle MEN B3

Gold	WU, Walter	CAN	4:21.08 NWR
Silver	NIELSEN, Ivan	DEN	4:40.03
Bronze	FOX, Christopher	GBR	4:41.56

200m Freestyle MEN S3

Gold	GUDMUNDSSON, Palmar	ISL	4:10.17 NWR
Silver	EDSTROM, Petter	SWE	4:10.82
Bronze	ANDRADE, Genezi	BRA	4:15.76

200m Freestyle MEN S4

Gold	ORIBE, Ricardo	ESP	3:11.00 NWR
Silver	PANCALLI, Luca	ITA	3:26.16
Bronze	THOMPSON, James	USA	3:29.18

200m Freestyle WOMEN S4

Gold	ESPENHAYN, Kay	GER	3:21.82 NWR
Silver	NARITA, Mayumi	JPN	3:22.47
Bronze	BRUDER, Aimee	USA	3:53.19

200m Freestyle MEN S5

Gold	LUERIG, Lars	GER	2:54.31 NWR
Silver	FUERTES, Juan	ESP	2:59.70
Bronze	SLECZKA, Krzysztof	POL	3:02.94

200m Freestyle WOMEN S5

Gold	HESS, Beatrice	FRA	3:01.18 NWR
Silver	AKOPYAN, Olena	UKR	3:17.71
Bronze	MCELENY, Margaret	GBR	3:20.51

200m Freestyle MEN S6

Gold	KALE, Duane	NZL	2:28.33 NWR
Silver	ANDERSEN, Peter	DEN	2:33.96
Bronze	PAVLINEC, Danijel	SLO	2:43.85

200m Freestyle WOMEN S6

Gold	NEWSTEAD, Jennifer	NZL	2:55.15 NWR
Silver	LOISEAU, Ludivine	FRA	2:58.44
Bronze	ESLING, Jeanette	GBR	3:04.73

100m Freestyle MEN MH

Gold	HOUTSMA, Alwin	NED	56.40 NWR
Silver	FITZPATRICK, Grant	AUS	59.32
Bronze	GROENEWALD, Craig	RSA	1:01.09

100m Freestyle WOMEN MH

Gold	WISCOMBE, Tracy	GBR	1:05.31 NWR
Silver	SULLIVAN, Carla	AUS	1:10.53
Bronze	BARKER, Petrea	AUS	1:10.91

50m Breaststroke MEN SB3

Gold	FRITSCHE, Christian	GER	50.07 NWR
Silver	PETERSSON, John	DEN	58.33
Bronze	HARRIS, Garth	CAN	1:00.22

50m Breaststroke WOMEN SB3

Gold	KAJIWARA, Noriko	JPN	54.21 NWR
Silver	MCELENY, Margaret	GBR	57.03
Bronze	ESPENHAYN, Kay	GER	1:04.91

100m Backstroke MEN S7

Gold	LINDMANN, Eric	FRA	1:19.28
Silver	LINDSEY, Andrew	GBR	1:19.37
Bronze	KIM, Soo	KOR	1:20.78

100m Backstroke WOMEN S7

Gold	HAKONARD, Kristin	ISL	1:26.41 NWR
Silver	NESHEIM, Eva	NOR	1:30.65
Bronze	WALKER, Elisabeth	CAN	1:33.22

100m Backstroke MEN S8

Gold	KIMMIG, Holger	GER	1:11.06 NPR
Silver	HANSEN, Kasper	DEN	1:12.55
Bronze	JAEHRIG, Geert	GER	1:12.70

100m Backstroke WOMEN S8

Gold	COOPER, Priya	AUS	1:23.43 NPR
Silver	VIVES, Silvia	ESP	1:31.73
Bronze	FALZON, Janelle	AUS	1:32.48

100m Backstroke MEN S9

Gold	BJORNSTAD, Helge	NOR	1:08.23 NPR
Silver	MALONE, David	IRL	1:08.98
Bronze	SCHMIDT, Detlef	GER	1:09.33

100m Backstroke WOMEN S9

Gold	NANNENBERG, J.	NED	1:18.13
Silver	MICHALCZYK, K.	POL	1:20.33
Bronze	CARLTON, Melissa	AUS	1:20.42

100m Backstroke MEN S10

Gold	DE GROOT, Alwin	NED	1:04.10 NWR
Silver	WOODS, Marc	GBR	1:06.48
Bronze	ENGELSMAN, Jurjen	NED	1:07.11

100m Backstroke WOMEN S10

Gold	BAILEY, Sarah	GBR	1:15.74
Silver	NORRIS, Karen	USA	1:16.23
Bronze	YOUNG, Judith	AUS	1:17.41

100m Freestyle MEN B1

Gold	KAWAI, Junichi	JPN	1:01.18
Silver	KELLY, Daniel	USA	1:16.23
Bronze	REDDISH, Timothy	GBR	1:03.82

100m Freestyle WOMEN B1

Gold	NILSSON, Eila	SWE	1:16.21
Silver	ROEHLE, Daniela	GER	1:18.69
Bronze	RINGERROOS, E.	FIN	1:19.34

100m Freestyle MEN B2

Gold	HOLMES, Christopher	GBR	58.42
Silver	BUGARIN, Kingsley	AUS	59.08
Bronze	BETTER, Ziv	ISR	1:00.01

100m Freestyle WOMEN B2

Gold	KORKJAS, Marge	EST	1:07.43
Silver	FERNANDEZ, Maria	ESP	1:07.75
Bronze	ZORN, Trischa	USA	1:08.34

100m Freestyle MEN B3

Gold	WU, Walter	CAN	57.63 NPR
Silver	KLEYNHANS, Ebert	RSA	58.77
Bronze	TCHESNOV, Vladimir	RUS	59.27

100m Freestyle WOMEN B3

Gold	HOPE, Yvonne	GER	59.88 NWR
Silver	HENKE, Daniela	GER	1:01.90
Bronze	ROSS, Marie Claire	CAN	1:02.37

4x50m Freestyle MEN S1, 2, 3, 4, 5, 6

Gold	BUTLER, Daniel	USA	2:38.13 NWR
	PAULSON, Aaron		
	BURNS, Gregory		
	PARKER, Martin		
Silver	FUERTES, Juan	ESP	2:41.33
	ORIBE, Ricardo		
	IGLESIAS, Jesus		
	TORRES, Javier		
Bronze	XIA, Kai	CHN	2:42.02
	ZENG, Huabin		
	MAO, Qiwen		
	ZHU, Weiming		

4x50m Freestyle WOMEN S1, 2, 3, 4, 5, 6

Gold	STIDEVER, Jane	GBR	2:52.36 NWR
	MCELENY, M.		
	ELSING, Jeanette		
	BOOTH, Jennifer		
Silver	D'URZO, Corine	FRA	2:53.55
	TRIPIER, V.		
	LOISERU, L.		
	HESS, Beatrice		
Bronze	BROOKS, S.	USA	3:08.27
	BRUDER, Aimee		
	HANEBRINK, S.		
	WADDELL, Camille		

50m Backstroke MEN S2

Gold	ANDERSON, James	GBR	1:13.66 NWR
Silver	PIESAK, Miroslaw	POL	1:15.37
Bronze	MCGREGOR, Alan	GBR	1:19.36

50m Backstroke WOMEN S2

Gold	CARRACELAS, Sara	ESP	1:30.89 NWR
Silver	BERRY, Mairead	IRL	1:31.45
Bronze	BASUALDO, Betiana	ARG	1:33.12

50m Backstroke MEN S3

Gold	BAKAEV, Albert	RUS	56.21
Silver	BADIE, Claude	FRA	56.34
Bronze	EDSTROM, Petter	SWE	57.52

50m Backstroke WOMEN S3

Gold	GONZALEZ, Aranzazu	ESP	1:02.82 NWR
Silver	BARROSO, S.	POR	1:06.45
Bronze	CONRADI, Annke	GER	1:07.78

50m Backstroke MEN S4

Gold	PANCALLI, Luca	ITA	49.23
Silver	BELLOT, Pierre	FRA	49.83
Bronze	LAUFENBERG, Craig	USA	54.01

50m Backstroke WOMEN S4

Gold	ESPENHAYN, Kay	GER	51.48 NPR
Silver	NARITA, Mayumi	JPN	54.87
Bronze	BRAEUMSO, Karen	DEN	1:03.21

50m Backstroke MEN S5

Gold	VERECZKEI, Zsolt	HUN	39.95 NWR
Silver	ATTIA, Essam	EGY	41.40
Bronze	PINARD, Pascal	FRA	42.63

50m Backstroke WOMEN S5

Gold	HESS, Beatrice	FRA	45.86 NWR
Silver	D'URZO, Corine	FRA	49.09
Bronze	STIDEVER, Jane	GBR	52.40

100m Backstroke MEN S6

Gold	ZHU, Weiming	CHN	1:21.12
Silver	BURNS, Gregory	USA	1:21.19
Bronze	KALE, Duane	NZL	1:23.51

100m Backstroke WOMEN S6

Gold	NEWSTEAD, Jennifer	NZL	1:37.96
Silver	DJOUROVA, Polina	BUL	1:40.43
Bronze	ZHOU, Xiangrong	CHN	1:42.31

100m Freestyle MEN S7

Gold	LINDMANN, Eric	FRA	1:07.13 NPR
Silver	ALEXANDER, Tony	CAN	1:08.29
Bronze	ANDRYUSHYN, Yuriy	UKR	1:08.60

100m Freestyle WOMEN S7

Gold	POHL, Daniela	GER	1:19.76
Silver	RIERA, Mireia	ESP	1:20.84
Bronze	HAKONARD, Kristin	ISL	1:22.87

100m Freestyle MEN S8

Gold	BRONDUM, Emil	DEN	1:03.87 NWR
Silver	KIMMIG, Holger	GER	1:04.06
Bronze	HANSEN, Kasper	DEN	1:05.34

100m Freestyle WOMEN S8

Gold	COOPER, Priya	AUS	1:12.08 NPR
Silver	THOMSEN, Pernille	DEN	1:18.76
Bronze	REUVEKAMP, Petra	NED	1:20.32

100m Freestyle MEN S9

Gold	ALICEA III, Luis	USA	1:01.04
Silver	STURKENBOOM, Rutger	NED	1:01.09
Bronze	EIRIKSSON, Olafur	ISL	1:01.69

100m Freestyle WOMEN S9

Gold	LUNCHER, Joyce	USA	1:08.16
Silver	CARLTON, Melissa	AUS	1:08.35
Bronze	BELLAVIA, Sabrina	BEL	1:08.52

100m Freestyle MEN S10

Gold	DE GROOT, Alwin	NED	57.26 NWR
Silver	LOEFFLER, Stefan	GER	57.86
Bronze	ENGELSMAN, Jurjen	NED	58.13

100m Freestyle WOMEN S10

Gold	HENGST, Claudia	GER	1:04.68 NPR
Silver	DASHWOOD, Gemma	AUS	1:05.82
Bronze	BAILEY, Sarah	GBR	1:06.04

4x100m Freestyle WOMEN B1, B2, B3

Gold	ROEHLE, Daniela	GER	4:33.52 NWR
	BEEKER, Birgit		
	HENKE, Daniela		
	HOPF, Yvonne		
Silver	STONEHAM, Kirsty	GBR	4:49.65
	BURTON, Janice		
	EDMANS, Leanne		
	EASTER, Melanie		
Bronze	ZORN, Trischa	USA	4:57.32
	SOMMER, Mandy		
	DUFFY, Dawn		
	SCOTT, Elizabeth		

100m Freestyle MEN S3

Gold	EDSTROM, Petter	SWE	1:59.21 NPR
Silver	GUDMUNDSSON, Palmar	ISL	1:59.82
Bronze	ANDRADE, Genezi	BRA	2:01.97

100m Freestyle WOMEN S3

Gold	GONZALEZ, Aranzazu	ESP	2:16.03 NWR
Silver	CONRADI, Annke	GER	2:19.78
Bronze	BARROSO, S.	POR	2:23.18

100m Freestyle MEN S4

Gold	ORIBE, Ricardo	ESP	1:31.35 NWR
Silver	PANCALLI, Luca	ITA	1:33.44
Bronze	PETERSSON, John	DEN	1:39.94
	AOKI, Akinobu	JPN	1:39.94

100m Freestyle WOMEN S4

Gold	NARITA, Mayumi	JPN	1:36.24 NWR
Silver	ESPENHAYN, Kay	GER	1:37.58
Bronze	BRUDER, Aimee	USA	1:53.27

100m Freestyle MEN S5

Gold	FUERTES, Juan	ESP	1:21.61 NWR
Silver	LUERIG, Lars	GER	1:22.51
Bronze	SLECZKA, Krystztof	POL	1:25.91

100m Freestyle WOMEN S5

Gold	HESS, Beatrice	FRA	1:23.84 NWR
Silver	AKOPYAN, Olena	UKR	1:28.59
Bronze	MCELENY, Margaret	GBR	1:34.82

100m Freestyle MEN S6

Gold	KALE, Duane	NZL	1:08.45 NWR
Silver	ANDERSEN, Peter	DEN	1:09.96
Bronze	PAVLINEC, Danijel	SLO	1:14.55

200m Breaststroke MEN B2

Gold	BUGARIN, Kingsley	AUS	2:35.21 NWR
Silver	BUNDGAARD, Christian	DEN	2:42.56
Bronze	KRYLOV, Vitali	RUS	2:44.08

200m Breaststroke WOMEN B2

Gold	VAN PUYVELDE, Carine	BEL	3:17.28
Silver	BARRETT, Elaine	GBR	3:18.57
Bronze	GARCIA-ARCICOLLAR	ESP	3:23.04

200m Breaststroke MEN B3

Gold	PEDERSEN, Noel	NOR	2:33.82 NWR
Silver	NEILSEN, Ivan	DEN	2:37.51
Bronze	NEFEDOV, Andrei	RUS	2:46.73

50m Freestyle MEN MH

Gold	HOUTSMA, Alwin	NED	26.18 NWR
Silver	FITZPATRICK, Grant	AUS	27.01
Bronze	GROENEWALD, Craig	RSA	27.32

50m Freestyle WOMEN MH

Gold	WISCOMBE, Tracy	GBR	31.73
Silver	KOKK, Eela	EST	33.14
Bronze	HRAFNSDOTTIR, Sigrun	ISL	33.29

4x100m Freestyle MEN S7, 8, 9, 10

Gold	KIMMIG, Holger	GER	4:08.50 NWR
	SCHMIDT, Detlef		
	ANDERS, Oliver		
	LOEFFLER, Stefan		
Silver	DE BURGH, C.	AUS	4:12.11
	COLLINS, Dominic		
	BURKETT, Brendan		
	BROCKENSHIRE, S.		
Bronze	MARTORELL, A.	ESP	4:14.36
	JIMENEZ, Juan		
	TORNERO, Enrique		
	SAAVEDRA, Pablo		

4x100m Freestyle WOMEN S7, 8, 9, 10

Gold	CARLTON, Melissa	AUS	4:45.65
	COOPER, Priya		
	FALZON, Janelle		
	DASHWOOD, Gemma		
Silver	LEVY, Brenda	USA	4:47.87
	NORRIS, Karen		
	PITTMAN, Allison		
	LUNCHER, Joyce		
Bronze	LOBENSTEIN, B.	GER	4:49.63
	POHL, Daniela		
	PUTZ, Stephanie		
	HENGST, Claudia		

50m Freestyle MEN S2

Gold	PIESAK, Miroslaw	POL	1:14.59 NWR
Silver	ANDERSON, James	GBR	1:17.63
Bronze	PEREIRA, Adriano	BRA	1:19.19

50m Freestyle WOMEN S2

Gold	CARRACELAS, Sara	ESP	1:29.77 NWR
Silver	BASUALDO, Betiana	ARG	1:31.66
Bronze	BROADRIBB, Victoria	GBR	1:31.72

50m Freestyle MEN S3

Gold	EULERT, Jaime	PER	51.95 NWR
Silver	BAKAEV, Albert	RUS	57.78
Bronze	EDSTROM, Petter	SWE	57.80

50m Freestyle WOMEN S3

Gold	GONZALEZ, Aranzazu	ESP	1:05.56 NWR
Silver	BARROSO, S.	POR	1:06.38
Bronze	CONRADI, Annke	GER	1:07.47

50m Freestyle MEN S4

Gold	ORIBE, Ricardo	ESP	41.85 NPR
Silver	PANCALLI, Luca	ITA	42.62
Bronze	AOKI, Akinobu	JPN	44.83

50m Freestyle WOMEN S4

Gold	NARITA, Mayumi	JPN	44.47 NWR
Silver	ESPENHAYN, Kay	GER	47.55
Bronze	BRAEUMSO, Karen	DEN	54.16

50m Freestyle MEN S5

Gold	FUERTES, Juan	ESP	37.52 NWR
Silver	LUERIG, Lars	GER	38.73
Bronze	SLECZKA, Krzysztof	POL	39.86

50m Freestyle WOMEN S5

Gold	HESS, Beatrice	FRA	39.47 NPR
Silver	AKOPYAN, Olena	UKR	40.82
Bronze	MCELENY, Margaret	GBR	43.81

100m Breaststroke MEN SB4

Gold	PINARD, Pascal	FRA	1:42.20 NWR
Silver	TEN, Ricardo	ESP	1:43.33
Bronze	VASCONCELOS, I.	BRA	1:46.55

100m Breaststroke WOMEN SB4

Gold	NEWSTEAD, Jennifer	NZL	1:55.49 NWR
Silver	OLOFSSON, Sara	SWE	2:07.92
Bronze	VIKGREN, Maria	SWE	2:09.50

100m Breaststroke MEN SB5

Gold	ENGEL, Kasper	NED	1:31.50
Silver	SLATTERY, Tadhg	RSA	1:38.59
Bronze	PAULSON, Aaron	USA	1:39.70

100m Breaststroke WOMEN SB5

Gold	WADDELL, Camille	USA	1:53.48
Silver	NESHEIM, Eva	NOR	2:01.66
Bronze	RACZKO, Gitta	HUN	2:03.07

100m Breaststroke MEN SB6

Gold	IGLESIAS, Jesus	ESP	1:31.78
Silver	BIDOIS, Aaron	NZL	1:33.62
Bronze	SCHLUBECK, Mathias	GER	1:34.92

100m Breaststroke WOMEN SB6

Gold	OKUPNIAK, Malgorzata	POL	1:56.65
Silver	OKOCZUK, Edyta	POL	1:57.95
Bronze	LAMPERS, Gerda	NED	2:01.58

100m Breaststroke MEN SB7

Gold	GONG, Baoren	CHN	1:25.92
Silver	KINDRED, Sascha	GBR	1:28.86
Bronze	VAN GEEL, Laurentius	NED	1:31.17

100m Breaststroke WOMEN SB7

Gold	HAKONARD, Kristin	ISL	1:39.34 NWR
Silver	SCHRETZMANN, Beate	GER	1:53.14
Bronze	REUVEKAMP, Petra	NED	1:59.45

100m Breaststroke MEN SB8

Gold	ULVANG, Rune	NOR	1:19.96 NWR
Silver	BJORNSTAD, Helge	NOR	1:22.80
Bronze	GUO, Yongzhong	CHN	1:23.70

100m Breaststroke WOMEN SB8

Gold	SHI, Tieyin	CHN	1:38.10
Silver	TRAMUNS, Laura	ESP	1:38.25
Bronze	VAN AMELSVOORT, S.	NED	1:39.38

100m Breaststroke MEN SB9

Gold	ENGELSMAN, Jurjen	NED	1:14.63 NWR
Silver	DE GROOT, Alwin	NED	1:18.19
Bronze	BESTUCHEV, Sergey	RUS	1:19.04

100m Breaststroke WOMEN SB9

Gold	COUFALOVA, Katerina	CZE	1:25.84
Silver	LUNCHER, Joyce	USA	1:29.21
Bronze	REINA, Begona	ESP	1:30.22

100m Breaststroke MEN SB10

Gold	LOEFFLER, Stefan	GER	1:13.50 NWR
Silver	KJELLQVIST, Tomas	SWE	1:18.41
Bronze	KOFLER, Mario	GER	1:18.93

100m Breaststroke WOMEN SB10

Gold	BAILEY, Sarah	GBR	1:26.97
Silver	YOUNG, Judith	AUS	1:29.89
Bronze	STENGER, Ricka	DEN	1:30.38

100m Backstroke MEN B1

Gold	KELLY, Dasniel	USA	1:09.92
Silver	KAWAI, Junichi	JPN	1:13.43
Bronze	GUNNARSSON, Birkir	ISL	1:17.74

100m Backstroke WOMEN B1

Gold	SAAVEDRA, Raquel	ESP	1:24.68 NWR
Silver	FINGERROOS, E.	FIN	1:25.50
Bronze	DONG, Qiming	CHN	1:26.37

100m Backstroke MEN B2

Gold	HOLMES, Christopher	GBR	1:07.29 NWR
Silver	SEGARRA, Francisco	ESP	1:11.08
Bronze	BETTER, Ziv	ISR	1:12.31

100m Backstroke WOMEN B2

Gold	ZORN, Trischa	USA	1:15.43
Silver	KORKJAS, Marge	EST	1:22.43
Bronze	GARCIA-ARCICOLLAR	ESP	1:23.82

100m Backstroke MEN B3

Gold	WU, Walter	CAN	1:04.80 NWR
Silver	PEDERSEN, Noel	NOR	1:07.47
Bronze	LENTINK, Jurgen	NED	1:11.30

100m Backstroke WOMEN B3

Gold	HOPF Yvonne	GER	1:09.28 NWR
Silver	ROSS, Marie Claire	CAN	1:13.50
Bronze	SCOTT, Elizabeth	USA	1:15.03

50m Freestyle MEN S6

Gold	ANDERSEN, Peter	DEN	31.26 NWR
Silver	KALE, Duane	NZL	31.41
Bronze	LIMA, Adriano	BRA	33.22

50m Freestyle WOMEN S6

Gold	LOISEAU, Ludivine	FRA	36.73 NWR
Silver	ESLING, Jeanette	GBR	38.63
Bronze	LIDDELL, Karni	AUS	39.56

50m Freestyle MEN S7

Gold	ALEXANDER, Tony	CAN	30.81
Silver	LINDMANN, Eric	FRA	31.23
Bronze	IGLESIAS, Jesus	ESP	31.28

50m Freestyle WOMEN S7

Gold	POHL, Daniela	GER	36.85
Silver	OLIVER, Tracey	AUS	37.18
Bronze	PROKEINOVA, Margita	SVK	37.34

50m Freestyle MEN S8

Gold	BRONDUM, Emil	DEN	28.84 NWR
Silver	FYKAS, Konstantinos	GRE	29.83
Bronze	KIMMIG, Holger	GER	29.85

50m Freestyle WOMEN S8

Gold	THOMSEN, Pernille	DEN	33.03 NWR
Silver	COOPER, Priya	AUS	34.17
Bronze	LEVY, Brenda	USA	35.38

50m Freestyle MEN S9

Gold	BURKETT, Brendan	AUS	28.09
Silver	STURKENBOOM, Rutger	NED	28.12
Bronze	ALICEA III, Luis	USA	28.16

50m Freestyle WOMEN S9

Gold	LUNCHER, Joyce	USA	31.36 NWR
Silver	BELLAVIA, Sabrina	BEL	31.56
Bronze	STENGER, Ricka	DEN	32.02

50m Freestyle MEN S10

Gold	DE GROOT, Alwin	NED	26.52
Silver	LOEFFLER, Stefan	GER	26.60
Bronze	BROCKENSHIRE, Scott	AUS	26.82

50m Freestyle WOMEN S10

Gold	HENGST, Claudia	GER	29.90
Silver	YOUNG, Judith	AUS	30.22
Bronze	PRINSLOO, Elizabeth	RSA	31.01

50m Freestyle MEN B1

Gold	KAWAI, Junichi	JPN	27.24
Silver	COHEN, Izhar	ISR	27.78
Bronze	KELLY, Daniel	USA	28.10

50m Freestyle WOMEN B1

Gold	NILSSON, Eila	SWE	33.02 NWR
Silver	CROSS, Tracey	AUS	34.41
Bronze	BURTON, Janice	GBR	35.16

50m Freestyle MEN B2

Gold	HOLMES, Christopher	GBR	26.61
Silver	CORRAL, Pablo	ESP	26.77
Bronze	BETTER, ziv	ISR	26.93

50m Freestyle WOMEN B2

Gold	KORKJAS, Marge	EST	29.90
Silver	ZORN, Trischa	USA	30.93
Bronze	FERNANDEZ, Maria	ESP	31.28

50m Freestyle MEN B3

Gold	KLEYNHANS, Ebert	RSA	26.06 NPR
Silver	PEDERSON, Noel	NOR	26.41
Bronze	WU, Walter	CAN	26.64

50m Freestyle WOMEN B3

Gold	HOPF, Yvonne	GER	27.38 NWR
Silver	HENKE, Daniela	GER	28.72
Bronze	ROSS, Marie Claire	CAN	28.87

4x50m Medley MEN S1, 2, 3, 4, 5, 6

Gold	BURNS, Gregory	USA	2:39.28 NWR
	PAULSON, Aaron		
	BUTLER, Daniel		
	PARKER, Martin		
Silver	ZHU, Weiming	CHN	2:46.35
	ZENG, Huabin		
	XIA, Kai		
	MAO, Qiwen		
Bronze	TEN, Ricardo	ESP	2:50.27
	IGLESIAS, Jesus		
	TORRES, Javier		
	FUERTES, Juan		

4x50m Medley WOMEN S1, 2, 3, 4, 5, 6

Gold	ZAMBO, Diana	HUN	3:22.65 NPR
	RACZKO, Gitta		
	JAROMI, Monika		
	ENGELHARDT, K.		
Silver	MOUCHA, Susan	USA	3:27.99
	WADDELL, Camille		
	NELSON, Jill		
	BROOKS, S.		
Bronze	STIDEVER, Jane	GBR	3:28.60
	MCELENY, M.		
	ESLING, Jeanette		
	BOOTH, Jennifer		

4x100m Medley MEN S7, 8, 9, 10

Gold	KIMMIG, Holger	GER	4:41.50
	LOEFFLER, Stefan		
	SCHMIDT, Detlef		
	ANDERS, Oliver		
Silver	UREN, Shaun	GBR	4:41.62
	MATTHEW, Iain		
	LONG, Giles		
	WOODS, Marc		
Bronze	VAN GEEL, L.	NED	4:46.06
	ENGELSMAN, J.		
	DE GROOT, Alwin		
	STURKENBOOM, R.		

4x100m Medley WOMEN S7, 8, 9, 10

Gold	NORRIS, Karen	USA	5:27.46 NWR
	STRAUB, Diane		
	LUNCHER, Joyce		
	PITTMAN, Allison		
Silver	LOBENSTEIN, B.	GER	5:28.39
	BRINCK, A.		
	HENGST, Claudia		
	POHL, Daniela		
Bronze	VIVES, Silvia	ESP	5:30.27
	REINA, Reina		
	BERNARDO, Ana		
	CERDA, Tania		

4x100m Medley WOMEN B1, 2, 3

Gold	ROEHLE, Daniela	GER	5:11.58 NWR
	BEEKER, Birgit		
	HOPF, Yvonne		
	HENKE, Daniela		
Silver	ZORN, Trischa	USA	5:29.71
	EDGAR, Katie		
	SCOTT, Elizabeth		
	SOMMER, Mandy		
Bronze	SAAVEDRA, Raquel	ESP	5:37.55
	GARCIA-ARCICOLL		
	GARCIA, Anais		
	FERNANDEZ, Maria		

TABLE TENNIS

Team MEN 3

Gold	KIM, Young	KOR
	AN, Jong	
	KIM, Ki	
Silver	DOLLMANN, M.	AUT
	ALTENDORFER, F.	
	STARL, Peter	
Bronze	RAWSON, James	GBR
	ROBINSON, Neil	
	DOERR, Werner	GER
	GUERTLER, Jan	

Team MEN 1-2

Gold	LAUNONEN, Matti	FIN
	KURKINEN, Jari	
Silver	HAJEK, Rudolf	AUT
	SCHARFE, Gerhard	
Bronze	ESSBACH, Dieter	GER
	KNAAK, Werner	
	POHLE, Udo	
	VILSMEIER, Otto	
	KANG, Sung	KOR
	LEE, Hae	
	PARK, Haun	
	KIM, Kyung	

Team MEN 4-5

Gold	GUSTAVSSON, Jan	SWE
	JOHANSSON, J.	
	HOGSTEDT, Patrik	
	BOLLDEN, Ernst	
Silver	PINNA, C.	FRA
	BENEDETTI, Bruno	
	DURAND, C.	
	TISSERANT, Guy	
Bronze	SUTTER, C.	AUT
	MANDL, Franz	
	GHION, Dimitri	BEL
	LE DOUX, Alain	
	PLETINCKX, J.	

Team MEN 6-8

Gold	SCHMIDT, Rainer	GER
	STELZNER, W.	
	KURFESS, Thomas	
	WOLLMERT, Jochen	
	SCHMITT, Thomas	
	MAISSENBACHER	
Silver	KARLSSON, M.	SWE
	ERIKSSON, Johnny	
	ANDERSSON, R.	
	VESTLING, Mikael	
	ANDREE, Magnus	
	LARSSON, Thomas	
Bronze	LEIBOVITZ, Tahl	USA
	SEIDENFELD, M.	

Team MEN 9-10

Gold	PICHON, Alain	FRA
	CHATEIGNER, O.	
	DE LA BOURDONNA	
	ROINE, Philippe	
Silver	FRACZYK, S.	AUT
	GOELLER, Thomas	

Bronze	SHMANDT, Andre	GER
	FAEHNRICH, Peter	
	MUELLER, Bernd	
	GASPAR, Ladislav	SVK
	DOVALOVSZKI, E.	

Individual MEN 1

Gold	LEE, Hae	KOR
Silver	LAUNONEN, Matti	FIN
Bronze	HAYLAN, Daniel	ARG
	KANG, Sung	KOR

Individual MEN 2

Gold	KIM, Kyung	KOR
Silver	BOURY, Vincent	FRA
Bronze	SCHARF, Gerhard	AUT
	KRUDINEN, Jari	FIN

Individual MEN 3

Gold	KESLER, Zlatko	YUG
Silver	ROBINSON, Neil	GBR
Bronze	ALTENDORFER, F.	AUT
	RAWSON, James	GBR

Individual MEN 4

Gold	BENEDETTI, Bruno	FRA
Silver	STEFANU, Michal	CZE
Bronze	SUTTER, Christian	AUT
	KREIDEL, Thomas	GER

Individual MEN 5

Gold	TISSERANT, Guy	FRA
Silver	KWONG, Kam	HKG
Bronze	BOLLDEN, Ernst	SWE
	CHOU, Chang-Shen	TPE

Individual MEN 6

Gold	NIELSEN, Brian	DEN
Silver	KARLSSON, Mattias	SWE
Bronze	KERSTEN, Harold	NED

Individual MEN 7

Gold	LEIBOVITZ, Tahl	USA
Silver	WOLLMERT, Jochen	GER
Bronze	KURFESS, Thomas	GER

Individual MEN 8

Gold	ANDREE, Magnus	SWE
Silver	SEIDENFELD, Mitchell	USA
Bronze	SUZUKI, Kenichi	JPN
	POLKANOV, Vladimir	MLD

Individual MEN 9

Gold	FRACZYK, Stanislaw	AUT
Silver	CHATIEGNER, Olivier	FRA
Bronze	PICHON, Alain	FRA
	GASPAR, Ladislav	SVK

Individual MEN 10

Gold	DE LA BOURDONNAYE	FRA
Silver	BADER, Robert	SWE
Bronze	AGUDO, Enrique	ESP
	JEONG, Kwang	KOR

Open MEN 1-5

Gold	KREIDEL, Thomas	GER
Silver	GHION, Dimitri	BEL
Bronze	BENEDETTI, Bruno	FRA
	SULE, Nasiru	NGR

Open MEN 6-10

Gold	FRACZYK, Stanislaw	AUT
Silver	GASPAR, Ladislav	SVK
Bronze	DE LA BOURDONNAYE	FRA
	HSU, Chin-Shan	TPE

Team WOMEN 3-5

Gold	SCHIPPMANN, B.	GER
	BARTHEIDEL, M.	
	PAPE, Christaine	
	SIKORA, Monika	
	POHLE, Gisela	
	ROOSEN, Gisela	
	STOSS, Helga	
Silver	FUNG, Yuet Wah	HKG
	WONG, Pui, Yi	
Bronze	DILORENZO, J.	USA
	JOHNSON, J.	
	TERRANOVA, T.	

Team WOMEN 6-10

Gold	ZHANG, Xiaoling	CHN
	LUO, Fuqun	
Silver	PROCHAZKOVA, H.	CZE
	PESTOVA, Eva	
	DAVIDKOVA, J.	
	MOJOVA, Jana	
Bronze	DARVAND, B.	FRA
	THIERRY, Martine	
	ODEIDE-SIMIAN	
	SEVIN, Michelle	

Individual WOMEN 3

Gold	SASVARINE, Paulik	HUN
Silver	BARTHEIDEL, Monika	GER
Bronze	POLLETT, Marie-Line	BEL

Individual WOMEN 4

Gold	JOHNSON, Jennifer	USA
Silver	PAPE, Christiane	GER
Bronze	LAEMERS, Gertrudis	NED

Individual WOMEN 5

Gold	SCHWENDTNER, S.	AUT
Silver	HOFFMANN, Maria	MEX
Bronze	POHLE, Gisela	GER
	NARDELLI, Maria	ITA

Individual WOMEN 9

Gold	LUO, Fuqun	CHN
Silver	ODEIDE-SIMIAN, M.	FRA
Bronze	NURUKI, Michiyo	JPN

Individual WOMEN 10

Gold	SEVIN, Michelle	FRA
Silver	DAVIDKOVA, Jolana	CZE
Bronze	JAGODZINSKA, K.	POL

Individual WOMEN 1-2

Gold	LAFAYE, Isabella	FRA
Silver	GIBELIN, Anne-Marie	FRA
Bronze	RODE, Baerbel	GER

Individual WOMEN 6-8

Gold	BORRE, Ingrid	BEL
Silver	THIERRY, Martine	FRA
Bronze	ZHANG, Xiaoling	CHN

Open WOMEN 1-5

Gold	PAPE, Christiane	GER
Silver	WONG, Pul Yi	HKG
Bronze	SCHWENDTNER, S.	AUT
	FUNG, Yuet Wah	HKG

Open WOMEN 6-10

Gold	ZHANG, Xiaoling	CHN
Silver	BORRE, Ingrid	BEL
Bronze	LUO, Fuqun	CHN
	ODEIDE-SIMIAN, M.	FRA

TENNIS

Doubles MEN

Gold	WELCH, Stephen	USA
	PARMELLY, Vance	
Silver	HALL, David	AUS
	CONNELL, Mick	
Bronze	MOLIER, Ricky	NED
	STUURMAN, E.	

Singles MEN

Gold	MOLIER, Ricky	NED
Silver	WELCH, Stephen	USA
Bronze	HALL, David	AUS

Doubles WOMEN

Gold	VANDIERENDONCK	NED
	KALKMAN-VAN DEN	
Silver	LEWELLEN, Hope	USA
	OLSON, Nancy	
Bronze	MARX, Oristelle	FRA
	RACINEUX, A.	

Singles WOMEN

Gold	SMIT, Maaike	NED
Silver	KALKMAN-VAN DEN B.	NED
Bronze	VANDIERENDONCK, C.	NED

VOLLEYBALL

STANDING

Gold	SCHWIETERING, R.	GER
	GIEBEL, Josef	
	SCHMIDL, Bernard	
	JOHANN, Andreas	
	MUELLER, Oliver	
	WEISSENFELS, K.	
	KAISER, Stefen	
	ALTMANN, Jens	
	SOMMER, Elmar	
	KOHL, Mansfred	
	GRGIC, Pavo	
	PAPAGEORGIOU, A.	
	KOSEL, Jurgen	
	KUTKENHORST-WEI	
Silver	MIHALCO, Jozef	SVK
	MOVOSAD, Lubomir	
	TOMSIK, Marek	
	SEDLAK, Pavol	
	MARCIN, Andrej	
	MORAVCIK, Peter	
	MAKOVNIK, J.	
	CSADER, Michal	
	BETIN, Pavol	
	NESTORIK, Michal	
	KOVAC, Richard	
	HANKOVA, Helma	
	STEFAK, Juraj	
Bronze	KRUSZELNICKI, J.	POL
	BOGUSZ, Tadeusz	
	MOSZCZYNSKI, P.	
	LEJA, Stanislaw	
	IWANIAK, Andrzej	
	WARDA, Marian	
	HUMERSKI, C.	
	ZAWISLAK, Adam	
	WOZNY, Tomasz	
	MOZDZYNSKI, K.	
	WANECKI, Roma	
	MLISZAK, Jan	
	GORA, Zygmunt	
	MANIAK, Monika	
	LEWICKI, Romnold	

SITTING

Gold	AKHAVANKHARAZI	IRI
	EIMRI, Jalil	
	BARATI SARBANDI	
	KASHFIA, Ali	
	SOLEIMANIKHORAM	
	GOLKAR AZGHANDI	
	SALAVATIAN, A.	
	ASHOURI, Farshid	
	SHAHI, Hassan	
	FIROUZI, Parvis	
	REZAEIKARAKANI	
	SHIVANI MAHJORI	
	KHALAFZADEH, Ja	
	KHOSRAVIVAFA, M.	
	DEGHANI, Dr.	
Silver	VENNESLAND, A.	NOR
	LYSE, Kaare	
	JENSEN, Lars	
	OLSEN, Oeivind	
	ABRAHAMSEN, B.	
	HALVORSEN, Erik	
	HODNEMYR, Ole	
	STRAND, Oeyvind	
	ROSTRUP, Gaute	
	NESHEIM, Tomas	
	HAUGSENG, Emil	
	LANNEM, Anne	
Bronze	NOROLA, Pekka	FIN
	HANNINEN, Keijo	
	SALONEN, Reijo	
	LAIN, Jukka	
	PULLI, Matti	
	KAPIAINEN, Petri	
	TERVO, Sami	
	MELANEN, Lauri	
	TUOMINEN, V.	
	VENALAINEN, L.	
	LIUKKONEN, Esa	
	HEINO, Jari	
	TIMO, Vare	
	JARMO, Karl	

YACHTING

Gold	CASSELL, Andrew	GBR
	DOWNS, Tony	
	CURTIS, Kevin	
	HARRISON, Ian	
Silver	COOK, David	CAN
	WESTERGAARD, Kirk	
	KELLY, Kenneth	
	MCROBERTS, John	
Bronze	ROSS-DUGGAN, John	USA
	MURPHY, Chris	
	LEATHERMAN, James	
	ESPARZA, Waldo	

WORLDWIDE SPONSORS

Coca-Cola • IBM • Motorola • Turner

OFFICIAL SPONSORS

ACOG • Sunrise Medical • The Home Depot • Kodak • Bell South • NAYA • Swatch

---

OFFICIAL SUPPLIERS
Georgia Power
Shepherd Center
O&P Athletic Fund Inc.
NationsBank
Delta Air Lines
Randstad Staffing Services
AT&T
XEROX
Ticket Master
Marta
UPS
The Atlanta Journal /The Atlanta Constitution
WSB-TV Atlanta
B98.5 FM Atlanta
Texaco
Metro Atlanta Chamber of Commerce

OFFICIAL SUPPORTERS
Paralyzed Veterans of America
Miramar Communications
SEMCO Productions
Sports Illustrated
Sport Supply Group
General Motors
United States Olympic Committee
Mettler-Toledo Inc.
Georgia Pacific
Lotus
Sportec
GES Exposition Services
Crenshaw Supply

NATIONAL PUBLICATION PATRONS
A Positive Approach
Ability Magazine
Accent on Living
ACCESS to Travel
Disability Product Postcards
Disability Today Publishing Group Inc.
Paralyzed Veterans of America Publications
Worldwide Association of Disabled Entrepreneurs

NATIONAL ORGANIZATION PATRONS
American Academy of Physical Medicine and Rehabilitation
American Alliance for Health, Physical Education, Recreation & Dance
American Association of Retired Persons
American Council of the Blind
American Occupational Therapy Association
American Paralysis Association
American Physical Therapy Association
American Rehabilitation Association
American Therapeutic Recreation Association
Amputee Coalition of America
Arthritis Foundation
Brain Injury Association
Disabled Sports, USA
Dwarf Athletic Association of America
Foundation for Physical Therapy
Health Industry Distributors Association
Health Industry Manufacturers Association
Junior League of Atlanta
Medical Rehabilitation Education Foundation
National Association of Activity Professionals
National Association for Medical Equipment Services
National Athletic Trainers Association
National Easter Seal Society
National Education Association
National Organization on Disability
National Parent Network on Disabilities
National Recreation and Park Association
National Rehabilitation Association
National Spinal Cord Injury Association
National Therapeutic Recreation Society
RESNA
Society for Human Resource Management
United Cerebral Palsy Associations, Inc.
United States Association for Blind Athletes
United States Cerebral Palsy Athletic Association
Wheelchair Sports, USA

ATLANTA PARALYMPIC ORGANIZING COMMITTEE OFFICERS

Chairman:
Harald Hansen, *Chairman & CEO, First Union National Bank of Georgia*

President & Chief Executive Officer:
G. Andrew Fleming

Executive Vice President & Chief Operating Officer:
David R. Simmons

Vice Chairman:
Al Mead, *Vice President Marketing, Alan Lerner Associates*

Treasurer:
Carl Knobloch, Jr., *Chairman & CEO, Production Operators Corporation*

Secretary:
Alana Shepherd,
Secretary of the Board, The Shepherd Center, Inc.

Senior Vice President & Chief Financial Officer:
Warren W. Quinley

Senior Vice President & Chief Marketing Officer:
Charles R. Edwards

Senior Vice President & Chief Games Operations Officer:
Michael P. Mushett

Vice President & Senior Counsel:
Annette Quinn

Vice President Communications & Creative Services:
Kay Branch McKenzie

Vice President Government Affairs & Development:
Dr. Jimmy Callaway

Vice President Consumer Marketing:
Marc Hamburger

Vice President Youth & Community Programs:
Barbara Trader

Vice President Technology:
John R. Schwartz

Vice President Sports:
Xavier Gonzalez

ATLANTA PARALYMPIC ORGANIZING COMMITTEE DIRECTORS

Fred Alias
Chairman, Sandcastle Resorts

David Apple, Jr., MD.
Medical Dir., The Shepherd Center, Inc.

Dan T. Cathy
President, Chic-Fil-A International

Cliff Crase
Editor & Publisher, Paralyzed Veterans of America Publications

Buddy Darden
Long, Aldridge & Norman

Paul DePace
Chairman, Wheelchair Sports USA

Curley M. Dossman, Jr.
President Elect, 100 Black Men of Atlanta, Inc.

Robert Harlin
ESQ., Chief Executive Partner, Powell, Goldstein Frazer & Murphy

Azira G. Hill
Retired Nurse, Atlanta Public Schools

Charles E. Harman
Vice President, Blue Cross and Blue Shield of Georgia

Lewis Holland, Sr.

Walter Huntley
President, Atlanta Economic Development Corporation

Dr. Samuel D. Jolley, Jr.
President, Morris Brown College

David B. Kenney
President, Kenney Hotel Group

Donald Leslie, MD.
Medical Director Outpatient Services, The Shepherd Center, Inc.

Kenneth T. Lombard
President, Magic Johnson Theaters

Abit Massey
Executive Director, Georgia Poultry Federation

L. Lowry Mays
Chairman & Chief Executive Officer, Clear Channel Communications

Karina Miller
Volunteer, The Shepherd Center, Inc.

Lou Moneymaker
Treasurer of the Board, United States Association of Blind Athletes

Carl V. Patton
President, Georgia State University

E. Earl Patton
Chairman & Chief Executive Officer, The Parkwood Group, Inc.

Andre Raes
Secretary General, International Paralympic Committee

James Shepherd
Chairman, The Shepherd Center, Inc.

Dr. Betty L. Siegel
President, Kennessaw State University

Taylor Smith
President, Atlanta Falcons Football Club

Harold Wade, Ph.D.
President, Atlanta Metropolitan College

Bruce L. Whitmer
Attorney-at-law, Disabled Sports USA

Charles R. Wolf
President, Wolf Camera & Video

Duncan Wyeth
United Cerebral Palsy Athletic Association, United States Olympic Committee

Trisha L. Zorn
Member, Athletes Advisory Committee

SPORT	VENUE	VENUE DIRECTOR	COMP. MGR.
Archery	Stone Mountain	Jack Hughes/Dan Mannix	Linda Rourke
Athletics	Centennial Olympic Stadium	Charles Sanders/S. Bresser	Skip Bresser
Basketball	Morehouse College	Ron Lykins	Dan Mannix
Boccia	Emory University	Howard Bailey	Howard Bailey
Cycling	Stone Mountain	Jack Hughes	David Williams
Equestrian	GA. International Horse Park	Cindy Hertel	Karen Lang
Fencing	Mercer University	Justin Hopper	Bill Murphy
Football	ClarkAtlanta University	Jaci Field	Jeff Ardis
Goalball	GeorgiaState University	Chris Rodriquez	Steve Kearney
Judo	Atlanta Metropolitan College	Shannon Bradley	Bill Rosenberg

SPORT	VENUE	VENUE DIRECTOR	COMP. MGR.
Lawn Bowls	Clark Atlanta University	Jaci Field	Joe & Patti Grabowski
Powerlifting	Marriott Marquis Hotel	Bill Carney	Curtis Leslie
Rugby	Atlanta Metropolitan College	Shannon Bradley	Shannon Bradley
Shooting	Wolf Creek	Cathy Reinhardt	Gary Anderson
Swiming	Georgia Tech Aquatic Center	Tasha Kaplan	Mark Ponzillo
Table Tennis	Gwinnett Civic Center	Rob Thompson	Richard Butler
Tennis	Stone Mountain	Ed Craver	Marc Nadel
Volleyball/Sitting	Clayton State College	Gene Higginbotham	Kathy Brenner
Volleyball/Standing	Alexander Memorial Colliseum	Stan Lockridge	Kathy Brenner
Yachting	Aqualand Marina, Lake Lanier	Bruce Barton	Linda Merkle

PARALYMPIC FAMILY

AALTO, RAIMO • ABASCAL, MARCELA • ABBEELE, RUDI • ACORN, BILL • ADAIR, PATRICK • ADLER, FRED • AGAIAVA, JAMIE • AGUIRRE, IZASKUN • AHMED, AHMED • AL-RUZ, HUSSEIN • ALBRIGHT, PAUL • ALCOCK, GWEN • ALL-RUNNER, CEDRIC • ALLAFORT, GHISLAINE • ALLEN, SONYA • ALLORGE, MICHEL • ALTHOFF, RON • ALZUBI, AZZAM • AMOS, JOHN • ANDERSEN, LEIGH • ANDERSEN, MORTEN • ANDERSON, CAROL • ANDERSON, MALCOLM • ANDERSON, STEVE • ANDERSSON, MATS • ANDJELKOVIC, PAUL • APPELBAUM, MEL • ARIAS, ALFONSO • ARNOLD, DICK • ASHBY, BRUCE • ASHTON, RENE • ATHA, BERNARD • AUBERGER, ANDRE • AULD, SCOOTER • AYALON, MICKY • AYLLON, JAVIER • BAERTELSEN, MARIANNE • BAKER, MARYLYNN • BALDING, LAURA • BALJAFLA, HAMAD • BARBERO, JOSE • BASKIN, DAVE • BASSI, BASSI • BAUMGART, GERRIE • BEASLEY, JOHN • BEASLEY, OCTAVIA • BECKER, JANET • BECKER, MARK • BECKMANN, AKSEL • BEHLING, JACK • BELL, JOHN • BENEDICK, JACK • BERG, MATTHIAS • BERKEBILE, JIM • BERTELING, JAN • BERTELING-HUISMAN, GREET • BESTILLEIRO, JORGE • BHAMBHANI, YAGESH • BIAVA, MICAELA • BIERING-SORENSEN, FIN • BIERKOWSKI, JACEK • BIGG, JUDI • BIRCHER, STEFAN • BLADES, ROGER • BLAKE, BILL • BLOUCH, GERRY • BOLTERSTEIN, LARRY • BORDAS, PAULINE • BOSTROM, ARNOLD • BOURKE, JOHN • BOWERS, SHARON • BRADY, STEVE • BRANDT, SIMON • BRICKLEY, RICHARD • BRIERE, GILLES • BRIERE, PIERRE-ALEXANDRE • BRINKER, KATHY • BRINKLEY, TRACIE • BROADBENT, BARRY • BROBST, BILL • BROMANN, JENS • BROOKS, SHARON • BROUWERS, GERARD • BROWN, PAULA • BROWN, SUSAN • BRUNS, JOHANNES • BRUTSCHER, ALICE • BRUTSCHER, JOHN • BRYANT, INGER • BUCHANAN, CLARK • BUKODI, ZSOLT • BULGER, DIANE • BURCHELL, ALISON • BURD, RAYMOND • BURD, RUTH • BURDETTE, ROBERT • BURDINE, MARILYN • BURDINE, PAUL • BURNS, NORMAN • BYNUM, MARY • CALVERT, NEILL • CAMITSCH, PAUL • CAMP, DON • CAMPBELL, BARBARA • CAMPBELL, ED • CAMPBELL, JOE • CAMPOS, SERGIO • CAOUETTE, KEN • CAPLA, MARTIN • CARDWELL, BOB • CARDWELL, KATHY • CAREY, PAM • CARMENI, BRUNO • CARMICHAEL, CARLA • CARR, ANDY • CARROLL, JR • CARTER, LINDON • CARUSO, JOSEPH • CASADO, LUIS • CASERTA, KAREN • CASTRO, CHRISTOPHER • CASWELL, PAT • CAVATAIO, F • CAVICCHIO, RAYMOND • CELOTTO, GIANCARLO • CHAMBERS, BARBARA • CHAMBERS, MICHAEL • CHAN, KAI • CHAPMAN, BERNARD • CHAPPEL, RUDI • CHEUNG, WILLIAM • CHI, KWIJOON • CHIBA, MIDORI • CHIRCHOV, STEPHAN • CHOW, INGA • CHOW, YORK • CHRANEWYCZ, GEORGE • CIOLO, ANTONIO • CLEMENS, CHRIS • COFFMAN, LOWELL • COHEN, CHRIS • COLBURN, ROBERT • COLDWELL, ROBERT • COLLE, PAUL • COLLEDGE, ROBERT • COLLINS, DIXIE • COMIER, RAY • CONCKLIN, RICHARD • CONOLLY, AL • CONSTANTINO, MIKE • CONYERS, DOUG • COOPER, RICHARD • COOPER, RICK • COOTS, AL • COOTS, MILLIE • CORCORAN, SUE • CORDES, CHRIS • CORNWELL, KATER • COSTA, HELDER • COTTON, DEREK • COUDENYS, LIEVEN • COURBARIAUX, BERNARD • COURBARIAUX, PIERRE • CRAENS, ALEXANDER • CRAVEN, JOCELYNE • CRAVEN, PHILIP • CRAWFORD, CLARENCE • CROW, LLOYD • CROWE, SHIRLEY • CRUICE, CHRISTINE • CRUZ, PAULO • CRUZ, RICARDO • CUBITT, JUDY • CULLEN, SHELLEY • CULVER, SANDY • CURTIS, KATHY • CUSACK, SUSAN • DALTON, PAT • DANZIGER, AHARON • DARBRE, MICHEL • DARLING, LINDA • DASCHKO, HEIDI • DAVIS, TIM • DE CORDOVA, FRANCISCO • DE CORDOVA, RAQUEL • DE DEMETER, DORRIT • DE KIMMENADE, NANCYE • DE KIMMENADE, WILL • DE LOO, HENK • DE RUYCK, TOM • DEAN, ALAN • DEANS, KERRY • DELANGE, ELLEN • DEMBROW, MATT • DENDY, ELIZABETH • DENNIS, JEANNINE • DEPAUW, KAREN • DEVILLE, ANDRE • DEWELL, ROSS • DIAS, JORGE • DICKINSON, BRIAN • DICKSON, ALAN • DINH, TRIEN • DODD, BUTCH • DOLL-TEPPER, GUDRUN • DOVICOVIC, DUSAN • DROLLA, JR • DRUWEL, JOHAN • DUBE, IAN • DUERR, FINN • DUGGER, JIM • DUMMER, GAIL • DUNN, JANET • DUNSTAN, GEORGE • DUPUIS, JEAN-PAUL • DURAN, CAMILLO • DURDALLER, JOAN • DUROJAIYE, MUSTAPHA • DUTILLE, FRANCIS • DUTKIEWICZ, TED • DWYER, RAYMOND • EARLE, SKIP • EDWARDS, DAVID • EGGERS, WIN • EGGLESTON, LARRY • EGLEY, LOREN • EIFLER, PETER • EKLUND, BJORN • ELIX, JAN • ELIZALDE, ALFREDO • ELNATANOV, VALERIY • ENGEL, INGRID • ENGLISH, BOB • ENTERLINE, JR • ENTRIKEN, AL • ESHENKO, VLAD • ESPIRITU, MANUEL • ESTRIN, ANISIM • EURE, BRUCE • EVERSON, SHARON • EVRARD, JEAN • EWING, ASHLEY • EZZELL, ANN • FABRITIUS, CAMILLA • FAGAN, PATRICK • FAIAS, JOAQUIM • FALLON, THOMAS • FARMER, PIERRE • FASTIGGI, ROBERT • FATT, DELANO • FELDMAN, SUSAN • FELSBERG, LEO • FERNANDES, PEDRO • FERNANDEZ, BARQUIN • FERRER, FERRER • FEWELL, DAVE • FISHER, BOB • FISHER, LOUIS • FLETCHER, FRED • FOREBACK, RAYMOND • FORTINI, DIANE • FOSTER, NICOLA • FOURNIER, DIANE • FRAMNES, LINDA • FRAS, PATRICIA • FREEBODY, JANE • FREW, MICHELLE • FRIEDRICH, KLAUS • FRITSCHI, JENNIFER • FUMADO, VICKY • FUNG-A-WING, ROEL • FUSADE, PIERRE • GAFFGA, LEN • GALE, IAN • GALE, ROSEMARY • GALINHA, LINA • GANTER, JOHN • GARNER, KIM • GATAKY, MARY • GERRY, DOUG • GIBBS, MIKE • GIBEAULT, HUGH • GIBSON, BILL • GILBERT, JACK • GILBERT, JO • GILLIS, LUCIAN • GILLMAN, BRUCE • GILTZ, MARY • GIRO, BEA • GLAESE, PETER • GLATZ, RUSS • GODET, PASCAL • GOLLEY, GRAHAM • GOMEZ-LIANO, PILAR • GONZALES, TONY • GRAPES, WAYNE • GRAYBEAL, LEE • GREEN, ANNE • GREY, JIM • GRIFFITHS, PAUL • GRIGGS, EMMITT • GROOT, CEES • GUEMATI, AIDA • GUY, BILL • HAIGLER, JEAN • HALE, JR • HALL, DEBORAH • HALLIDAY, ROBERT • HALSTEAD, DAVE • HANSON, DAVID • HARGREAVES, ALISON • HARING, ERICH • HARMS, AD • HARRIS, TOM • HARRISON, IAN • HARRISON, PAULINE • HART, CLAIRE • HART, TAMMY • HARTIGAN, BEA • HARTZ, BILL • HARVEY, MARTHA • HASLINGER, FRANZ • HATSUYAMA, YASUHIRO • HATZMANN, RIEKUS • HEAD, JOHN • HEFKA, MARIAN • HEINZLE, CORINNA • HELSLOOT, ERIC • HERRICK, DOC • HERRICK, STELLA • HERUTI, RAFI • HEYA, NORIO • HIBBERT, GLYN • HILDEN, BILL • HILDEN, NOREEN • HINES, TIMBER • HIRD, MATT • HITE, JIM • HJALF, GRETE • HJALTESTED, THOR • HODGES-HITE, JOYCE • HOFFMANN, HELMUT • HOLLAND, JACK • HOLLAND, LEONA • HOLM, BROR • HOOD, JAMES • HOOPER, VIV • HOPPEN, JEFF • HORNE, DAVID • HOROWITZ, NANCY • HORTON, JIM • HORVATH, CSABA • HOUCK, AL • HRANIC, ZDRAVKO • HUBBELL, PAULINE • HUGHES, PAUL • HURLEY, RITA • HUTCHINS, DENISE • IAZOUNITCHEVA, TATIANA • IBRAHIM, AZMY • III, BUDDY • III, STEVE • III, TRES • ILLMAN, ARNOLD • INLOW, GEORGE • ISLER, LARRY • JACOBSEN, MARIE • JAKOBSEN, BIRCK • JANITZ, ATTILA • JANSEN, FRED • JAREMA, JOHN • JENNEJAHN, CHRIS • JENNEJAHN, ROD • JINKS, ED • JOHANSON, EMILY • JOHNSON, JESSE • JOHNSON, LYMAN • JOHNSON, MARVIN • JOHNSON, SCOTT • JONES, ALLISON • JOON, PIETER • JORDAN, BEN • JORGENSEN, EVAN • JOSEPH, JOSEPH • JR, FRANK • JR, JOE • JUNKINS, PETE • KAHN, LARRY • KAIRY, RUBEN • KALISZEWSKI, KELLI • KANESHIRO, KEVIN • KEARNEY, BEVERLY • KEARNEY, STEVE • KELLY, FREDERICK • KENDALL, JENTRY • KERSHAW, KEITH • KHOEINI, HOSSEIN • KIM, KYU • KITCHEN, PAUL • KIVITS, WIM • KLEIN, FRITS • KLEPPE, THOR • KNAAP, JOHAN • KNAPINSKI, JANE • KNECHT, ALEXANDER • KNUDSEN, HANNE • KNUDSEN, MARY • KNUDSEN, VIBEKE • KO, RUSSELL • KOCHMAN, RAND • KOLODZIEJCZYK, JANUSZ • KOLOMBATOVICH, GEORGE • KONCNIK, PETER • KOPPER, HAROLD • KOSHEWA, PAUL • KREMER, HAROLD • KRISTIANSSON, EVA • KROMBHOLZ, GERTRUDE • KRUIMER, AART • KUCERA, NORBERT • KUEPFER, CATHY • KUYKENDALL, RANDY • KVEIL, FREDRIK • KYLE, DOUG • LABANOWICH, STAN • LAMMINPAA, REIJO • LAMPI, AULIS • LAPICOLA, PHYLLIS • LAPOLLA, TONY • LARSEN, MORTEN • LATHAM, CINDY • LAUB, RUSS • LAURIDSEN, INGRID • LAVEBORN, MATS • LAVEBORN, MATS • LAVERGNE, CONNIE • LAWRENCE, GILLIAN • LEASK, JIM • LEDERMAN, CYRIL • LEE, BRENT • LEE, DAVID • LEE, RENAY • LEECH, KARL • LEGG, DAVID • LEJINS, ZIG • LENAERTS, WALTER • LENYK, JO • LEONAVICIUTE, GITA • LEPORTE, GEORGE • LERNOUT, JAN • LEWIS, BEVERLEY • LEWIS, CRYSTAL • LEWIS, JOE • LIGGINS, ALPHONZO • LIKEY-OTT, LEN • LILLO, ARACELI • LILOV, VLADIMIR • LIM, TAI • LINDSEY, JAY • LINDSTROM, HANS • LITTLE, MARIE • LOISELLE, DICK • LOPEZ, BOB • LOPEZ, DOMINGO • LOTAN, GABRIEL • LOVE, GREG • LOWE, BOB • LOWE, CATHY • LOWE, ELAINE • LOWERY, CLARKE • LUNCHER, RAY • LYNCH, ERIC • LYNN, GAY • LYTTBACKA, ANNELIE • MACARLE, MARIA • MACDOUGAL, MAC • MACKAY, JOAN • MACKINNON, BILL • MACWILLIAMS, BERT • MACWILLIAMS, EDE • MAGOON, EMILY • MAILHOT, SUE • MAIN, NORMAN • MAKRIS, VASILIS • MANCINI, SR • MANIGAULT, ART • MANN, RICHARD • MANSELL, MARTIN • MANTON, SUE • MARCUS, BOB • MARCUS, STAN • MARKSON, ED • MARTIN, EMERIC • MARTINEZ, ALBERTO • MARTINEZ, MARIO • MARTINEZ-CAYERE, RAFY • MASINGALE, MARILYNN • MATTHEWS, JOAN • MATZLER, WILFRIED • MCBEE, TAWNI • MCCARTAN, MIKE • MCCULLOCH, JANET • MCDOUGAL, TREVA • MCGUIRE, MICK • MCKANNA, STEVE • MCKEE, BRIAN • MCKEOWN, KOLLENE • MCKIERNAN, SUE • MCLAUGHLIN, JEANNE • MCLAUGHLIN, OLLIE • MCLEAN, RONALD • MCLEOD, LORI • MCNAMARA, BILL • MCNAMARA, OLIVE • MCNEW, PAT • MCSHANE, MICK • MEADEN, CHRIS • MELZER, LINDA • MENDEZ, JAVIER • MENDEZ, PABLO • MERRICK, CAROLYN • MERRICK, DON • MEZIANI, KAMEL • MICAHNIK, DAVE • MICHELINI, LUCA • MICHELINI, LUCA • MIKITA, DAREK • MILBRODT, DEBBIE • MILLER, JOHN • MILLER, RON • MILLER, TOM • MITCHELL, JOANNE • MITCHELL, KEITH • MITCHELL, LOUIS • MONGOVAN, BILL • MONTEMURRO, BARB • MONTEMURRO, SCOTT • MORENO, RICARDO • MORGAN, MARIANNE • MORRIS, STAN • MOSKOWITZ, MANNY • MOSS, DICK • MOSS, JONATHAN • MOSTAFA, HOSSAM • MULLER, GERHARD • MURDIE, DINA • MURDIE, IAN • MURPHY, DARLENE • MUSHETT, CAROL • MUSHETT, JILL • MYRICK, NANCY • NALLS, TAD • NASH, LARRY • NEALE, GORDON • NEGROPONTIS, PETER • NELSEN, MARK • NEVIN, RAY • NILSSON, LEIF-AKE • NOVAK, PETER • NOVECOSKY, LAURA • NOWICKI, JOHN • NUSS, THOMAS • O'DELL, BRUCE • O'NEILL, DON • OCHOA, NICOLAS • OGILVIE, DONNA • OGILVIE, JOE • OLENIK, LISA • OLINGER, VANE • OLINGER, VANITTA • OLIVA, FRANCISCO • ORCHARD, MAUREEN • ORDONEZ, CARMEN • ORMAN, PAUL • ORR, AL • ORTH, GLENDA • OTT, WOLFGANG • OTT, WOLFGANG • OTTO, STEFAN • OTTO, ULLI • OWEN, STEVE • OZKAN, METIN • PALAU, JUAN • PALM, BARBARA • PARDINI, PIERANGELO • PARIS, TARA • PARISI, DAN • PARK, YONG • PARMELE, LINDA • PARNHAM, JUNE • PASCUAL, TONI • PATE, JACK • PATTI, CATHY • PEPIN, SERGE • PEREDA, LUIS • PERRY, JEROME • PERRY, LARRY • PERRY, MIKE • PETERS, JOANN • PETERSEN, STEEN • PETERSON, BOB • PETERSON, CYNTHIA • PIERCE, CURTIS • PILKINGTON, SCOTT • PINELLI, ED • PINELLI, PIERRE • PINELLI, PIERRE • PINTOS, JORGE • PIO, SCOTT • PIRKLE, JR • PLEAU-GAUTHIER, SEBASTIEN • POLANSKY, SUE • POLKEY, BARRY • POLLEFEIZ, MARI • PORTER, ROBERT • POSSE, FEDERICO • PRALL, WINNIE • PRICE, STACEY • PRIEBE, CHARLES • PROBST, ANTON • PRUITT, NORMAN • PRUITT, SANDY • PRYCE, DAVE • PULLIAM, LARRY • QASRAWI, BASSAM • RABENSTEIN, SANDRA • RABY, GAIL • RAES, ANDRE • RAES, LUC • RAKOWITZ, JIM • RAMOS, RAY • RAMOT, ITZCHAK • RAMSAY, JOHN • RANSOME, FRANK • REED, JIM • REICHL, GESINE • RENKEN, BOB • RICHARDSON, ALFRED • RICHTER, KEN • RIDING, MICHAEL • RIERA, CRISTINA • RILEY, GRAHAM • RITCHIE, KEN • RIVEIROS, FERNANDO • RIVERA, CAROLE • ROBERTS, DARREN • ROBERTS, GREG • ROBINS, DWIGHT • ROBINSON, GARNET • ROBINSON, HAL • ROCQUE, FRED • ROCHE, SARAH • RODRIGUEZ, CARLOS • RODRIGUEZ-LAUBERT, CONRADO • ROGERS, MALCOLM • ROGERS, NED • ROGUT, E • ROJEK, DEAN • ROSENTHAL, RADU • ROYER, DONALD • RUIZ, CARMEN • RUTER, CHARLIE • RUTTERKAMP, HERMAN • RYAN, TIM • SABEL, ASH • SABIR, MANSOUR • SACCO, TOM • SAEZ, GERARD • SAGER, RUSS • SALAM, ALY • SALEM, NABIL • SALGADO, SHEILA • SALISBURY, CHAMP • SALISBURY, PEGGY • SALOMON, NELLY • SALTZMAN, EDWARD • SAMFORD, BILL • SAMS, CAROL • SAND, ARLENE • SANDERS, ROGER • SANZ, ENRIQUE • SARDARI, AMIR • SARJANOVIC, IVAN • SATOH, MITSUYA • SAVELKOUL, GENE • SAXBY, DAN • SAXTON, BOB • SCHMIDT, EMILY • SCHONSTEINER, JURGEN • SCHWARTZ, SUE • SCHWITTAI, JUERGEN • SCOBIE, BRIAN • SCOTT, GREG • SCOTT, PAUL • SEABASTY, THOMAS • SEARS-LEASK, LORI • SEIDEN, JEFF • SEMENIUK, JEANNETTE • SERRACANTA, PAU • SEWELL, DAVID • SHAW, MARILYN • SHAW, TONY • SHEA, CATHY • SHEPPARD, CHARLIE • SHERILL, CLAUDINE • SHOOK, RON • SLANGEN, LOU • SLAYTON, CINDY • SMIT, CEES • SMITH, DON • SMITH, FORREST • SMITH, FRANK • SMITH, GREGG • SMITH, LARRY • SMITH, PATTI • SMITH, RANDI • SMITH, TREVA • SNOW, LORNA • SNYDER, BILL • SNYDER, SUSAN • SODERHOLM, SEPPO • SODERSTROM, PETER • SODERSTROM, RAYLEEN • SOLT, JONQUIL • SOLVANG, JAN • SOOMRO, ASHIQUE • SORKKILA, EEVA • SOUTHAM, MARK • SOUZA, RICARDO • SPEERS, STEPHEN • SPELIERS, FERNAND • SPENCER, CLIVE • SPENCER, DODIE • SPENLAU, RON • SPICER, PAULA • SPRATT, RALPH • STAHL, C • STAM, ANNEKE • STEADWARD, ROBERT • STEELE-MILLS, JOAN • STEIN, JULIAN • STEPHENS, JOHN • STEPONCHEV, BUTCH • STERLING, KURT • STEVENSON, MARY • STEWART, DAN • STEWART, JOHN • STONE, JEAN • STRANGE, MAURA • STROHKENDL, HORST • STROM, AUDREY • STUBBS, MIKE • SUCHOWER, ANDY • SUGIYAMA, KANEYOSHI • SULLIVAN, MICK • SUTTON, JOE • SYNOR, HENRY • SZEKER, LO'CI • TAKEMORI, JAMES • TALTON, BILLY • TAMBERINO, MICHAEL • TARABYKINE, ALEKSANDR • TARBERT, JOHN • TASS, ATTILA • TAYLERT, AL • TAYLOR, ANGIE • TAYLOR, BILL • TAYLOR, FAY • TETREAULT, JANICE • THEISEN, GARY • THIBOUTOT, JR • THIBOUTOT, MICHELE • THIBOUTOT, PATRICIA • THOMAS, BILL • THOMAS, JOE • THOMAS, JR • THOMSON, BILL • THORKILDSEN, TORALV • THORNTON, FLETCHER • TIITTANEN, JAAKUO • TINYSZIN, ROMAN • TIPPINS, BILL • TODD, ALLEN • TODD, JACK • TOLMATCHEV, ROMAN • TOMLINSON, JOHN • TORNE', JOAN • TORRES, PETE • TRACY, AL • TRANNINGER, SANDRA • TREVINO, MARGIE • TROTMAN, PH • TSAPOS, MISAIL • TUOMI, VIRPI • TURK, III • TURMAN, MARIANNE • TURMAN, RAY • TURNER, HARRY • TUSQUETS, ELENA • UM, SUNG-HO • VAMOSH, ARIC • VAN AANHOLT, COR • VAN AANHOLT, PETER • VAN HAASTEREN, HENK • VAN HOOREWEGHE, RAYMOND • VAN HOYWEGHEN, EUGEEN • VAN MEENEN, PIERRE • VANCE, NICKI • VANLANDEWYCK, YVES • VANTHOURNOUT, NERA • VARDY, PHIL • VEIT, JR • VENCKUTONIS, RIMAS • VIEWEGER-STROHKENDL, VERONIKA • VILA, VILA • VISHOOT, EMI • VLAMINCK, WALTHER • VOGT, ELKE • VOIGHT, LEISA • VOLKMER, IRINA • VON ARBIN, CHARLOTTE • VON NOTTBECK, DETLEV • VUTE, RAJKO • WADE, ROBERT • WADE, ROBERT • WAINIO-OATO, GUY • WALDIE, ROSEMARY • WALKEMEYER, BILLY • WALKER, JR • WALKER, WILL • WALLAART, EDWIN • WALLACE, DAVE • WALLACE, LESLIE • WALLER, JOHN • WALSH, JANE • WALTON, STEVE • WANG, CARL • WARD, RON • WARREN, JANE • WARREN, RHEA • WASHINGTON, CAREY • WATKINS, JR • WATSON, BARRY • WATSON, FRED • WAUTERMARTENS, POL • WAYS, GEORGE • WEBB, ANN • WEBBER, HAROLD • WEBSTER, IRENE • WEBSTER, JIM • WEHR, AL • WEHR, PEGGY • WEIN, PEGGY • WEISS, KEN • WEISSMAN, BARB • WELLS, "D" • WELLS, JR • WELSCH, WALT • WEST, DONNA • WEST, GEORGE • WEST, MARALYN • WESTON, GERRY • WHEELER, GARRY • WHITE, JAMES • WHITLOW, HERB • WHYTE, BRUCE • WILLIAMS, SR • WILLIAMS, TREVOR • WILLIAMSON, DOUG • WILLIFORD, DANNY • WILLOWS, DEB • WILSON, JOHN • WILSON, LIZ • WILSON, STEPHEN • WINGFIELD, BILL • WINGFIELD, CHRISTA • WINTERSTEIN, DIANE • WIRSCHING, JOHAN • WITHROW, ROGER • WOLFERMAN, JAY • WONG, EDMUND • WOOD, DON • WOOD, MYRA • WOODRUM, CHIP • WU, SHENG • WU, YU-TUNG • WUNDER, KATHERINE • WUNDERLE, MAGGIE • WUNDERLICH, EDIE • YOE, DEE • ZBIERANOWSKI, PAWEL • ZIDULIAK, KAROL • ZIRKLE, TIM • ZUCKER, BRAD • ZUTTERMAN, THIERY • ZWERINA, HEINZ

STAFF & VOLUNTEERS

ABBATE, MAUREEN • ABBENSETT, ROBERT • ABBEY, CAROLINE • ABBEY, JOHN • ABBOTT, DARBY • ABBOTT, PAULA • ABDUR-RAHMAN, KHADIJAH • ABDY, LURENA • ABERNATHY, DEBORAH • ABERNATHY, KENNETH • ABERSON, JAMES • ABOULAFIA, ALBERT • ABRAMOWITZ, MICHAEL • ABRAMS, JON • ACKERSON, JENNIFER • ACOSTA, TERRI • ADAMI, LISA • ADAMS, ARDEN • ADAMS, BECKY • ADAMS, BUNNY • ADAMS, CARLA • ADAMS, DAVID • ADAMS, GALE • ADAMS, GARY • ADAMS, GERALD • ADAMS, GINNY • ADAMS, HARRIETT • ADAMS, JANET • ADAMS, JAYME • ADAMS, JENNIFER • ADAMS, JERRY • ADAMS, JIM • ADAMS, JO • ADAMS, KIM • ADAMS, KIMBERLEY • ADAMS, LARRY • ADAMS, LEMOND • ADAMS, SARA • ADAMS, SKIP • ADAMS, TERRIE • ADAMS, WILLIAM • ADAMSON, JO • ADCOCK, ERIC • ADEZIO, JOSEPH • ADEFOPE, FOLAHAN • ADEKUNLE, MOSUN • ADELMAN, DENISE • ADELMAN, SHEILA • ADESANYA, AFOLABI • ADKINS, CELIA • ADKINS, MATTIE • ADKINS-WARD, ANDRE • ADLER, RICHARD • ADLER, SCOTT • ADRIAN, NATHAN • AGGREY, SYLVIA • AGUILAR, ELIZABETH • AGUILAR, IRAN • AGUILERA, MARTIN • AGUILGRA, HUGO • AHLEN, ANNA • AHMED, AMIR • AHMED, KASHIF • AHONEN, DANIEL • AHRENDT, LURAE • AHRENS, KAREN • AHSAN, SANIYA • AIKEN, JERRY • AIKENS, KEITH • AKHTER, AAMER • AKIN, NANCY • AKSEL, INNA • AKSEL, SEMEN • AL-HAKEEM, SAADIQ • ALAGANO, MARIA • ALANIZ, MIKE • ALASIN, SALLY • ALBERGA, ALLAN • ALBERT, JON • ALBERT, MICHAEL • ALBRITTON, KAMYLLA • ALCANTARA, PAULA • ALDAY, MARGARET • ALDRETE, RUBEN • ALDRIDGE, RUBY • ALDRIDGE, STEPHANIE • ALEKOZAI, SHARIFA • ALEXANDER, DAWN • ALEXANDER, DOUGLAS • ALEXANDER, EBONI • ALEXANDER, EDWARD • ALEXANDER, LIA • ALEXANDER, MARSHA • ALEXANDER, QUINCY • ALEXANDER, SADIE • ALEXANDER, SARAH • ALEXANDER, SONYA • ALEXANDER, TODD • ALEXANDER, TRACY • ALEXANDER, WILLIE • ALFORD, JIM • ALFORD, STEVEN • ALGER, BILL • ALGER, KATHY • ALI, SEKOU • ALIFFI, JESSICA • ALIFFI, SARAH • ALLEMAN, RUSSELL • ALLEN, ANNE • ALLEN, ANNIE • ALLEN, CHRISTINE • ALLEN, DALE • ALLEN, GEORGE • ALLEN, HELEN • ALLEN, JACKIE • ALLEN, JAN • ALLEN, JENNIFER • ALLEN, JENNY • ALLEN, JO • ALLEN, KEVIN • ALLEN, KIM • ALLEN, MICHAEL • ALLEN, MIKE • ALLEN, NANCY • ALLEN, PATRICK • ALLEN, SKIP • ALLEN, VICTORIA • ALLEN, WILLIAM • ALLENDE-HENRY, MAGALIS • ALLIGOOD, MARY • ALLIGOOD, MIKE • ALLISON, JUAN • ALLOR, CHARLES • ALLRED, SCOTT • ALLSOPP, TIM • ALLSWANG, MARGO • ALLY, DEANNA • ALMOND, TONYA • ALONY, PAT • ALSAJJAR, MUBEL • ALSAGER, CHARMAINE • ALSBERRY, ANGELA • ALSENTZER, ULRICH • ALSTON, RACHEL • ALTWASSER, COLETTE • ALVARADO, CARLOS • ALVAREZ, JOHN • ALVAREZ, SHEILA • ALVEREZ, THERESA • ALVERSON, CAROLE • ALVERSON, SUSAN • AMANO, HARUKA • AMBROSE, AMY • AMERSON, BERNADETTE • AMERSON, MIKE • AMIN, MUSTAFA • AMLANIE, ABDUL • AMMONS, FREDERICK • AMMUMUIA, LEPAPA • AMOS, DAY-DAY • AMOS, JANICE • AMOS, MICHAEL • AMOS, POOH-BOY • AMOS, WANDA • AMOS-HANNON, EMMA • AN, JOHNNY • ANDERSEN, DAVID • ANDERSEN, DOUGLAS • ANDERSEN, LISA • ANDERSEN, RYAN • ANDERSON, AARON • ANDERSON, ANDY • ANDERSON, BETTY • ANDERSON, BRADY • ANDERSON, BRITTANY • ANDERSON, CANDACE • ANDERSON, CATHY • ANDERSON, CHARLES • ANDERSON, CHERISH • ANDERSON, CHRIS • ANDERSON, CYNTHIA • ANDERSON, EARTHA • ANDERSON, ERIK • ANDERSON, FREDRICA • ANDERSON, GARY • ANDERSON, GRAYLIN • ANDERSON, GREGORY • ANDERSON, HOLLY • ANDERSON, JOSH • ANDERSON, JOY • ANDERSON, JUDY • ANDERSON, KATHERINE • ANDERSON, LATONYA • ANDERSON, LAURIE • ANDERSON, LAVERTA • ANDERSON, LISA • ANDERSON, LORETTA • ANDERSON, MARSHA • ANDERSON, NAOMI • ANDERSON, PATRICIA • ANDERSON, ROBERT • ANDERSON, SALLYE • ANDERSON, SANDRA • ANDERSON, SENETHA • ANDERSON, SHERRI • ANDERSON, THOMAS • ANDERSON, TIKI • ANDERSON, TODD • ANDERSON, TRACI • ANDERSON, TRENT • ANDERSON, VALDEZ • ANDRADE, LIONEL • ANDREOTTI, JANIA • ANDRES, LORENA • ANDERSON, MARK • ANDREWS, ANITA • ANDREWS, CHRIS • ANDREWS, MONTE • ANDREWS, SARAH • ANDREWS, TIMOTHY • ANDREWS, TIMOTHY • ANDREWS, TRICIA • ANDRUS, ETHAN • ANGEL, LAURIE • ANGEL, SHARON • ANGELICO, JOHN • ANNELL, ERIK • ANSARI, DAWUD • ANTHONY, JOSEPH • ANTHONY, KELLY • ANTHONY, RODNEY • ANTHONY, TIMOTHY • ANTHONY, WISTERIA • ANTOS, TIFFANY • ANTOUR, LAURIE • ANWEILER, BRIAN • BARRETT, VERONICA • BARRINGTON, CARL • BARRON, ALEX • BARRON, KAREN • BARRONETTA, ANNETTE • BARROS, GILROY • BARROW, AMY • BARROW, HUMBERTO • BARSKY, ROBYN • BARTEL, LARRY • BARTH, GEOFF • BARTHOLOMAI, CRISTINA • BARTMAN, IAN • BARTNIKOWSKI, ALEXANDRA • BARTNIKOWSKI, CHRISTINA • BARTON, BRUCE • BARTON, PHILLIP • BARTOW, ROSS • BARTRAM, ERIC • BARTSCH, DANIELLE • BASS, BARBARA • BASS, JON • BASSETT, DEBBIE • BASSETT, SARA • BAST, FELIX • BASTIDAS, MARISELA • BATES, GERALD • BATES, JAMES • BATES, TRACY • BATINE, PATRICIA • BATOR, EDMUND • BATTEN, BRIGID • BATTEN, JEANNE • BATTLE, STEPHANIE • BATTS, EY • BAUCOM, HARRIET • BAUER, KARLA • BAUGH, LENA • BAUGHMAN, KATIE • BAUM, KIMBERLY • BAUMAN, DIANE • BAUMGARTEN, JOCELYN • BAUMGARTEN, WIL • BAX, SUSAN • BAXTER, AMY • BAXTER, DICK • BAXTER, SUSAN • BAYBECK, BRAD • BAYCI, MICHAEL • BAYER, ED • BAYER, JOHN • BAYERL, CARLA • BAYERL, CARLA • BAYNE, JOYCE • BAYRON, NORMA • BAZAN, ALBERTO • BAZEMORE, CURT • BAZILE, KIMBERLYN • BEACH, ROBERT • BEACH, SHARON • BEACH, STEPHANIE • BEAL, TIA • BEALE-NORRIS, DARLENE • BEALKO, COURTENEY • BEALL, NATALIE • BEAMON, HEIDI • BEAN, JUDY • BEARD, HELEN • BEARSLEY, TY • BEARY, SHARON • BEASLEY, HOWARD • BEASLEY, MEGAN • BEASLEY, YOLANDA • BEAUCAIRE, RONALD • BEAVERS, MELISSA • BEAVERS, PAMELA • BECCO, GINNY • BECERRA, HORTENSIA • BECERRA, JUAN • BECHER, TANYA • BECK, GINNY • BECK, HELEN • BECKER, RON • BECKFORD, MELANIE • BECKMAN, J • BECKMAN, KAREN • BECQUET, PAIGE • BEDFORD, CHARLES • BEDFORD, NANCY • BEEBE, ANN • BEEKS, TONI • BEER, PAM • BEHAN, SHARON • BEHR, MICHAEL • BEHRINGER, RACHEL • BEIDLEMAN, ANNE • BEIRNE, CHRIS • BEISWENGER, BILL • BELANGER, PASCALE • BELCHER, RUSSELL • BELESS, DANIEL • BELFRAGE, RUPERT • BELGUM, GRETCHEN • BELK, DENISE • BELKEN, LAURA • BELL, AL • BELL, ANGELA • BELL, BOB • BELL, CONNIE • MICHAEL, ERIC • BELL, GLEN • BELL, HOPE • BELL, JENNIFER • BELL, JENNIFER • BELL, JULIE • BELL, KAY • BELL, LAKITA • BELL, LATISHA • BELL, LINDA • BELL, LINDA • BELL, MARGARET • BELL, MEGAN • BELL, NANCY • BELL, PATRICIA • BELL, ROBERT • BELL, SHERRY • BELL, VANESSA • BELLAMY, KATY • BELLAVITA, CHRISTOPHER • BELMAN, MARY • BELVISO, MARCELA • BENSOREK, SHARONA • BENAVIDESS, ALEJANDRO • BENCICH, VIVIAN • BENDER, JEFFREY • BENDER, LARRY • BENDER, MICHAEL • BENEDICT, ROBYN • BENFIELD, ANDREA • BENFIELD, LYNN • BENFORD, TERRILYN • BENHAM, RENEE • BENJAMIN, RICHELLE • BENNETT, ANTHONY • BENNETT, BLYTHE • BENNETT, JENNIFER • BENNETT, MARK • BENNETT, NANCY • BENNETT, ROSEMARY • BENNINGTON, ROBIN • BENOIT, MICHAEL • BENSLEY, DANNY • BENSLEY, TRACI • BENSON, EVAN • BENSON, WENDY • BENTLEY, LYNFORD • BENTLEY, MARION • BENTLEY, SHERRELL • BENTON, ANNIE • BENTON, CHRISTY • BENTON, THELMA • BENTZ, PETER • BERARD, DAVID • BERASSA, EULA • BERDEEN, NAOMI • BERENSON, MATT • BERGER, BRIAN • BERGER, JASON • BERGER, JONATHAN • BERGER, SARA • BERGERON, JOSEPH • BERGERON, SAMANTHA • BERGERSEN, LAURA • BERKALL, BENJAMIN • BERMUDEZ, ANGELA • BERNHARDT, JAN • BERNLOEHR, GEORGE • BERNOT, MICHAEL • BERNTSEN, PAULA • BERRY, ALLYSON • BERRY, CHARLES • BERRY, DAVID • BERTINO, LINDA • BERTRAM, SUSAN • BESAL, HELEN • BESCHER, MYRNA • BESECKER, SUZANNE • BESHERS, MELANIE • BESKIN, JAMES • BESSENT, SHELDONIA • BESSEY, SUSAN • BESSEY, TIM • BESSINGER, DEBORAH • BEST, JAMES • BEST, KEN • BESTER, HELEN • BETHEA, JAN • BETZ, ANDREW • BEUTEL, SABINA • BHIMULL, DARRIN • BIAS, WILLIAM • BICKES, JESSICA • BICKES, MARY • BICKES, TOM • BICKMAN, CINDY • BICKMAN, MICHAEL • BIEBER, DORTE • BIEGER, DON • BIERENFELD, BARBARA • BIERI, LAURA • BIGSBY, DOMINIQUE • BILES, JACKIE • BILLINGS, CHRISTEN • BILLINGSLEA, GRADY • BILLINGSLEY, TRACY • BILLIPS, M • BILLOCK, JOHN • BILLUPS, III • BILSTROM, DAVID • BINDAS, JAN • BINGHAM, ANGELA • BINGHAM, HERMAN • BINGLEY, ANTHONY • BIRCHALL, PAULA • BIROTTE, ROSALIND • BIROZES, RENEE • BISCH, JIM • BISH, CHRIS • BISH, ROBYN • BISHKO, ROBYN • BISHOP, ANN • BISHOP, JUANITA • BISHOP, MARK • BISHOP, WILL • BISSAINTHE, WILNER • BISSELL, NORMAN • BITTEL, ELLA • BITTNER, AURELIA • BITZER, THOMAS • BIVINS, DEANGELO • BIZZELL, MARY • BIZZOCO, BRUCE • BLACK, BEVERLY • BLACK, CALVIN • BLACK, CLAIRE • BLACK, DAN • BLACK, KIMBERLYN • BLACK, LINDA • BLACK, LYNETTE • BLACK, MARGIE • BLACK, MARY • BLACK, NICKIE • BLACK, SHELLY • BLACKBURN, BERT • BLACKBURN, DONNA • BLACKBURN, II • BLACKBURN, SHERRY • BLACKBURN, THELLAMELIA • BLACKMON, CHRISTINA • BLACKNELL, ANDREA • BLACKWELL, ALISON • BLACKWELL, RENEE • BLACKWELL, SAUNDRA • BLADEN, JOHN • BLAGG, LAWANNA • BLAINE, SEMAJ • BLAIR, CLAY • BLAIR, DAVID • BLAIR, JAN • BLAIR, JANE • BLAIR, SARA-ELIZABETH • BLAIS, JANE • BLAKE, ANDY • BLAKE, BARBARA • BLAKE, CHRISTINE • BLAKE, KATHY • BLAKE, ROSEMARY • BLAKE, STEPHANIE • BLAKE, VANIA • BLAKELEY, MARION • BLALOCK, ANNE • BLALOCK, LINDA • BLANC, SYLVIA • BLANCHARD, ALBERT • BLANCHARD, NANCY • BLANCHET, BUDDY • BLANCO, GEORGE • BLAND, BERNICE • BLANDING, MARCIA • BLANKENBURG, OLAF • BLANKENSHIP, AARON • BLANKENSHIP, DANIELLE • BLANKENSHIP, IZABEL • BLANKENSHIP, JOHN • BLANKENSHIP, KIMBERLY • BLANTON, DEBBIE • BLASINGAME, ANGIE • BLATT, TYLER • BLAZON, SANDRA • BLEDSOE, MICHAEL • BLISS, AMBER • BLISS, JEAN • BLISS, PAM • BLOCK, VICTOR • BLOCKER, DOTTIE • BLODGETT, CHUCK • BLOIS, KIMBERLY • BLOIS, MELINDA • BLOKDIJK, MARLOES • BLOOM, BITSY • BLOOM, JOSHUA • BLOOMBERG, TOBY • BLOUNT, DANIEL • BLUM, BILL • BLUMBERG, KIMBERLY • BLYTHE, ANN • BOATRIGHT, TONY • BOATWRIGHT, KEVIN • BOCHICCHIO, B • BODDIE, JANICE • BODDIE-DUNCAN, JULIA • BODDY, FIONA • BODE, JAMES • BODE, MARANDA • BODIFORD, KEITH • BODINE, CHRISTOPHER • BOEDTS, BARBARA • BOEL, WERNER • BOEMKER, RON • BOFF, KEN • BOGDAN, DAVID • BOGROW, CHARLOTTE • BOGROW, HAROLD • BOHAM, BRETT • BOHAM, BRIAN • BOHM, HERBERT • BOHN, JAMES • BOHORQUEZ, GILBERT • BOHRES, BOB • BOHRES, SHERRY • BOITET, KARA • BOIVIN, AMANDA • BOJARSKI, ELISABETH • BOLAND, SUSAN • BOLANDER, BO • BOLDING, GLADYS • BOLDUC, DARRYL • BOLENDER, PAULA • BOLES, MARLON • BOLGLA, LORI • BOLIN, ROD • BOLLEN, DORIS • BOLSTAD, KERRY • BOLTON, CRYSTA • BOLTON, DAVE • BOLTON, HAROLD • BOLTON, TRISH • BOMBARD, JIM • BOND, BILL • BOND, CLARA • BOND, CYNTHIA • BOND, ERNIE • BONDURANT, FRAN • BONDURANT, LOUIS • BONEBERGER, DENISE • BONET, ANGEL • BONHAM, GEORGE • BONILLA, ALEX • BONNER, JILL • BONITO, GEORGE • BOOKER, JUANITA • BOOKER, MARY • BOOKER, PERETHA • BOONE, DANCE • BOONE, JENNIFER • BOOTH, ELIZABETH • BORASCH, DIANA • BORASCH, MATT • BORCHERING, BARRY • BORDERS, HANSON • BORDNER, JASON • BORJA, MARVIN • BORN, ERIN • BORNES, FELICIA • BORRUSO, JOSEPH • BORST, PHOEBE • BORSTAD, SIG • BORY, PATTI • BORYK, RICK • BOS, BOSMAN • BOSCH, EMILY • BOSMAN, LARRY • BOST, ADAM • BOST, SHARON • BOSTIC, BETTY • BOSTIC, DONALD • BOSTICK, BEVERLY • BOSTICK, SAM • BOSTROM, SANDRA • BOUCHARD, DON • BOUCKAERT, NATALIE • BOUCKAERT, STEPHANIE • BOUDA, BRET • BOULAY, JACQUES • BOURASSA, JASON • BOURASSA, JEAN • BOURASSA, JEFF • BOURBON, SANDRA • BOURGOYNE, DOUGLAS • BOUTER, JEROEN • BOUTIN, ELLIE • BOWBLISS, STEVE • BOWDEN, DENISSA • BOWDEN, ANDY • BOWEN, BILL • BOWEN, BONNIE • BOWEN, KERIN • BOWEN, MARGIE • BOWEN, PAUL • BOWERS, BECKY • BOWERS, JULIA • BOWES, SANDY • BOWIE, CATHIE • BOWKER, EDWARD • BOWLAND, S • BOWLING, GEORGIA • BOWLING, SUE • BOWMAN, BROCK • BOWMAN, CATHY • BOWMAN, GLENDA • BOWMAN, MONICA • BOWMAN, RON • BOWSER, STEVEN • BOWZER, ANETA • BOX, DAVID • BOX, KEVIN • BOX, LEE • BOX, NINA • BOYCE, GARY • BOYCE, RENDELL • BOYCE, SHIRLEY • BOYD, GENIE • BOYD, JANE • BOYD, MARIANNE • BOYD, ROSETTA • BOYD, SUE • BOYD, THIOT • BOYDSTON, GINNY • BOYE, ED • BOYER, DAN • BOYER, KAREN • BOYER, KEVIN • BOYKIN, MELLIE • BOZEMAN, BRENDA • BOZEMAN, TIMOTHY • BRACKETT, RICK • BRADBURY, YAEL • BRADFORD, EARL • BRADFORD, PAMELA • BRADFORD, RICKY • BRADLEY, CHARLES • BRADLEY, ELISABETH • BRADLEY, GRAEME • BRADLEY, HOMMIE • BRADLEY, JEROME • BRADLEY, KEN • BRADLEY, NATHANIEL • BRADLEY, SCOTT • BRADLEY, SHANNON • BRADSHAW, JOEY • BRADSHAW, LISA • BRADY, SUSANA • BRADY, TIM • BRAIMAH, JANET • BRAKEBUSCH, SHEILA • BRAKEVILLE, ROSS • BRAMLETT, DAVID • BRAMLETT, MARTIN • BRANAM, KATHY • BRANCH, ALEX • BRANCH, BRENDA • BRANCH, JAMES • BRANCH, SCOTT • BRAND, TAYLOR • BRANDT, JOHN • BRANHAM, TONNA-ARON • BRANNAN, BRET • BRANNAN, CHARLES • BRANNAN, JENNY • BRANNAN, MARJI • BRANNER, RICHARD • BRANNON, JEANNA • BRANNON, NANCY • BRANNON, SHERRY • BRANSON, RACHELE • BRANTS, LUCY • BRASWELL, JANIE • BRATCHER, ELAINE • BRATEMAN, DEBBIE • BRAUN, PAUL • BRAUN, ROSS • BRAUN, TIM • BRAWNER, DORIS • BRAXTON, WENDY • BRAY, IAN • BRAY, JAMES • BRAY, LATRESSE • BRAY, LOUIS • BRAY, RONALD • BRAYTON, FERNANDO • BREAUX, KATHRYN • BREDOW, RONALD • BREEDEN, TRACY • BREEDLOVE, CYNTHIA • BREEN, BRIAN • BREESER, SKIP • BREHM, TAMMY • BREITENBACH, BEE • BREJDA, ANDREW • BRENNAMAN, ADAM • BRENNAN, BETSY • BRENNAN, KATHLEEN • BRENNAN, KATHRYN • BRENNAN, LINDEE • BRENNER, KATHY • BRENNER, RON • BRETTELL, DAVID • BREWER, BELITA • BREWER, DAVID • BREWER, SHELLIE • BREWINGTON, ELIZABETH • BREYER, CAROL • BREZNAI, FRANK • BRICKER, STACY • BRIDGES, DANA • BRIDGES, DARRYL • BRIDGES, LARRY • BRIDGES, LINDA • BRIDGES, LORI • BRIDGES, ORLANDO • BRIDGES, TRACEY • BRIELEY, TEDDY • BRIGGS, CHARLOTTE • BRIGGS, ELLEN • BRIGHAM, NICK • BRIGHTMAN, KITTY • BRIGHTMON, MICHAEL • BRILEY, CHRISTOPHER • BRINDELL, ANN • BRINDELL, MARY • BRINSON, KATHY • BRION, KIMBERLEY • BRISCO, MEGAN • BRISIGHELLI, MARCELA • BRISTOL, HANNAH • BRISTOL, TED • BRITT, AMY • BRITT, EMILY • BRITT, PATSY • BRITT, SHARON • BRITTAIN, KATIE • BRITTINGHAM, PEGGY • BROADRICK, KEVIN • BROADRICK, MELANIE • BROADWAY, ALISON • BROADWAY, HELEN • BROCK, DOTTI • BROCK, KIMBERLY • BROD, CHRISTEL • BRODIE, CATHERINE • BRODIE, FREDRICK • BROK, ANKE • BROKAW, MALINDA • BROOKE, JULIA • BROOKE, TERRI • BROOKFIELD, DAVID • BROOKINS, MONA • BROOKS, BLAIRE • BROOKS, CORNEITHA • BROOKS, DANIELLE • BROOKS, EMILY • BROOKS, HEATHER • BROOKS, REGINALD • BROOKS, ROBBYE • BROOKS, ROBIN • BROOKS, SANDRA • BROOKS, TINA • BROOKS-HARRIS, TERRI • BROOKSHIRE, CURTIS • BROTHERS, WALTER • BROUGHTON, ROBIN • BROUGHTON-DILLARD, TERESA • BROUSSARD, DWAYNE • BROUSSARD, ROSE • BROUSSARD, SUZANNE • BROWN, ALAN • BROWN, ALAN • BROWN, AMY • BROWN, ANDREA • BROWN, ANDREW • BROWN, ANYA • BROWN, BETH • BROWN, BRIDGET • BROWN, CALVIN • BROWN, CECIL • BROWN, CHRISTOPHER • BROWN, CINDY • BROWN, COREY • BROWN, DANIEL • BROWN, DEBBIE • BROWN, DELICIA • BROWN, ELIZABETH • BROWN, GARY • BROWN, GREGORY • BROWN, HARRIET • BROWN, HOLLIE • BROWN, JANETTE • BROWN, JANICE • BROWN, JASON • BROWN, JEROME • BROWN, JERRY • BROWN, JIMMY • BROWN, JODIE • BROWN, JOHN • BROWN, JOHN • BROWN, JOSEPH • BROWN, KATHERINE • BROWN, KAY • BROWN, KELLY • BROWN, LAKESHA • BROWN, LAURIE • BROWN, LENEAR • BROWN, LISA • BROWN, LORI • BROWN, LORI • BROWN, MARVIN • BROWN, MARY • BROWN, MARY • BROWN, MELANIE • BROWN, MELINDA • BROWN, MERI • BROWN, NANCY • BROWN, NICOLE • BROWN, ODESSA • BROWN, ONIKA • BROWN, PATRICK • BROWN, RENEE • BROWN, ROBERT • BROWN, ROBERT • BROWN, SANDRA • BROWN, SARAH • BROWN, SUSIE • BROWN, TARRENCE • BROWN, TESSIE • BROWN, TODD • BROWN, TONI • BROWN, TRUDY • BROWN, VANESSA • BROWN, VIRGINIA • BROWN, YVONNE • BROWN-WADDY, DEBORAH • BROWNE, BARBARA • BROWNE, DONNA • BROWNING, JUDY • BROWNING, LEON • BROWNING, MELISANDRE • BROWNING, PAMELA • BROWNLEE, JOHN • BROWNLEE, SHIRLEY • BROZ, DAVID • BRUCE, BARBARA • BRUCE, GREGORY • BRUCE, JAMES • BRUECK, CANDICE • BRUEGGEMANN, JAYSON • BRUFFEY, BOB • BRUMBALOW, WENDELL • BRUMBELOE, KATIE • BRUNO, LISA • BRUNSON, BARBARA • BRUNSON, CECIL • BRUNSON, JOHN • BRUNSON, MARTY • BRUNSON, TERESA • BRUNTON, MARY • BRYAN, DAMION • BRYAN, ELLOUISE • BRYAN, EMERSON • BRYAN, JESSE • BRYAN, JOHN • BRYAN, MARY • BRYAN, TERENCE • BRYANT, ALAN • BRYANT, BOBBY • BRYANT, ELEANOR • BRYANT, JASMINE • BRYANT, JIM • BRYANT, JOANNE • BRYANT, JOHN • BRYANT, LOUISE • BRYANT, MARK • BRYANT, NETTIE • BRYANT, PAMELA • BRYANT, RODERICK • BRYANT, SYLETHIA • BRYANT, WILLIAM • BRYE, CAMMIE • BRYER, MIKE • BUAFO, SHIRLEY • BUBB, WENDY • BUCCIERO, ROBERTO • BUCCIGROSSI, MICHELLE • BUCHAN, BARB • BUCHANAN, ALBERTA • BUCHANAN, ALICE • BUCHANAN, CHRISTOPHER • BUCHANAN, GLORIA • BUCHANAN, JENNIFER • BUCHANAN, MAXINE • BUCHANAN, RUSSELL • BUCHANAN, SUSAN • BUCK, KARIN • BUCK, MARIA • BUCK, STEPHANIE • BUCKLAND, PAMELA • BUCKLAND, ROBERT • BUCKLAND, WHITNEY • BUCKLEY, ERIN • BUCKLEY, JIM • BUCKLEY, STEPHANIE • BUCKMASTER, MATT • BUCKMASTER, REBECCA • BUCKNER, PAUL • BUCKNER, SCOTT • BUCKNER, STEPHEN • BUDAY, JENNIFER • BUDD, PERRI • BUDKA, CHRISTINE • BUECHLE, LEE • BUELL, R • BUERGER, LYNN • BUETTNER, DIERDRE • BUFFINGTON, LINDA • BUICE, KATIE • BUICE, LAWANNA • BUIST, ALICE • BUK, ANNETTE • BULLOCK, JANELLE • BUNEK, EMIL • BURCH, JAKE • BURCHETT, CAROL • BURCHETT, LARRY • BURCHETTE, JOE • BURDEN, LANI • BURDEN, SARAH • BURDETT, RICHARD • BURDETT, VELVET • BURDETTE, ASHLEY • BURDETTE, BILLY • BURDETTE, FREDERICK • BURENTTE, FATE • BURGE, ANNA • BURGER, SHERYLE • BURGESS, ANGELIA • BURGESS, BARBARA • BURGESS, BOB • BURGESS, CHRIS • BURGESS, DUQUOIN • BURGESS, SHARON • BURGESS, VERONICA • BURGIN, KELLY • BURHANS, LAURA • BURIEL, LIZ • BURING, RALPH • BURK, BOBBI • BURKE, AKEISHA • BURKE, BETHANY • BURKE, CATHARINE • BURKE, DOROTHY • BURKE, ELIZABETH • BURKE, NEAL • BURKE, JENERO • BURKEL, ARCHIE • BURKEL, JOHN • BURKHALTER, JAMES • BURKHART, BILLY • BURKHOUR, CINDY • BURLEIGH, LINDA • BURLING, DOUGLAS • BURNAUGH, BRIAN • BURNETT, AL • BURNETT, BARBARA • BURNETT, BETTY • BURNETT, CYNTHIA • BURNETT, G • BURNETT, RODNEY • BURNETT, SYLVIA • BURNETTE, ANGIE • BURNETTE, LEE • BURNS, ALICEN • BURNS, BOB • BURNS, DIANNE • BURNS, ELBERT • BURNS, GRETTA • BURNS, JIM • BURNS, JODY • BURNS, JONATHAN • BURNS, JOY • BURNS, LILLIE • BURNS, SHARRON • BURNS, STEPHANIE • BURNS, VIVIAN • BURNS-JENKINS, MIRIAM • BURNSIDE, ROSIE • BUROKER, RACHEL • BURR, BOB • BURR, MELISSA • BURRASCANO, MICHAEL • BURRELL, TOM • BURRIS, ELWIN • BURROUGHS, BRENDA • BURROUGHS, CAROL • BURROWS, JASON • BURROWS, NADINE • BURSTEIN, MICHAEL • BURTON, ADAM • BURTON, BARBARA • BURTON, EMILY • BURTON, GARY • BURTON, HELEN • BURTON, HOLLY • BURTON, JACKIE • BURTON, MARILEA • BURTON, MELBA • BURTON, NORMAN • BUSBEE, DONNA • BUTLER, STEPHANIE • BURY, PATTY • BURY, PHILLIP • BUSBY, MERRELL • BUSBY, TOMMY • BUSH, ANGELA • BUSH, DONNA • BUSH, JACK • BUSH, PHIL • BUSH, VICKIE • BUSING, DEBRA • BUSING, JOHN • BUSING, RYAN • BUSKEY, DAWN • BUSTOS, LOU • BUTHORN, JAMIE • BUTLER, DAWN • BUTLER, GLORIA • BUTLER, HERB • BUTLER, JACKIE • BUTLER, MARILEA • BUTLER, MIKE • BUTLER, NORMAN • BUTLER, RICHARD • BUTLER, SUE • BUTLER, TERRI • BUTTREY, DONALD • BUTTREY, RICK • BUTTS, GLADYS • BUTTS, MIKE • BUTTS, PAMELA • BUTTS, SALLY • BUXTON, TONI • BYARD, MILTON • BYARS, ELEANOR • BYBEE, ERIC • BYBEE, J • BYERS-GRANITO, KIM • BYESS, BRENDA • BYNUM, GORDON • BYNUM, NADINE • BYRD, EDWARD • BYRD, LISA • BYRD, SCOTT • BYRD, VANESSA • BYRNE, CATHERINE • BYRNE, CHRYSTI • BYRNE, JOSEPH • BYRNES, MARTIN • CABRAL, DANIEL • CADDIS, DONNA • CADENHEAD, CLARENCE • CADWALLADER, ROBYN • CADY, LOIS • CADY, STEVEN • CAGE, JASON • CAGLEY, DENISE • CAIACCIO, CAROL • CAIN, FRANCIS • CAIN, JOHN • CAIN, SHANNON • CALDERON, CESAR • CALDWELL, CLARE • CALDWELL, MARILYN • CALDWELL, MELVIN • CALHOUN, EUGENE • CALHOUN, CRAIG • CALHOUN, DEBRA • CALHOUN, MARCUS • CALHOUN, UELLA • CALISE, JIM • CALIX, LEONARD • CALL, EVAN • CALLAHAN, BRYANT • CALLAHAN, CARY • CALLAHAN, CHRISTY • CALLAHAN, JACQUELINE • CALLAN, CANDANCE • CALLAWAY, HELEN • CALLAWAY, JANET • CALLAWAY, JEAN • CALLAWAY, RAYMOND • CALLEN, ASHLEY • CALLEN, FRANCES • CALLOWAY, CAROLINE • CALLOWAY, DOROTHY • CALLOWAY, JIMMY • CALMES, ERIC • CALVANO, PETER • CALVERT, SEMMES • CAMELA, SARAH • CAMP, BETTY • CAMP, JAMES • CAMP, LINDA • CAMP, LYNN • CAMP, SHEILA • CAMPANARO, BOBBIE • CAMPBELL, CATHY • CAMPBELL, DAVID • CAMPBELL, ELLEN • CAMPBELL, JEAN • CAMPBELL, JENNIFER • CAMPBELL, JIM • CAMPBELL, JON • CAMPBELL, JULIE • CAMPBELL, KATHRYN • CAMPBELL, MABLE • CAMPBELL, MILTON • CAMPBELL, NANCY • CAMPBELL, SHANNON • CAMPBELL, SHERRIE • CAMPBELL, WILLIAM • CAMPER, NIXON • CAMPION, LYNN • CAMPOS, MELVIN • CANADA, ANITA • CANADY, BILL • CANADY, SUE • CANADY, WALTER • CANNON, AUDREY • CANNON, CONNIE • CANNON, MARIRUTH • CANNON, RICHARD • CANNON, RICHARD • CANNON, STEVEN • CANTERBURY, BENJAMIN • CANTRELL, BRIANT • CANTRELL, JILL • CANTRELL, SARAH • CANTRELL, VANCE • CANTRELLE, DON • CANTWELL, SHARON • CAPERTON, KATHERINE • CAPO, CHRIS • CAPONE, LEA • CAPPS, CATHERINE • CARASI, SILVINA • CARD, DOT • CARD, SHAWN • CARDOSO, MARCELA • CAREY, JOHNNIE • CARINO, JOSEPHINE • CARISLE, ERIC • CARLEY, BETH • CARLEY, CAROLINE • CARLIN, STEWART • CARLISLE, JAMES • CARLISLE, KEE • CARLISLE, LINDA • CARLISLE, WAYNE • CARLOUGH, PETER • CARLSON, JOHN • CARLSON, JOHN • CARLSON, SHAWN • CARLSON, JOHN • CARLTON, RENAE • CARMACK, IKE • CARMICHAEL, DELENA • CARMICHAEL, HARRY • CARMICHAEL, SHAUNDRAE • CARNES, HARRIET • CARNES, TERRY • CARNEY, BILL • CAROLLO, LISA • CARPENTER, MARK • CARPENTER, MIKE • CARPENTER, PAT • CARPENTER, STEPHANIE • CARPER, JEFF • CARR, ADAM • CARR, DEBRA • CARR, LISA • CARR, ROBIN • CARR, SUSIE • CARRAWAY, BRUCE • CARRERE, RONALD • CARROLL, GERRY • CARROLL, JENNY • CARROLL, JOHN • CARROLL, JOHN • CARROLL, KELLI • CARROLL, LINDA • CARROLL, RONALD • CARROLL, SUSAN • CARROLL, YOLANDA • CARROW, ALLISON • CARSON, CANDY • CARSON, CANDY • CARSON, ERIC • CARSON, KELLY • CARSON, SUZY • CARSTARPHEN, SHEILA • CARSWELL, DELLA • CARSWELL, WANDA • CARTER, ADRIAN • CARTER, ALLISON • CARTER, ARTHUR • CARTER, ATLENA • CARTER, BEN • CARTER, BRYAN • CARTER, CARLA • CARTER, CAROLE • CARTER, CHARLES • CARTER, CHIP • CARTER, COLLEEN • CARTER, CYNTHIA • CARTER, DAVID • CARTER, DEBORAH • CARTER, DON • CARTER, DOROTHY • CARTER, EVELYN • CARTER, GESINA • CARTER, IRENE • CARTER, JACQUELINE • CARTER, JOHN • CARTER, JOY • CARTER, JUANITA • CARTER, JULIETTE • CARTER, KATHERINE • CARTER, KEISHA • CARTER, MICHAEL • CARTER, NAT • CARTER, NICK • CARTER, SUSAN • CARTER-STINSON, M • CARTLEDGE, GRACE • CARTWRIGHT, DOUGLAS • CARUSO, CHRISTY • CARUSO, RICK • CARWILE, ALLISON • CASABONNE, HOLLY • CASAJUANA, ALEXIS • CASAJUANA, JOAQUIN • CASANOVA, CHRISSY • CASANOVA, DAVID • CASE, LYNDA • CASEY, ANGELA • CASEY, FITE • CASEY, MOLLY • CASEY, SANDRA • CASH, SANDY • CASH, SONJA • CASILLO, JASON • CASILLO, ROBIN • CASIMIR, TERRY • CASON, LONNIE • CASPERSEN, WAYNE • CASS, CARRIE • CASTEEL, FRED • CASTEEL, MICHAEL • CASTEJON, CARLOS • CASTLE, ELIZABETH • CASTLEBERRY, CLIFF • CASTLIN, BELINDA • CASTRO, AFONSO • CASTRO, LOUIS • CASTRO, MARLON • CASTRO-SCHNEIDER, SIEGLINDE • CASTRUCCI, BRIAN • CATCHINGS, CATCH • CATER, GINA • CATES, PHIL • CATO, KATE • CATO, LESLIE • CATO, MARCIA • CATO, RENEE • CATO, VERNICE • CAUDILL, BRADLEY • CAUTHEN, LEIGH • CAVALLARO, JOE • CAVALLO, MEGAN • CAVANAGH, VERONICA • CAVANAUGH, JOHN • CAWTHORNE, WINIFRED • CEBULA, LOUISE • CECIL, AMY • CECOGNA, BEA • CEJA, SERGIO • CELO, KATHY • CEMBOR, BRIAN • CERAVOLO, MARK • CERDAS, JAVIER • CERISOLES, HERVE • CERISOLES, TERRY • CESARI, COURTNEY • CHAAPEL, CHADWICK, RONALD • CHADWICK, MELANIE • CHAE, JESEUNG • CHAFFIN, ANNETTE • CHAMBERLIN, GEORGE • CHAMBERS, ANNIE • CHAMBERS, CYNTHIA • CHAMBERS, JOHN • CHAMBERS, MEG • CHAMBERS, ROOSEVELT • CHAMBERS, TINETTE • CHAMBERS, YOLANDA • CHAMP, KATHLEEN • CHAMPAGNE, KAREN • CHAMPLAIN, CATHY • CHAN, BRINDISI • CHAN, JOHN • CHAN, MICAH • CHANDLER, BETH • CHANDLER, DAN • CHANDLER, DAVE • CHANDLER, DEAN • CHANDLER, ERICK • CHANDLER, JENNIFER • CHANDLER, JULIE • CHANDLER, MACK • CHANDLER, PAIGE • CHANDLER, PENNY • CHANEY, PERRY • CHANG, AI-WEN • CHAPIN, JESSIE • CHAPLES, KEVIN • CHAPLIN, VIRGINIA • CHAPMAN, ASHLEY • CHAPMAN, CAMPBELL • CHAPMAN, DONNIE • CHAPMAN, LYNDA • CHAPMAN, MARILYN • CHAPMAN, NANCIE • CHAPMAN, SARA • CHAPMAN, TIM • CHAPMAN, WAYNE • CHAPPELL, TOMIKA • CHAPPUIS, JAMES • CHARD, GIL • CHARD, JUNE • CHARETTE, DONNA • CHARLES, GINA • CHARLES, JOHN • CHARNEY, ADAM • CHARUK, GEORGE • CHASTAIN, ANN • CHASTAIN, PAULA • CHASTAIN, THOMAS • CHATTERTON, ANNE • CHATTIN, JOHN • CHATTIN, NANCY • CHAUHAN, RAJ • CHAVDA, JAYMEN • CHAVERS, AUSTINA • CHAVEZ, DANNY • CHAVEZ, FRANCISCO • CHEASTY, CATRIONA • CHEE-AWAI, RONALD • CHEN, D • CHEN, DANNY • CHEN, HUI-CHENG • CHEN, KIM • CHEN, TIM • CHENEVERT, AISHA • CHENG, DAI-LIN • CHENG, NITA • CHERMAN, DESIRAE • CHERMAN, MARISA • CHERRY, CHARLES • CHERRY, DORCUS • CHERRY, WAYNE • CHESHIRE, ROBERT • CHESKES, SILVIA • CHESNES, COLLEEN • CHESTER, GLADYS • CHEYNEY, MARGARET • CHIAPPE, LORI • CHILAZI, CLAIRE • CHILCUTT, JEFF • CHILD, MARTHA • CHILDERS, CHARLIE • CHILDERS, STEPHANIE • CHILDRESS, MARILYN • CHILDS, TUWANDA • CHILIMIGRAS, PANORITA • CHIN, RICHARD • CHIN-A-FOENG, GERARD • CHING, PAMELA • CHINIK, II • CHINNERY, TESS • CHISHOLM, JANE • CHISHOLM, WANDA • CHIU, JULIE • CHLOTGAOUER, ED • CHO, ANNA • CHOATE, DOREEN • CHOATES, BETTY • CHOO, JUANNY • CHOU, JOYCE • CHRANOWSKI, DEBBIE • CHRISHON, ROBBIE • CHRISTENSEN, LORI • CHRISTIAN, CHARLOTTE • CHRISTIAN, CHRISTI • CHRISTIAN, NEAL • CHRISTIAN-VAUGHN, ANGELA • CHRISTIE, GREG • CHRONIC, CATHY • CHRONISTER, MICKIE • CHUMLEY, APRIL • CHUNG, JOHN • CHUNG, MINGHAN • CHURCH, DAVE • CHURCH, JEFFREY • CHURCHES, DAVID • CIABATTONE, VINCE • CICHONSKI, ANA • CICOGNA, BEA • CICOLA, KERRI • CIELEC, JENNIFER • CIGANEK, DAVID • CIRINO, DONALD • CISCO, ADRAIN • CITCHIE, PATRICK • CIVETTA, NANCY • CLAIR, CAROL • CLAMON, CATHRINE • CLARK, ARTHUR • CLARK, BEAU • CLARK, BRANDON • CLARK, BRANDY • CLARK, CALVERT • CLARK, DANNO • CLARK, DEIDRE • CLARK, DEL • CLARK, DOROTHY • CLARK, EDWARD • CLARK, GARY • CLARK, JAMES • CLARK, JUDY • CLARK, KATHERINE • CLARK, KENNETH • CLARK, MARY • CLARK, PETER • CLARK, PHOEBE • CLARK, ROBERT • CLARK, ROBERT • CLARK, ROD • CLARK, ROSIE • CLARK, SONJA • CLARK, STACIE • CLARK, TAMMY • CLARK, VELMA • CLARK, VICKIE • CLARK, ZAN • CLARK-WHITLOCK, LECLARA • CLARKE, GORDON • CLARKE, LOYAL • CLAY, ARBAR • CLAY, BRADLEY • CLAY, DAVID • CLEAVELAND, MELISSA • CLEAVES, BRADFORD • CLEAVES, HENRY • CLEMENS, SHARI • CLEMENTS, VIRGINIA • CLEMONS, PAT • CLEMMONS, TIMOTHY • CLEMONS, TROY • CLEVELAND, JUDITH • CLEVELAND, THOMAS • CLIFTON, ALVIN • CLIFTON, BECKY • CLIFTON, RAE • CLIFTON, RITA • CLIFTON, TRACY • CLINE, JOHN • CLINKENBEARD, JEANNIE • CLISSOLD, GENEVIEVE • CLOCK, KAREY • CLOMAN, TANZANIA • CLOPPER, BEN • CLOSE, CHRISTOPHER • CLOSE, LINDA • CLOSE, OLIVIA • CLOUD, MICHELLE • CLUES, SAM • CLUNIE, RAYMOND • CLYCE, CHRISTINA • CMIEL, KEVIN • COAKLEY, SCOTT • COAN, NORA • COATES, LINDA • COBB, ALISON • COBB, AMY • COBB, CARLTON • COBB, FRANCES • COBB, JUDY • COBB, PATTY • COBERLY, DANIELLE • COCHRAN, ANNE • COCHRAN, BELINDA • COCHRAN, CAROLYN • COCHRAN, KEN • COCKERHAM, CLIFFORD • COCKERHAM-BISCH, TARA • CODDINGTON, KAYE • CODY, JOCE • CODY, ANN • COE, TRICIA • COFFEE, LISA • COFFEL, BETTY • COFFEY, DIANE • COFFMAN, RAYMOND • COHELEACH, JOHN • COHELEACH, LINDA • COHELEACH, ROBERT • COHEN, JASON • COHEN, JUDY • COHEN, MARK • COHEN, PATRICIA • COHEN, RICHARD • COHOON, MEREDITH • COHORST, KATIE • COILE, HAZEL • COKER, PAUL • COLAVITA, CHRISTINE • COLBATH, JEFFREY • COLBERT, BRIDGET • COLBERT, GARY • COLCOCK, ANGELE • COLE, BRUCE • COLE, EDDIE • COLE, J • COLE, JUDITH • COLE, MITCHELL • COLE, SAMUEL • COLE, TERESA • COLEMAN, JAMES • COLEMAN, KELLY • COLEMAN, KIM • COLEMAN, KYLE • COLEMAN, LEANNE • COLEMAN, MARCHELL • COLEMAN, ROBERT • COLEMAN, SHANELLE • COLES, TERENCE • COLESANTI, BOB • COLLANDER, KEVIN • COLLANDER, NANCY • COLLIER, LISA • COLLIER, MARY • COLLIER, WARREN • COLLINGTON, MARTIN • COLLINS, ALICE • COLLINS, BRIAN • COLLINS, CHRISTINE • COLLINS, CINDY • COLLINS, DAN • COLLINS, DAVE • COLLINS, DICK • COLLINS, GARY • COLLINS, JAMES • COLLINS, JEN • COLLINS, JERRY • COLLINS, JODI • COLLINS, JOE • COLLINS, LINDSEY • COLLINS, MICHAEL • COLLINS, RAYMOND • COLLINS, SHAUN • COLLINS, SHEREE • COLLINS, STEPHANIE • COLLINS, STEVE • COLLINS, TOM • COLLINS, WESLEY • COLWELL, PAIGE • COLYN, TANYA • COMBS, DEBBIE • COMER, HOLLY • COMER, SALLY • COMERFORD, ROBERT • COMERY, ELAINE • CONAWAY, DAVID • CONCEPCION, EMILY • CONDON, DEB • CONDUFF, BUDDY • CONINE, DIANE • CONKLIN, NOREENA • CONLEY, ALLY • CONLEY, JOHN • CONLEY, RICHARD • CONLEY, WILLIAM • CONLON, SUSANNE • CONN, KELLY • CONN, MICHAEL • CONNELL, KATE • CONNELLY, DALEY • CONNER, AMANDA • CONNER, CONSUELO • CONNER, DIANA • CONNER, KELLY • CONNER, PENNY • CONNOLLY, TOM • CONNOR, KERRY • CONNORS, PATRICK • CONRAD, MARLENE • CONROY, GERRY • CONSOLINI, TAMMI • CONSOLINI, TRACI • CONTI, KIM • CONTI, RICHARD • CONWAY, PAM • COOGAN, KATHI • COOK, ARTHUS • COOK, BEN • COOK, CHARLES • COOK, DEBBIE • COOK, DEEANNE • COOK, EDWARD • COOK, ERIC • COOK, IVERSON • COOK, LINDA • COOK, LISA • COOK, LYNDA • COOK, MAREICE • COOK, SANDRA • COOK, SHANE • COOK, TAMIE • COOK, TARA • COOK, TONYA • COOK, TYSAUN • COOK, WHITNEY • COOKS, APRIL • COOKS, CARLA • COOKS-HILL, ORA • COOLEY, AMY • COOLEY, SHIROD • COOLS, AONNA • COOMBS, MARY • COONEY, JIM • COOPER, AARON • COOPER, ANGELA • COOPER, BRIAN • COOPER, BUD • COOPER, CAROL • COOPER, DONNA • COOPER, JENNY • COOPER, MELISSA • COOPER, PATRICIA • COOPER, PRESHIOUS • COOPER, ROBERT • COPE, CHARLES • COPE, DEBBIE • COPE, JOHN • COPE, KARI • COPELAND, ANGIE • COPELAND, INGA • COPELAND, JULIE • COPELAND, YOLANDE • COPES, KEN • COPPOLA, NICHOLAS • CORBETT, SCOTT • CORBETT, MEREDITH • CORBETT, VERA • CORBITT, AMBER • CORBITT, GWENDOLYN • CORCORAN, JESSICA • CORDELL, RON • CORDES, CARL • CORK, CHAD • CORK, SANDRA • CORKRAN, JULIUS • CORNELL, DEE • CORNELL, JESSE • CORNWELL, BRIAN • CORRAL, ERNEST • CORTES, CHRISTINA • CORTES, IRIS • CORTES, IVAN • CORTES, YOLANDA • CORTEZ, BECKY • COSSEL, ANTHONY • COSTELLOE, MARGARET • COSTLOW, WILLIAM • COTTER, MIKE • COTTON, SARAH • COUCH, SYBIL • COUEY, NICOLE • COUGHLIN, COLLEEN • COULTER, STEPHANIE • COULTER-O'BERRY, COLLEEN • COURSE, JULIE • COURTENAY, KIRK • COURTNEY, ANN • COURTNEY, KIM • COURTNEY, YOLANDA • COUSINS, ALLEN • COUSLIN, MELINDA • COUTCH, BRIAN • COUTURIER, SHEILA • COWAN, ANTHONY • COWANS, RICKY • COWARD, LOREN • COWARD, STEPHEN • COWART, PAT • COWLES, JOHN • COWN, PAMELA • COX, CHARLIE • COX, DENNIS • COX, FELICIA • COX, MALISSA • COX, MARTHA • COX, MARY • COX, ONDREA • COX, RITA • COX, STACY • COX, TANYA • COX, TYRONE • COYLE, CYNDEE • COYLE, JACK • COYLE, LORRAINE • CRABTREE, LEE • CRABTREE, ROB • CRADDOCK, RODNEY • CRAFT, GARY • CRAIG, DONALD • CRAIG, HEATHER • CRAIG, MELANIE • CRAIG, TIM • CRANDELL, DAVID • CRANE, FREDA • CRANE, NATHAN • CRANFORD, HEATHER • CRAST, BILL • CRATON, CHRISTINA • CRAVENS, PAT • CRAWFORD, BRENDA • CRAWFORD, HELEN • CRAWFORD, LAURA • CRAWFORD, LUNCINO • CRAWFORD, MARY • CRAYTON, CHARYLENE • CRAYTON, SHERRY • CREECH, CHRIS • CREECH, VANESSA • CREEL, SUSAN • CRESCIMBENI, JAYNE • CREVIER, ROBERT • CREWS, BETTY • CREWS, KIMBERLY • CRIGLER, MELANIE • CRISP, KIM • CRITCHFIELD, BRENT • CRITES, DAVID • CROCHET, DONALD • CROCKETT, ANDY • CROCKETT, DALE • CROCKETT, KELLI • CROCKETT, SANDEE • CROMARTY, LEXY • CROMER, SANDI • CRONIC, DANNY • CRONIN, CHARLES • CRONIN, DIANA • CRONIN, GAYE • CRONIN, MARGARET • CRONIN, TODD • CROPPER, MIKE • CROSBY, SHIRL • CROSBY, SUZANNE • CROSS, CHRISTINA • CROSS, FRANK • CROSS, GINA • CROSS, PAM • CROSS, RITA • CROSSLAND, KATY • CROSSLAND, MARY • CROSSLEY, KELLY • CROUSE, AMY • CROUSE, DONNA • CROUSE, LAURA • CROW, ANDREW • CROW, ANTHONY • CROWDER, JARED • CROWE, JAMIE • CROWE, LYN • CROWE, PAT • CROWE, SAM • CROWLEY, CATHY • CROWLEY, FELICIA • CROWSON, WILLIAM • CRUMPTON, LISA • CRUZ, ELAINE • CRUZ, GLORIA • CRUZ, LARA • CRYOR, SHARON • CSICSILA, JENNIFER • CUDD, CARMEN • CUDDIHY, JOE • CUDDY, AL • CUDDY, KATHRYN • CUDMORE, ART • CULBERSON, BRIANNA • CULBREATH, CARLOS • CULLEN, CHRISTIAN • CULLEN, JULIE • CULLEY, RUTH • CULLINAN, TIMOTHY • CULP, CAROL • CULP, SHARON • CULP, TERRY • CULVER, RICK • CUMBERBATCH, CARLEEN • CUMBIE, MICHAEL • CUMMING, JIM • CUMMINGS, AYESHA • CUMMINGS, JACK • CUMMINGS, JOHN • CUMMINS, TAMMY • CUNHA, ROBERT • CUNIC, ANNE • CUNNINGHAM, BOB • CUNNINGHAM, CLARISSA • CUNNINGHAM, GRACE • CUNNINGHAM, KEVIN • CUNNINGHAM, MICHAEL • CUNNINGHAM, VERDERY • CUPPLES, SHIRLEY • CURCIO, BARBARA • CURETON, JAMES • CURL, JACK • CURNYN, MARY-ELLIN • CURRIE, RAB • CURRY, MARGIE • CURRY, MICHAEL • CURRY, REGINALD • CURRY, REGINALD • CURRY, REGINALD • CURTI, FRANK • CURTIS, BROOKE • CURTIS, SHERRIE • CURTIS, TERRY • CURTISS, FRANCES • CUSHING, JERRY • CUSHING, SANDY • CUTLER, MINDY • CUTRIGHT, JESSICA • CYPHER, GREGORY • CZERWENSKYI, RAISSA • CZERWONKY, BRADFORD • D, DWAYNE • D, JANETTA • D'ADAMO, ANN • D'AMBROSIO, GEORGE • D'AMICO, VICKI • D'ANDREA, JERRY • D'ANDREA, LOIS • D'ANTONIO, CHRIS • D'AURIA, RALPH • D'ZAMKO, CHRIS • DA SILVA, BENEDICTO • DAANE, ANN • DACEY, MARGUERITE • DACHMAN, NELLO • DACOSTA, ROBERT • DAHL, JACK • DAHLSTROM, CARL • DAILEY, MEG • DALE, PETER • DALEY, ROBERT • DALLAS, JIMMY • DALLOUL, FAWZI • DALLOUL, GHASSAN • DALLOUL, ISSAM • DALMEIDA, SU • DALRYMPLE, MIA • DALTON, BETSY • DALY, HANK • DALY, MILES • DANCHETZ, KHRISTINA • DANDRIDGE, JOSHUA • DANFORTH, MICHAEL • DANFORTH, SUSAN • DANIEL, KENDRA • DANIEL, LEE • DANIEL, LEROY • DANIEL, LIZ • DANIEL, MARY • DANIEL, MELISSA • DANIEL, MILLARD • DANIEL, PATRICIA • DANIEL, REBON • DANIEL, RICHARD • DANIEL, STANLEY • DANIELLY, ANTHONY • DANIELS, RONALD • DANIELSON, DEE • DANKEL, CAROLYN • DANKINS, JACQUELIN • DANNEHL, KARL • DANNELLY, KRISTI • DANNEMAN, DALE • DANSBY, SYLVIA • DANTES, ZACHARY • DANTRE, AMY • DANYO, DANIEL • DAO, MO • DAOK, KATHERINE • DARBY, DONNA • DARBY, SAMANTHA • DARLAND, RICK • DARLEY, PAT • DARLING, ALMA • DARLING, ZOE • DARNELL, ROBIN • DARTEZ, FRANK • DARTEZ, WILMA • DASHEVSKAYA, ELLA • DASHEVSKIY, LEONID • DASILVA, TONY • DASTI, SALMAN • DATTLER, JUDY • DAUBE, DIRK • DAUBE, MARY • DAUGHERTY, AMY • DAUGHERTY, FRED • DAUGHERTY, MARTI • DAUGHERTY, RUBY • DAUPHINAIS, NICOLE • DAVENPORT, ALLEN • DAVENPORT, JAN • DAVENPORT, MARC • DAVENPORT, MARILEE • DAVENPORT, SHANNON • DAVENPORT, SONYA • DAVES, JEAN • DAVID, • DAVIDSON, ELEANOR • DAVIDSON, GAIL • DAVIDSON, GLENDA • DAVIDSON, KEITH • DAVIDSON, LAURIE • DAVIDSON, SHARON • DAVIOU, AL • DAVIOU, PAT • DAVIS, AMANDA • DAVIS, AMBER • DAVIS, ANGELA • DAVIS, ANTHONY • DAVIS, ARNITA •

DAVIS, BEVERLY • DAVIS, CAROLYN • DAVIS, CARRIE • DAVIS, CECIL • DAVIS, CHARLES • DAVIS, CHRIS • DAVIS, CHRISTINE • DAVIS, CHRISTOPHER • DAVIS, CLAUDIA • DAVIS, CONNIE • DAVIS, DAPHNE • DAVIS, DEBBIE • DAVIS, DEBORAH • DAVIS, DEE • DAVIS, DEEYA • DAVIS, DONNA • DAVIS, DORIS • DAVIS, DUANE • DAVIS, ELLIE • DAVIS, GLENDA • DAVIS, GLORIA • DAVIS, GRETCHEN • DAVIS, GWEN • DAVIS, HOLLY • DAVIS, IRENE •
DAVIS, JANE • DAVIS, JANELLE • DAVIS, JASON • DAVIS, JENNIFER • DAVIS, JERRY • DAVIS, KAREN • DAVIS, KARL • DAVIS, KATHY • DAVIS, KEN • DAVIS, KENT • DAVIS, KENT • DAVIS, KIM • DAVIS, LETITIA • DAVIS, LILLIAN • DAVIS, LILLIE • DAVIS, LYNN • DAVIS, MARGARETA • DAVIS, MATILDA • DAVIS, MATT • DAVIS, NANCY • DAVIS, PATRICIA • DAVIS, PRISCILLA • DAVIS, REG • DAVIS, RITA • DAVIS, ROBERT • DAVIS,
ROBERT • DAVIS, ROBIN • DAVIS, ROMAN • DAVIS, RON • DAVIS, RUTH • DAVIS, SHAUN • DAVIS, SUE • DAVIS, TIMOTHY • DAVIS, TOMMY • DAVIS, TRESEA • DAVISON, DEBORAH • DAVISON, PAUL • DAVY, GERALD • DAWAN, WESLEY • DAWKINS, BRONWYN • DAWKINS, JANET • DAWSON, DEBORAH • DAWSON, DEMETRIUS • DAY, ELAINE • DAY, GEORGE • DAY, LAURA • DAY, REBECCA • DAY, ROY • DAY, SHAWN • DAYLEY, JOHN • DAY-
LEY, MARIA • DE BARDELABEN, KELLY • DE BOURGOIN, CELINE • DE FOUCAULT, JEAN-MARC • DE JUAN, MANUEL • DE KIEWIT, NEL • DE LOACH, JANICE • DE MELLO, VALERIA • DE SART, MARCI • DEAKINS, KEITH • DEAL, FRANKLIN • DEAMS, JENNIFER • DEAN, CARMELL • DEAN, MARK • DEAN, MIKE • DEAN, RAYMOND • DEAN, TRACEY • DEAN-GILLS, NEACHEILE • DEANGELO, GAETANA • DEAS, HELEN • DEASON, EDWARD • DEATON,
BARBARA • DEBERRY, CHERYL • DEBORD, CORY • DEBOSE, BARBARA • DECAMP, MARCIA • DECARLO, LINDA • DECASTRO, JOE • DECHAINE, DANIEL • DECKARD, ROBERT • DECKER, DAVE • DECKER, ERILYNNE • DECKER, JON • DECKER, LINDA • DECKER, PATRICIA • DECKER, SUE • DECONINCK, FRANKLIN • DECUIR, MARQUETTE • DEEDS, DARRELL • DEEDS, DAVID • DEGUISEPPI, MARIA • DEILY, TIM • DEISENROTH, JOSH • DEIVERT,
RICHARD • DEJESUS, DONNA • DEJONG, WENDY • DEJOURNO, PAMELA • DEKINE, SHERRY • DELAGE, PASCALE • DELAINE, DIANN • DELANO, CHIP • DELAPENIA, LES • DELATORRE, STEPHANA • DELBRIDGE, LARRY • DELEON, CRISTINA • DELEON, RICARDO • DELEOT, KIT • DELGADO, MERCEDES • DELGADO, FERNANDO • DELL, TRACEY • DELL'ORTO, LUKE • DELLING-EISELT, KATHLEEN • DELLINGER, MATT • DELOACH, DARRIN •
DELONEY, JUANZEN • DELORME, MYRIAM • DELROSARIO, JOSE • DEMARCO, MICHAEL • DEMER, JOAN • DEMOSS, STEVE • DEMPSEY, BRENDA • DEMPSEY, PEGGY • DEN, ANNA • DENCKEWITZ, BIRKE • DENNARD, MELANIE • DENNEY, JENNIFER • DENNIS, INETTA • DENNIS, JACKIE • DENNIS, LARRY • DENNIS, TOM • DENNISON, ANN • DENNISON, JOE • DENNISTON, MARY • DENNY, DONNA • DENSTER, MICHELLE • DENT, KIRKLAND •
DENTON, MARCELLA • DEPEW, CARRIE • DEPPEN, DEANNA • DEPROSPERO, CLARICE • DERBES, SHELLY • DEROSA, SERENA • DEROUEN, CRAIG • DERRICHO, ED • DERRICK, MELISSA • DERROW, MARIE • DESBERG, TODD • DESHETLER, DENISE • DESIMINI, DINA • DESIMINI, JOHN • DESKEY, DEREK • DESOUZA, HORACIO • DESPIAU, ZOBEIDA • DESTOMBES, JULIETTE • DEVANE, DON • DEVERA, JOHN • DEWALT, SHERRI • DEWBRE, NORMA
• DEWESE, VICTOR • DEWEY, ANNE • DEWEY, GENE • DEWITT, CLIFF • DEWITT, HOLLY • DEWITTY, GORDON • DEXTER, MARGO • DIAMOND, HEATHER • DIAMOND, JACK • DIAMOND, LEONARD • DIAMOND, MONA • DIAMOND, RUTH • DIAZ, CLOTILDE • DIAZ, DAVID • DIAZ, PABLO • DIBACCO, RACHELE • DICEMBRE, ANNA • DICKERSON, GORDON • DICKERSON, JANET • DICKERSON, JIM • DICKERSON, JOELL •
DICKERSON, JOHN • DICKERSON, RYAN • DICKINSON, JANET • DICKINSON, KAY • DIEHL, MARTY • DIETER, BETH • DIETZ, HARRIETT • DIETZ, KRISTIN • DILBECK, DEBORAH • DILLARD, CLAUDETTE • DILLON, DOROTHY • DILLON, JANA • DILLON, JEFFREY • DILLON, SHAWN • DINEDA, WILLIAMS • DINERMAN, BRIAN • DINICOLA, ALICE • DIOMANDE, DOUTY • DION, KATIE • DIONNE, KENNETH • DIRST, STEPHANIE • DIX, CATHY • DIX, HELEN • DIX,
ROBIN • DIX, SCOTT • DIXON, CAROLYN • DIXON, CEDRIC • DIXON, CHARLES • DIXON, DAVID • DIXON, ELIZABETH • DIXON, ERNEST • DIXON, GUS • DIXON, JESSICA • DIXON, KIM • DIXON, MARGO • DIXON, MEREDITH • DIXON, WILLIAM • DIXON, WILLIE • DIXON-LEWIS, JOANN • DIXSON, ELIZABETH • DLOUGHY, MARIE • DOAN, DIANNE • DOBBINS, DEBBIE • DOBBINS, HENRY • DOBBS, MARGARET • DOBBS, RANDY • DOBBS, TRISH •
DOBROVOLKSKY, SYLVIA • DOCKERY, JAMES • DODGE, CHRISTOPHER • DODGE, EMILY • DODGEN, NANNIE • DODSON, JR • DODSON, LINDA • DODSON, MARY • DOE, ANGELA • DOEVE, ALBERT • DOKEH, JIRO • DOLAN, JIM • DOLAN, KELLY • DOLBEER, ALAN • DOLENSEK, SHARON • DOLEZAL, EMILY • DOLGOPOLOVA, ZHANNA • DOLIN, DAVE • DOLL, ABIGAIL • DOLLAR, DAMASCUS • DOMBY, SARAH • DOMINECK, TEIRRA • DOMINGUEZ,
GRISELDA • DOMVILLE, KEVIN • DONALDSON, CHRISTI • DONALDSON, KAREN • DONALDSON, SANDRA • DONALDSON, SUSAN • DONAT, KIM • DONLAN, STEPHANIE • DONNELL, MAE • DONNELLY, ROYANNE • DONNELLY, WENDY • DONNER, THOMAS • DONNIGAN, ERIN • DONOGHUE, LORA • DOOLEY, BURYL • DOOLITTLE, ASHLEY • DOOLITTLE, DAVE • DORAME, FELIPE • DORCH, CYNTHIA • DOREMIRE, CATHERINE • DORMAN, JUDY •
DORMAN, VINNETTE • DORRIS, DORIS • DORSEY, CURTIS • DORSEY, DEBRA • DORSEY, MICHAEL • DORSEY, SARAH • DOTA, SANDY • DOUCETTE, JENNIFER • DOUGHERTY, CHRISTINE • DOUGHERTY, HELEN • DOUGHERTY, JOHN • DOUGHERTY, PEGGY • DOUGLAS, LARRY • DOUGLAS, MELINDA • DOUGLAS, MONICA • DOUGLAS, SHALANDA • DOUGLASS, ROBERT • DOVER, JOYCE • DOVERS, JUDY • DOW, DAVID •
DOWELL, HENRY • DOWNEY, WILLIAM • DOWNS, MARSHALL • DOWNS, RICK • DOYLE, JULIE • DOYLE, MARY • DOZIER-BRYANT, RENEE • DRAEGER, BURT • DRAGON, RANDAL • DRAHEIM, NANCY • DRAKE, ALISON • DRAKE, BARBARA • DRAKE, DEBORAH • DRAKE, DONA • DRAKE, JANIS • DRAKE, VALDEMAREST • DRAKE, VICKIE • DRECHSLER, LOUISE • DREISZIS, THOMAS • DRESCHER, ALEXANDRE • DRESDNER, MICHAEL • DREW,
COLLEEN • DREW, DENNIS • DREW, DIANE • DREW, GREG • DREWRY, CRISTINE • DREWRY, PEGS • DRISDELL, RUBY • DRISKELL, SHERYL • DROST, ADAM • DROST, ANNA • DRUCKER, NEAL • DRUIN, ERICA • DRUMMOND, DON • DRUMMOND, O • DRYGAS, TED • DUBBELL, LARRY • DUBLIN, GLORIA • DUBOW, CATHRYN • DUBOW, GREG • DUBBELL, LARRY • DUDA, PAUL • DUDA, STAN • DUDLEY, BRIAN • DUDLEY, KATHRYN • DUFFIELD,
MARK • DUGAL, JAMES • DUGIN, TIMOTHY • DUGUAY, JIM • DUJSIK, SEANIE • DUKE, DENNIS • DUKES, CYNTHIA • DUKES, DARLENE • DUKES, JEFFERY • DUKES, JEFFREY • DULANSEY, MARY • DULANY, LISSA • DUMAS, ANDREW • DUMAS, PANDORA • DUMAS, PENNY • DUMBLETON, KEN • DUMMETT, LAVYONE • DUNAHOO, CRYSTAL • DUNAHOO, RAY • DUNAJSKY-BELL, ANITA • DUNBAR, GEORGE • DUNCAN, DAWN • DUNCAN, FRANCES
• DUNCAN, IMOGENE • DUNCAN, JAMES • DUNCAN, JIM • DUNCAN, LEE • DUNCAN, SUZANNE • DUNCAN, SUZANNE • DUNHAM, CHRISTOPHER • DUNLAP, CHRIS • DUNLAP, DORIS • DUNN, CHARLES • DUNN, DIANE • DUNN, GLENDA • DUNN, LINDA • DUNN, MARY • DUNN, MAUREEN • DUNN, STEVE • DUNN, STEVEN • DUNN, WILLA • DUNNIGAN, GARY • DUNPHY, PATRICK • DUNWODY, EMILY • DUPONT, LAURIE • DUPONT, ROBERT •
DUPREE, JERRY • DURAN, JJ • DURAN, JULIO • DURANT, KELLY • DURANT, REGINA • DURANTE, DEANNA • DURDEN, CAROLINE • DURDEN, SESSER • DURDEN, TRACEY • DURDEN, WANDA • DURFEE, KAREN • DURFEE, PAUL • DURHAM, SCOTT • DURHAM, STEPHANIE • DURKEE, KENTON • DUSENBERY, REBECCA • DUTRO, JAIME • DUVERNOIS, ALICE • DWAILEEBE, LAURIE • DWYER, JUDITH • DYAR, SANDY • DYE, CANDIA • DYE, DAVID •
DYE, MARILYNN • DYER, ALIX • DYER, ELLA • DYER, NATE • DYER, NORMA • DYER, SHANNON • DYKES, PERRY • DYLAN, HENRY • DZIEJOWSKI, JENNIFER • EADNUS, LISA • EAD, FAOUZI • EASLIN, PAULE • EALEY, VERONICA • EARLE, MITCH • EARNEST, PATRICE • EASLEY, MARY • EASON, DAVID • EASON, JERRY • EASON, LEIGH • EAST, GARVIN • EASTERLING, BARBARA • EASTERLY, DALLAS • EASTON, DAN • EATON,
FRED • EATON, MIKE • EATON, SCOTT • EBERHART, PIA • EBERLEIN, SANDY • EBERSBACH, PETER • EBERSOLE, GREGORY • EBERWEIN, KELLY • ECHOLS, GREG • ECHOLS, MARTHA • ECKENROD, CAY • ECKERT, BRADLEY • EDDY, • EDELSTEIN, NICHOLAS • EDENBURN, KEVIN • EDGE, BOBBIE • EDGE, DENNIS • EDISON, KARI • EDMAN, SARAH • EDMOND, CHRISTINE • EDMONDS, VIVIAN • EDMONSON, DONNA • EDMUNDS, BETSY •
EDWARDS, AL • EDWARDS, CAROL • EDWARDS, CAROL • EDWARDS, CHUCK • EDWARDS, DAPHNE • EDWARDS, GERALD • EDWARDS, JAMES • EDWARDS, JOHN • EDWARDS, KATHRYN • EDWARDS, LARRY • EDWARDS, LURLEEN • EDWARDS, PATTI • EDWARDS, PHIL • EDWARDS, SONYA • EDWARDS, SUSIE • EDWARDS, TERRY • EDWARDS, WILLIAM • EFFINGER, LAURA • EFFINGER, MILLAR • EGRESITZ, JOE • EHRIG, GAYLE • EHRIG, GAYLEN
• EICHELBERGER, KATHRYN • EIDEX, JEANNE • EIDSON, SYBIL • EIKERMANN, TIMOTHY • EISELT, KURT • EISENHAUER, JOHN • EKLUND, ERIK • EKLUND, JENNIFER • EKTVEDT, MATS • ELANGO, PEGGY • ELDER, LUE • ELDER, ROD • ELDRIDGE, REG • ELEY, JAMES • ELGAR, JIM • ELGART, MARK • ELIE, ED • ELIE, PAT • ELIZONDO, BASILIO • ELLINGER, ANN • ELLINGTON, HEATHER • ELLIOT, ADDIE • ELLIOT, RODNEY • ELLIOT, SUSIE •
ELLIOTT, ALLISON • ELLIOTT, ANGELA • ELLIOTT, CHRIS • ELLIOTT, GINNY • ELLIOTT, HOLLY • ELLIOTT, JACKIE • ELLIOTT, JEANETTE • ELLIOTT, KEISHA • ELLIOTT, MARY • ELLIOTT, ONDREA • ELLIS, KATHERINE • ELLIS, LINDA • ELLISON, FRANCES • ELLISON, SHEA • ELLISTON, CHARLENE • ELLSWORTH, JANNA • ELLWANGER, GREGG • ELROD, JULIANNA • ELSNER, ROBYN • ELSTON, SUSAN • ELTANEY, PERRY • ELWOOD, KENNETH •
EMEOTT, SANDY • EMERSON, SANDY • EMETERIO, BETH • EMMERICH, MARK • EMMERT, VERNON • EMPERT, JOE • ENDERS, JOHN • ENDICOTT, SUSANNE • ENDRES, DAVID • ENGDAHL, ALLYSON • ENGELHARDT, BILL • ENGLAND, CHERYL • ENGLAND, PAMELA • ENGLE, MADONNA • ENGLE, PAUL • ENGLEMANN, FRITZ • ENGLISH, ALEX • ENGLISH, ANN • ENGLISH, DON • ENGLISH, MARY • ENGLISH, SANDRA • ENGLISH, STAR • ENGSTROM,
RYAN • ENHOLM, BOB • ENLOE, STUART • ENOCH, TONYA • EPLEY, DEWAYNE • ERB, HEIDI • ERICKSEN, BETSY • ERICKSON, TRACEY • ERICSON, DEAN • ERNE, KEVIN • ERNST, LORRIE • ERNST, MARYELLEN • ERNST, REBECCA • ERVIN, D • ERVIN, SANTONIA • ERVIN, SILVINA • ERWIN, SUZANNE • ERWIN, VERNA • ESARTIA, KHATIA • ESCALERE, JACQUES • ESCOBAR, ARCADIO • ESCOBAR, JOSE • ESHEE, DARLENE • ESPLANA, MICHAEL
• ESQUEDA, TONY • ESSIENNE, CHRISTINE • ESTEPP, THOMAS • ESTEVEZ, JULIANA • ETHEREDGE, GLORIA • ETTERMAN, MARGE • ETURRALDE, WOODY • ETZLER, KARA • EUBANKS, ELIZABETH • EUBANKS, YVONNE • EUSTIS, BRIAN • EVANGELISTA, ERNESTO • EVANS, ANN • EVANS, BARBARA • EVANS, BRADLEY • EVANS, CAROL • EVANS, CEE • EVANS, DOROTHY • EVANS, JAN • EVANS, JOSEPH • EVANS, MARY • EVANS, NICKY • EVANS,
PATTI • EVANS, ROGERS • EVANS, ZARA • EVATT, DIJ • EVENRUD, ANN • EVERSON, CHRIS • EVICK, LEA • EWALT, JOHN • EWING, CHILLY • EWING, MARGARET • EWING, PETER • EXUM, BENNIE • EYLER, DON • EZEKEL, GARY • FABER, KRISTEN • FABER, LINDA • FACKLER, KEN • FACKLER, MICHELE • FAGAN, SEAN • FAGIN, DAVID • FAGRELL, INGA • FAHRNEY, JAMES • FAIR, MARTHA • FAIRCLOUGH, PATRICIA • FAIRWEATHER, G • FAI-
SON, KAREN • FAKHARIAN, GUS • FAKHARIAN, MARY • FALBO, CHIQUI • FALK, LAURIE • FALLER, DAVE • FALLIGAN, AL • FALLON, CHARLOTTE • FALLON, STACEY • FALLS, KATHRYN • FANIA, CARL • FANK, JILL • FANNING, CLAUDIA • FARAH, KAMAL • FARHIDVASH, FARIBA • FARINA, KRISTINE • FARLEY, COLLEEN • FARMER, ANNETTE • FARMER, ASHLEY • FARMER, JANET • FARMER, JILL • FARMER, VERNA • FARNES, WARREN • FARNSWORTH,
TROY • FARO, KELLIE • FARRELL, BRIAN • FARRELL, CHRISTINE • FARRELL, KATHERINE • FARRELL, MICHAEL • FARRELL, ROBERT • FARRELLY, IRENE • FARRIS, KATH • FARROW, STEVEN • FARWELL, TIM • FASANO, PETER • FAULKNER, LAURA • FAUSTO, FIDEL • FAVA, SHEILA • FAVORS, BENJAMIN • FAY, TERESA • FAZECAS, CARMEN • FEARNEY, SUE • FEARNEY, TIM • FEARS, MICHAEL • FEATHER, DJ • FEDELES, JANET • FEDELL, TIFFANY
• FEDER, KAREN • FEDERAL, MEGAN • FEDEYKO, HOLLY • FEE, GLENN • FEENEY, TONY • FEIR, DEBORAH • FELD, SANDY • FELDKAMP, SUE • FELDMAN, DICK • FELDPAUSCH, LEE • FELLABAUM, MATT • FELTON, DEBRA • FELTS, ANNE • FENNELL, BRIDGIT • FENTON, TRICIA • FERDINAND, TROY • FERGASON, JOHN • FERGASON, KAREN • FERGUSON, ANGIE • FERGUSON, BEN • FERGUSON, BRANDY • FERGUSON,
BRUCE • FERGUSON, CALVIN • FERGUSON, CAROLE • FERGUSON, DAWN • FERGUSON, HELEN • FERGUSON, MARY • FERGUSON, PAUL • FERGUSON, RENAE • FERGUSON, ROSE • FERMIN, SAN • FERNANDES, HELEN • FERNANDEZ, FRANK • FERNANDEZ, RICARDO • FERRARA, LINDA • FERRARA, MIKE • FERRELL, JILL • FETTE, SUZANNE • FETTERMAN, AUDREY • FETTIG, PATRICIA • FEYERLEIM, CHARLOTTE • FICK, RODERICK • FICKE,
CATHY • FICKENWORTH, MICHAEL • FIEDLER, ELAINA • FIELD, DEBORAH • FIELD, JACI • FIELD, MARY • FIELD-TURNER, ROBIN • FIELDS, ANTONIOUS • FIELDS, BILL • FIELDS, DANA • FIELDS, LAURA • FIELDS-PERRY, DOROTHY • FIELDS-RYAN, SHELLY • FIERRO, RICHARD • FIGA, DARYL • FIKE, CATHY • FILART, ROSEMARIE • FILIP, KEITH • FILLON, EMILIE • FILSON, SARAH • FINCHAM, MEGAN • FINCHER, JANICE • FINE, ARIC • FINE, FINE •
FINKELSTEIN, DICK • FINKELSTEIN, MICHAEL • FINKELSTEIN, SUSAN • FINKLE, DOLORES • FINLAY, BRIAN • FINLEY, CHARLES • FINN, ELIZABETH • FINNERAN, MARY • FINNEY, ADRIAN • FINNEY, DARYL • FINNIE, KAREN • FIORENTINO, TONY • FIORESI, MAUREEN • FISCHELS, PEYTIE • FISCHER, AMY • FISCHER, CAROL • FISCHER, ROB • FISCHER, VIRGINIA • FISHCO, W • FISHER, CRAIG • FISHER, DENISE • FISHER, GEORGE • FISHER, JOHN
• FISHER, LINDA • FISHER, STEVE • FITTON, BERNARD • FITZGERALD, DANIEL • FITZGERALD, LINDA • FITZGERALD, MEGAN • FITZGERALD, RHONDALEA • FITZGERALD, ROBERT • FITZGERALD, SHARON • FITZGERALD, TOM • FIYAKSEL, ANNA • FLACK, MARYANN • FLAGEUL, ALEXANDRE • FLAGG, MICHELLE • FLAHIVE, BRENDAN • FLANAGAN, JOEY • FLANIGAN, YETOI • FLATHE, KAREN • FLAVIN, LAURA • FLECKENSTEIN, SCOT • FLEDER,
ANGIE • FLEMING, ANDY • FLEMING, ANNE • FLEMING, CAROL • FLEMING, HARRY • FLEMING, MARY • FLEMING, MATT • FLEMING, NIKI • FLEMISTER, LESLIE • FLEMISTER, WAYNE • FLETCHER, BRYAN • FLETCHER, JENNIFER • FLETCHER, KATHERINE • FLETCHER, KRISTIE • FLETCHER, MARCIA • FLETCHER, MARK • FLETCHER, MARTHA • FLETCHER, REGINA • FLICEK, DIANA • FLICKINGER, ERIC • FLICKINGER, KEN • FLICKINGER, WILLIAM
• FLINDERS, GREG • FLINN, SUZANNE • FLINT, MARLENE • FLINT, ROBERT • FLOERSHEIM, MARCI • FLOM, GARY • FLOOD, BARRY • FLOOD, JONATHAN • FLORENCE, D'JEANNE • FLORENCE, DEBORAH • FLORES, DANIEL • FLORES, MIGUEL • FLOURNOY, DEBORAH • FLOURNOY, VERA • FLOWERS, FERN • FLOYD, FELICIA • FLOYD, LYNN • FLOYD, WILMA • FLYNN, ALAN • FOALE, DEBORAH • FOERDERER, FRANK • FOERSTER, ROBERT •
FOERTSCH, LUISE • FOLEY, JUDITH • FOLEY, LYNDSAY • FOLSOM, DIANE • FOLTZ, RANDY • FONTANILLA, ROBERT • FONTENOT, DAVID • FOOR, JESSICA • FOPPIANO, JUDY • FOPPIANO, LES • FORBES, AL • FORBES, CECILIA • FORBUSH, ROBERT • FORD, ANN • FORD, DEREK • FORD, GERALD • FORD, GUY • FOREMAN, DEBBIE • FORLANDER, DAVID • FORMER, CEPHUS • FORNEK, GERRY • FORNEK, SUSAN • FORNELL, REMEI • FORNERET,
GEORGE • FORNO, TIM • FORNWALT, MARK • FORNWALT, ROBIN • FORRESTER, BETTY • FORRESTER, BRYCE • FORRESTER, JILL • FORRESTER, JON • FORRESTER, PAMELA • FORSYTHE, ERIC • FORT, HEATHER • FORT, MARTHA • FORTE', PATRICIA • FOSKEY, MARILYN • FOSKEY, WANDA • FOSSUM, KYLE • FOSSUM, PAULA • FOSTER, DAPHNE • FOSTER, JOHN • FOSTER, KAREN • FOSTER, KEVIN • FOSTER, LARRY • FOSTER, MARSHALL •
FOSTER, NANCY • FOSTER, NEIL • FOSTER, RITA • FOSTER, SANDRA • FOSTER, WILLIAM • FOTOS, JIMMY • FOTOVAT, KATRINA • FOUNTAIN, ALICEON • FOUNTAIN, JANE • FOUNTAIN, KIMBERLY • FOUNTAIN, PHYLLIS • FOUSHAY, HENREY • FOWLER, ANNA • FOWLER, JO • FOWLER, LAUREN • FOWLER, PATTON • FOWLER, RAY • FOWLER, ROBERT • FOWLER, SUSAN • FOWLER, WANDA • FOX, BETSY • FOX, BRIAN • FOX, DAVID • FOX, TOM
• FOXLEY, KALLE • FRANCHI, FRED • FRANCIS, ANNEMARIE • FRANCIS, BRYANT • FRANCIS, CHARLENE • FRANCIS, KELLI • FRANCIS, LORNA • FRANCIS, RAY • FRANCISCO, SHERMAN • FRANK, JILL • FRANK, M • FRANK, MICHELE • FRANKIEWICZ, MARY • FRANKIEWICZ, RON • FRANKLIN, GAYLE • FRANKLIN, GEOFFREY • FRANKLIN, JANET • FRANKLIN, JASON • FRANKLIN,
KATHY • FRANKLIN, LADARYL • FRANKLIN, MARK • FRANKLIN, THOMAS • FRANKSTONE, SUSAN • FRANSEN, LINDA • FRANSWORTH, KATHLEEN • FRANTZ, MARIA • FRANZEN, CAROL • FRASE, SHARA • FRASER, BARRY • FRAZIER, CLARENCE • FRAZIER, DEDREA • FRAZIER, GARY • FRAZIER, JEANETTE • FRAZIER, LATANISHA • FREDDOSO, JOE • FREDERICK, STEVE • FREEDLAND, AMY • FREED-
MAN, JONATHAN • FREEDMAN, NOAH • FREELAND, NOELLE • FREELAND, TILLIE • FREEMAN, ANTHONY • FREEMAN, BOBBIE • FREEMAN, CORNELIUS • FREEMAN, JAMES • FREEMAN, JAMES • FREEMAN, KAREN • FREEMAN, MELVIN • FREEMAN, PAM • FREEMAN, PEGGY • FREEMAN, REBECCA • FREEMAN, TONYA • FREESEMAN, DAVE • FREESE, ZACH • FRENCH, BEVERLY • FRENCH, LACEY • FRENCH, RONNI • FRERICH, VINCE • FREUND,
JAN • FRIEDENBERG, PAULA • FRIEDERICH, BARBARA • FRIEDLY, ERIK • FRIEDMAN, BRENNAN • FRIEDMAN, DONNA • FRIEDMAN, RUSSELL • FRIEDMAN, SHEILA • FRIENDLY, LATONYA • FRIENDLY, MINNIE • FRIERSON, MICHAEL • FRIESEN, DIANE • FRIESEN, HAROLD • FRIESEN, MARTHA • FRITCHMAN, TRACY • FRITSCH, LINDA • FRITSCH, NEIL • FRITZ, AMANDA • FRITZ, IRMI • FRITZ, JODY • FRITZ, NANCY • FROHLICH, KAITLIN • FROMAL,
KIMBERLY • FRUEND, THOMAS • FRY, JIM • FUCHS, JERRY • FUENTES, ROBERT • FUKAYA, MAKIKO • FULCHER, DOROTHY • FULCHER, RHONWYN • FULD, TONY • FULKERSON, WILLIAM • FULLARD, BARBARA • FULLER, YOLANDA • FULMER, TERRY • FULTON, ANGELA • FUNDERBUNK, LISA • FUNDERBURK, JOHN • FUNDERBURKE, SUE • FUNK, LORA • FURBISH, BARBARA • FURBISH, BILL • FURCHA, JOHN • FURCHA, RAE • FURLAN,
MARCELO • FURLONG, MARILYN • FURTNEY, SUSAN • FURUKAWA, SHINKO • FUSSELL, ALISON • FUTCH, SHELLY • FUTTER, FREDERICK • GAAN, LEIA • GAASCH, DEBBI • GABLE, DEBRA • GABLE, NANCY • GABRIEL, MARY • GADDY, OLLIE • GADE, BILL • GADSEN, SAYL • GAFFNEY, KEISHA • GAFNEA, SARAH • GAGE, JAMES • GAHAFER, LEO • GAILLARD, BILL • GALAZ, JEAN • GALBREATH, PAUL • GALES, JULIA • GAL-
IZIO, LYNDSIE • GALLAGHER, KATE • GALLIPPI, TONY • GALLOIS, PAUL • GALLON, HATTIE • GALLOP, SHELIA • GALLOWAY, JULIE • GAMBLE, CHARLES • GAMBLE, FLORA • GAMBLE, JAN • GAMBRELL, CATHY • GAMMON, STEVEN • GANDY, GORDON • GANN, CAROLYN • GANOE, FRED • GAO, YANSHA • GAON, LESLIE • GARBE, KATHIE • GARCIA, DAVID • GARCIA, DEANNA • GARCIA, DENISE • GARCIA, GROVER • GARCIA, JESUS • GAR-
CIA, MARIA • GARCIA, MARIA • GARCIA, PHILLIP • GARCIA, RAMIRO • GARCIA, SETH • GARDNER, JEFFREY • GARDNER, KAREN • GARDNER, MARIAN • GARDOCKI, VICKI • GARLAND, SUZANNE • GARLAND, TINA • GARNER, ANTHONY • GARNER, GINA • GARNER, JUDI • GARNER, MIKE • GARON, BRUCE • GARRET, ROGER • GARRETT, BESS • GARRETT, BRAD • GARRETT, CHERYL • GARRETT, KRISTY • GARRETT, MICHAEL • GARRETT, REBA
• GARRETT, TANYA • GARRIOTT-WHITE, NOELLE • GARRISON, MARGIE • GARRISON, SHARON • GARRISON, SHARON • GARRISS, SUE • GARRY, JACQUE • GARTON, ANGIE • GARVEY, WILLIAM • GARVIN, PAMELA • GARVIN, SEAN • GARY, KELLEY • GARY, META • GARY, ROD • GASPAROVIC, FRANK • GASTELUM, VICTOR • GASTON, CASSANDRA • GASTON, LISA • GATES, DURLEY • GATES, FLAVIA • GATES, GLENDA • GATES, LORENA • GATE-
WOOD, GEORGE • GATINS, EILEEN • GATLING, DONNA • GATTO, MIKE • GAULKE, JIM • GAULKE, RUTH • GAULT, CHRIS • GAUSE, JEREMY • GAUTHIER, KRISTIN • GAVANT, KELLI • GAVIN, PAT • GAVINI, MAMATHA • GAVZY, MATTHEW • GAY, HILTON • GAY, KEVIN • GAY, MALINDA • GAY, MARY • GAY, PATRICK • GAY, PATTI • GAY, PRECIOUS • GAY, SANDRA • GAY, TERRA • GEARING, CAROL • GEBNAR, CHRISTINE • GEBRIAN, MICHELLE
• GEDDES, CATHERINE • GEE, LOCKHART • GEIGER, ELAINE • GEIGER, EMORY • GEIS, CAROLYN • GEISE, SCOTT • GEISLER, ADAM • GEISLER, FRED • GEISLER, ROBERT • GELLERSTEDT, MARY • GELLMAN, MARCI • GELUSO, NICOLE • GENO, DIANE • GENO, ROY • GEORGE, DEBBIE • GEORGE, DUANE • GEORGE, KAREN • GEORGE, MARKELLE • GEORGE, MEGAN • GEORGE, PATRICIA • GEORGE, THOMAS • GEORGINO, JENNIFER • GER-
GEN, CATHY • GERHARDT, JEFF • GERI, CONNIE • GERKER, BOB • GERMAN, DICK • GERVAIS, KEVIN • GERWICK, BRANDI • GETAHUN, ENDALE • GETTIS, MELISSA • GETZ, PATSY • GHIRARDI, JAVIER • GIAMBO, CINDY • GIANGRECO, BARBRO • GIARDINA, DOMINIC • GIBBS, BARBARA • GIBBS, E • GIBBS, JOHN • GIBBS, KATIE • GIBBS, LOIS • GIBBS, NORWOOD • GIBBS, SYLVIA • GIBILTERRA, STACEY • GIBSON, ANNA
• GIBSON, BARRIE • GIBSON, BRIAN • GIBSON, EMMA • GIBSON, JAMES • GIBSON, JUANITA • GIBSON, LESLIE • GIBSON, TARA • GIERS, WILLIAM • GILBERT, GEORGIA • GILBERT, IVY • GILBERT, LINDA • GILBERT, RAYMOND • GILBERT, REESHEDA • GILBERT, SHERRI • GILBERT, TERRIA • GILBERT, WILLIAM • GILBREATH, MARY • GILES, DANL • GILES, HILDA • GILES, RENEE • GILL, AARON • GILL, ROGER • GILLARD, GWENDOLYN • GILLARD,
SHARIEFF • GILLESPIE, KIMBERLY • GILLESPIE, MIKE • GILLESPIE, VANESSA • GILLIAM, BRIANA • GILLIAM, JONATHAN • GILLIG, MINDY • GILLING, KATHLEEN • GILLIOM, MIKE • GILLIS, PAUL • GILMORE, MILES • GILNER, ABE • GILNER, ANITA • GILNER, CELIA • GILNER, DAWNENE • GILREATH, MELISSA • GINN, CHARLES • GINN, DANA • GIPPNER, PATRICIA • GIPSON, BARBARA • GIRASOLE, GARY • GIROUARD, LEISA • GIRTEN, SANDRA • GIT-
TER, GREG • GIVENS, KATHY • GLADBACH, CHRIS • GLADNEY, JAMES • GLAGOLA, NANCY • GLANTZ, MEG • GLASCO, LISA • GLASCO, RANDI • GLASER, CHERYL • GLASER, KEVIN • GLASER, KIMBERLY • GLASS, CONTESSA • GLASS, DAN • GLASSCOCK, GWYNN • GLASSCOTT, MARTINE • GLATZE, KAREN • GLENN, ALLI • GLENN, BETTY • GLENN, KATRINA • GLENN, MARTHA • GLODOWSKI, NANCY • GLON, NICOLAS • GLOTZBACH, BRIAN
• GLOVER, AZALINE • GLOVER, JANE • GLOVER, SAMPSON • GLOVER, SAMSHIA • GLOVER, STEPHANIE • GLOVER, WILLIAM • GLUCK, JOHN • GLUCK, LAURIE • GLUDE, KELLY • GOAD, RACHELL • GOANS, PAM • GOCHANOUR, AMANDA • GODBEY, SHERRILL • GODDARD, BOBBY • GODDARD, ERIN • GODFREY, ANNIE • GODFREY, SHAWN • GODWIN, JIMMY • GOECKER, ROBERT • GOEMAN, CYNDEE • GOFF, STEPHANIE • GOFTON, LORNA
• GOGOL, CATE • GOGOL, DAVID • GOGOL, NIK • GOHN, JASON • GOINS, RAYMOND • GOKARN, RAJUL • GOLD, MORTON • GOLDBACH, MARIANNE • GOLDBERG, HELANE • GOLDBERG, JEFFREY • GOLDBERG, STEVE • GOLDEN, CARL • GOLDEN, DEBBIE • GOLDEN, KIM • GOLDEN, PATRICK • GOLDEN, SHIRLEY • GOLDENBERG, ROY • GOLDMACHER, JOEL • GOLDMAN, BILL • GOLDMAN, JULIE • GOLDSMITH, CAROL • GOLDSMITH, FAE
• GOLDSMITH, LORI • GOLDSMITH, MARVIN • GOLDSTEIN, ALISON • GOLDSTEIN, BARBARA • GOLDSTEIN, JEFFREY • GOLDSTEIN, MARALYN • GOLDSTEIN, MICHELE • GOLDSTEIN, RICHARD • GOLDWATER, DENNIS • GOMER, JENNIFER • GOMEZ, JOSE • GOMEZ, RENE • GOMEZ-GARCIA, MAGDA • GONSALVES, LASCHUNN • GONZALES, ABEL • GONZALEZ, JUANA • GONZALEZ, RENE • GONZALEZ, XAVIER • GOOCH, SUZETTE • GOOD,
MATTHEW • GOODE, APRIL • GOODMAN, JACQUELYN • GOODMAN, JAY • GOODMAN, WINNIE • GOODNOW, HOLLY • GOODRICH, JULIE • GOODRICH, MARILYN • GOODRICH, TERI • GOODSON, JOSEPH • GOODSON, MICHAEL • GOODSTEIN, BARRY • GOODWIN, HARRIET • GOODWIN, KIM • GOOLSBY, TRESONJA • GORDON, CHERYL • GORDON, JUSTINA • GORDON, NICOLE • GORDON, ROBERT • GORDON, SHERRY • GORDON, THEODORA
• GORDON, XAVIER • GORE, CHARLES • GORE, ROBERT • GORMAN, MARK • GORMAN, PETER • GORMAN, THOMAS • GOSS, JUANITA • GOSSETT, JILL • GOTT, RACHEL • GOTTLIEB, LYDIA • GOTTLIEB, MATTHEW • GOTTLIEB, RHONDA • GOULD, DERRICK • GOULDING, CHARLOTTE • GOULDING, JULIE • GOULDING, RANDOLPH • GOWDER, BEVERLY • GRABOW, DAVE • GRABOWSKI, JOE • GRABOWSKI, PATTI • GRACEY, KATHRYN • GRAF,
TINA • GRAFFEO, KIMBERLY • GRAFFEO, MARK • GRAFTON, JOHN • GRAHAM, BALLARD • GRAHAM, CHARLIE • GRAHAM, CHERYL • GRAHAM, FREDERICK • GRAHAM, LESLEY • GRAHAM, LILLA • GRAHAM, LINDSAY • GRAHAM, MICHAELA • GRAHAM, PAM • GRAHAM, TOM • GRAHAM, TRAVIS • GRAITCER, SAMUEL • GRANAAS, NINA • GRANADOS, HECTOR • GRANBERRY, PAT • GRANGE, MICHAEL • GRANT, H • GRANT, JOY • GRANT,
LINDSEY • GRANT, LOIS • GRANT, PATRICIA • GRANT, ROBERT • GRANT, ROSE • GRANT, WILL • GRANTHAM, CARON • GRASSIN, NOLWEN • GRASSMYER, BARBARA • GRASSMYER, BOB • GRASSMYER, NORA • GRAVELY, SUSAN • GRAVER, ASNE • GRAVES, ANNIE • GRAVES, LEIGH • GRAY, BELINDA • GRAY, JENNIFER • GRAY, LORA • GRAY, MATTHEW • GRAY, MIESHA • GRAY, PATTY • GRAY, SANDRA • GRAY, TERRA • GRAYSON, CYNTHIA
• GRAYSON, ELIZABETH • GREABER, F • GRECO, FLORENCIA • GREELY, GAIL • GREEN, BETTY • GREEN, CLARICE • GREEN, DUANE • GREEN, EMILY • GREEN, JOSEPH • GREEN, KEITH • GREEN, LISA • GREEN, MANERVIA • GREEN, MARIA • GREEN, MARIKO • GREEN, MICHAEL • GREEN, PATRICIA • GREEN, ROSEBUD • GREEN, SANDY • GREEN, STACY • GREEN, STUART • GREEN, SUZY • GREENBERG, LESLIE • GREENBERG, MARILYN
• GREENE, CHRIS • GREENE, FRANK • GREENE, JACQUIE • GREENE, SHARON • GREENE, STEVEN • GREENE, TINA • GREENE, VICTOR • GREENFIELD, SUSAN • GREENING, PATRICIA • GREENWALD, DAVID • GREENWALT, DAVID • GREENWAY, GREG • GREENWOOD, LORRAINE • GREENWOOD, RAELYNN • GREER, LYNDA • GREGG, EMILY • GREGO, DEBORAH • GREGOR, CHARLENE • GREGOR, SUSEEN • GREGORY, ALAN •
GREGORY, ANNA • GREGORY, MONIQUE • GREGORY, SUSAN • GREINER, PAMELA • GRESHAM, APRIL • GRESHAM, LESLIE • GRETH, BONNIE • GREUTERT, ANNETTE • GRIBBLE, DWAYNE • GRIDER, HILLARIE • GRIER, ADAM • GRIER, ELAINE • GRIER, JIM • GRIER, LYNDA • GRIER, ROBERT • GRIER, ROMAN • GRIER-HENDERSON, JACKIE • GRIES, KAREN • GRIFFIN, CAROLYN • GRIFFIN, DAVID • GRIFFIN, ELIZABETH • GRIFFIN, ETTY • GRIF-
FIN, JAMES • GRIFFIN, KATIE • GRIFFIN, MARSHA • GRIFFIN, MARY • GRIFFIN, MATTIE • GRIFFIN, MEGAN • GRIFFIN, SYLVIA • GRIFFIN, TERRY • GRIFFING, PAUL • GRIFFIS, CLAUDIA • GRIFFITH, BARBARA • GRIFFITH, MICHAEL • GRIFFITHS, DEBBIE • GRIGGS, DEANDRA • GRIGGS, TRACY • GRIMES, BOB • GRIMES, GRANT • GRIMES, PEGGY • GRIMES, SHALANDA • GRIMES, TRISH • GRIMSLEY, BARBARA • GRINCE, SCOTT • GRINDSTAFF,
LEONARD • GRINER, KRISTINE • GRINER, THOMAS • GRIS, SAMSON • GRISSOM, SAM • GROAH, SUZIE • GROCER, STEPHEN • GROEZINGER, JILL • GROFF, DIANE • GROH, JEFF • GROOVER, RENEE • GROSS, CLAUDIA • GROSS, FLOYD • GROSS, JESSICA • GROSS, KRISTIN • GROSS, LINDA • GROSSMAN, SUSAN • GROVE, KATHRYN • GROVES, NANCY • GRUBB, SHARON • GRUBBS, JIM • GRUBBS, MEREDITH • GRUEZO, MARIA • GRUIDL,
JOAN • GRUIDL, MARY • GRUSON, KERRY • GUAJARDO, CINDY • GUEHRING, ERIK • GUERIN, LAURA • GUERRIERI, LISA • GUEST, LAURA • GUEVARRA, EUGENE • GUILBAULT, DONNA • GUILLAUMET, JOSEPH • GUILLERMIN, MICHELLE • GULLETT, WAYNE • GULLEY, PAT • GULLY, SAM • GUMMIG, MONICA • GUNN, MARVELETTE • GUNN, RICARDO • GUNNERSEN, DEE • GUNTER, BILLY • GUNTER, JEFF • GUNTER, LARRY • GUNTER, MARTHA
• GUPTA, SUSHMA • GURROLA, THOMAS • GURUCHARRI, KAREN • GUSTAFSON, AMY • GUSTAVSSON, CAMILLA • GUSTIN, LETY • GUSTIN, SALLY • GUSTKE, PAUL • GUTH, THOMAS • GUTHERIE, PETER • GUTHRIE, GLENN • GUTHRIE, MARJORIE • GUTHRIE, REED • GUTIERREZ, ALICIA • GUTIERREZ, TONY • GUTMAN, TRUDY • GUTSCHENRITTER, DOROTHY • GUY, DAN • GUY, VINCENT • GUY, WANDA • HAAS, D • HAAS, KARL • HAAS,
VIRGINIA • HABER, JAN • HABIBI, AZITA • HABIBI, PARISA • HABINA, JOYCE • HADFIELD, CHRIS • HADFIELD, LYNN • HADINGER, MITCHEL • HADLEY, DANA • HAEFELE, MARGARET • HAFER, BONNIE • HAGEN, DAWN • HAGG, RACHAEL • HAHLEN, KAUREL • HAHN, CONNIE • HAILE, ANNA • HAILE, CAROLYN • HAILEY, SHARYN • HAIN, PEGGY • HAIRE, STEVEN • HAIRSTON, SEBASTIAN • HAIRSTON, TERESA • HAJDUK, JAYE • HAJDUK, MARY
• HALASCHEK-WEINER, FRANZ • HALBERT, WILLIAM • HALBIN, KAREY • HALE, ASKIA • HALEY, BRENT • HALKER, TREY • HALL, ANGELA • HALL, ASHLEY • HALL, DONNA • HALL, ELLIE • HALL, HARRY • HALL, HOWARD • HALL, JACQUELINE • HALL, JIM • HALL, KEE • HALL, LAURA • HALL, LISA • HALL, MARK • HALL, MONTAREE • HALL, PAT • HALL, PETER • HALL, PHILLIP • HALL, PHYLLIS • HALL, QUENDALL • HALL, RACHEL
• HALL, RECKAY • HALL, RICHARD • HALL, SHIRLEY • HALL, SUSAN • HALL, SUZANNE • HALL, TIM • HALL, WALTER • HALL-BOYER, KATHY • HALLAM, BRIAN • HALTER, STAN • HALTER, SUE • HALUSKA, PHILIP • HAM, DEBBIE • HAM, RACHEL • HAMANN, AMANDA • HAMBRICK, BETTY • HAMBURGER, DOROTHY • HAMBURGER, MARC • HAMBY, CYNTHIA • HAMBY, JESSICA • HAMBY, KAREN • HAMES, MELISSA • HAMILTON, JUDIE •
HAMILTON, LESLIE • HAMILTON, MARY • HAMILTON, OTHEYA • HAMILTON, ROY • HAMM, BRUCE • HAMM, CHRISTINE • HAMM, ROGER • HAMMANN, LINDA • HAMMELL, JOE • HAMMELL, SHELLEY • HAMMETT, CAROL • HAMMOND, CALVIN • HAMMOND, DIANA • HAMMOND, JESSICA • HAMMONDS, JARVIS • HAMMONTREE, KEN • HAMONTREE, STEVEN • HAMPTON, DONALD • HAMPTON, DOREEN • HAMPTON, JASON • HAMPTON, SHEILA • HAMRE,
SCOTT • HANBERY, GARY • HAMRICK, HEATHER • HAMRICK, LINDA • HAMRICK, PEGGY • HAMRICK, ROBBIE • HAN, DAVID • HAN, ELIZABETH • HAN, HYUN-SUK • HAN, JEANNIE • HANCOCK, JULIE • HANCOCK, PAT • HANCOCK, STEPHANIE • HAND, ASHLI • HAND, HOPE • HAND, JOSEPH • HANEDA, KAZUMASA • HANEVOLD, BARBARA • HANEY, DAMIAN • HANEY, TIFFANY • HANEY, TRACY • HANKINS, SUSAN • HANLEY, KERA • HANLEY
MARCELLO • HANLEY, SEAN • HANN, HEATHER • HANN, KATHY • HANNA, MATT • HANNAN, JOAN • HANSEN, LAURA • HANSEN, MARIANNE • HANSON, CAROL • HANSON, CLARE • HANSON, LISA • HANSON, NANCY • HANSON, TED • HANTHORN, JUDITH • HANZAK, JOHN • HAPE, LYNN • HAQ, FAYYAZ • HARAMALIS, JOHN • HARBER, BETH • HARBER, KATHY • HARBUCK, DON • HARDEN, BETTIE • HARDEN, SHERRY • HARDEN, VALENCIA •
HARDEN, VALERIE • HARDIN, JOE • HARDIN, JOSEPH • HARDIN, MAE • HARDIN, SALLY • HARDISON, KRIS • HARDNEY, MIKE • HARDRICK, RENEE • HARDY, CAROLYN • HARDY, CHERYL • HARDY, HEATHER • HARDY, VALERIE • HARE, ELISE • HARGADON, KELLY • HARKNESS, GEORGE • HARLAND, ANN • HARMAN, AMELIA • HARMAN, KATHY • HARMER, KEVIN • HARMON, ALLEN • HARMON, JULIE • HARMON, MICHELLE
• HARMON, NEIL • HARMS, RON • HARMS, STEPHANIE • HARNER, TAMMY • HARNEY, KEVIN • HARP, ALAN • HARP, STEPHANIE • HARPER, ALLYSON • HARPER, CASEY • HARPER, COREY • HARPER, DEREK • HARPER, JACK • HARPER, JAMES • HARPER, RONALD • HARRELL, BILL • HARRELL, FRAN • HARRELL, JOLENE • HARRELL, MARK • HARRELL, MARTHA • HARRELL, MICHAEL • HARRELL, TRISHA • HARRELSON, JR • HARRIES, JEFF •
HARRINGTON, ROXIE • HARRINGTON, VICTOR • HARRIS, BETTYE • HARRIS, BEV • HARRIS, CEDRIC • HARRIS, CHERYL • HARRIS, DAMIEN • HARRIS, DARNACEA • HARRIS, DARRYL • HARRIS, DEREK • HARRIS, ELLEN • HARRIS, ERICA • HARRIS, EWINA • HARRIS, FRANK • HARRIS, GLEN • HARRIS, HEIDI • HARRIS, IRVING • HARRIS, JAMES • HARRIS, JAN • HARRIS, JANET • HARRIS, JIMI • HARRIS, JOHN • HARRIS, JOYCE • HARRIS, JULIE •
HARRIS, KIKI • HARRIS, KIMBERLIE • HARRIS, LORI • HARRIS, MATTIE • HARRIS, NAKITA • HARRIS, RICHARD • HARRIS, ROSE • HARRIS, SHARONDA • HARRIS, SHARONDA • HARRIS, STANLEY • HARRIS, STEPHANIE • HARRIS, SUKI • HARRIS, SUZETTE • HARRIS, THOMAS • HARRIS, TONI • HARRIS, VIRGINIA • HARRIS, WILLIE • HARRISON, ANSLEY • HARRISON, ANTHONY • HARRISON, CAROLYN • HARRISON, CHERYLE • HARRISON, DEANI •
HARRISON, DENNY • HARRISON, E • HARRISON, ELENA • HARRISON, HARRY • HARRISON, KIMBERLY • HARRISON, LEE • HARRISON, PAULETTE • HARRISON, TERESA • HARSTAD, DAVE • HART, BETH • HART, MARY • HART, MELINDA • HART, NICHOLA • HART, RICH • HART, ROSA • HARTING, JAN • HARTLEY, CYNTHIA • HARTLEY, MISSY • HARTMAN, ELROY • HARTMANN, LISA • HARTSFIELD, VANESSA • HARTWELL, DAREN • HARTZELL,
ANITA • HARUTUNYAN, VAHAN • HARVEL, NATHAN • HARVEY, CHIP • HARVEY, JIMMY • HARVEY, JOYCE • HARVEY, MARIE • HARVEY, NEKO • HARVEY, TODD • HARWOOD, MALLORY • HASHBARGER, ED • HASHBARGER, YORIKO • HASKINS, VIRGINIA • HASSIB, ASHRAF • HASTINGS, ALDEAN • HASTINGS, BRENT • HATCH, CHRISTOPHER • HATCH, DOUGLAS • HATCH, MEREDITH • HATCHER, LORI • HATCHER, MONROE • HATCHER, SHEILA
• HATCHER, TONI • HATFIELD, ANNE-LOUISE • HATFIELD, DIAN • HATFIELD, ROSA • HATHER, STEVE • HATTINGH, JAN • HAUSER, JOANN • HAUSER, KIMBERLY • HAVERTY, JOHN • HAVLAK, SHIRLEY • HAWKINS, DOUGLAS • HAWKINS, J • HAWKINS, LATASHA • HAWKINS, LINDA • HAWTHORNE, LARRY • HAY, DAVID • HAY, TONIQUA • HAYDEN, ROBERT • HAYDEN, SHARON • HAYES, BECCA • HAYES, CHRISTOPHER • HAYES, CHRISTY •
HAYES, DIANE • HAYES, HENRY • HAYES, JENNIFER • HAYES, MARY • HAYES, MELINDA • HAYES, ZACKARY • HAYMON, JAMAL • HAYMON, REGINA • HAYNES, RAMONIA • HAYNES, WILLIAM • HAYWARD, GARY • HAYWOOD, WANDA • HAZEN, DAVID • HAZLETT, DAN • HAZLETT, WILLIAM • HAZLITT, PEGGY • HAZZARD, VIVIAN • HEAD, GILBERT • HEAD, JAIME • HEAD, KRISTEN • HEAD, RENONNA • HEAD, ROSA • HEAD, SHELLY • HEADEN,
TOMMY • HEALEY, THOMAS • HEALY, MARY • HEARD, RANDALL • HEARD, SELERY • HEARN, ANDREW • HEATH, DIANE • HEATH, DORIS • HEATH, ELIZABETH • HEATH, JIMMY • HEATH, JOHNNY • HEBDA, JERRY • HEBDA, SUSAN • HECHT, DAVID • HECHT, EDYTHE • HECKMASTER, SHAUN • HECKSTALL, ANDREA • HEERY, CORIE • HEFFERNAN, BETH • HEFFERNAN, CHRISTOPHER • HEIDT, LAURA • HEIGHTS, DEBORAH • HEIN, MIKE • HEIN
LEIN, JOSEPH • HEINRICH, JERRY • HEINTZ, MARY • HEINTZ, NORM • HEINZE, JOHN • HEINZEN, MALENA • HEISER, SANDRA • HELFERS, DARRIN • HELLEMALM-ASHFIELD, JARL • HELLER, SARAH • HELMICH, RICHARD • HELTON, JAMES • HENDERSON, BETH • HENDERSON, JANEE • HENDERSON, LAVERNE • HENDERSON, MARTHA • HENDERSON, RON • HENDERSON, SUZANNE • HENDERSON, THOMAS • HENDLEY
NEODESHA • HENDRICK, SUSAN • HENDRICKS, ED • HENDRICKS, FRED • HENDRICKS, WILLIAM • HENDRICKSON, CHRISSIE • HENDRICKSON, SHARON • HENDRIX, JASON • HENDRIX, JR • HENDRIX, LAWRENCE • HENDRIX, MARK • HENDRIX, THOMAS • HENEGAN, DORCAS • HENEGAN, KENNY • HENKEL, CAROL • HENKEL, JOHN • HENLEY, EARLIE • HENNEK, DARCI • HENNEK, LYNNE • HENRY, AMY • HENRY, DIANE • HENRY, DYLAN •
HENRY, EMMA • HENRY, GREGORY • HENRY, JOHN • HENRY, KEN • HENRY, KRISTEN • HENRY, KYLA • HENRY, SONJA • HENRY, SUSAN • HENRY, WILLARD • HENSEL, PAULA • HENSON, LINDA • HERBERMANN, JOHN • HERBERT, ANITA • HERBERT, CATHY • HERBERT, MARY • HERBST, MARY • HERHOLZ, JULIE • HERKERT, LORI • HERMAN, EMILY • HERMAN, PHILIP • HERNANDEZ, ELIGIO • HERNANDEZ, MIGUEL • HERNDON, JAMES • HER-
RERA, LEONARDO • HERRING, KAREN • HERRING, NOREEN • HERRLEIN, ROBERT • HERRMANN, SUZI • HERRON, BOB • HERRON, CHARLES • HERRON, KATHLEEN • HERRON, ROSE • HERSEY, SARAH • HERSHEY, MELANIE • HERSHMAN, ROBIN • HERTEL, CINDY • HERZBERG, GARY • HERZBERG, PEGGY • HERZOG, DEBBIE • HERZOG, SARAH • HESLA, THOR • HESS, CINDY • HESS, WILLIAM • HESSEL, EVAN • HESTER, BUD • HESTER,
CHRIS • HESTER, JENNIFER • HESTER, JUANITA • HESTER, LEIGH • HESTER, ROBIN • HETHERINGTON, DEBBIE • HETHERINGTON, DON • HEWITT, PEG • HIAM, PAUL • HIBBS, BETH • HICKEY, CAROL • HICKEY, LAINE • HICKEY, PATRICIA • HICKMAN, AIMEE • HICKMOTT, JOSEPH • HICKS, ALLISON • HICKS, DANETTA • HICKS, KEITH • HICKS, KENNETH • HICKS, LISA • HICKS, MIA • HICKS, ROBERT • HIDLE, ANDY • HIESTAND, TREVOR • HIETT,
BETTY • HIGDON, WYN • HIGGINBOTHAM, GENE • HIGGINS, ANNE • HIGGINS, ELFI • HIGGINS, KEN • HIGGINS, MADONNA • HIGGINS, PATTI • HIGGISON, LYNN • HIGGS, PAUL • HIGHTOWER, CHRIS • HIGHTOWER, DEBBIE • HIGHTOWER, JERRY • HILAIRE, NICOLE • HILDEBRANDT, LUER • HILGER, BRENDA • HILKE, BARBARA • HILL, ANNE • HILL, BETSY • HILL, BOB • HILL, CALVIN • HILL, CAROLE • HILL, CAROLYN • HILL, CYNTHIA • HILL,
DANIEL • HILL, DAVID • HILL, DONALD • HILL, ELOISE • HILL, GREGORY • HILL, JESSIE • HILL, LARRY • HILL, LISA • HILL, LUCILLE • HILL, MATTHEW • HILL, NINA • HILL, NORMAN • HILL, PATRICIA • HILL, SUSAN • HILL, SUSIE • HILL, TERRY • HILL, TIMOTHY • HILL, TONYA • HILLIARD, BARBARA • HILLIARD, JOYCE • HILLMAN, SHARON • HILLMON, CAROLYN • HILLMON, DESIREE • HILLYER, BRENDA • HILOW, CAROL • HILSCHER, SEAN • HIN-
DES, JANINE • HINDMAN, JEAN • HINDSON, LISA • HINERMAN, LISA • HINES, LILANA • HINES, ORLANDO • HINES, PEGGY • HINES, ROBIN • HINES, ROGER • HINES, SHEILA • HINES, TIFFANY • HINGERTY, SUSAN • HINKEL, AMY • HINNANT, NICOLE • HINTON, KIMBERLY • HINTON, VINICE • HIPP, STAN • HIPP, SYBIL • HIRAM, UNIQUE • HIRES, SPENSER • HIRKALA, DAVID • HIRSCH, JOSEPH • HIRSCHHORN, JOEL • HIRSHBERG, MARY • HITCH-
COCK, BARBARA • HITCHCOCK, DONALD • HITCHCOCK, ROGER • HITT, JARROD • HIXON, ALBERTA • HLOTYAK, STEVE • HO, ROSALIND • HO, SHIRLEY • HO, THERESA • HOADE, JIMMY • HOBBS, TAMMY • HOBBS, TOM • HOBSON, KARRI • HOCHGERTLE, DOROTHY • HOCHGERTLE, JAMES • HODGDON, BARBARA • HODGE, CHAS • HODGES, BARRY • HODGES, CAROL • HODGES, KEVIN • HODGES, LISA • HODGES, STAN • HODGKINS,
DENNIS • HOECKENDORF, LENI • HOERZ, KARL • HOFF, MICHAEL • HOFFER, MIKE • HOFFMAN, ANN • HOFFMAN, KARA • HOFFMAN, KAT • HOFFMAN, KRISTEN • HOFFMAN, PAM • HOFFMAN, ROGER • HOFFMANN, JANET • HOFFMANN, SONJA • HOGAN, DENISE • HOGAN, JULIA • HOGAN, THOMAS • HOGE, GAIL • HOGLE, PATI • HOGSED, KEITH • HOHN, JEFFREY • HOLBROOK, COZETTE • HOLBROOK, SALLY • HOLBROOKS, OSEPH • HOLBY,
ALISON • HOLBY, BILL • HOLBY, LANE • HOLBY, STEPHANIE • HOLCOMBE, TONY • HOLDEN, JILL • HOLLAND, BILLIE • HOLLAND, ENA • HOLLAND, JAMEESE • HOLLAND, KEITH • HOLLAND, LISA • HOLLAND, WILLIAM • HOLLAR, SANDI • HOLLEY, FRANCIS • HOLLINGSWORTH, LARRY • HOLLINGSWORTH, LORI • HOLLIS, ADRIENNE • HOLLOMAN, WILLIAM • HOLLOWAY, JOHNSIE • HOLLOWAY, PHYLLIS • HOLLOWELL, BILLY • HOLMAN,
DAVID • HOLMAN, NANCY • HOLMAN, ROBERT • HOLMAN, WILLIAM • HOLMES, CALEB • HOLMES, DIANE • HOLMES, MARIO • HOLMES, SHELLEY • HOLMES, WILLIAM • HOLMGREN, ERIC • HOLTON, DOLLIE • HOLTZCLAW, GRACE • HOLYCROSS, PHIL • HOOD, CHERYL • HOOD, CHRIS • HOOD, GREG • HOOD, JUDY • HOOKS, ERNEST • HOOKS, EVAN • HOOPER, DJ • HOOPER, JASON • HOOPER, MELVIN • HOOTEN, RONNIE • HOOVER, AMANDA • HOOVER,
JIM • HOOVER, SUZANNE • HOPKINS, GABE • HOPKINS, MARILYN • HOPKINS, TRACIE • HOPPER, JASON • HOPPER, JUSTIN • HOPPER, MARGARET • HOPPER, RACHEL • HOPPING, MARGARET • HOPSON, DIANE • HOPSON, LOU • HORAN, SHIRLEY • HORN, CAMI • HORNE, HARVEY • HORNE, JENNIFER • HORNE, KATRINA • HORNE, KELLY • HORNER, CHRISTINE • HORNER, CHUCK • HORNS, ANDREA • HORNSBY, CINDY • HORNSBY, PATTY
• HOROWITZ, JERRY • HOROWITZ, PEARLANN • HORTENSTINE, RAH • HORTON, ACHIM • HORTON, CHRISTOPHER • HORTON, MARCUS • HORTON, NAKIA • HORTON-NAHARI, VICKI • HORVATH, ANDREA • HOSSAIN-ABRAHAMI, ALLIE • HOTCHKISS, STUART • HOUCHINS, DEE • HOUCHINS, TOM • HOUCK, TRACEY • HOUGH, TRUDY • HOUGLAND, RODGER • HOUK, JILL • HOUSE, JOHN • HOUSER, ANITA • HOUSLEY,
LYNNE • HOUSTON, DAVID • HOWARD, BILL • HOWARD, BOB • HOWARD, DEIRDRA • HOWARD, DEREK • HOWARD, GENEVA • HOWARD, JEANETTE • HOWARD, JESSE • HOWARD, JOHN • HOWARD, LEONARD • HOWARD, MONTEZ • HOWARD, NICK • HOWARD, REBECCA • HOWARD, RUBELLE • HOWARD, SARAH • HOWARD, TIM • HOWARD, VAL • HOWE, EMMETT • HOWE, KRISTIN • HOWE, PAUL • HOWELL, CHARLES • HOWELL, CLAIRE
• HOWELL, TODD • HOWETT, CIANNAT • HOWIE, LAWRENCE • HOWSON, TOM • HREN, DOUGLAS • HSIAO, CONNIE • HUANG, ED • HUANG, HAIYING • HUBBARD, CATHY • HUBBARD, SARA • HUBERT, IVEY • HUDDLESTON, JOHNNIE • HUDGENS, DANA • HUDGINS, JAMES • HUDKINS, ALCY • HUDLER, GARRICK • HUDSON, BARBARA • HUDSON, DAVID • HUDSON, ELEANOR • HUDSON, GWEN • HUDSON, JOHN • HUD-
SON, JOHNNIE • HUDSON, KELLY • HUDSON, MALCOLM • HUDSON, MARIANNE • HUDSON, MICHAEL • HUDSON, PAM • HUDSON, PEPE • HUELS, CHUCK • HUFF, WYNNE • HUFFORD, MATT • HUGGINS, DARRYL • HUGHES, ALICE • HUGHES, BETTYEE • HUGHES, BRIAN • HUGHES, DWIGHT • HUGHES, JACK • HUGHES, JIM • HUGHES, LLOYD • HUGHES, TERESA • HUGHES, TERRY • HUGHES, TIFFANY • HUGUELEY, SUZANNE • HUGUENIN,
AYIESHA • HUGUINEA, NIAKESHA • HULL, BETTY • HULL, BURNETT • HULL, HELEN • HULL, MICHAEL • HULL, RALPH • HULSENBECK, CHARLOTTE • HULSENBECK, PAULETTE • HULT, ALLISON • HUMBLES, ANGELA • HUMENANSKY, ADAM • HUMES, RICHARD • HUMPHREY, BRAIN • HUMPHREY, DONDIL • HUMPHREY, ROBERT • HUMPHREY, SUE • HUMPHREYS, FRANK • HUMPHREYS, GARDNER • HUMPHRIES, HARVEY • HUMPHRIES, WENDY
• HUMS, MARY • HUNCZAK, FAY • HUNDLEY, JERRY • HUNKIN, PAULINE • HUNSAKER, CAROL • HUNSINGER, DAVID • HUNT, ADELE • HUNT, CATHY • HUNT, EMANUEL • HUNT, EMMA • HUNT, FREDERICK • HUNT, HARLAN • HUNT, JAMES • HUNT, JIM • HUNT, MELISSA • HUNT, MONIQUE • HUNT, SABRINA • HUNT, SCOTT • HUNT, WYNELL • HUNTER, AMY • HUNTER, CLARENCE • HUNTER, DEE • HUNTER, FRASURE • HUNTER, HELEN •
HUNTER, HELGA • HUNTER, WILLIAM • HUNTZ, KIP • HURFORD, TRISH • HURLEY, ROSLAND • HURSEY, AMANDA • HURSEY, ETHEL • HURSEY, MELISSA • HURST, KAY • HUTCHERSON, HAZELE • HUTCHERSON, MONNORA • HUTCHINGS, GARTH • HUTCHINGS, TODD • HUTCHINSON, BRIAN • HUTCHINSON, JAMES • HUTCHINSON, MARCUS • HUTCHISON, PAULINE • HUTH, SHANNON • HUTSON, VALERIE • HUTTENBACH, LAURA • HUTTEN-
BACH, MARISA • HWANG, STEPHEN • HYATT, TONYA • HYRE, WESLEY • HYSNI, CRAIG • IANDOLI, JOE • IBARGUEN, ALI • IBEBUNJO, NNAMDI • ICKES, TIM • IFFLAND, FRED • II, PHILLIP • II, ROBERT • IIDA, KEITA • III, EDWARD • III, HAWLEY • III, WES • III, WM • IKEMIYA, JUNKO • ILANO, ELI • ILINE, MIKHAIL • ILLES, LILIA • IMAI, KAZU • INGRAFFIA, BRENDA • INGRAHAM, CYNTHIA • INGRAM, EMILY • INGRAM, MARY • INGRAM,
TERESA • INGRAM-COTTRELL, LINDA • INMAN, MARY • IRISH, MITCH • IRMINGER, JILL • IRVER, SHARON • IRVIN, BREE • IRVIN, LINDSAY • IRVING, STELLA • IRWIN, MICHAEL • ISAAC, ANN • ISAACSON, JEAN • ISABEL, LINDA • ISOM, LINDSAY • ISON, GENIE • ISRAEL, CONNIE • ISREAL, ANDREI • ITO, ROBERT • IV, MAURICIO • IVEY, DEBRA • IVEY, WILLIE • IVY, CATHERINE • IWANE, IWANE • IWANE, NORMA • IZA, DEBBIE • JABAL-
TEREK • JABLONOWSKI, ADAM • JABLONOWSKI, ANDREW • JACKSON, ANNIE • JACKSON, AUDRAINE • JACKSON, BENJAMIN • JACKSON, CAROL • JACKSON, CAROLYN • JACKSON, CHERYL • JACKSON, COREY • JACKSON, DAN • JACKSON, DAVID • JACKSON, DONALD • JACKSON, DOUGLAS • JACKSON, ECONOMY • JACKSON, GEORGIA • JACKSON, GLORIA • JACKSON, JACQUELYN • JACKSON, JAY • JACK-
SON, JENNIFER • JACKSON, JOYCELYN • JACKSON, KATRINA • JACKSON, LA • JACKSON, LAURIE • JACKSON, LAURIE • JACKSON, LINDA • JACKSON, LIZ • JACKSON, MATTHEW • JACKSON, MELISSA • JACKSON, NATHANIEL • JACKSON, OMEGA • JACKSON, PATRICIA • JACKSON, PATRICK • JACKSON, RALPH • JACKSON, REGINAL • JACKSON, ROCHELLE • JACKSON, RON • JACKSON, ROZ • JACKSON, SANDRA • JACKSON, SHERRY • JACKSON, SONYA • JACK-
SON, STEVEN • JACKSON, TAMARA • JACKSON, TERRY • JACOBS, DANIEL • JACOBS, JANICE • JACOBS, JIM • JACOBS, JUDITH • JACOBS, LESLIE • JACOBS, PRICE • JACOBS, VICKI • JACOBSEN, PAUL • JACOBSON, ERIN • JACOBSON, KRISTIN • JAFFEE, LOUISE • JAGGER, KRISTEN • JAKUBECY, JEFF • JAMARUSTY, LALENA • JAMES, CARLTON • JAMES, DAVID • JAMES, DEAN • JAMES, DEBORAH •
JAMES, JEFFREY • JAMES, KEVIN • JAMES, M • JAMES, MICHAEL • JAMES, RON • JAMESON, MONTY • JAMISON, BRIAN • JANIS, CHARLOTTE • JANN, BRIGETTE • JANOWSKI, MARK • JARVIS, INGRID • JASPER, JAMES • JAUDON, MELANIE • JAY, ADAM • JAYARAMAN, SUNI • JAYSON, MICHAEL • JAYSON, NANCY • JEAN-FRANCOIS, BERLINE • JEFFERSON, CHRISTOPHER • JEFFERY, LESLIE • JEFFERY, SHARON • JEFFREYS,
EMMETT • JEFFREYS, JIM • JEHLE, LEONARD • JELLETS, JEFFREY • JEMMOTT, MICHELLE • JENKINS, BERNITA • JENKINS, COREY • JENKINS, DANA • JENKINS, ESAW • JENKINS, HERMAN • JENKINS, IRIE • JENKINS, JAN • JENKINS, KELLI • JENKINS, MICHAEL • JENKINS, PAMELA • JENKINS, PAT • JENKINS, RONALD • JENN, JESSICA • JENNES, JENNIFER • JENNINGS, CAROLYN • JENNINGS, DANA • JENNINGS, ERIC • JENNINGS, LESLIE • JEN-
NINGS, RICHARD • JENSEN, MELANIE • JENSEN, MELISSA • JENSEN, ROGER • JENSEN, TAYLOR • JEPSON, KURT • JEREZ, HUMBERTO • JERNIGAN, MARK • JESENSKY, DEBRA • JESIFERS, KAREN • JESSIE, YVETTE • JESTER, SUE • JETER, LORI • JETT, BRIAN • JETT, KRISTI • JIHAD, JAMILLA • JIKIEMI, EDRIC • JIM, EJ • JIMENEZ, FEDERICO • JIMENEZ, LYNNE • JOBSON, JENNIFER • JOE, ALEXANDER • JOHARY, ALBERT • JOHNSON, A • JOHN-
SON, ALAN • JOHNSON, ALLENA • JOHNSON, ANDREA • JOHNSON, ANGELA • JOHNSON, ARLANDUS • JOHNSON, BRENDA • JOHNSON, BRENDA • JOHNSON, BRUCE • JOHNSON, CAROL • JOHNSON, COLLEEN • JOHNSON, CORA • JOHNSON, CYNTHIA • JOHNSON, DEANTHONY • JOHNSON, DERNESSA • JOHNSON, DOLORES • JOHNSON, DON • JOHNSON, DOTTIE • JOHNSON, DUSHAUN • JOHNSON, ERIC • JOHNSON, GEORGE • JOHN-
SON, GLEN • JOHNSON, GREG • JOHNSON, HEINZ • JOHNSON, HENRY • JOHNSON, HOJO • JOHNSON, JAMES • JOHNSON, JANE • JOHNSON, JAQUELINE • JOHNSON, JARVIS • JOHNSON, JEANETTE • JOHNSON, JEANNETTE • JOHNSON, JERRY • JOHNSON, JESSE • JOHNSON, JETTIE • JOHNSON, JOHN • JOHNSON, JOYCELYN • JOHNSON, JUDD • JOHNSON, KAREN • JOHNSON, KATIE • JOHNSON, KELLY • JOHNSON, KENNETH •
JOHNSON, KENDALL • JOHNSON, KRISTINE • JOHNSON, LADARRELL • JOHNSON, LAURA • JOHNSON, LEE • JOHNSON, LEE • JOHNSON, MARIE • JOHNSON, MARK • JOHNSON, MARY • JOHNSON, MELANIE • JOHNSON, MELISSA • JOHNSON, MICHELLE • JOHNSON, MOSES • JOHNSON, MYRA • JOHNSON, PAUL • JOHNSON, RANDY • JOHNSON, RENEE • JOHNSON, RETHA • JOHNSON, RETTA • JOHNSON, ROBERT • JOHNSON, ROBERT •
JOHNSON, RYAN • JOHNSON, SAMUEL • JOHNSON, SCOTT • JOHNSON, SCOTT • JOHNSON, SHERITA • JOHNSON, STEPHEN • JOHNSON, STEPHEN • JOHNSON, STEVEN • JOHNSON, STUART • JOHNSON, TERI • JOHNSON, TONI • JOHNSON, WALTER • JOHNSON, WILLIAM • JOHNSON, ZEARRIOUS • JOHNSON-WRIGHT, LESLEY • JOHNSTON, ALAN • JOHNSTON, AMANDA • JOHNSTON, DIANE • JOHNSTON, KIRBY • JOHNSTON, MARGARET • JOHNSTON,
MARIA • JOHNSTON, MELISSA • JOHNSTON, MONICA • JOHNSTON, RICHARD • JOHNSTON, SIDNEY • JOHNSTON, SYLVIA • JOHNSTONE, MEGAN • JOHSON, ERIN • JOINER, CHARI • JOLIVETTE, TONY • JONES, ALVIN • JONES, ASLEY • JONES, BARBARA • JONES, BERYSE • JONES, BETH • JONES, BRADLEY • JONES, BRENDA • JONES, BRENT • JONES, BRETT • JONES, BRODERICK • JONES, CAMMIE • JONES, CARL • JONES, CAROL • JONES,
CARRIE • JONES, CHRISTOPHER • JONES, CYNTHIA • JONES, CYNTHIA • JONES, DANA • JONES, DANELLE • JONES, DANIEL • JONES, DANNY • JONES, DARON • JONES, DARYL • JONES, DAVID • JONES, EVE • JONES, GARY • JONES, GLORIA • JONES, GREGORY • JONES, HEATHER • JONES, JACQUELINE • JONES, JAN • JONES, JEANETTE • JONES, JENNIFER • JONES, JO • JONES, JOHN • JONES, JULIE • JONES, KATHY • JONES, KIM •
LARRY • JONES, LINDA • JONES, LINDA • JONES, MANDY • JONES, MARIAN • JONES, MARLENE • JONES, MARTIN • JONES, MELINDA • JONES, MICHAEL • JONES, MICHAEL • JONES, MICHAEL • JONES, NATASHA • JONES, PAUL • JONES, PEGGY • JONES, QUENTIN • JONES, RAHFIYA • JONES, RALPH • JONES, REBECCA • JONES, RHONDA • JONES, RUSTY • JONES, SABRINA • JONES, SCOTT • JONES, SHELTON • JONES,
• JONES, STACY • JONES, STEVE • JONES, SUE • JONES, TAVA • JONES, VINCENT • JONES, WINCE • JONES-LEWIS, GERALDINE • JORDAN, JERRIE • JORDAN, KEVIN • JORDAN, LYNNE • JORDAN, MICHAEL • JORDAN, PEARLIE • JORDAN, TROY • JORDAN, WILLIAM • JORDON, JO • JORDY, SHAWN • JORGENSON, EMILY • JOSEPH, RANDY • JOSEY, ANDREA • JOS-
MARK • JOSSELSON, ROBYN • JOUBERT, PATRICIA • JOWDY, ELIZABETH • JOWDY, JAMES • JOWETT, SUSAN • JOYCE, ERIN • JOYCE, MIKE • JOYNER, JUDY • JR, ED • JR, FRED • JR, JOE • JR, JOHN • JR, JOHN • JR, LARRY • JR, PAUL • JR, ROBERT • JR, ROY • JR, SAM • JR, WILLIE • JUBON, DOROTHY • JUBON, JAN • JUDKINS, DEMETRIUS • JUE, ALLEN • JUETT, LESLIE • JULIAN, HYUN • JUNG, STEPHEN • JUSTESEN, JAMES • JUSTICE, KATE •
• JUSTICE, SANDRA • JUSTINIANO, ANTONIANO • KADERLY, KIMBERLY • KAGAN, RON • KAISER, JIM • KAISER, JULIET • KALAIDJIAN, WILLA • KALCSO, JOSEPH • KALEDA, MARY • KALISH, STAN • KALUA, ISAAC • KAM, ENID • KAM, HAL • KAMERON, MARSHA • KAMINSKY, KIMBERLY • KAMMER, PETE • KAMMEYER, BRYCE • KAMMEYER, MINDY • KAMMEYER, SHELBY • KANAZAWA, JOHN • KANEL, LYNNE • KANG, HELEN • KANG, JACOB
KANICS, INGRID • KANTOR, STEPHANIE • KANY, KRISTIN • KAPLAN, BARBARA • KAPLAN, JON • KAPLAN, JULIE • KAPLAN, TASHA • KAPPEL, KATHY • KAPPEL, PAUL • KAPPLER, JESSICA • KARAI, SASSAN • KARCH, JOHN • KARICH, TAMETHA • KARIUKI, NJOKI • KARNOWSKI, JOHN • KASAK, JOANNE • KASCHALK, SUE • KASTEL, CYNTHIA • KASTIGAR, BETH • KATCHER, SAULO • KATES, ROOSEVELT • KATSMA, LEWIS • KATTO, YURI •
BARBARA • KATZ, DALE • KATZ, JENNIFER • KATZ, MICAH • KATZ, SUE • KATZ, TAMI • KAUFMANN, BOBBY • KAULBACH, LAURIE • KAVANAUGH, NANCY • KAY, CARMEN • KAY, CYNTHIA • KAY, GEORGE • KAYE, RAYMOND • KAYE, SUE • KAYE, SYLVIA • KAYSE, YASHU • KEARNEY, MARY • KEARNEY, STEPHEN • KEARSON, HEATHER • KEATON, CATHRYN • KEATON, COSANDRA • KEATON, PATTI • KECK, ANNAMARIE • KEDERSHA, SCOTT
• KEEBLE, JENNIFER • KEEBLER, DON • KEEL, JEFF • KEEN, ERICKA • KEEN, PRITTI • KEEN, WAYNE • KEEN, DOUG • KEIM, MARTHA • KEITH, JAN • KEITH, JANNIE • KEITH, SANDRA • KELLER, BOB • KELLER, MARK • KELLER, WENDY • KELLEY, DANIEL • KELLEY, DONALD • KELLEY, JOHN • KELLEY, LEE • KELLEY, MARY • KELLEY, PAT • KELLEY, ROBERT • KELLUM, ARNOLD • KELLY, ALMA • KELLY, BETTY • KELLY, CHERYL
KELLY, COYOTITO • KELLY, DARLENE • KELLY, DEBRA • KELLY, ERIN • KELLY, GEORGE • KELLY, JIM • KELLY, JOHN • KELLY, KATHLEEN • KELLY, LINDA • KELLY, NANCY • KELLY, PHILIP • KELLY, ROB • KELLY, ROSEMARY • KELLY, TERRY • KELNHOFER, REBECCA • KELTERBORN, DOUG • KEMP, AUDIE • KEMP, CANDACE • KEMP, NEDRICK • KENDALL, THERON • KENDRICKS, CONNIE • KENEIPP, WAYNE • KENNA, CHERYL • KENNEDY,
MICHAEL • KENNEDY, DEBORAH • KENNEDY, JAMES • KENNEDY, JOHN • KENNEDY, MAUREEN • KENNEDY, PATRICIA • KENNEDY, SANDRA • KENNEDY, TANI • KENNEL, VIVIAN • KENNERLEY, ANITA • KENNERLEY, PATRICE • KENNY, MARY • KENT, PATRICIA • KENT, SUSAN • KEOGH, HELEN • KEOGH, JOAN • KERBY, CLAIRE • KERCHER, ALAN • KERMOYAN, DAVID • KERN, LEE • KERNES, JULIET • KERNIZAN, SHEREE • KERR, DALE •
JOHN • KERR, MARY • KERRY, DARYL • KERSH, BRADLEE • KESSEL, JOHN • KESSLER, ERIK • KESSLER, HOLLY • KESSLER, KARA • KESSLER, KEITH • KESSLER, LINDA • KESSLER, LORI • KESTER, KRIS • KETCH, BRUCE • KETTLES, KELLY • KETTS, KEVIN • KEVIN, COFFEY • KEY, ERICA • KEY, ERNEST • KEY, MARILYN • KEY, TERESA • KEYTON, JANICE • KEYWOOD, GENNY • KEYWOOD, JULIE • KEYWORTH, CRAIG • KHALFAN, NOORANI
KHAS, TONI • KIBBE, DEBRA • KIDD, CHAD • KIDD, DAVID • KIDD, SHAWN • KIDDY, KEITH • KIDWELL, BETSY • KIEFER, MARGARET • KIERNAN, KEVIN • KIHARA, ESTHER • KIHARA, NEHEMY • KIKTA, RON • KILBANE, LISA • KILGO, LUCILLE • KILGO, SUZY • KILGORE, DEBBIE • KILGORE, KARIN • KILGORE, LAUREA • KILLEEN, TONY • KILPATRICK, ANNE • KILPATRICK, JOHN • KILPATRICK, THOMAS • KIM, IN • KIM, JASON • KIM, JAY • KIM
JEANNIE • KIM, JENNIFER • KIM, MIN • KIM, NOOLIE • KIM, PAULA • KIM, SUE • KIMBALL, ALICE • KIMBLE, TERRI • KIMZEY, GEORGETTE • KINARD, CONNIE • KINCAID, JENNIFER • KINCAID, SARAH • KIND, CHRISTOPHER • KING, BARB • KING, CHARLES • KING, CHARLES • KING, CHRISTINE • KING, CINDY • KING, GEORGE • KING, H • KING, III • KING, KELLY • KING, KRISTI • KING, PAT • KING, RANDY • KING, RAY • KING, REBECCA • KIN
RICHARD • KING, SHELIA • KING, STEVEN • KING, TRICIA • KINGSLEY, DAN • KINNEBREW, KETISHA • KINNERSON, CONNIE • KINNEY, MARY • KINNEY, MATTHEW • KINNEY, WILLARD • KINSEY, VANESSA • KINZEL, JULIE • KIPHART, JANET • KIRBY, DEANNA • KIRBY, TERRY • KIRCHGESSNER, RENATE • KIRK, MICHELE • KIRKLAND, ELIZABETH • KIRKLAND, NICOLE • KIRKMAN, CHARLES • KIRLIN, JOE • KIRSHNER, RICK •
• KIRWAN, JOSEPH • KISS, SANDOR • KITELINGER, JAMES • KITTOK, MARY • KITTREDGE, MARJORIE • KIVETT, ANN • KLANAC, TRACY • KLAPDOHR, KARIN • KLAPPER, JOSH • KLARIC, GARY • KLAVOHN, DEBRA • KLAYMAN, SUSAN • KLECKA, ANTHONY • KLEEMAN, GEORGE • KLEIMAN, MARGARET • KLEIN, AMANDA • KLEIN, JENNIFER • KLEIN, KATHY • KLEIN, PATTI • KLEINE, SUSAN • KLINE, JEFFREY • KLINE, MEGAN • KLINE, MICHEL
• KLING, DAN • KLING, RYAN • KLING, SUZY • KLINGBELL, FRED • KLINGENBERG, CAROL • KLINGENSMITH, BOB • KLINGER, JANN • KLISZKA, DANI • KLITZKE, THIAGO • KLOMPE, JANNEKE • KLOPP, JACIN • KLOSTERMANN, BOBBIE • KLOSTERMANN, MIKE • KLOUSER, ANN • KNAPP, GENIE • KNAPP, KIM • KNAPP, RAY • KNASIAK, JOHANNA • KNEISS, AMY • KNEISS, KATHY • KNIAT, KEN • KNICK, JEANE • KNICK, TOM • KNIESTEDT, KARL
• KNIGHT, ARVIL • KNIGHT, JAMES • KNIGHT, LINDA • KNIGHT, LINDA • KNIGHTON, YASMIN • KNISKERN, JOY • KNOPF, MICHAEL • KNOPP, ANNIE • KNOPP, ROY • KNOWLES, CHERYL • KNOWLES, PAUL • KNOX, CHINAETTA • KNOX, CLAUDIA • KNOX, JAMES • KNOX, SHERRY • KNUREK, DEBBIE • KNUTSEN, CHUCK • KNUTSON, GEEGEE • KOBERNA, LAURA • KOBYLKA, ANJA • KOCH, CAROLYN • KOCH, FRED • KOCH, RON • KOCHNE
JUDY • KOCHNER, KATIE • KOCS, SHANNA • KOEPPEL, CHRISTOPHER • KOESTER, HOLLY • KOGER, MICHAEL • KOHLBACH, DOT • KOHM, JAMIE • KOHTALA, ANNE • KOIVU, MICHELLE • KOKENY, KRISZTA • KOLAR, JILL • KOLSHAK, ANN • KOLSHAK, JENNI • KOOPMAN, GAY • KOPLETSKI, JOYCE • KOPP, PETER • KORNFELD, SHERRI • KOSARIC, FATIMA • KOSCO, HOLLIS • KOSTAKOS, KATHERINE • KOTLAN, DELY • KOTLER, KATHLEEN
KOWALSKY, DON • KOZICKI, MARIA • KRABAK, BRIAN • KRAFKA, JOHN • KRAFT, MIKE • KRAHAM, SUSAN • KRAKER, PHILIP • KRAMER, JEFF • KRAMER, MICHAEL • KRASSEN, JOSH • KRASSEN, KRIS • KRATZER-REEVE, SUSAN • KRAUSS, CHRIS • KRAUSS, JENNIFER • KRAVITZ, JENNIFER • KRAWCZAK, DOUGLAS • KRECKMAN, GAYLE • KREIDER, ROBIN • KREMER, GRACE • KRESSER, PETULA • KREST, HOLLY • KREUTER, PHIL • KRIDE

SUSAN • KRIEBEL, KATY • KRIEBEL, ROBERT • KRIEG, CARRIE • KRIEGER, GLENN • KRISE, JEANNE • KRISEL, GLORIA • KROEGER, ELLEN • KRONICK, GARY • KROTENBERG, DEBORAH • KROTENBERG, ETHEL • KROTENBERG, MARVIN • KROUSER, EMMA • KRUEGER, BILL • KRUEGER, JR • KRUG, PAMELA • KRUGER, DAVI • KRUGER, ELIAS • KRUGER, GAYLE • KRUSZKA, AMY • KRYSAK, BILL • KRYZAK, PATRICIA • KSIASKIEWITZ, JOSEPH • KUBOTA, MASAKO • KUCSERA, ELLEN • KUDLACEK, MARTIN • KUHN, EMILY • KUHN, PAULA • KUHN, SAMUEL • KUHN, ZACHARY • KUHNE, SCOTT • KULERS, GIL • KUMAR, LAKSHMI • KUMAR, MUTHU • KUMAR, USHA • KUNERTH, KATHY • KUNIANSKY, SONIA • KUNISAWA, RINA • KUO, JOHN • KURKJIAN, BETTY • KURTZ, GLENN • KURYLA, ROSEANN • KUZNICKI, GISELA • KWON, SOON • KYBURZ, KELLEY • KYLE, BETTY • KYSER, EMILY • LABARA, SAMUEL • LABARBERA, JACKIE • LABENNE, KAREN • LABHAHU, SUSAN • LABOVITZ, ANDREW • LABREC, SANDY • LACKEY, HEATHER • LACY, ALLAN • LACY, CAROL • LACY, TIM • LADHA, MONA • LADINSKY, ROBYN • LAFLAMME, RAE • LAFONT, DAVID • LAFONTAINE, NANCY • LAFORGIA, ELISE • LAGO, MERRILL • LAIFSKY, SUZANNE • LAIRD, ERNEST • LAMAR, JENNIFER • LAMB, BAILEY • LAMB, ELIZABETH • LAMB, GEORGE • LAMB, JAMES • LAMB, JANET • LAMB, KELLIE • LAMBRETTA, PAUL • LAMMERT, JOHN • LAMONTAGNE, ALBERT • LAMONTTE, BILLY • LAMOTTE, BILLY • LAMY, RICHARD • LANCASTER, MICHAEL • LANCE, BRIAN • LANCE, VALARIE • LANDERS, APRIL • LANDERS, BOB • LANDERS, MICHAEL • LANDERS, NANCY • LANDERS, TOM • LANDES, PAT • LANDIN, ROBERT • LANDRY, ISRAEL • LANG, AMY • LANG, BOB • LANG, KAREN • LANGARICA, DANNY • LANGDON, LINDA • LANGFORD, SANDRA • LANGLEY, ANNE • LANGLEY, JOANN • LANGLEY, MICHELLE • LANGLEY, PHYLLIS • LANGLEY, SIBYL • LANGLEY, TIFFANY • LANGLEY, WHITNEY • LANIER, JOHN • LANIER, LENNEICE • LANIER, MELODY • LANIER, VICTOR • LANOUETTE, MICHELLE • LAPLANTE, EDWARD • LAPLANTE, JANET • LAPORTE, KATHY • LAPREAD, TAMMY • LARGENT, BARBARA • LARKINS, VERNA • LAROCHELLE, MAGUY • LARSEN, KARI • LARSEN, MARY • LARSEN, MELISSA • LARSEN, SUDI • LARSEN, VICTOR • LARSON, EDWARD • LARY, ANN • LASALLE, DEVIN • LASATER, JANET • LASSETER, ELLEN • LASTINGER, HOLLY • LATCH, SUE • LATHAM, GREGORY • LATHAM, JOSEPH • LATHAM, MARK • LATHAM, STEPHEN • LATIMER, GLENN • LATIMER, SANDRA • LATTANZIO, JAMES • LATZKO, ALEXANDER • LAUER, CINDY • LAUER, GREGG • LAUFER, DAVID • LAUFER, GERI • LAUFER, LARRY • LAUFER, VINCENT • LAUGHLIN, JIM • LAURA, BRIAN • LAUREL, DEBORAH • LAURETTA, LYNN • LAURIA, LOU • LAURICH, JOHN • LAURSEN, MARTIN • LAURY, JACK • LAVENDER, JACK • LAVINE, BRYAN • LAVOICE, MARLA • LAWAND, VIVIAN • LAWICKI, DOROTHY • LAWLER, CINDY • LAWLER, MARCELLA • LAWRIE, PATRISH • LAWRIE, TOM • LAWSON, ANNA • LAWSON, JANE • LAWSON, JESSIE • LAWSON, SHIRLEY • LAWSON, WENDI • LAWSON, YARI • LAWTON, DOUG • LAYTON, DERRICK • LAZENBERRY, CHRYSTAL • LAZENBY, GENIA • LEACH, HEATHER • LEACH, JR • LEACH, MEL • LEACHMAN, DANETTE • LEAKE, PACE • LEAPHART, SUZETTE • LEATHERMAN, NANCY • LEATHERWOOD, TAMARA • LEBBIE, GLENNA • LEBBIE, TAMBA • LEBLANC, MAX • LEBLOND, ROBERT • LECORN, LARRY • LEDOUX, JOSEPH • LEDOUX, PHIL • LEE, BRANDON • LEE, CARMEN • LEE, CHERYL • LEE, CHRISTOPHER • LEE, CYNTHIA • LEE, DANIEL • LEE, DEANNA • LEE, DOUG • LEE, ELDRIDGE • LEE, ELIZABETH • LEE, GRACE • LEE, JACQUELINE • LEE, JAE • LEE, JAMES • LEE, JEE • LEE, JEFF • LEE, JIN • LEE, JOHN • LEE, KI-TAE • LEE, LAO • LEE, MARIANNA • LEE, MICHELLE • LEE, RICHARD • LEE, RON • LEE, SHERRIE • LEE, SUSANNA • LEE, SUZY • LEE, TAMMY • LEE, WALTER • LEE, YEUN-JOO • LEETH, ROBERT • LEFKOFF, MARVIN • LEGGETT, LAURI • LEGGOE, ANNE • LEHNER, KAREN • LEHR, TAMARA • LEIGHTON, LESLIE • LEINAAR, KAREN • LEIPOLD, CINDY • LEMANSKI, HOLLY • LEMASTER, JEFF • LEMMON, PHYZ • LEMMOND, KATHRYN • LEMMOND, STEPHANIE • LEMOINE, VAL • LEMON, MEADOW • LEMONS, LOVELL • LENAHAN, JOAN • LEND, MICHELE • LENHARD, JOAN • LENKEIT, ANITA • LENKEIT, WILLI • LENYK, SCOTT • LENYK, SHERI • LENZ, BETTY • LENZNER, MARK • LEO, ANNA • LEONARD, ANGELA • LEPAK, JEFFREY • LERER, STEPHANIE • LEROUX, AMY • LEROY, ADRIANE • LEROY, GEORGE • LEROY, JASON • LEROY, SHARON • LERZO, ROBERT • LESLIE, CURTIS • LESTER, ARMY • LETA, DAVID • LETOHA, RUSS • LETT, CELIA • LETT, DWAYNE • LETZ, JIM • LEVEILLE, LAURA • LEVERENZ, DARREN • LEVERSEDGE, FRASER • LEVINE, BALFOURA • LEVISON, DANNY • LEVITT, GARY • LEVITT, IAN • LEVITT, MICHAEL • LEWALLEN, TRACI • LEWANDOWSKI, FRANK • LEWANDOWSKI, RICHARD • LEWELLYN, DONNA • LEWERS, DEBBIE • LEWIS, BERNARD • LEWIS, BERNITA • LEWIS, BEVERLY • LEWIS, CHARLIE • LEWIS, CHRISTOPHER • LEWIS, CLAUDETTE • LEWIS, DONNA • LEWIS, EUNICE • LEWIS, JERRY • LEWIS, JOANNE • LEWIS, JOEL • LEWIS, KEVIN • LEWIS, KIMBERLY • LEWIS, KIRSTY • LEWIS, LINDA • LEWIS, LISA • LEWIS, LIZ • LEWIS, MARGARET • LEWIS, MARY • LEWIS, REGINALD • LEWIS, RONNIE • LEWIS, STEVE • LEWIS, TONI • LEWIS, VALERIA • LEWIS, YVONNE • LEWIS, YVETTE • LEY, CATHY • LEYSATH, ED • LI, THEODORE • LIBOWSKY, BEN • LICHT, ALICIA • LICHTERMANN, KRISTEN • LICKFELD, DARLENE • LIDDELL, JANICE • LIEB, TOM • LIEBOWITZ, DANIEL • LIEN, PETER • LIENDO, ANTONIO • LIGGON, GWENDOLYN • LIGHT, JIMMY • LILIENTHAL, ANDREW • LILLEROOS, CHRISTIAN • LIMA, BARBARA • LIMBRID, THOMAS • LIMEHOUSE, JEAN • LINCH, JOHN • LINDBERG, KEVIN • LINDEMANN, CARLA • LINDEMANN, ROBIN • LINDER, BRUTENE • LINDER, DAWNYELL • LINDNER, KAREN • LINDNER, MIKE • LINDSEY, KRISTIN • LINDSTROM, REBECCA • LINDSTROM, SUE • LINDSTROM, TIMOTHY • LINK, KAREN • LIPCHIN, LYNDA • LIPHAM, CHRISTY • LIPPY, DENNIS • LIPTON, JENNIFER • LISBY, SHEILA • LISS, DEBBIE • LISSIMORE, LESLIE • LISTON, GEORGE • LISTON, JIM • LITARDO, FRANK • LITTEN, ELIZABETH • LITTLE, DOLORES • LITTLE, JIM • LITTLE, TERRY • LITTLE, VINITA • LITTLESTONE, ARTHUR • LITTLESTONE, BARBARA • LITTLESTONE, JODI • LIU, JEFFERY • LIVINGSTON, ANGEL • LIVINGSTON, HOLLI • LIVINGSTON, KIMBERLEY • LIVINGSTON, TARA • LIVSEY, CAROLINE • LLEWELLYN, MICHAEL • LLOYD, DAVE • LLOYD, MATTHEW • LOBE, LOU • LOBLEY, SARAH • LOCKETT, MAURICE • LOCKHART, CHRIS • LOCKHART, KAREN • LOCKHART, LUCI • LOCKHART, TONYA • LOCKMAN, ROBERT • LOCKMAN, SHIRLEY • LOCKRIDGE, STAN • LOCKWOOD, ABBY • LOCKWOOD, MARY • LOCSIN, MELISSA • LOCSIN, NEIL • LODDEN, FRED • LODGE, SASH • LOEBSACK, JESSE • LOEFFLER, LYNN • LOESCH, ANN • LOFSTRAND, ROCHELLE • LOFTUS, INGRID • LOGAN, LEOLA • LOHNES, BILL • LOHNES, PAULA • LOKER, ANDREA • LOLLEY, DEBBIE • LOMAX, DELPHYNE • LOMAX, DWIGHT • LOMAX, EDDIE • LOMBARDI, JOSEPH • LONG, BRIAN • LONG, CAROL • LONG, CEDRIC • LONG, CYNTHIA • LONG, DUSTIN • LONG, EDA • LONG, GLADYS • LONG, JOHN • LONG, LELA • LONG, MARTHA • LONG, MICHAEL • LONG, RALPH • LONG, SHERON • LONG, STACY • LONG, TIMOTHY • LONGAMORE, BARBARA • LONGAMORE, STEVE • LONGLEY, MARY • LONGO, PEGGY • LOO, BRAD • LOPER, ROBERT • LOPES, AL • LOPEZ, GLORIA • LOPEZ, MARK • LOPEZ-CANCEL, REINALDO • LORD, CAROL • LORIER, JUDY • LOTT, DENISE • LOTT, GINNY • LOTT, JERNISE • LOTT, JUANITA • LOTT, MICHAEL • LOUDER, SHEILA • LOUGHLIN, JENNIE • LOUGHLIN, NEIL • LOUHIVIRTA, LAURI • LOUIE, DAVE • LOUTHAN, CHUCK • LOVE, ALLISAH • LOVE, BETH • LOVE, CHERYL • LOVE, DAWN • LOVE, GAIL • LOVE, JERRY • LOVE, MICHAEL • LOVEDAY, DEBRA • LOVEJOY, CURTIS • LOVELADY, ANN • LOVELESS, HEATHER • LOVELESS, MICHEAL • LOVELL, LAURA • LOVERING, CALVIN • LOVERN, RACHEL • LOVETTE, MARVIN • LOWE, ANDRE • LOWE, BRENDA • LOWE, JENNIFER • LOWE, PHYLLIS • LOWE, SYLVIA • LOYD, JOHN • LOYLESS, HELEN • LOZADA, JOSE • LU, ALICE • LUBLINK, RON • LUCAS, ANGELA • LUCAS, CAROLYN • LUCAS, MARY • LUCAS, NICKI • LUCHENE, CHERYLE • LUCKEY, RYAN • LUCKY, VINCENT • LUDENA, HAYDEE • LUDOVICI, ALAN • LUDWIG, SCOTT • LUDY, JACKIE • LUDY, RICH • LUGAR, JUDY • LUKE, KATHRINE • LUJAN-HOFFMAN, JOSE • LUJAN-HOFFMAN, SERGIO • LUJAN-MEDINA, SERGIO • LUJANO, BOB • LUKER, DONNY • LUMBRA, GARY • LUNA, THOMAS • LUND, SUMMER • LUNDGREN, KATHERINE • LUNDIN, REBECCA • LUNDY, ELAINE • LUNDY, RICHARD • LUNSFORD, HEIDI • LUSSIER, CHARLIE • LUTHER, BETSY • LUTHER, JOHN • LUTOMSKI, JR • LUTTRELL, SHIRLEY • LUTTRELL, TANJA • LUTZ, HEIDI • LYERLY, KAYE • LYKINS, JUDY • LYKINS, RON • LYLE, JAMES • LYLE, NANCY • LYNCH, ANTHONY • LYNCH, DEBORAH • LYNCH, HUGH • LYNCH, MARCIA • LYNCH, SUSAN • LYNCH, TERESA • LYNCH-HALUSKA, BETTY • LYNN, DRUE • LYNN, FRANKLIN • LYNN, GAIL • LYNN, JUDY • LYNN, TERRY • LYON, ANDY • LYON, KATHRYN • LYONS, DEREK • LYONS, III • LYONS, JANE • LYONS, KATE • LYTLE, JESSE • LYTLE, RHONDA • LYTLE, WILLIAM • MABRY, TODD • MACCONNELL, GREG • MACHADO, CAETANO • MACIAS, WILLIAM • MACIUNAS, ALGIS • MACK, B • MACK, CATHERINE • MACK, KATHY • MACKAY, COLLEEN • MACKEY, LIZ • MACKLER, ANDREW • MACNAMARA, JOHN • MACNEIL, MARCIA • MACOMBER, JACQUELINE • MACONACHY, MARGERY • MACTAVISH, BRET • MACTAVISH, REID • MADARIS, MARIANNE • MADDOX, ROXANN • MADDOX, BILL • MADDOX, JAN • MADDOX, LACRECIA • MADEAN, CHERYL • MADIGAN, SHERRY • MADISON, HARRISON • MADISON, JACQUELINE • MADISON, SHONNA • MADRIGAL, JESUS • MADRO, RICHARD • MAEDA, CINDY • MAFFAI, FARRAH • MAGEE, DANNY • MAGNANT, CHRIS • MAHAN, KIM • MAHER, BETH • MAHER, MOLLY • MAHER, PHIL • MAHON, TINA • MAHONE, NEDRA • MAHONEY, DAVETA • MAHONEY, MOLLY • MAHONEY, SHARON • MAIER, MARGARET • MAIN, JULIE • MAIN, P • MAINERI, ALBERTA • MAIRS, RUSSELL • MAJESKA, ERIC • MAJESKA, KEVIN • MAJESKA, RIC • MAJETT, KERMIT • MAJOR, FRANK • MAKILYA, HENDRIKA • MALA-BANAN, RICHARD • MALATINO, EILEEN • MALCOM, KRISTY • MALDEN, BILLY • MALENCH, SHARON • MALES, BETTINA • MALINO, DENISE • MALLASCH, MARY • MALLES, GRETCHEN • MALLOCH, LISA • MALLORY, DIANE • MALONE, CASEY • MALONE, ERIN • MALONE, MIKE • MALONE, PATRICIA • MALONE, PATRONIA • MALONE, VIRGINIA • MALONEY, BONNIE • MALOOF, STEVE • MALOY, HEIDI • MALSBY, SUSAN • MALONEY, TRAVIS • MALPANI, DEEPA • MALTA-BEY, LOUIS • MANAGO, TERRY • MANCINI, CHRISTOPHER • MANCUSO, ELIZABETH • MANCUSO, MARY • MANCUSO, TODD • MANDEL, ELISSA • MANGAWANG, BENJAMIN • MANGHAM, BILL • MANIGAULT, JOHN • MANISCALCO, VINCENT • MANLEY, BEN • MANLOW, STEVE • MANN, BRUCE • MANN, DOYLE • MANN, HARRIETT • MANN, NATALIE • MANNING, ALEX • MANNING, GLENN • MANNING, JACKIE • MANNING, JAMIE • MANNING, KRISTI • MANNING, MARY • MANNING, MAUREEN • MANNING, SCOTT • MANNING, SUSAN • MANNIS, WILLIAM • MANNIX, DAN • MANSFIELD, SHARAN • MANTYCH, CHRISTINE • MANUEL, MONICA • MANZEY, ANATACIO • MAPLESTONE, WENDY • MARA, NICOLE • MARABLE, JACKIE • MARAN, BOB • MARANKLE, JERI • MARAZZO, ALFRED • MARBUT, LIZ • MARCELIC, TAYLOR • MARCHANT, STEPHANIE • MARCHISELLO, SHARON • MARCRUM, EMILY • MARCUS, BOB • MARCUS, DAVID • MARGOLIN, BOB • MARGOLIN, REYO • MARIANES, BILL • MARIBEI, CAROLINE • MARINE, BILL • MARION, MARION • MARIOS, LORI • MARITZ, SUZANNE • MARJANOWICZ, NICOLE • MARKEY, DAVID • MARKEY, FAYE • MARKHAM, LORNA • MARKHAM, RUDOLPH • MARKHAM, WILLIA • MARKIEWICZ, ADAM • MARKLE, JAMES • MARKO, BARBARA • MARKOTT, BEV • MARKS, BESSIE • MARKS, KAREN • MARKS, SUSAN • MARKS, TANYA • MARKS, THOMAS • MARLOW, WILLIAM • MARNER, DARA • MARQUEZ, ISRAEL • MARQUEZ, MARIA • MARQUEZ, MICHELLE • MARQUEZ, YOLANDA • MARQUIS, BRENDA • MARRERO, BRIAN • MARRIN, ALICE • MARRIN, NANCY • MARRIOTT, DIANE • MARROQUIN, SANDRA • MARSELIS-MOORE, WILLIE • MARSH, MELANIE • MARSH, NANCY • MARSH, RICHARD • MAR-SHALL, ARTHUR • MARSHALL, DOROTHY • MARSHALL, EVELYN • MARSHALL, JAMAAL • MARSHALL, JERRY • MARSHALL, KATHY • MARSHALL, LASONJI • MARTIN, AMY • MARTIN, ANNE • MARTIN, BURNETT • MARTIN, CINDY • MARTIN, DAVID • MARTIN, DAVID • MARTIN, DJ • MARTIN, EDNA • MARTIN, JAN • MARTIN, JANET • MARTIN, JOHN • MARTIN, JUAN • MARTIN, LAWRENCE • MARTIN, LORNA • MARTIN, MAURINE • MARTIN, NANCY • MARTIN, RANDY • MARTIN, SERGE • MARTIN, SHERI • MARTIN, THERESA • MARTIN, TOM • MARTIN, VALERIE • MARTIN, VIRGINIA • MARTINEZ, ADALBERTO • MARTINEZ, JUAN • MARTINEZ, OLIVER • MARTINEZ, ROLANDO • MARTINEZ-DILERNIA, SANDRA • MARTING, AIMEE • MARTING, TOM • MARX, RICHARD • MASBRUCH, MELVIN • MASBRUCH, SYLVIA • MASHUTA, CAROL • MASI, BRYAN • MASON, AMBER • MASON, ANTHONY • MASON, CAROLYN • MASON, JONATHAN • MASON, KATHERINE • MASON, LANTRY • MASON, LINDA • MASON, MATTHEW • MASON, WALT • MASSAGLI, CYNTHIA • MASSEY, JR • MASSEY, RAYMOND • MASSEY, RICHENDA • MASSIAH, CLEMENCIA • MASTEN, BUCK • MASTERS, NEIL • MASTRODONATO, GARY • MASTRODONATO, JORDAN • MASTROGIOVANNI, MARY • MATHESON, EDWIN • MATHEWS, DIANE • MATHEWS, DON • MATHESON, DAVID • MATHIS, DONALD • MATHIS, GEORGE • MATHIS, GLORIA • MATHIS, JAMES • MATHIS, KESHA • MATHIS, NELLIE • MATOS, MIGUEL • MATSUMOTO, YUKO • MATTHEWS, MATTIE • MATTHEWS, MELANEE • MATTHEWS, YUKI • MATTHIS, GINGER • MATTINGLY, DIANA • MATTISON, BARBARA • MATTOX, DEBORAH • MATTSON, GREG • MATTSON, KEVIN • MATTSON, SKIPPY • MATUKAITIS, LAUREN • MATUSEVICH, MIKHAIL • MATUUSERICH, MARIA • MAURA, ANNE • MAURER, CINDY • MAURICE, BEVERLY • MAXHAM, JAMES • MAXIE, LEON • MAXWELL, JAY • MAY, BELLA • MAY, CHONITA • MAY, KAREN • MAYANI, VIREN • MAYBEN, DEVIN • MAYBERRY, NOAH • MAYBERRY, TERRI • MAYERIK, CHERYL • MAYERS, NATASHA • MAYKUTH, PAT • MAYLE, DENISE • MAYNARD, OLIVER • MAYO, DONELL • MAYO, MICHAEL • MAYO, MICHAEL • MAYO, PAM • MAYO, SHEILA • MAYS, CLYDE • MAYS, RICHARD • MAYS, RUTH • MAZELIN, ROBERT • MAZIAR, MELODY • MAZLINA, MINDEL • MAZZA, ALEJANDRA • MAZZA, JESSE • MBOGO, WENDY • MCABEE-REHER, C • MCAFEE, DIANE • MCAFEE, RICHARD • MCAFEE, SARAH • MCARTHUR, SHERRY • MCBRIDE, JANE • MCCABE, MAXINE • MCCALEB, BARRY • MCCALL, CLINT • MCCALL, KRISTA • MCCALL, YVONNE • MCCALLUM, DIANE • MCCAMPBELL, CLYDE • MCCANCE, MAURICE • MCCANCE, MAURICE • MCCANN, CARRIE • MCCANT, BARBARA • MCCARL, MARIANNE • MCCARLEY, AARON • MCCART, JEANNE • MCCARTER, JENNIFER • MCCARTHY, FRANK • MCCARTHY, JOSH • MCCARTNEY, MELISSA • MCCARTHY, STEPHANIE • MCCATTY, MAURICE • MCCAUL, DARRELL • MCCLARY, JENNA • MCCLEARY, JENNIFER • MCCLELLAN, MARY • MCCLELLAN, SUE • MCCLELLAND, BRENDA • MCCLELLAND, STEVEN • MCCLIN-TON, STEPHANIE • MCCLERKLIN, ETHEL • MCCLESTER, SUSAN • MCCLOUD, SUSAN • MCCLURE, ANDY • MCCLURE, JACK • MCCLURE, KAREN • MCCLURE, SUSAN • MCCLUSKY, DUNCAN • MCCOLLAM, STEPHEN • MCCOLLOUGH, CYNTHIA • MCCOLLUM, DAVID • MCCONNELL, SUE • MCCORMACK, DOUG • MCCORMACK, JEANNIE • MCCORT, LYNN • MCCORT, ROBERT • MCCORVEY, JESSE • MCCOY, MARC • MCCOY, RICHARD • MCCRACK-EN, EARL • MCCRAE, SABRINA • MCCRARY, KA • MCCRAY, BRANDON • MCCRAY, SEAN • MCCREARY, CAREN • MCCRIMMON, ANNIE • MCCULLAGH, MARY • MCCULLOUGH, AMIR • MCCULLOUGH, CHERYL • MCCULLOUGH, JEAN • MCCULLOUGH, SARAH • MCCULLY, C • MCDANIEL, BURTON • MCDANIEL, GLEN • MCDANIEL, LARRY • MCDANIEL, SARA • MCDANIEL, STEVEN • MCDANIEL, WESLEY • MCDANIEL-VANHIEL, LESLIE • MCDAN-NALD, HUNT • MCDERMOTT, CYNDI • MCDONALD, ALLEN • MCDONALD, CHANCE • MCDONALD, JACKIE • MCDONALD, JANETTE • MCDONALD, JIMMY • MCDONALD, LESLIE • MCDONALD-BROOKS, MARILYNN • MCDOUGAL, KATHRYN • MCDOUGAL, PAUL • MCDOWELL, CHRISTY • MCDOWELL, MARY • MCDOWELL, SHARI • MCDUGALD, GLENDA • MCDUGALD, TOM • MCELHINEY, MICHAEL • MCELREATH, KIRK • MCELROY, PATRICIA • MCELVEEN, HARRY • MCEUEN, JOY • MCEUEN, MIKE • MCEUEN, MINDY • MCFALL, BRENDA • MCFANN, ALISSA • MCFARLAND, CARLTON • MCFARLANE, DONALD • MCFARLIN, FRED • MCFARLING, GINNA • MCFARLING, KELLY • MCGARITY, TAMMY • MCGARR, ROGER • MCGEE, STEPHEN • MCGEHEE, BILL • MCGILL, KAY • MCGLORN, LEE • MCGOWAN, NATE • MCGREEVEY, JOHN • MCGREEVY, DENNIS • MCGUE, JOY • MCGUFFOG, BRIDGET • MCGUFFOG, NORM • MCGUIRE, DAN • MCGUIRE, LAURA • MCGUIRE, PATRICK • MCHALE, CATHY • MCHALE, CINDY • MCHENRY, JEN • MCHUGH, JEANNE • MCINERNY, KRIS • MCINNISH, PAUL • MCINTIRE, JOHNATHAN • MCINTOSH, ANTHONY • MCINTOSH, KAREN • MCINTOSH, LINDA • MCINTYRE, OLIVIA • MCIVER, PATRICIA • MCIVER, RUSSELL • MCKAIN, JUDY • MCKALPAIN, DAMON • MCKAY, CECIL • MCKEE, EVELYN • MCKEE, HEATHER • MCKEEN, JENNI • MCKELLER, JUDYTH • MCKELVEY, JOHN • MCKENNEY, GLENN • MCKENZIE, DIONA • MCKENZIE, GRAY • MCKENZIE, JANICE • MCKENZIE, KAY • MCKENZIE, LAURIE • MCKENZIE, LEONARD • MCKENZIE, MARIE • MCKEON, DONALD • MCKESSY, DAN • MCKIBBON, LISA • MCKILLIP, GLENN • MCKIM, MEREDITH • MCKINNEY, DAVID • MCKITHEN, GLORIA • MCKNIGHT, CAROLYN • MCKNIGHT, CINDY • MCKNIGHT, GEORGE • MCKNIGHT, TOM • MCLACHLAN, GARY • MCLACHLAN, JEAN • MCLARTY, TERRY • MCLEAN, BILL • MCLEAN, CATHY • MCLEMORE, JERRY • MCLENDON, BOBBY • MCLENDON, OMAR • MCLENDON, SANDY • MCLEOD, SARA • MCLEOD, VICTORIA • MCLEROY, JAMES • MCLEROY, JUDITH • MCLENDEN, TOM • MCMAHAN, BRAD • MCMAHON, JANE • MCMAHON, MOLLY • MCMAKIN, GARVIN • MCMANUS, MATT • MCME-NAMIN, DONALD • MCMICHAEL, MERRY • MCMILLAN, BARBARA • MCMILLAN, JOHN • MCMILLAN, LINDA • MCMILLIN, SUSAN • MCMULLAN, SUE • MCMULLEN, LEE • MCMULLEN, RON • MCNABB, DWIGHT • MCNEAL, DENNIS • MCNEAL, DOUG • MCNEAL, JILL • MCNEAL, SUSAN • MCNEAL, VICKEY • MCNEESE, JENNIFER • MCNEESE, MARTIN • MCNEILL, JIMMY • MCOWEN, DONNA • MCPARLANE, JACKIE • MCPEAKE, MEGAN • MCPHER-SON, ARLENE • MCPHERSON, JANET • MCPHERSON, PHONISIA • MCPHERSON-RICE, STACEY • MCQUEEN, KIRK • MCQUEENEY, BRYAN • MCQUIRE, MARGUERITE • MCRAE, JEAN • MCRAE, RENITA • MCRAE, TONIKA • MCRANEY, LAURA • MCSWAIN, HELEN • MCTIGHE, SHANNON • MCVEY, MICHAEL • MCWHORTER, TONI • MCWILLIAMS, DANA • MCWILLIAMS, JULEE • MEACHAM, TONY • MEADOR, KELLY • MEADOWCROFT, JOSEPH • MEAD-OWS, ERIC • MEAGHER, RITA • MEANEY, JOE • MEANEY, SALLY • MEANS, JACQUELYN • MEANS, SEAN • MEANS, TAMERA • MEDEIROS, JOHN • MEDERNACH, KEN • MEDERS, MARILYN • MEDINA, MANUEL • MEDINA, MANUEL • MEDINA, RAFAEL • MEDLEY, WILLIAM • MEDLIN, LAURA • MEDOFF, HOWARD • MEDORI, MELISSA • MEDORI, MICHELE • MEEK, STEPHANIE • MEEKS, MIKE • MEEUWSEN, ANNA • MEGEL, MICHELE • MEGEL, NICOLE • MEIER, TAMRA • MEIR, DANIELLE • MELLADO, MONICA • MELTON, GRACE • MELTON, JACQUELINE • MELTON, JOHN • MELTON, KIM • MELTON, TRIPP • MELVIN, MEVIN • MELVIN, GEOFF • MENARD, LELAND • MENCHAN, GREGORY • MENDEN, ANNE • MENDENHALL, BRENT • MENDOZA, LINDA • MENDOZA, VIRNA • MENENDEZ, PHIL • MENGER, ERICH • MENON, MICHAEL • MENSCH, MARK • MENSE, CAROLINA • MENZIES, ALLISON • MENZIES, DONNA • MERCER, HILARY • MERCER, JENENE • MERCER, KELLY • MERCER, MICHELLE • MERCER, RICK • MERCER-HOUSTON, TERRI • MERCHANT, SEAN • MERIWEATHER, WILLIAM • MERKLE, JOE • MERKLE, LINDA • MERRICK, DORCAS • MERRIFIELD, FRANK • MERRILL, KEYRUN • MERRILL, ROBIN • MERRITT, WILLIAM • MERTZ, SUSAN • MERZ, PAULINE • MESCHICK, CHARLES • MESSER, LAURIE • MESSERVY, TED • METALLO, RICHARD • METCALF, STACY • MEUSE, LA • MEYER, AMBER • MEYER, EVA • MEYER, HAYLEY • MEYER, KEVIN • MEYER, ROBYN • MEYER, TROY • MEYERS, DAVE • MEYERS, SHERON • MIAO, JUN • MICALE, ANTHONY • MICHAEL, JAMES • MICHAEL, JOHN • MICHAEL, MD • MICHAELIDES, MARGARET • MICHALS, JOYLYNN • MICHALSKI, KATHY • MICHEL, KATHLEEN • MICHELETTI, JOYCE • MICKELSON, DENNIS • MICKNICZ, PAUL • MIDDLEBROOKS, SABRINA • MIDDLETON, GORDON • MIDDLETON, MICHAEL • MIDDLETON, RUTH • MIDDLETON, SASHA • MIEARS, DAN • MIELNIK, JAMES • MIESNER, SANDRA • MIETTINEN, HELI • MIKITA, KELLY • MIKOVSKY, ED • MILAM, SHARON • MILBOURN, DONNA • MILBURN, FRED • MILCHUS, KAREN • MILES, ANGINEEKI • MILEY, PAT • MILIAN, CUSTODIO • MILLARD, SHARON • MILLER, ADRIENNE • MILLER, ATIAN • MILLER, BARBARA • MILLER, BARBARA • MILLER, BERNICE • MILLER, BOB • MILLER, BRIAN • MILLER, CAROL • MILLER, CAROL • MILLER, CASS • MILLER, CHERI • MILLER, CINDY • MILLER, DOUG • MILLER, GRACE • MILLER, JOE • MILLER, JULIE • MILLER, KEVIN • MILLER, LAURA • MILLER, LYNN • MILLER, MARK • MILLER, MELISSA • MILLER, MICHAEL • MILLER, MICHAEL • MILLER, MONA • MILLER, NICOLE • MILLER, NIKKI • MILLER, NORA • MILLER, PAT • MILLER, PAT • MILLER, PATRICIA • MILLER, PRINCETTA • MILLER, RAYMOND • MILLER, RENEE • MILLER, ROBERT • MILLER, ROBERT • MILLER, RONALD • MILLER, SUE • MILLER, TIM • MILLER, TOBY • MILLER, WAYNE • MILLER, WHITNEY • MILLGARD, JACK • MILLIANS, JULIE • MILLICHAP, DENISE • MILLIGAN, HELEN • MILLIGAN, JOSEPH • MILLIGAN, MARILYN • MILLS, ANNI-TA • MILLS, BYRON • MILLS, DIANE • MILLS, JANE • MILLS, JEANNE • MILLS, KEO • MILLS, MATTHEW • MILLS, RANDY • MILLS, ROSS • MILLS, THOMAS • MILLS, THOMAS • MILLSAP, KEN • MILLSAPS, F • MILNE, AMY • MILNE, CYNTHIA • MILNER, LILLIE • MILSAP, JAMES • MILTIADES, VICTOR • MILTON, JON • MILTON, KATHRYN • MILTON, SHARON • MIMS, GLORIA • MIMS, SAMUEL • MIN, CHRISTINE • MIN, ERICK • MIN, KIM • MIN, SONG • MINALL, DAWN • MINCEY, BILLIE • MINCEY, CYNTHIA • MINDA, KARI • MINGLE, SCOTT • MINNICH, CORTLANDT • MINNICH, SHERRY • MINOR, MARVA • MINOR, SCOTT • MINOR, WILLIAM • MINORS, CHARLES • MINOS, JULIE • MINTO, BOB • MINTON, FLORENCE • MINTON, SUSAN • MINTON, WILLIAM • MINTZ, SARAH • MIR, ROGER • MIRELES, JOSE • MIRON, BRUCE • MITCHELL, ALLAN • MITCHELL, AMY • MITCHELL, BILLIE • MITCHELL, CLYDE • MITCHELL, DEBRA • MITCHELL, EDITH • MITCHELL, ELLEN • MITCHELL, ELNETTA • MITCHELL, INEZ • MITCHELL, JAMES • MITCHELL, JANE • MITCHELL, JEFF • MITCHELL, JOYCE • MITCHELL, MICHELE • MITCHELL, MICKEY • MITCHELL, PAT • MITCHELL, RANDY • MITCHELL, REGAN • MITCHELL, ROBIN • MITCHELL, STEVEN • MITCHELL, TERRELL • MITCHELL, VICKIE • MITCHELL, VICTORIA • MITCHEM, GREGORY • MITCHEM, GRE-GORY • MITTONG, MARY • MIXON, GLORIA • MIZELL, TOM • MIZERA, ANGELIQUE • MOAT, SCOTT • MOBLEY, BRIDGETTE • MOBLEY, MARY • MOCHIZUKI, NAOKO • MOCK, SUSAN • MODLER, ANTOINETTE • MODZELEWSKI, CINDY • MOE, MARY • MOELLER, REINHILD • MOFFETT, MICHAEL • MOFFI, DIANE • MOFFLY, SARA • MOGHADDAS, ALI • MOGIL, CINDY • MOHDSALLEH, MURNI • MOHR, WALT • MOHRLE, ANDREA • MOHRMANN, KIMBERLY • MOJARRA, VICTOR • MOLLICA, HARRY • MOLLOY, JUSTIN • MOLLOY, RUTHANN • MOMPART, SARA • MONCUS, MACK • MONEY, MARIO • MONEY, NISHA • MONGIELLO, RICHARD • MONIZ, ASHLEY • MONTE, TOM • MONKHOUSE, TIM • MONN, STACEY • MONRO, SIRIBOA • MONROE, JACKIE • MONS, WENDY • MONTANE, ROSS • MONTAYNE, JACQUELYN • MONTGOMERY, DIANNE • MONTGOMERY, JOHN • MONTGOMERY, JUDITH • MONT-GOMERY, ROWENE • MONTGOMERY, TIMOTHY • MONTOYA, KATIE • MOODY, CHANDRA • MOODY, PEARLIE • MOOG, RENEE • MOON, JULIE • MOON, JUN • MOON, RONNIE • MOON, SHARON • MOORE, ARNOLD • MOORE, CORRIE • MOORE, DEBORAH • MOORE, DORIE • MOORE, EUGENE • MOORE, GENE • MOORE, GLENDA • MOORE, HAROLD • MOORE, HARVEY • MOORE, JAMES • MOORE, JANE • MOORE, JENNIFER • MOORE, JOYCE • MOORE, LINDA • MOORE, LISA • MOORE, LIZ • MOORE, MARGARET • MOORE, MARGIE • MOORE, MARTHA • MOORE, MICHAEL • MOORE, NAN • MOORE, RICHARD • MOORE, SARAH • MOORE, THOMAS • MOORE, TIMOTHY • MOORE, TOM • MOORE, TONY • MOOSE, BETSY • MOR, SHERIE • MORA, ALAN • MORA, JOE • MORAES, ROBERTO • MORALES, DAGOBERTO • MORALES, FREDDY • MORAN, CARLISS • MORAN, JEAN • MORAN, JOSEPH • MORAN, KIP • MORAN, LEE • MORAN, SEAN • MORAST, VIRGINIA • MORDER, MARY • MORDER, NELIA • MORDER, SR • MORE, DENISE • MORGAN, AUDREY • MORGAN, BRENDA • MORGAN, CANDACE • MORGAN, DAN • MORGAN, DARRYL • MORGAN, GREG • MORGAN, JAMES • MORGAN, JANE • MORGAN, JENNIFER • MORGAN, JOHNNY • MOR-GAN, MARLON • MORGAN, MELISSA • MORGAN, MICHAEL • MORGAN, MIKE • MORGAN, PAULA • MORGAN, ROBBI • MORGAN, RUTHIE • MORGAN, WANDA • MORGAN, WENDY • MORIARITY, JOHN • MORIN, BETH • MORIN, DENITA • MORINE, DALE • MORLEY, VERDI • MORRILL, AUDREY • MORRIS, ANGIE • MORRIS, ANN • MORRIS, ANNE • MORRIS, ANTONIO • MORRIS, CAROL • MORRIS, DENA • MORRIS, DON • MORRIS, ERIKA • MORRIS, FELICIA • MORRIS, HERB • MORRIS, IRIS • MORRIS, JONATHAN • MORRIS, KELLY • MORRIS, NAYSA • MORRIS, PAM • MORRIS, RENETTA • MORRIS, SHAY • MORRIS, SHELDON • MORRIS, TUWANNA • MORRIS, VALERIE • MORRISON, CAROL • MORRISON, E • MORRISON, JIM • MORRISON, KAYE • MORRISON, KIM • MORRISON, RAY • MORRISON, THOMAS • MORRISSEY, BLAISE • MORRISSEY, JEAN • MORROW, MERRY • MORSBERGER, RICHARD • MORSE, CHRISTOPHER • MORSE, RYAN • MORTENSEN, GEORGE • MORTENSEN, JULE • MORTEZ, ARTHUR • MORTON, GEORGETTE • MORTON, GLORIA • MORTON, JERRICO • MORTON, SANDRA • MORTON, SCOTT • MOSBY, LYNN • MOSEBY, JOHN • MOSELEY, ANNA • MOSER, KELLY • MOSES, PATRICIA • MOSHER, SCOTT • MOSKOW, BERNIE • MOSLEY, STEVE • MOSLEY, WANDA • MOSS, ANNETTE • MOSS, BARBARA • MOSS, CATHY • MOSS, CHRISTOPHER • MOSS, HARRY • MOSS, JUDY • MOSS, KIM • MOSS, VANESSA • MOSS, YONZETTA • MOTE, DOYLE • MOTEGI, KIYOMI • MOTHERSHED, ROBB • MOTLEY, EVE • MOTON, ROBERT • MOTT, ROSEMARY • MOUCHET, DEBORAH • MOUDY, TARA • MOULDER, DAVID • MOULDS, MICHELLE • MOW, MICHAEL • MOWERY, ALLISON • MOWERY, TOM • MOWREY, JULIET • MOWRY, BRENDA • MOWRY, IKE • MOYLAN, JOE • MOYLAN, ROSEMARY • MU, MICHAEL • MUBARAK, ALEYAH • MUCHENJE, MAREVA • MUDAHY, PHILIP • MUELLER, BRENDA • MUELLER, BRIGITTE • MUELLER, GEORG • MUHAMMAD, DEBORAH • MUHAMMAD, JESSICA • MUIR, LAUNA • MUJAHID, ATTIYYA • MUJICA, NORBERTO • MUJICA, YVETTE • MULCAHY, DEBORAH • MULCAY, DANNY • MULHARE, EILEEN • MULLANEY, VERA • MULLEN, LILLIAN • MULLEN, SHANNON • MULLINAX, JESSICA • MULLINGS, BARRINGTON • MULLINS, BONNIE • MULLINS, CLARENCE • MULLINS, CLARENCE • MULLINS, IAN • MULLINS, JOHN • MULLINS, MARCUS • MULLINS, MICHAEL • MULLINS, PAT • MULLINS, SHARON • MULLINS, THERESA • MULLIS, PHYLLIS • MULLOY, CHRISTY • MULVANERTY, BARBARA • MUNIE, KIM • MUNN, ALEX • MUNN, BRYAN • MUNOZ, CEASAR • MUNOZ, GIL • MUNROE, JENNIFER • MURCHISON, YOLAND • MURDOCK, PATRICIA • MURKISON, JENNIFER • MURPHY, ARTHUR • MURPHY, BILL • MURPHY, BOB • MURPHY, CAROL • MURPHY, JACK • MURPHY, JEAN • MURPHY, JENNIFER • MURPHY, JULIA • MURPHY, KERRY • MURPHY, MARGARET • MURPHY, MIKE • MURPHY, PABLO • MURPHY, PETER • MURPHY, THEA • MURPHY, TINE • MURRAY, DEBBI • MURRAY, DWAYNE • MURRAY, ELAINE • MURRAY, HERNDON • MURRAY, JASON • MURRAY, JOCK • MURRAY, MARK • MURRAY, MEGHAN • MURRAY, RANDALL • MURRAY, RICHARD • MURRAY, SARA • MURRAY-CLEMON, LOURETTA • MURRY, JOHN • MUSHETT, MICHAEL • MUSHETT, TONY • MUSICK, JESSICA • MUSKA, ANNE • MUSSELLS, CONNIE • MUTHEKI, DORCAS • MUTISYA, MARTIN • MYERS, BILLY • MYERS, CRAIG • MYERS, DONALD • MYERS, JANELL • MYERS, KIM • MYERS, LINDA • MYERS, LISA • MYERS, RICK • MYERS, ROBERT • MYERS, SHARON • MYERS, TRACI • NAHRENDORF, KNUTE • NAIL, ANNE • NALEPA, JENNIFER • NAPELL, ELSA • NADEL, JENNIFER • NADEL, MARC • NADER, LEANN • NAEGEL, SONJA • NAFT, JONATHAN • NAGARKER, PADMA • NAGARKER, VINNIE • NAGATA, BRETT • NAGEL, DENISE • NAGLE, CANDY • NAKAGAWA, DEBBIE • NAKAHARA, MARC • NAKAMURA, MARCIA • NAKASHIMA, CAROL • NANCE, JAMES • NANTZ, CARROLL • NANNIS, MARCIA • NAPOLI, CAROL • NASH, KIMBERLY • NASH, THURMON • NASH, WILLIAM • NASPINSKI, PAUL • NASSAR, JOCELYNE • NATARAJAN, ANUSHA • NAUMANN, BRENDA • NAUT, EDGAR • NAVARRO, M • NAVARRO, NILBERTO • NAVARRO, TIM • NAVE, JUDY • NAYLOR, PAT • NAZARIO, VICTOR • NAZWORTH, DAVE • NEAL, CLAUDETTE • NEAL, JANIE • NEAL, PERRY • NEALEY, KRISTIN • NEBERGALL, BOB • NEELY, BUTCHIE • NEELY, JAMES • NEER, EMILY • NEESE, RICHARD • NEGRON, JANICE • NEGRON, LUIS • NELMS, SHIRELY • NELSON, BEVERLY • NELSON, DEBORAH • NELSON, HARVEY • NELSON, HOLLIE • NELSON, JOYCE • NELSON, LINDA • NELSON, MARY • NELSON, MELANIE • NELSON, MICHELE • NELSON, MILDRED • NELSON, PEGGY • NELSON, RONALD • NELSON, TAMEIKA • NELSON, TRINA • NEMO, CAROL • NERHOOD, HEATHER • NERO, NOEL • NES-BIT, CHERYL • NESBITT, STACY • NESMITH, CHRISTINE • NETHERTON, LINDA • NETKO, SCOTT • NEU, MOLLY • NEUFELD, JAY • NEUMANN, CHERYL • NEUMARK, JUNE • NEUNABER, DON • NEVERS, ERIN • NEVERS, STAN • NEWAY, MODEL • NEWBOLD, CLARA • NEWBOLDS, DAVID • NEWELL, DOVIE • NEWELL, KAREN • NEWHOUSE, THOMAS • NEWKIRK, LINDA • NEWLON, DENISE • NEWMAN, BETH • NEWMAN, BRIANNE • NEWMAN, CHERYL • NEWMAN, JOHN • NEWMAN, MIKE • NEWNAM, BARRY • NEWSOME, THERESA • NEWTON, DOUGLAS • NEWTON, FRANCES • NEWTON, JAMES • NEWTON, SHIRLEY • NG, JODIE • NGO, ANNETTE • NGUYEN, THAI-AN • NGUYEN, THY • NIAKO, EUSEBIA • NICHOLAS, GAYNELL • NICHOLAS, PATRICIA • NICHOLAS, TERRI • NICHOLLS, LAUREN • NICHOLS, DOTT • NICHOLS, ELLEN • NICHOLS, LIZ • NICHOLSON, BROOKS • NICHOLSON, MICHELLE • NICKENS, CLAUDINE • NICKITAS, ATHENA • NICKLAS, CLAIRE • NICKLES, JANET • NICOLAI, LYNN • NIELAND, JANE • NIELAND, JILL • NIELSEN, CATHERINE • NIELSEN, CINDY • NIELSEN, KLAUS • NIEMEYER, CHARLES • NIEMEYER, JON • NIGH, JOHNNA • NIKITIN, KEITH • NILSEN, ARNIE • NILSSON, JAKOB • NILSSON, PIA • NIMONS, NISBET, WILLIAM • NISH, ANDY • NISHI, MOTOKO • NISONGER, ANNA • NIX, AMY • NIX, CHARLENE • NIX, JAMES • NIXON, HARVEY • NIXON, KERRY • NIXON-PEREZ, SIBRENA • NJOROGE, LUCIE • NOBLES, SARAH • NOBUNAGA, AUSTIN • NOCERITO, FRANK • NODA, AKIKO • NOEL, JOHNY • NOEL, SCOTT • NOLAN, FARRAH • NOLAN, SUSAN • NOLLNER, BILL • NOMA, FUMIE • NONEMAKER, LORI • NOONE, JEN • NOORMOHID, SHAHAB • NORDFORS, JUDI • NORMAL, DERRICK • NORMAN, ARNISHA • NORMAN, BERNICE • NORMAN, KIM • NOR-MAN, MARGARET • NORMAN, MELISSA • NORMAN, TOM • NORRED, JEANETTE • NORRIS, ALLIE • NORRIS, KEN • NORRIS, MARGARET • NORRIS, MEG • NORRIS, TONYA • NORTH, MANDY • NORTHROP, BABETTE • NORTON, ANN • NORTON, CHARLOTTE • NORTON, JERRY • NORTON, KIMBERLY • NORTON, MARYLOU • NOSEGBE, CLARA • NOSEGBE, EDMUND • NOTT, TARA • NOURI, MARY • NOVAK, JILL • NOVAK, PHIL • NOVAK, RANDY • NOVAK, SETH • NOVAK-DAIZ, CATHERINE • NOWACK, ROBERT • NOWAK, DENIS • NOWICKI, JENNIFER • NOWOTNY, NANCY • NUCCIO, VINCE • NUETZI, TONY • NUGENT, CAROLYN • NUGENT, DAN • NUNLEYROACH, VERONIKA • NUNNALLY, CHARLES • NUNNALLY, N • NUPPNAU, TODD • NUSBAUM, BEVERLY • NUSE, ABBY • NUSE, GAIL • NYSTROM, ELSA • O'BANION, CAROLYN • O'BRIEN, BRUCE • O'BRIEN, CONNIE • O'BRIEN, GENE • O'BRIEN, JEANNE • O'BRIEN, MARRIETTA • O'CALLAGHAN, JEAN • O'CALLAGHAN, KNOX • O'CONNOR, EILEEN • O'CONNOR, JACKIE • O'CONNOR, JOHN • O'CONNOR, KEEVA • O'CONNOR, O • O'CONNOR, SEAN • O'CONNOR, TOM • O'DAY, LAURA • O'DELL, DIXIE • O'DONNELL, MAUREEN • O'GRADY, MICHAEL • O'HAGAN, ROCHELLE • O'HARA, M • O'HAVER, LYN • O'HAVER, STEPHANIE • O'KELLEY, ATRAVIUS • O'LEARY, MIKE • O'NEAL, REBECCA • O'NEAL, SANDRA • O'NEILL, TIMOTHY • O'NEILL, CHARLIE • O'NEILL, KELLEY • O'NEILL, ROSE • O'NIEL, KELLY • O'REAR, BOLIVAR • O'SHAUGHNESSY, SEANA • O'SHEA, GERRY • O'STEEN, HANK • OAKLEY, TOM • OATES, JAMES • OBAL, JACKIE • OBERDORFER, GENE • OBERFELD, BENNETT • OBRANOWICZ, CHARLIE • OBREGON, BETTY • OBREGON, MICHELLE • OCALLAGHAN, THEODORE • ODA, TAEKO • ODEN, WAYNE • ODENDAHL, JOHN • ODENDAHL, LISA • ODOM, JAMASON • OFFENBACH-VANKLEEK, LISETTE • OFFILL, MARK • OGBORN, VICKI • OGBURE, BENSON • OGLESBY, DAN • OGLESBY, SUSAN • OH, CORRIE • OH, HELEN • OH, KYLE • OH, MYUNG • OH, PHYLLIS • OH, SEUNG • OH, SHERRY • OHSE, TAMARA • OKAMOTO, BRIDGET • OKAMOTO, SHIGEMITSU • OKEEFE, JEANNE • OLANDER, RICHARD • OLDEN, KIM • OKA, MARK • OHNO, MIEKO • ODEN, BRITTANY • OKAWA, DAISUKE • OKAZAKI, ROTO • OKAMA, KIYOKO, TANYA, FRANCES ...

RAMON • SAKS, RACHEL • SAKS, WILLIAM • SALAS, ANTOINETTE • SALATA, ELIZABETH • SALAZAR, LORETTA • SALLEY, ROBERT • SALOMON, ALLICIA • SALSBURG, DENA • SALSBURG, DENA • SALTER, ADOLPHUS • SALTER, EDWARD • SALTER, JAMES • SALVARAS, JUDY • SALVATORE, KARLA • SALZBERG, BRUCE • SAM, ANTHONY • SAM, TASHIMA • SAM, TASHIMA • SAMBER, DOUGLAS • SAMBER, KIM • SAMOSE, EMILY • SAMPLES, STACEY • SAMPSON, AMY • SAMPSON, RICK • SAMPSON, THERYON • SAMPSON, WOODY • SAMS, JERRY • SAMS, NICOLE • SAMSON, SUZANNE • SAMUEL, DONDRA • SAMUELS, DAWN • SAMUELS, LYNN • SANCHES, CINDY • SANCHEZ, ABRIL • SANDE, WILLIAM • SANDELL, KIMBERLY • SANDER, MARK • SANDERS, BENNIE • SANDERS, CARLTON • SANDERS, CHARLES • SANDERS, DEBBIE • SANDERS, EDWARD • SANDERS, GEORGE • SANDERS, GEORGIA • SANDERS, JIMMY • SANDERS, JON • SANDERS, NATHAN • SANDERS, PAT • SANDERS, REGINA • SANDERS, SHANNON • SANDERS, STUART • SANDMAN, AMY • SANDOVAL, ANTONIO • SANDRI, DANIEL • SANDY, VERONICA • SANFORD, GORDON • SANFORD, MURRAY • SANFORD, RICKY • SANG, JENNY • SANTANA, ANDREA • SANTIAGO, FELIX • SANTO, ANN • SANTO, JOHN • SANTOYO, ADOLF • SANTROCK, KELLY • SAPIR, MARCIE • SAPP, IRWIN • SAPP, RICHARD • SAPP, TERRI • SAPP, TINA • SARGENT, DAVID • SARGENT, TOM • SARRELS, ANGELA • SASNETT, MARIE • SASSER, RAINE • SASTRY, PADMA • SATTERFIELD, TOMMY • SATTERLY, LORA • SAUER, EDWIN • SAUER, SUSANNE • SAULS, MISSY • SAUNDERS, MARY • SAUNDERS, PENNY • SAUNDERS, SARA • SAUSVILLE, KEITH • SAVAGE, BRIAN • SAVARESE, IRENE • SAVARESE, RONALD • SAVOLT, JOAN • SAWYER, DANNY • SAWYER, JOHN • SAWYER, MELVIN • SAWYER, TRACY • SAYANI, NAVROZ • SAYE, LINDA • SAYER, NONA • SBARRA, AMY • SCAGLIONE, CHARLES • SCALES, ANGELA • SCALES, EDWIN • SCALES, LILLIAN • SCALES, SABRINA • SCARBOROUGH, CHRISTINA • SCARBOROUGH, DON-CARLOS • SCARBOROUGH, JANICE • SCARBROUGH, JANET • SCARBROUGH, STEVE • SCARDINO, JOE • SCARFF, ROB • SCARTASCINI, MARIEL • SCHACHTEL, DONNA • SCHAEFER, JEAN • SCHAEFER, KATHLEEN • SCHAF, PAM • SCHAFF, TERRI • SCHAFFER, ERIK • SCHALTENBRAND, STEPHEN • SCHAMHART, TAMAR • SCHAUER, MARY • SCHEAR, JUSTIN • SCHECHTEL, LYN • SCHECHTEL, RAYMOND • SCHEETZ, DOUGLAS • SCHEFFEL, IRIS • SCHEFFLER, WALT • SCHEFFLER, JOSHUA • SCHEID, CHUCK • SCHEIDEL, DANIEL • SCHEIDT, DEREK • SCHEIDTMANN, TRACY • SCHEINPFLUG, LARRY • SCHELL, GEORGIA • SCHELL, KARLA • SCHELL-HARO, JEANNE • SCHERER, AMY • SCHERER, DIANNA • SCHESTOPOL, BENJAMIN • SCHEUER, SIGMUND • SCHIFF, DAVID • SCHIFFMAN, JESSICA • SCHIFFMAN, KER-JINGHWEI • SCHILBERG, DANIEL • SCHILLINGS, KAREN • SCHINDLER, JUDITH • SCHIPPER, DAN • SCHLEGEL, DAVID • SCHLEICHER, STEPHANIE • SCHLOSSER, DOUG • SCHLOSSER, JENNIFER • SCHMIDT, ANN • SCHMIDT, CYNTHIA • SCHMIDT, DAVE • SCHMIDT, MARK • SCHMIDT, MIKE • SCHMIDT, MILTON • SCHMIDT, REBBECCA • SCHMIDT, SIBYL • SCHMIDT, TODD • SCHMITT, GRETCHEN • SCHMITT, KATHY • SCHMITT, TAMARA • SCHNABEL, WOLFGANG • SCHNALL, LARRY • SCHNAUDT, ANDRE • SCHNEIDER, GLENDA • SCHNEIDER, SANNE • SCHNETZER, JENNIFER • SCHNITZER, MARIA • SCHOMBER, AXEL • SCHOONMAKER, LISA • SCHORER, KIMBERLY • SCHORER, KRISTEN • SCHORER, LONNIE • SCHOTT, WENDY • SCHRADE, SARA • SCHRADER, MONICA • SCHRAFF, RICHARD • SCHRAMM, CHERYLL • SCHRAMM, LARRY • SCHRAUTH, KEVIN • SCHREIBER, AGNES • SCHREIBER, CATHY • SCHRODE, COREY • SCHROEDER, DAVID • SCHROEDER, FRAN • SCHROEDER, MARCIA • SCHROER, PAT • SCHROPP, PATTI • SCHUBERT, ALFRED • SCHUCH, MIKE • SCHUG, CHIP • SCHULER, ELIZABETH • SCHULER, TRACEY • SCHULTE, STEPHEN • SCHULTHEISS, DIANE • SCHULTHEISS, STEPHANIE • SCHULTZ, JOHN • SCHULZ, ED • SCHULZ, JACKIE • SCHULZE, ALEXIS • SCHULZE, BARBARA • SCHUMACHER, JENE • SCHUMACHER, RICHMON • SCHUTTE, RAY • SCHUYLER, JIM • SCHUYLER, SALLY • SCHWAB, AMY • SCHWARTZ, CHARLY • SCHWARTZ, COLBY • SCHWARTZ, JOHN • SCHWARTZ, NANCY • SCHWARTZ, SUE • SCHWARTZ, SYLVIA • SCHWARTZMAN, GRACIE • SCHWEERS, JANE • SCHWENNESEN, CHRISTY • SCOGGIN, ETHELDRA • SCOGGINS, SANDY • SCOTT, ANITA • SCOTT, CATHY • SCOTT, CHARLES • SCOTT, DAVID • SCOTT, DEBRA • SCOTT, ELIZABETH • SCOTT, GENIE • SCOTT, HELEN • SCOTT, JULIAN • SCOTT, KIMBERLY • SCOTT, LINDA • SCOTT, MARY • SCOTT, MICHAEL • SCOTT, PARRISHA • SCOTT, ROBERT • SCOTT, SHANNON • SCOTT, SUZETTE • SCOTT, TIMOTHY • SCOTT, TONY • SCRIBER, KENT • SCRIVENS, CHARLES • SCRIVERNS, JANYNE • SCRUGGS, PRINEST • SEAHOLM, RENA • SEARCY, DONALD • SEARS, TRICIA • SEAY, BECKY • SEAY, HEATHER • SECRIST, DAWN • SEDLACKO, EUGENE • SEDNEY, JESSICA • SEEBURGER, JACQUELINE • SEGAR, CLIFF • SEGARS, DONNA • SEIFERT, LARRY • SEIFERT, NANCE • SEIFERT, NANCY • SELF, DIANNE • SELHORST, LAURA • SELIG, STANLEY • SELK, JACOB • SELL, MARY • SELLERS, ERIN • SELLERS, KATE • SELLMAN, GAYLE • SELLMAN, PAM • SELLS, LINNETTE • SELMAN, SUSAN • SELOVER, AMY • SELTZER, MARYLOU • SEMINARA, DONNA • SENGSOUVONG, PAN • SENGSTOCK, KIP • SENS, ALOISIUS • SEO, KO • SEOANES, ANNETTE • SEPIN, JOANNE • SERGENT, DOUG • SERINA, MEG • SERRANO, MARTIN • SETHI, ASHA • SETHI, KAMAL • SETTLE, DENISE • SEVILLIAN, DUANE • SEWARD, HOLLEY • SEWARD, TERRY • SEXTON, EILEEN • SEXTON, RICHARD • SEYMOUR, CARNIE • SEYMOUR, DUNCAN • SHADEL, JOAN • SHADLE, MICHAEL • SHAFER, ELLEN • SHAFFER, EMMETT • SHAFFER, SYLVIA • SHAFROTH, JANE • SHAH, MANISH • SHAH, NEETU • SHAH, NIMISH • SHAHHEYDARI, MO • SHAIDNAGLE, NANCY • SHAKHBAZYAN, SEDA • SHAMBURGER, SANDRA • SHANKS, MONICA • SHANNON, TYRONE • SHAPIRO, LORI • SHAPLEY, JOHN • SHARANSKIY, YURIY • SHARIFF, KARIM • SHARKASI, MUEIN • SHARMA, BERNADETTE • SHARP, JASON • SHARP, REUBEN • SHARPE, KENNETH • SHARPTON, CHARLES • SHARPTON, JUDY • SHAVER, CHARLES • SHAW, ANGIE • SHAW, DANNY • SHAW, JENNIFER • SHAW, LOUISE • SHAW, RICARDO • SHAW, RICK • SHAYLOR, SUSAN • SHAYNE, PHILIP • SHEALY, ERIN • SHEALY, HALLIE • SHEALY, LENORA • SHEALY, MARILYN • SHEARON, MICHELLE • SHEARHOUSE, NEB • SHEARS, SELEMAR • SHEEDY, KERRY • SHEEHAN, CHRISTEEN • SHEETS, KELLY • SHELAR, SCOTT • SHELBY, ASHLEIGH • SHELLEBARGER, BONNIE • SHELLEBARGER, JERE • SHELOR, RAYMOND • SHELTON, ARTIE • SHELTON, BUSHAWN • SHELTON, JANICE • SHELTON, THOM • SHENSKY, DAVIDA • SHEPARD, BRIDGET • SHEPARD, EMILY • SHEPARD, JOSHUA • SHEPARD, MICHELLE • SHEPHARD, YVETTE • SHEPHERD, FREDRICK • SHEPHERD, KELLY • SHEPHERD, O • SHEPLEY, NATHAN • SHEPPARD, ADAM • SHEPPARD, JEFFREY • SHEPPARD, MICHAEL • SHERBERGER, ESTHER • SHERMAN, KERI • SHERRARD, DAVID • SHERRILL, NOVELLA • SHERRY, JESSICA • SHETTERLY, DAVID • SHETTERLY, DUDE • SHICK, AMANDA • SHIELDS, BEVERLEY • SHIELDS, BRIAN • SHIELDS, GAIL • SHIELDS, GARIELLE • SHIELDS, GARY • SHIELDS, SIDNEY • SHIMIZU, YUICHIRO • SHINHOLSTER, TODD • SHINLIVER, SERITA • SHIPE, MARY • SHIPP, PETER • SHIRAZI, YUSAF • SHIRLEY, BARRY • SHIRLEY, DAVID • SHIRLEY, PATSY • SHIVER, MARIANNE • SHIVERS, DELORIS • SHIVERS, STEVEN • SHOAI, MARY • SHOCKLEY, LINDA • SHOEMAKER, BONNIE • SHOEMAKER, JIM • SHOFFNER, JOHN • SHOLTES, MARK • SHOOK, CHRISTOPHER • SHOOK, HEIDI • SHOPE, STACIE • SHOPP, PEGGY • SHOWS, KIMBERLY • SHREIBER, ANNE • SHRINE, CAROLYN • SHRINE, GAIL • SHU, ANNIE • SHUFORD, JUDY • SHULER, KAREN • SHULER, SANDRA • SHURTLEFF, CHARLA • SHURTLEFF, TIM • SHUSTER, SANDY • SIBERT, SASHA • SIBLEY, FORREST • SIBLEY, MARVIN • SIBLEY, RECARDO • SIEGEL, DAVID • SIEGEL, DAVID • SIEGEL, RANDIE • SIEGEL, SONDRA • SIEJA, STEVEN • SIEVERS, MELISSA • SIGETY, MIRANDA • SIGMAN, CATHY • SIGMAN, MARY • SIGMAN, MIKE • SIGMON, ALISON • SIGMUND, REBECCA • SIKES, DELL • SILER, CATHY • SILER, CINDY • SILER, DIRRICK • SILER, STEVEN • SILFEE, CHERYL • SILVER, ALISON • SILVER-BERNSTEIN, CARRIE • SILVERMAN, BARRY • SILVIA, HEIDI • SIMAO, ANDREA • SIMBURG, SIMONE • SIMISTER, DAVID • SIMM, ALEXANDRA • SIMMONS, CAROLYN • SIMMONS, CHANTEL • SIMMONS, DAVID • SIMMONS, DEBBIE • SIMMONS, DEE • SIMMONS, DIANA • SIMMONS, DOROTHY • SIMMONS, FAYE • SIMMONS, LAURA • SIMMONS, MARGUERITE • SIMMONS, NEWANDA • SIMMONS, RANDY • SIMMONS, ROSALYN • SIMMONS, SHARON • SIMMONS, STEVE • SIMMONS, ZETTA • SIMMS, DORI • SIMOGLOU, COSTAS • SIMON, BUD • SIMON, ERNESTINE • SIMON, SABU • SIMON, TRAVIS • SIMONS, DEBRA • SIMONS, SHARON • SIMONS, TRACY • SIMONTON, JAY • SIMOT, PAM • SIMPSON, BILL • SIMPSON, CYNTHIA • SIMPSON, LILLIE • SIMPSON, MARTHA • SIMPSON, STEPHANIE • SIMS, BEN • SIMS, BRAD • SIMS, CELESTE • SIMS, FELESSA • SIMS, MICHAEL • SIMS, RANDALL • SIMS, SHELBY • SIMS, VIRDELL • SIMS, WILLIE • SINATRA, PAUL • SINCLAIR, CAROL • SINCLAIR, PHEON • SINGER, VIRGINIA • SINGLETON, ALDVETTA • SINGLETON, KATHLEEN • SINGLETON, LAWANDA • SINGLETON, ROBIN • SINGLEY, SARA • SINTON, ROBIN • SIRMANS, JOHN • SISSON, SUSAN • SKAGGS, BARRETT • SKANDALAKIS, VIDA • SKEEN, JAMES • SKEETE, BRIAN • SKERIK, NORM • SKINNER, BRAD • SKINNER, COLBY • SKINNER, DEBBIE • SKIPPER, NATHAN • SKOLSKY, ROBIN • SKORA, STEVEN • SLACK, ANTHONY • SLACK, ROD • SLACK, VIRGINIA • SLADE, ROSE • SLADE, STEVE • SLAPE, ALICE • SLASKI, JOE • SLAUGHTER, RALPH • SLAYTON, LAVINIA • SLAYTON, LINDA • SLEDGE, KAREN • SLEETH, LEEANNE • SLEETH, MARYLEE • SLEMP, SHEILA • SLOAN, SUSAN • SLOAN, W • SLONE, STEPHANIE • SLOUGH, KATHY • SLOWIACZEK, CHARLES • SLUPECKI, KAREN • SLYKER, TAMARA • SMALL, BARBARA • SMALL, ROGELIO • SMALLEY, MARY • SMALLINS, SHANNA • SMALLWOOD, JOE • SMALT, STEVE • SMALT, SUZY • SMART, PAULETTE • SMITH, ABBIE • SMITH, ALICE • SMITH, ALONZO • SMITH, ANNE • SMITH, ASHLEY • SMITH, AUSTIN • SMITH, B • SMITH, BERKELEY • SMITH, BETTYE • SMITH, BOBBI • SMITH, BOYNTON • SMITH, BRIAN • SMITH, BUDDY • SMITH, CALVIN • SMITH, CARL • SMITH, CARLA • SMITH, CAROL • SMITH, CATHY • SMITH, CHARLES • SMITH, CHARMAINE • SMITH, CHERYL • SMITH, CINDY • SMITH, CLARA • SMITH, CLARKE • SMITH, CONNIE • SMITH, CONNIE • SMITH, COURTNEY • SMITH, CRIS • SMITH, DANIELLE • SMITH, DANNY • SMITH, DAVE • SMITH, DAVID • SMITH, DINAH • SMITH, DONALD • SMITH, DONNA • SMITH, DOROTHY • SMITH, DOUG • SMITH, DOUGLAS • SMITH, EARNEST • SMITH, EDWARD • SMITH, ELIZABETH • SMITH, ELIZABETH • SMITH, ELLA • SMITH, ELLEN • SMITH, ERICA • SMITH, GARY • SMITH, GERALD • SMITH, GERALD • SMITH, GERALD • SMITH, GLORIA • SMITH, GLORIA • SMITH, HERMAN • SMITH, JANIE • SMITH, JARISSA • SMITH, JEANNE • SMITH, JEROME • SMITH, JERRY • SMITH, JOAN • SMITH, JOCELYN • SMITH, JOHNIFER • SMITH, JONATHAN • SMITH, JR • SMITH, KEITH • SMITH, KEN • SMITH, KEVIN • SMITH, KIMBERLY • SMITH, KRISTIN • SMITH, LAUREN • SMITH, LENNON • SMITH, LINN • SMITH, LISA • SMITH, LOUISE • SMITH, LUCY • SMITH, MARLA • SMITH, MARY • SMITH, MARY • SMITH, MARY • SMITH, MARY • SMITH, MEG • SMITH, MEGHAN • SMITH, MELISSA • SMITH, MICHAEL • SMITH, MICHAEL • SMITH, NAOMI • SMITH, PAM • SMITH, PAMELA • SMITH, PATRICIA • SMITH, PENNY • SMITH, RACHEL • SMITH, RANDY • SMITH, RANDY • SMITH, RENDA • SMITH, RENEE • SMITH, REYNA • SMITH, RICHARD • SMITH, RICKY • SMITH, RITCH • SMITH, ROBERT • SMITH, ROBERT • SMITH, ROSE • SMITH, RUBY • SMITH, RUSSELL • SMITH, RYAN • SMITH, SANFORD • SMITH, SCOTTY • SMITH, SHAY • SMITH, SHELLEY • SMITH, SHENAN • SMITH, SHIRLEY • SMITH, SHIRLEY • SMITH, SPENCER • SMITH, STEPHANIE • SMITH, STEPHEN • SMITH, STEWARD • SMITH, TIMOTHY • SMITH, TOM • SMITH, TONY • SMITH, VANESSA • SMITH, VINCENT • SMITH, WADE • SMITH, WADE • SMITH-TYLER, HELEN • SMOTHERMAN, CAROL • SMOTHERS, ESTERINE • SMOTHERS, SHANAAL • SMOTHERS-HILL, NICHOLE • SNAPE, JIM • SNELLING, CHARLIE • SNELSON, MARY • SNIDER, LISA • SNIDER, NICK • SNIDER, REBECCA • SNIPES, MICHAEL • SNIPES, WHITNEY • SNODDY, LEMONT • SNOW, GLEN • SNOW, KELLY • SNOW, LEANN • SNOWBALL, HALINA • SNOWDEN, LORETTA • SNYDER, BURNIE • SNYDER, DAWN • SNYDER, PAIGE • SNYDER, SARA • SOARES, LUCIANA • SOBELMAN, NANCY • SOBELSON, BARI • SOBELSON, BONNIE • SOFFIN, ANNE • SOHN, EUGENEA • SOLIVAN, ADAM • SOLOMON, LAMONT • SOLOMON, TARA • SOLONCHE, LILA • SOLYMOSSY, LINDA • SOMOGYI, DAN • SONG, CHARLIE • SOPER, BECKY • SOPER, JANET • SOPHIA, MIKE • SORENSON, KRISTIN • SOREY, MARY • SORG, ROGER • SORGATZ, MARY • SORIE, ANNE • SORLIE, DENISE • SORRELLS, HOPE • SOSEBEE, MARTHA • SOSEBEE, ROBERT • SOSKIN, BEEDEE • SOSKIN, KATIE • SOTO, ANGIE • SOUCHEK, KEN • SOUCIE, LINDA • SOULINTHONG, THANOUSINH • SOUTH, LISA • SOUTHARD, CARRIE • SOUTHERLAND, CHRIS • SOW, SOULEYMANE • SPALDING, EUGENE • SPANGLER, BENJAMIN • SPANGLER, LYNDA • SPANO, STEPHANIE • SPARKS, CHRIS • SPARKS, DYNA • SPARKS, STEPHANIE • SPATES, RIETTA • SPATES, ROBERT • SPAULDING, BILL • SPAULDING, DE'LORES • SPAULDING, ROBERT • SPEARS, MARIA • SPEARS, MARLA • SPEARS, PAUL • SPEED, MIKE • SPENCER, DEONNE • SPENCER, DONNA • SPENCER, RICHARD • SPENCER, TORI • SPICER, LINDA • SPIELMAN, KAREN • SPIGGS, ROBERT • SPIGNER, DORIS • SPIGNER, JAMES • SPILLANE, ROBERT • SPIVEY, DAVID • SPILLER, SABRINA • SPRAGUE, PAMELA • SPRATLIN, JEFF • SPRATLING, JACQUI • SPRINGS, LINDSEY • SPRING, SHELLEY • SPRUCE, JOHN • SPRUELL, RUTHIE • SPRY, BENNIE • SR, DAVID • SR, RUSTY • SRIDARAN, SRIDAR • SRINIVASAN, SURESH • ST CLAIR, DAVE • STACHERA, STEVEN • STACHOLY, PETER • STAFF, MARATHON • STAFF, MARATHON • STAFFORD, ROBERT • STAILEY, CHRISTINE • STALEY, ANN • STAMAS, LOUIS • STAMBERGER, TARA • STAMM, DENNIS • STAMPS, HASSAAN • STANDARD, TAMI • STANEK, DANA • STANFIELD, BILL • STANG, LAURA • STANG, RICHARD • STANLEY, CHRISTY • STANLEY, LISA • STANLEY, MAUREEN • STANLEY, ROBERT • STANLEY, SHEILA • STANLEY, VANESSA • STANONIK, MATTEA • STANPHILL, BUTCH • STANSEL, MARJORIE • STANTON, JACKIE • STANTON, KATIE • STAPLES, CHERYL • STAPLETON, KAY • STAPLETON, RICK • STARCHER, SAMUEL • STARCHEVSKIY, VICTOR • STARE, MICHEAL • STARK, BILL • STARK, LYNNE • STARK, TOM • STARLIN, REBECCA • STARLING, MICHAEL • STARNES, CINDY • STARR, CHRIS • STARR, ELLEN • STARR, FREDERICK • STARR, SHANDRA • STARY, KAREN • STATEN, KATHY • STATEN, TERRI • STATHAM, DIANE • STATHAM, SOMMER • STAWICK, MELISSA • STECKLER, LESLIE • STEDMAN, KEITH • STEELE, CHARLIE • STEELE, JEFFREY • STEELE, RONALD • STEELE, STEVE • STEELMAN, KIM • STEFFENHAGEN, DAVID • STEGALL, NICOLE • STEGALL, PAM • STEGER, MICHAEL • STEHMAN, HEATHER • STEIN, ANGELINE • STEIN, SANDRA • STEINBERG, LAUREN • STEINBERG, RON • STEINBRENNER, RIE • STEINGOLD, STAN • STEINHAUSER, ANDY • STEMP, SHEILA • STENGELHOFEN, THEO • STENGER, SALLY • STEPHAN, ANDY • STEPHAN, KATHY • STEPHAN, MELANIE • STEPHENS, CLIFFORD • STEPHENS, ELAINE • STEPHENS, EVA • STEPHENS, FAN • STEPHENS, JULIE • STEPHENS, KINDELL • STEPHENS, LAURA • STEPHENS, M • STEPHENS, MICHAEL • STEPHENS, RICHARD • STEPHENS, SHANE • STEPHENS, THERESA • STEPHENS, VICKI • STEPHENS, VIRGINIA • STEPHENSON, JOHN • STEPHENSON, TOMMY • STERCHI, ANNE • STERLING, KELLY • STERLING, TRENESE • STERNBERG, MARIS • STESHKO, MOLLY • STEUBEN, JOEL • STEUWE, KATHY • STEVENS, CAROL • STEVENS, EDDIE • STEVENS, JANICE • STEVENS, JEANNETTE • STEVENS, PATTY • STEVENS, ROBIN • STEVENSON, DAVID • STEVENSON, JAN • STEVENSON, JOHN • STEVENSON, PATRICE • STEWARD, JACK • STEWARD, JOSEPH • STEWARD, MICHAEL • STEWARD, NANCY • STEWARD, WANDI • STEWART, CINDY • STEWART, CLAY • STEWART, COURTNEY • STEWART, DAVID • STEWART, DEBRA • STEWART, GARY • STEWART, JAMES • STEWART, JUDY • STEWART, LOLITA • STEWART, PAT • STEWART, QUINCY • STEWART, SAMUEL • STEWART, THOMAS • STICKLES, DENA • STIEFVATER, JOHN • STIEL, DANNY • STIERLEN, CONSTANCE • STIKES, NANCY • STILGER, VINCE • STILL, ROBIN • STILLMAN, SUSAN • STILLWELL, TAMMIE • STILWILL, JILL • STIMMEL, MARY • STOBBE, JULIE • STOBBE, TIM • STOCKTON, PHYLLIS • STOGNER, BILLY • STOGNER, JOHN • STOGNER, NICKY • STOGNER, SANDY • STOKES, DEBRA • STOKES, JEANETTE • STONE, CARRIE • STONE, ELLEN • STONE, GREGORY • STONE, JOHN • STONE, LINDA • STONE, MICHAEL • STONE, PHYLLIS • STONE, SUZANNE • STONEHOUSE, FRANCINE • STOPKA, CHRIS • STOREY, VICTORIA • STORY, HEATH • STORY, ROBERT • STORY, WAYMON • STORY, WINSHIP • STOTT, DANA • STOTTS, BRIAN • STOUT, TAFFEY • STOVER, ANNA • STRAKA, STACY • STRAND, BRIANA • STRANGE, CHUCK • STRANGE, ROSIE • STRATTON, MELISSA • STRATTON, THOMAS • STRAUCH, MISSY • STRAUSS, ESTELLE • STRAUSS, LISA • STRAYER, JONATHAN • STRAYER, LORI • STRAZAR-SAUNDERS, TRISH • STREIB, DAVID • STRELEC, CYNTHIA • STRICKLAND, CHRIS • STRICKLAND, DENNIS • STRICKLAND, FRANK • STRICKLAND, HATTIE • STRICKLAND, JUDY • STRICKLAND, LAURA • STRICKLAND, STUART • STRICKLETT, JOHN • STRICKLETT, JOHN • STRICKMAN-LEVITAS, CRAIG • STRIPLING, CAROL • STRIPLING, ELIZABETH • STROCK, LISA • STRONG, DANIEL • STROOBANTS, HILDE • STROTHER, MARK • STROUD, CHRISTOPHER • STRUBLE, STACY • STUART, JAMES • STUBBLEFIELD, LAINIE • STUBBS, AMY • STUMP, KEVIN • STUMP, MEGAN • STURGIS, BYRON • STUTTS, KEITH • STYLES, MICHAEL • STYLES, RACHEL • STYLES, ROSE • SU, SA • SUAREZ, VICTOR • SUBRAMANIAN, MANI • SUDDETH, LESLIE • SUFFRIN, KENNETH • SUGGS, KEN • SUGGS, LINDA • SUHR, KENNETH • SULLARDS, SHANE • SULLARDS, STEPHANIE • SULLEN, MENIZE • SULLIVAN, DEBBY • SULLIVAN, DENNIS • SULLIVAN, DIANNE • SULLIVAN, JOSHUA • SULLIVAN, KENNETH • SULLIVAN, LANIE • SULLIVAN, MEGHAN • SULLIVAN, PEARLINE • SUMLIN, HULETT • SUMMERS, DAVID • SUMMERS, KATHLEEN • SUMMERS, MARGIE • SUMMERSILL, ANN • SUMMERSON, LILLIAN • SUMMERVILLE, CARLA • SUMPTER, DAVID • SUNDARAM, SAKU • SUPARDI, DOLLIE • SUTHERLAND, DAVID • SUTTERFIELD, LAUREN • SUTTON, CAROLYN • SUTTON, DAVID • SUTTON, KYRA • SUTTON, VERONICA • SUTYLO, LINDA • SVANBERGSSON, KRISTJAN • SVETLY, BETH • SWADER, MARY • SWAFFORD, JUDITH • SWAFFORD, RONALD • SWAILS, SHIRLEY • SWAMINATHAN, MANGAL • SWAMINATHAN, NIKHIL • SWAN, PAT • SWANGER, LARRY • SWANK, JOSEPH • SWANN, ELEANOR • SWANN, RODNEY • SWANSON, JONATHAN • SWARTZ, JOHN • SWARTZENTRUBER, MARLIN • SWEDLOW, LAURA • SWEENEY, JIM • SWEENEY, PERRY • SWEIGART, CARL • SWENSON, CATHY • SWIFT, ED • SWIFT, ROBIN • SWIFT, RYAN • SWISHER, CAROL • SWOGER, TIMOTHY • SWOPE, ALLYSON • SWYER, DAVID • SWYER, MONIQUE • SYFERT, MANDI • SYKES, CHUCK • SYKES, JENNA • SYKES, MICHAEL • SYLER, RHONDA • SYLVER, PRISCILLA • SYLVESTER, AARON • SYLVIA, JR • SYMONDS, ALICE • SYVINSKI, STEVEN • SZYMAN, DAN • TAAFFE, LEILA • TADAYON, MO • TADROS, WADIE • TAFEL, ALLAN • TAFEL, MICHAEL • TAFFEL, NANCY • TAFT, DAVID • TAKATSUKI, ALISSA • TAKEGAHARA, HIDEKI • TALAVERA, SAMUEL • TALLER, ANNEMARIE • TALLEY, CHES • TALLMAN, DUANE • TALLON, MATT • TALMADGE, BETTY • TAMBURELLO, PAULA • TAMURA, ARATA • TAMURA, KAZUMI • TAN, ROWENA • TANG, DON • TANG, RC • TANKERSLEY, JENNY • TANNER, JODY • TANNER, LISA • TANNETT, DONNA • TANTILLO, MARY • TANTIVEJKUL, KWANCHANOK • TANZOSCH, FELICIA • TAQI-EDDIN, MUYESSER • TAQUECHEL, BETH • TARKENTON, FRED • TARKENTON, JACKIE • TAROLI, FRED • TARRANT, KAREN • TARSITANO, LEE • TATE, CHRISTOPHER • TATE, CINDY • TATE, ELIZABETH • TATE, ELVIRA • TATE, HUNTER • TATE, I • TATE, WILL • TATE-HOLLOWAY, PAMELA • TATMAN, ROBERT • TATUM, CHRISTINE • TAULMAN, SUSAN • TAVARES, HANK • TAVERAS, LUIS • TAYLOR, ALEX • TAYLOR, ANTHONY • TAYLOR, BILL • TAYLOR, BRANDON • TAYLOR, BUD • TAYLOR, CAMERON • TAYLOR, CHANIKA • TAYLOR, CHARLYE • TAYLOR, CHESTER • TAYLOR, CHET • TAYLOR, CHRIS • TAYLOR, CHRISTIAN • TAYLOR, CLYDE • TAYLOR, DAN • TAYLOR, DONNA • TAYLOR, DOUGLAS • TAYLOR, ELIZABETH • TAYLOR, ELVIS • TAYLOR, EMILY • TAYLOR, EVELYN • TAYLOR, JERMAINE • TAYLOR, JESSE • TAYLOR, JIM • TAYLOR, JIMI • TAYLOR, JUANITA • TAYLOR, KAREN • TAYLOR, KAVIN • TAYLOR, LARRY • TAYLOR, LEISA • TAYLOR, LESLIE • TAYLOR, LINDA • TAYLOR, LISA • TAYLOR, MOLLY • TAYLOR, NORMA • TAYLOR, PEGGY • TAYLOR, RICHARD • TAYLOR, ROBERT • TAYLOR, SAMANTHA • TAYLOR, SHEA • TAYLOR, SHEILA • TAYLOR, SONJA • TAYLOR, THOMAS • TAYLOR, VERONICA • TAYLOR, VIVIAN • TAYLOR, WES • TAYLOR-THOMPSON, MICHELLE • TEAGUE, BILL • TEAGUE, BRIAN • TEAGUE, MARILYN • TEAGUE, TANGYE • TEAL, JAMES • TEAL, JANET • TEAL, ROBERT • TEAL, TOMMY • TEBAY, RANDALL • TEDARDS, TOM • TEDDER, JO • TEDDLIE, ANNE • TEDESCHI, DOT • TEDESCHI, LESLIE • TEDESCHI, VINCENT • TEDFORD, CHERYL • TEEGARDEN, BILL • TEEVAN, JOHN • TEGELAAR, DAVID • TEKENBROEK, ROLAND • TELENKO, NIEATA • TELLINGTON-JONES, LINDA • TELTOE, AMBER • TEMONEY, FRANCES • TEMPLE, DEBORAH • TEMPLES, SHARON • TEMPLETON, ALAN • TENHOOR, TERRI • TERESE, MARLO • TERLAJE, RAY • TERRANCE, CAROLYN • TERRELL, CHRISTY • TERRELL, FRANCES • TERRELL, JOYCE • TERRELL, REGINA • TERRY, DAVID • TERRY, KAREEM • TERRY, OCTAVIUS • TESHERA, NICHOLE • TESTANI, IWONA • TESTON, WENDY • TESZLER, SUDIE • TEVES, JONATHAN • THACKREY, KENT • THAYER, D • THEISEN, KRISTY • THEKKUMPURAM, VELAMA • THEODOS, JOHN • THERRIEN, MIKE • THIBODEAU, MARC • THIESSEN, DAVE • THODESON, FRED • THOMAN, LARRY • THOMAS, ABBEY • THOMAS, ANTHONY • THOMAS, ANTHONY • THOMAS, ASHINDRA • THOMAS, BARBARA • THOMAS, CARMEN • THOMAS, CLAY • THOMAS, DANYELL • THOMAS, DAWN • THOMAS, DEMETRIUS • THOMAS, ED • THOMAS, ESTHER • THOMAS, GARI • THOMAS, GEORGE • THOMAS, HATTIE • THOMAS, HAZEL • THOMAS, HIAWATHA • THOMAS, JAY • THOMAS, JENNIFER • THOMAS, JERMICE • THOMAS, JERRY • THOMAS, JOHN • THOMAS, JOHNNY • THOMAS, JON-MICHAEL • THOMAS, JULIUS • THOMAS, LAURA • THOMAS, LAWREN • THOMAS, LORENZO • THOMAS, MELISSA • THOMAS, MYRTLE • THOMAS, NANCY • THOMAS, PAM • THOMAS, ROBERT • THOMAS, ROGERIA • THOMAS, ROSIE • THOMAS, RYAN • THOMAS, SALLY • THOMAS, SANDRA • THOMAS, SHARONDA • THOMAS, SHARONDA • THOMAS, SUNSHINE • THOMAS, TANGELITA • THOMAS, TERRY • THOMAS, VALENCIA • THOMPSON, BETH • THOMPSON, BLAKE • THOMPSON, BRENDA • THOMPSON, BRIGETTE • THOMPSON, CAROLE • THOMPSON, CHRIS • THOMPSON, CLIFFTON • THOMPSON, DONA • THOMPSON, DONNA • THOMPSON, GREGORY • THOMPSON, HANNAH • THOMPSON, JANIE • THOMPSON, JIMMY • THOMPSON, KENITH • THOMPSON, KRISTI • THOMPSON, LEWIS • THOMPSON, PATRICE • THOMPSON, PHIL • THOMPSON, RICHARD • THOMPSON, ROB • THOMPSON, ROXANE • THOMPSON, RUSSELL • THOMPSON, SAM • THOMPSON, SANDRA • THOMPSON, SHEILA • THOMPSON, SHELLEY • THOMPSON, STARR • THOMPSON, STEFANI • THOMPSON, SUSAN • THOMPSON, TONI • THOMPSON, WALTER • THOMPSON, WILLIE • THOMSEN, ERICA • THOMSEN, LIZ • THOMSEN, NANCY • THOMSEN, VICTOR • THOMSON, WILLIAM • THOR, JOSEPH • THORN, KENDRA • THORNBURY, LOYCE • THORNE, BEN • THORNE, DICK • THORNE, JANICE • THORNTON, ALEXIA • THORNTON, BRENDA • THORNTON, CHEVAI • THORNTON, DEBORAH • THORNTON, DON • THORNTON, KATIE • THORNTON, KELLI • THORNTON, MATTHEW • THORNTON, TREVERA • THORPE, JEANNE • THORPE, ALAINA • THORPE, JEFFERY • THORSTAD, ROGER • THRASHER, CURTIS • THRELKELD, KELLY • THRIVIKRAMAN, JYOTHI • THROCKMORTON, CHRIS • THUMA, ALICE • THURMAN, JOHNNY • THURMAN, MONICA • THURMOND, SADIE • TIDWELL, DONNA • TIDWELL, JIM • TIEMAN, BETH • TILDEN, HELEN • TILGHMAN, DONNIE • TILGHMAN, MARY • TILLEY, MARK • TILLMAN, JOHN • TILLMAN, TRISH • TIMES, NANCY • TIMM, ALICIA • TIMM, ANDREW • TIMM, KENT • TIMMIS, NICOLE • TIMPERIO, LAURA • TINDELL, JAY • TINLEY, STEPHANIE • TINSLEY, BROOKS • TINSLEY, PHILIP • TIRELLA, ROBERT • TIRRELL, MAUREEN • TIRUMS, LYNN • TIS, LAURIE • TISCARENO, MARY • TISCHLER, INGRID • TITTA, ANN • TOBACK, MONICA • TOBIAS, KRISTEN • TOBIN, TAMI • TODD, DAWN • TODD, JENNIE • TODD, WILLIE • TODOROV, ALEXANDER • TOKUOKA, K • TOLBERT, JAMES • TOLEDO, SANDRO • TOLER, MELISSA • TOLES, TERRY • TOLIVER, ANDREA • TOLOTTA, MARIA • TOM, MIMI • TOMASKO, ALAN • TOMBERLIN, ALLISON • TOMLIN, ANNE • TOMLIN, CHARLES • TOMLINSON, JT • TOMPKINS, TREY • TONN, LYDIA • TONNE, ANDREA • TORAIN, ERIC • TORCHIA, THOMAS • TORNIAINEN, MERVI • TORRES, FERNANDO • TORRES, JORGE • TORRES, JOSE • TORRES, LEMUEL • TORRES, LUIS • TORRES, SUZANNE • TOTTEN, BETTY • TOWEY, MATTHEW • TOWLER, POLLY • TOWNER, MARGARETTE • TOYODA, IKUYO • TRACY, KENNETH • TRACY, SEAN • TRACY, SUZIE • TRADER, BARB • TRAMMELL, DANA • TRANSUE, MARYBETH • TRASKA, ANTHONY • TRAUGOT, ANDREW • TRAVIS, NOELLE • TRAYLOR, KATHY • TRAYNIN, GENRIKH • TREA, CONNIE • TREADWAY, DIANA • TREADWELL, STEPHEN • TRENT, TERRY • TRESSLER, JACK • TREVINO, AUDELIA • TREVINO, KEITH • TRIMBLE, BOB • TRIMBLE, CHARNETTE • TRIMBLE, TERESA • TRINH, PHOUNG • TRINH, PHUONG • TRIPLETT, MICHAEL • TRIPP, EDWINA • TRIPP, NANCY • TRITINGER, MICHAEL • TROLLINGER, JUDY • TROWER, TED • TRUAN, MEGAN • TRUCHAN, STEPHANIE • TRUELL, CORINNE • TRUESDALE, ELAINE • TRUMP, TRENT • TRUNDLE, JANET • TSAI, PETER • TSETSE, KANDACE • TSUDA, SHINTARO • TSUI, JASON • TUBBS, ALVIN • TUCKER, CALOISE • TUCKER, CEDRICK • TUCKER, DEBORAH • TUCKER, ELLIOTT • TUCKER, GREGORY • TUCKER, MATTHEW • TUDOR, ROBIN • TUGGLE, RONALD • TUHKANEN, INKERI • TUITE, DONNA • TULLER, BRANDIE • TULLER, DANIEL • TULLY, CELIA • TULLY, DENNIS • TUNNELL, MARGARET • TUNSTALL, EVELYN • TURBYVILLE, GAIL • TURCOTTE, LICHELLE • TURCOTTE, MICHAEL • TUREK, ELLEN • TURKHEIMER, STEFAN • TURKO, EILEEN • TURNER, ALLISON • TURNER, ANGELLE • TURNER, BARZELLA • TURNER, BETTY • TURNER, BRYAN • TURNER, CHESLEY • TURNER, DEBORAH • TURNER, ERICA • TURNER, FRANCIE • TURNER, GEORGE • TURNER, GLORIA • TURNER, JACK • TURNER, JAMES • TURNER, JUANITA • TURNER, JULIE • TURNER, LEE • TURNER, LESLEY • TURNER, LINDA • TURNER, LISA • TURNER, MARK • TURNER, MAURA • TURNER, PAM • TURNER, ROBERT • TURNER, SANDRA • TURNER, SCOTT • TURNER, SHANA • TURNER, TOM • TURNER, TRACEY • TURNER, ANN • TURPIN, TOM • TUSQUETS, JACOBO • TVEAT, RYAN • TWADDELL, BOB • TWADDELL, LINDA • TWEED, DORA • TWEED, WILLIAM • TWINE, J • TYBURSKI, KEN • TYERS, KIRSTEN • TYLER, TAMMIE • TYLER, WILL • TYLOR, LISA • TYRER, ALISON • TYROFF, SHARON • TYSON, HUGO • TYSON, SYNGE • TYSON, WENDY • UBERTO, PETER • UEGAKI, KIMI • UGENYI, VICTOR • UHLER, BRENDA • UHLER, JASON • ULICNY, GARY • ULICNY, SALLY • ULMAN, RICHARD • ULRICH, CHAD • ULRICH, HEIDI • UMPHLETT, JOHN • UNDERWOOD, BETTY • UNDERWOOD, GLADYS • UNDERWOOD, HERBERT • UNDERWOOD, REBECCA • UNGER, TED • UNSER, CHRISTY • UNSER, EDWARD • UNSWORTH, GAIL • UPTON, YVETTE • URTEAGA, LUIS • USY, JOHN • UZUNAY, SELEN • VACCARO, LAURA • VACCARO, RALPH • VADNAIS, GINA • VADNAIS, TOM • VAKSELIS, DENNIS • VALDEZ, VICTOR • VALENTI, CAROLE • VALENTINE, BOBBIE • VALENTINE, TODD • VALENZUELA, LINDA • VALESKE, JULI • VALLEJO, RICHARD • VALTAVAARA, JUHA • VAN ALSTINE, ANGELA • VAN GORP, HOLLY • VAN MATER, MARY • VAN PELT, DUNCAN • VAN PHAM, LE • VAN SICKLE, MERRY • VAN TINE, FRAN • VAN VACHON, VAN WERDEN, DOUGLAS • VAN ZANT, VERNON • VANAUKEN, CYNTHIA • VANBEVERS, JAMIE • VANCE, GWEN • VANCE, SANDRA • VANDERBILT, K • VANDERBOOM, RENEE • VANDERHORST, CHRISTINA • VANDERHORST, PAT • VANDERMARK, DOUGLAS • VANDERVEEN, BRAD • VANDERYT, KIRBY • VANDIVER, SCOTT • VANDORN, LUKEITHA • VANFLEET, BETH • VANGAS, SHARON • VANN, MARY • VANPELT, ERIC • VANREELL, RONALD • VANSADERS, SHEILA • VANVOORHIS, GAIL • VANZANT, RAQUILAH • VARADY, DIANE • VARCOE, REE • VARDYA, SMITA • VARELA, VICTORIA • VARGAS, ONIX • VARGHESE, LISA • VARLEY, NOLINA • VARNEDOE, BARBARA • VARNER, GLORIA • VARNER, JOHN • VARNER, LEE • VARNEY, LINDA • VARSHA, BOB • VASON, KEITH • VASSOS-LILLIE, IRENE • VAUGHAN, JIM • VAUGHN, ANTHONY • VAUGHN, CHERYL-ANN • VAUGHN, JIL • VAUGHN, PEGGY • VAUGHN-HUTCHINSON, MINDI • VAUPEL, JERROD • VAVASOUR, KERRY • VAZIN, VIRGINIA • VAZQUEZ, ROSE • VEAL, REX • VEERLING, DEBBIE • VEGA, ANTHONY • VELAZQUEZ, GEORGE • VELENZ, ROBERTO • VENABLE, JASON • VENEGAS, REBECA • VENSON, SJANA • VERNA, MIKE • VERPILLOT, ALICIA • VERRET, SUZANNE • VERST, AMY • VERST, DANIELLE • VERZINSKIE, RONALD • VETTER, STEPHEN • VEZETINSKI, DENICE • VEZETINSKI, PATRICK • VIBERG, ANNE • VIBERG, SARA • VICENTE, VICTOR • VICTORY, RICHARD • VIDEON, TRACY • VIDRO-MARTINEZ, WILFREDO • VIEBROCK, ERIC • VIELHABER, DENNIS • VIGILANCE, TROY • VIGNERI, MARI • VIGNOLI, MAXIMILLIAN • VILLAMARZO, MARIA • VILLARREAL, JR • VILLEGAS, CARLOS • VINA, E • VINCENT, BARBARA • VINCENT, DEBRA • VINCENT, HEATHER • VINCENT, MICHELE • VINCENT, RACHEL • VINCENT, THERESA • VINCENT, WAYNE • VINCENT, WINCHEL • VINE, DELORES • VINES, CALVIN • VINES, CHERYL • VINGERLING, ELISABETH • VINSON, ELIZABETH • VINSON, NATALIE • VINSON, SHARON • VIRANI, FATIMA • VITRANO, TONY • VITULLI, TONY • VOEGTLY, TODD • VOGEL, ADAM • VOGEL, JEFFEREY • VOGEL-BROWN, CONNIE • VOGELMANN, MARKUS • VOGT, KEN • VOGT, WENDY • VON NORDHEIM, STEVE • VON SELZAM, EVA-MARIA • VON SELZAM, HARALD • VONG, QUAN • VOORT, HOLLY • VORCE, MARY • VORTICE, JOYCE • VOSS, DOUGLAS • VOSS, PATRICIA • VOUTT, REGEENA • VOYLES, LINDA • VOYLES, RICHARD • VOYMAS, BENJAMIN • VRANKOVA, EVA • VRIONIS, JOHN • VU, HIEN • WABICH, CHER • WADDINGTON, PAMELA • WADDLE, BECKY • WADE, ALICE • WADE, CHRIS • WADE, JASON • WADE, JIM • WADE, JOHNNY • WADE, TIA • WADE, TRAY • WADE, VERNA • WAEGHE, NADINE • WAGNER, CINDY • WAGNER, EMILY • WAGNER, FRANCES • WAGNER, JAMES • WAGNER, LOUIS • WAGNER, PETER • WAGNER, RALPH • WAGONER, ANALISA • WAGONER, THERESA • WAHL, RICHARD • WAINRIGHT, SUSANNE • WAITS, KEVIN • WAKID, KATHERINE • WALDING, GUY • WALDROP, MARLAN • WALDSCHUETZ, NIKKI • WALKER, ALICIA • WALKER, ANSLEY • WALKER, ANTHONY • WALKER, BEN • WALKER, CAROL • WALKER, CAROLYN • WALKER, CONNIE • WALKER, CRYSTAL • WALKER, DEBORA • WALKER, DOLORES • WALKER, DONNA • WALKER, DORI • WALKER, ERNESTINE • WALKER, FLOYD • WALKER, GAYE • WALKER, J • WALKER, JAIME • WALKER, JANET • WALKER, JODEE • WALKER, JUNE • WALKER, KATRINA • WALKER, KIM • WALKER, LYDIA • WALKER, MAURICE • WALKER, RAMSAY • WALKER, ROBERTA • WALKER, ROSIE • WALKER, SAKHYEH • WALKER, SAMANTHA • WALKER, SHARON • WALKER, SHAUN • WALKER, SUSAN • WALKER, TAMMI • WALKER, TERMAYNE • WALKER, VANICE • WALKER, VIRGIL • WALKER, ZACHARY • WALKO, KAREN • WALKUP, TRACY • WALL, BEN • WALLACE, ANISE • WALLACE, BETSY • WALLACE, DEENA • WALLACE, EDGIE • WALLACE, ERIKA • WALLACE, GENE • WALLACE, JAMES • WALLACE, JOANNE • WALLACE, MELISSA • WALLACE, MICHEAL • WALLACE, PAMELA • WALLACE, SHERRY • WALLACE, SUSAN • WALLACE, YOLANDA • WALLEN, DEB • WALLER, CHANDA • WALLER, CHANTE • WALLER, THERESA • WALP, BRIAN • WALSH, EAMON • WALSH, JANE • WALSH, JEANETTE • WALSH, KELLY • WALSH, MICHELLE • WALSH, MOOSE • WALSH, SHAUN • WALSH, SHAWN • WALSH, STEVEN • WALSH, TIM • WALSH, TOM • WALTER, EVA • WALTER, JEAN • WALTON, AMY • WALTON, EMILY • WALTON, JONATHAN • WALTON, PAT • WALTON, SANDRA • WALTZ, WILLIAM • WALTZ-ALLEN, OZANNA • WANAMAKER, BENHUR • WANG, ANGELA • WANG, CATHERINE • WANG, JOHN • WANG, PATTY • WANG, RUI • WARD, ALLISON • WARD, EDDIE • WARD, FRANK • WARD, JOHN • WARD, JOY • WARD, JR • WARD, LAURA • WARD, TONY • WARD, TRISHA • WARD, WILL • WARE, LINDA • WARFIELD, DAVID • WARFIELD, DONNA • WARLEY, ANNE • WARLEY, TERESA • WARNE, KIM • WARNER, LEFONGIA • WARNER, LEONARD • WARNER, LINDA • WARNER, VIRGINIA • WARREN, BARBARA • WARREN, CAROLYN • WARREN, JOSH • WARREN, KELLY-ANN • WARREN, PATSY • WARREN, SARA • WARREN, STANLEY • WARREN, SUSAN • WASHBURN, SUNNY • WASHINGTON, CARMELITA • WASHINGTON, CHERY • WASHINGTON, J • WASHINGTON, ROMAINE • WASHINGTON, RUDY • WASHINGTON-CRESPY, MILDRED • WASLEY, ELAINE • WASNER, MIEKE • WASS, KEVIN • WASSEL, COLLEEN • WASSEL, MARY • WASSELL, AMANDA • WASSON, BARBARA • WATERFALL, PEGGY • WATERS, CONNIE • WATERS, MARCUS • WATERS, PENNY • WATERS, SHANNON • WATKINS, BRENDA • WATKINS, HARDIN • WATKINS, LATRICE • WATKINS, MARION • WATKINS, MARY • WATKINS, YRA • WATSON, AMY • WATSON, BOB • WATSON, BONNIE • WATSON, BRENDA • WATSON, DIANA • WATSON, DOUGLAS • WATSON, HEATHER • WATSON, JANE • WATSON, JEREMY • WATSON, KELLY • WATSON, MICHAEL • WATSON, RICHARD • WATSON, ROBIN • WATSON, RONALD • WATSON, SHERIE • WATSON, TOM • WATSON, VICKIE • WATSON, VICKIE • WATTERS, ROXANNA • WATTLES, RAY • WATTS, MARY • WATTS, TANIESHA • WAYDA, VALERIE • WAYNE, JIM • WAYNE, LINDA • WAYNE, TODD • WAYNICK, JERI • WAYNICK, PAIGE • WAYS, ALISHA • WEATHERS, BARBARA • WEAVER, ALVIN • WEAVER, CHARLES • WEAVER, CHRISTOPHER • WEAVER, CINDY • WEAVER, DEBORAH • WEAVER, DESMOND • WEAVER, JR • WEAVER, JULIA • WEAVER, ROSEMARY • WEAVER, SANDY • WEBB, ANN • WEBB, BRUCE • WEBB, DEN • WEBB, DENNY • WEBB, JACQUELYN • WEBB, JOE • WEBB, JOHN • WEBB, LAWRENCE • WEBB, MARJORIE • WEBB, MIRIAM • WEBB, PENNY • WEBB, PHYLLIS • WEBBER, VANESSA • WEBER, CONNIE • WEBER, GENE • WEBER, JENNIFER • WEBER, LORRAINE • WEBER, MARK • WEBER, NICOLE • WEBER, THERESA • WEBER, TOM • WEBER, WILLIAM • WEBSTER, GAIL • WEBSTER, JULIE • WEBSTER, RICHARD • WEDDING, PAM • WEDGE, TORREY • WEED, KEVIN • WEEKS, KRIS • WEESE, ERIK • WEESE, KELLY • WEESE, LORI • WEIDENAAR, KAREN • WEIDLER, DONNA • WEILER, WEIRDO • WEIMER, RAE • WEIN, BETH • WEINBERG, MARY • WEINKLE, ROBERT • WEINRAUB, ANITA • WEISBROD, ALEXIS • WEISBROD, STEVE • WEISENFELS, JANET • WEISER, STACEY • WEISMANN, BETH • WEISMANN, JOE • WEISS, ANDY • WEISS, ELKE • WEISS, KATHY • WEISSENBURGER, CONNIE • WEISSMAN, BARB • WEISSMAN, DAN • WEIST, CHARLES • WELCH, BETH • WELCH, LINDA • WELCH, RENEE • WELCH, STEPHANIE • WELDEN, GARY • WELDEN, KATHRYN • WELDON, JENNIFER • WELDON, JOE • WELLER, ANDREW • WELLER, JUDI • WELLER, KATHERINE • WELLER, LUKE • WELLER, MARK • WELLS, JOHN • WELLS, LESLIE • WELLS, MARY • WELLS, ROBERT • WELLS, STEPHANIE • WELLS, T • WELSH, JASON • WELTI, MARIA • WELTY, CHAD • WENDELL, GRAY • WENK, ELLE • WENNEKER, CAROLYN • WENNEKER, ROBIN • WENNEKER, RONALD • WENZEL, RANEE • WEPFER, KATIE • WEPFER, LYNNE • WERDHAUSEN, TRACY • WERNER, GREG • WERNER, SARAH • WERTHEIM, PAULA • WERUM, REGINA • WESLEY, DINO • WESLEY, KEVIN • WESOLOWSKI, CORRIE • WESOLOWSKI, KRISTI • WESSINGER, BILL • WESSLING, CHRIS • WEST, BENJAMIN • WEST, BETTY • WEST, BRUCE • WEST, CINDY • WEST, ERIC • WEST, MARGARET • WEST, STEPHANIE • WEST, TALLY • WEST, TERI • WEST, WINDY • WESTBERRY, LINDA • WESTBROOK, LAWRENCE • WESTBROOK, STEPHEN • WESTCOTT, JOHN • WESTCOTT, MARK • WESTERN, FEDERICO • WESTFALL, DANIEL • WESTIN, LISA • WESTIN, PETER • WESTRICH, MARY • WESTRICK, RICHARD • WEYANDT, JR • WEYANDT, MATT • WEYDERT, JERRY • WHALEN, JILL • WHALEN-SHAW, PATRICIA • WHALEY, BART • WHEATLEY, JAMES • WHEELER, JOHN • WHALEY, TOMMY • WHEATON, DEBBIE • WHEATON, KIM • WHEELER, BRYAN • WHEELER, CHERYL • WHEELER, ELLIE • WHEELER, GLORIA • WHEELER, MARY • WHEELER, WENDY • WHELAN, KATHLEEN • WHELAN, RICHARD • WHELAN, TOM • WHELCHEL, DEBORAH • WHELESS, KATHERINE • WHITAKER, LOUVENIA • WHITAKER, MICHAEL • WHITE, ANN • WHITE, ANNETTE • WHITE, BRANDON • WHITE, CHARLES • WHITE, DANA • WHITE, DINA • WHITE, DONALD • WHITE, DONNA • WHITE, DOUGLAS • WHITE, GEORGE • WHITE, GLORIA • WHITE, HATTIE • WHITE, HUGH • WHITE, JANIE • WHITE, JIM • WHITE, JOE • WHITE, JOHN • WHITE, JOYCE • WHITE, KAREN • WHITE, KAREN • WHITE, KEN • WHITE, LARRON • WHITE, LAURA • WHITE, MACKENZIE • WHITE, MARY • WHITE, NICKY • WHITE, NICKY • WHITE, O • WHITE, PORTIAH • WHITE, ROBIN • WHITE, RYAN • WHITE, SALLY • WHITE, SANDY • WHITE, SHERI • WHITE, STEFANIE • WHITE, SUSAN • WHITE, TRACY • WHITE, TYRONE • WHITE, TYRONNIA • WHITE, TYRONNIA • WHITE-ROBERSON, MIRANDA • WHITED, GEORGE • WHITEHEAD, CATHY • WHITEHURST, CAROLINE • WHITENER, ANDY • WHITE, TERE, KERRY • WHITFIELD, MARSHARN • WHITFIELD, STAN • WHITFIELD, TYLER • WHITHAM, GAY • WHITLEY, ODELL • WHITLEY, SHARON • WHITMAN, JAMES • WHITMER, WHIT • WHITMIRE, TERESA • WHITMIRE, TRINA • WHITMORE, JACQUELINE • WHITNEY, MARK • WHITNEY, THOMAS • WHITNEY, VICKI • WHITNEY, WES • WHITSON, MARCUS • WHITT, GLENDA • WHITTAKER, CHUCK • WHITTAKER, JACK • WHITTAKER, WILLIAM • WHITTEN, CLIFTON • WHITTEN, KINA • WHITTENBURG, JEANE • WHITTINGTON, BOB • WHITTINGTON, CONNIE • WHITTLE, ANNA • WHOBREY, PAMELA • WHYE, CAROLYN • WHYTE, ANYE • WIBANKES, JAMES • WICK, MARIE • WICKER, RUSSELL • WICKMAN, TERRANCE • WICKS, CHARLENE • WICKS, COLEMAN • WIDMANN, CARL • WIDMER, GEORGIANA • WIDMER, THERY • WIEDER, BETH • WIEDER, GREG • WIENECKE, CLAYTON • WIESCHHOFF, KITTY • WIETING, MIKE • WIETING, SHELLEY • WIGGINS, ADRIENNE • WIGGINS, CARIN • WIGGINS, CHARLES • WIGGINS, CLAY • WIGGINS, DAWN • WIGGINS, SANDRA • WIGGS, BOB • WIGGS, SUZI • WIGLEY, JEFF • WIGLEY, TERRI • WIITA, ARUN • WILCE, MAUREEN • WILCOX, CYNTHIA • WILDER, MARGO • WILDER, SUZANNE • WILDERMUTH, KATHY • WILES, COURTNEY • WILEY, JUDITH • WILHITE, BARB • WILHITE, SHERRY • WILKEN, ULF • WILKENS, SUSAN • WILKERSON, MICHELLE • WILKERSON, WILLIE • WILKES, JAMES • WILKES, MICHAEL • WILKIE, BILL • WILKINS, CHRISTOPHER • WILKINS, JAMES • WILKINS, NANCY • WILLCOXON, DAVID • WILLCOXON, ELSPETH • WILLIAMS, LISA • WILLIAMS, A • WILLIAMS, AL • WILLIAMS, ALEC • WILLIAMS, ALICIA • WILLIAMS, ANSON • WILLIAMS, BASIL • WILLIAMS, BECKY • WILLIAMS, BRENDA • WILLIAMS, BRENT • WILLIAMS, CANDICE • WILLIAMS, CATHY • WILLIAMS, CHARLES • WILLIAMS, CHARLOTTE • WILLIAMS, CHRISTOPHER • WILLIAMS, CLARA • WILLIAMS, CORRINE • WILLIAMS, COURI • WILLIAMS, DARIUS • WILLIAMS, DAVID • WILLIAMS, DAVID • WILLIAMS, EDWARD • WILLIAMS, ELIZABETH • WILLIAMS, EVAN • WILLIAMS, EVETTE • WILLIAMS, FRANK • WILLIAMS, GERALDINE • WILLIAMS, HERMAN • WILLIAMS, HOWARD • WILLIAMS, JACKIE • WILLIAMS, JACQUELINE • WILLIAMS, JAMEE • WILLIAMS, JAMES • WILLIAMS, JANIE • WILLIAMS, JEFFEREY • WILLIAMS, JENNIFER • WILLIAMS, JENNY • WILLIAMS, JOHNNIE • WILLIAMS, JOY • WILLIAMS, KASTINA • WILLIAMS, KENNETH • WILLIAMS, KEVIN • WILLIAMS, L • WILLIAMS, LADASIA • WILLIAMS, LARRY • WILLIAMS, LATRINA • WILLIAMS, LINDA • WILLIAMS, LINDA • WILLIAMS, LIZ • WILLIAMS, LYNETTE • WILLIAMS, MARY • WILLIAMS, MARY • WILLIAMS, MARY • WILLIAMS, MICHAEL • WILLIAMS, MICHELE • WILLIAMS, NAKISHA • WILLIAMS, NANCY • WILLIAMS, NATASHA • WILLIAMS, NIKKI • WILLIAMS, PEGGY • WILLIAMS, RICHARD • WILLIAMS, RICK • WILLIAMS, RON • WILLIAMS, RONALD • WILLIAMS, SHELLY • WILLIAMS, SHIRLEY • WILLIAMS, STACI • WILLIAMS, STEPHANIE • WILLIAMS, TERESSA • WILLIAMS, TJ • WILLIAMS, VERONICA • WILLIAMS, YOLANDA • WILLIAMS, YVONNE • WILLIAMS-SMITH, JUANITA • WILLIAMSON, BRENDA • WILLIAMSON, DANNY • WILLIAMSON, ELAINE • WILLIAMSON, HELYN • WILLIAMSON, JOHN • WILLIAMSON, LINDA • WILLIAMSON, TOMMIE • WILLIS, BRYAN • WILLIS, HOPE • WILLIS, JILL • WILLIS, JIMMY • WILLIS, KEN • WILLIS, KERRY • WILLIS, KIMBERLY • WILLOCKS, BILLY • WILLOUGHBY, CALVIN • WILLS, RICHARD • WILMER, CHARLES • WILPERS, MATT • WILPERS, RITA • WILSON, BEN • WILSON, BRENDA • WILSON, BRIAN • WILSON, CAROLYN • WILSON, CARY • WILSON, CHAD • WILSON, CHARLES • WILSON, CHARLES • WILSON, CLORETTA • WILSON, CYNTHIA • WILSON, DANNY • WILSON, DAVID • WILSON, DEBBIE • WILSON, DONNA • WILSON, GARY • WILSON, HAYES • WILSON, HEATHER • WILSON, JAY • WILSON, JERROLD • WILSON, JINAKI • WILSON, JOSE • WILSON, KATHE • WILSON, KELLY • WILSON, KIMBERLEY • WILSON, LARRY • WILSON, LAURA • WILSON, LORI • WILSON, MARVIN • WILSON, PAUL • WILSON, RAMONA • WILSON, REGINALD • WILSON, RITA • WILSON, SAUNDRA • WILSON, SHELONDA • WILSON, SHIRLEY • WILSON, TIMOTHY • WILSON, TORRANCE • WILSON, TRACIE • WILSON, VERONICA • WILSON, VICKY • WILSON, WILLIAM • WILSON, WILLIE • WILT, LAURA • WILTZ, URSULA • WIMBUSH, BRIDGET • WIMBUSH, SANDRA • WIMBUSH, WILLIE • WINBUSH, BRIDGETTE • WINCHELL, CHARLES • WINDHAM, DANIEL • WINEBARGER, STEFANIE • WINER, DAVID • WINER, RICK • WINER, SCOTT • WINFREE, JEFFREY • WINGATE, AMEER • WINGATE, GIGI • WINGATE, KAREN • WINSLOW, MARY • WINSOR, NED • WINSTEAD, BETH • WINTER, MARYLISA • WINTERS, DEMETERIUS • WINTERS, SONIA • WINTERS, TORI • WINTERS, WAYNE • WINTERSTEIN, SARAH • WINTHROP, EDWARD • WIRTH, ALVA • WIRTH, KENNETH • WISCHERATH, DAVID • WISE, CHRIS • WISE, ELIJAH • WISE, PAULA • WISEMAN, GARY • WISNIEWSKI, VALARIE • WISOR, DOUGLAS • WITHAM, LISA • WITHERINGTON, PAULA • WITKOWSKI, JESSE • WITT, DAVE • WITT, EILEEN • WITT, MIRA • WITTER, ERIC • WITZMAN, VANESSA • WOELZ, KEREN • WOELZ, SARAH • WOELZ, TOMER • WOJCIK, JEAN • WOJTASZEK, CHRISTINE • WOLAVER, NICHOLAS • WOLF, LAURIE • WOLF, MIKE • WOLFARTH, LAURA • WOLFF, MARIJA • WOLFF, MICHAEL • WOLFGANG, FRANK • WOLFORD, VIVIAN • WOLKIN, DENNIS • WOLKING, JANE • WOLNA, KARIN • WOLOWICZ, ELIZABETH • WONG, DONNA • WONG, ERIC • WONG, STEPHEN • WONG, VALERIE • WOO, AMIE • WOOD, BARBARA • WOOD, CHIP • WOOD, FLOYD • WOOD, GAIL • WOOD, HELEN • WOOD, JR • WOOD, JUDY • WOOD, KARLA • WOOD, M • WOOD, TYRONE • WOODALL, JANNIE • WOODARD, GLYNDA • WOODARD, JACQUELYN • WOODARD, JEFF • WOODARD, MONA • WOODFORD, ERICA • WOODFORD, LORI • WOODS, CAMERON • WOODS, DAVID • WOODS, DICK • WOODS, EMILY • WOODS, JOANNE • WOODS, REGINA • WOODWARD, BONNIE • WOODWARD, COURT • WOODWARD, JC • WOODWARD, JIMMY • WOODWARD, JOHN • WOODWARD, LYNNE • WOODWARD, PAUL • WOODWARD, TRACY • WOODY, TAMMY • WOOLEY, CAROL • WOOLVERTON, MARY • WOOSNAM, PHIL • WOOSTER, BOB • WOOTEN, LYDIA • WOOTEN, STEPHEN • WORKMAN, JUDY • WORTH, JR • WORTHINGTON, KAREN • WORTHY, ROBIN • WORTHY, VERNON • WREGE, MELISSA • WRENN, MARGARET • WRENN, ESTES, BETH • WRIGHT, 'WRIGHT' • WRIGHT, BRENT • WRIGHT, DANA • WRIGHT, DAVID • WRIGHT, DENISE • WRIGHT, DENISE • WRIGHT, DON • WRIGHT, IVEN • WRIGHT, JOHN • WRIGHT, KARAN • WRIGHT, KIRSTEN • WRIGHT, LEONARD • WRIGHT, LETITIA • WRIGHT, LINDA • WRIGHT, MARK • WRIGHT, MARY • WRIGHT, PAULETTE • WRIGHT, PEGGY • WRIGHT, SHANNON • WRIGHT, SONYA • WRIGHT, TERESA • WRIGHT, TOM • WRIGHT, WILLIAM • WRIGHT, WILLIAM • WRIGHT, WILLIAM • WU, SUNNY • WU, YIN • WYATT, ANNE • WYATT, DAWN • WYATT, JAMES • WYATT, JOHN • WYATT-LAING, ANGELA • WYCHE, RUSSELL • WYCKOFF, AILEEN • WYGLADALSKI, FRAN • WYNKOOP, MARY • WYNN, TOM • WYNNE, MICHELLE • YAGER, HOWARD • YAMADA, YUKARI • YANCEY, EVELYN • YANCEY, HUNTER • YANCEY, PHYLLIS • YANG, GRACE • YANG, JAE • YARBROUGH, PHIL • YAROVA, NANCY • YARWASKY, LAURI • YASCHIK, JEFFREY • YASUDA, ERI • YATES, KATHERINE • YAWN, PAMELA • YBARRA, FRANCESCO • YEARGIN, BONNIE • YEARGIN, BRENT • YEE, ANGELA • YEE, BRENDA • YEE, HENRY • YONG, KAI • YORG, JAMES • YORK, KRISTY • YORK, PAT • YORK, SUSAN • YORKE, JOY • YOSHIDA, MIKI • YOSHIKAWA, YURIKA • YOSS, BARBARA • YOUNG, ALICE • YOUNG, ALLYSON • YOUNG, ANDREA • YOUNG, ASHLEY • YOUNG, BATINA • YOUNG, ELIZABETH • YOUNG, EMILY • YOUNG, FALLON • YOUNG, JERRY • YOUNG, JOE • YOUNG, LUIS • YOUNG, MELANIE • YOUNG, RHONDA • YOUNG, TANYA • YOUNG-ROGERS, DENINE • YOUNG-TOATLEY, DEBORAH • YOUNT, PAUL • YU, PETER • YUSZKIEWICZ, DON • ZACCONE, MATT • ZACHAR, SID • ZACHARY, CHERRIE • ZACHARY, YVONNE • ZACHOK, STEVEN • ZAHAROPOULOS, LIZ • ZAJAC, JULIE • ZAJDEL, JEFFREY • ZAMPROGNA, LAURA • ZANDT, AUGUST • ZARETSKY, BASIA • ZARYSKI, JR • ZDENEK, ERICKA • ZEIGLER, LAURA • ZEIGLER, SUSAN • ZEITMAN, BARRY • ZELLMAN, ANTON • ZEMAN, CHERYL • ZEMAN, JERRY • ZENAS, DANIEL • ZENDT, PAM • ZENNARO, MARY • ZESKE, KIM • ZETTLEMOYER, JASON • ZHU, BIN • ZIMBRICK, ANGIE • ZIMMER, MARK • ZIMMERMAN, CATHY • ZIMMERMAN, CYNTHIA • ZIMMERMAN, ERIC • ZIMMERMAN, NORMAN • ZIMMERMAN, STUART • ZINK, DUSTIN • ZINKE, MONICA • ZINN, BECKY • ZINN, LESLIE • ZIPKES, ANNE • ZOEHNER, YVONNE • ZOLAD, KATHY • ZOLLER, JEAN • ZOLLER, KENT • ZOOK, DAVE • ZOOK, HELEN • ZOOK, MICHELLE • ZROLKA, BOB • ZUBKE, ELLEN • ZUIDEMA, CHRISTINA • ZULU, NKOSINKULU • ZULUAGA, FERNANDO • ZUROW, MIKKI • ZWIRLEIN, LINDA • ZYLMA, JOHN • ZYSTRA, ROBERT.

DELEGATIONS

AFGHANISTAN: AFZAL, GUL • COTTER, TERRY • KHAN, ZABET • TOURIALAY, BASEER • **ALGERIA:** ABDI, SAMIR • ABI, OMAR • ABOURA, RABAH • AICHAINE, ZOUBIR • ALLEK, MOHAMED • BELAOUNI, ABDELKADER • BELLELE, FOUZI • BENCHENANE, ABDERRAHMANE • BOUDJELTIA, YOUCEF • KHELLADI, AMINE-MED • MEGHNAI, MOHAMED • OUIDDIR, MOHAND-OUL-HADJ • SAADOUNE, HOCINE • YAHIAOUI, HAKIM • ZERGOUN, BACHIR • **ANGOLA:** CAFUCHI, JOAQUIM • COSTA, FERNANDO • DA FONSECA, VASCO • LONDACA, ANGELO • **ARGENTINA:** ACHIDIAK, ACHIDIAK • ALVAREZ, MARCELO • ANRIQUEZ, MARIO • ARANDA, JUAN • ARISTEGUI, JORGE • BASCIONI, HORACIO • BASUALDO, BETIANA • BIGLIONE, MALVINA • BRANDOLI, VICTOR • CAMPO, JOSE • CARDARELI, CARLOS • CARLOMAGNO, FERNANDO • CASTILLA, FABIAN • CASTINEIRA, ALVARO • CATACATA, SANTIAGO • CEBALLOS, JOSE • CECCATI, ALEJANDRO • CETTOUR, DIEGO • CIARROCHI, ELIANA • COMETTO, LAURA • CREMIEUX, GUSTAVO • DE BRILLA, ANA • DE PAUL, ALICIA • DELELLA, NICOLAS • DIAZ, OSCAR • DUCRET, DANTE • FERRERO, HUGO • FERREYRA, LUIS • FRENDE, ANDREA • GARCETE, RAMON • GODOY, JORGE • GOMEZ, EDUARDO • GUILLAUME, DIEGO • HAYLAN, DANIEL • HERRERA, ROBERTO • IANI, GUSTAVO • JEREZ, JUAN • KIRSTEIN, NATALIO • LEGORBURU, LIDIA • LEGORBURU, ROSA • LIJO, SEBASTIAN • LOPEZ, EMILIANO • MACIEL, MARCELO • MAMANI, CANDELARIO • MARINO, JOSE • MARINO, LEONARDO • MARINO, MARTA • MASARA, VICENTE • MIRAS, HECTOR • MISOL, OSUALDO • MONSALVO, ALEJANDRO • MORRONE, SANTIAGO • NATTKEMPER, ALBERTO • NESTOR, SUAREZ • ORTIZ, GUILLERMO • PARODI, ALBERTO • PEDRAZA, ALBERTO • PERDIGUERO, RICARDO • PEREZLINDO, ALEJANDRA • POCHETTINO, OMAR • RAMIREZ, FABIAN • RAMIREZ, PROF • REYNOSO, MARIO • RIZZO, PABLO • RODRIGUEZ, MARIA • RODRIGUEZ, OMAR • ROJO, ARIEL • ROMERO, ROMERO • RUIZ, SERGIO • SANCHEZ, MARCELO • SCALA, EMILIA • SOSA, MARIO • SOTELO, MARCOS • STERLI, EDUARDO • TOMMASEO, ENRIQUE • TORRES, GASTON • VALENZUELA, LUIS • VERA, MARCELO • VIDELA, PABLO • YAMAMOTO, YORIYUKI • **ARMENIA:** ABGARYAN, HAIK • ABRAHAMIAN, HAMLET • ABRAHAMYAN, ARMEN • AIVAZIAN, ARAM • ARAKELYAN, LEVON • ARZUMANYAN, SAMVEL • BALABEKIAN, GRIGORY • DUMANYAN, ANTON • GABRIELYAN, SAMVEL • GHOUGASIAN, ARSHAG • GEVORKIAN, MURAD • GRIGORYAN, GRIGORY • HOVHANNISYAN, SEVAK • HOVSEPYAN, NARINE • KOCHARYAN, ARMEN • MANUKYAN, SAMVEL • MARGARYAN, ARTUR • MARTIROSYAN, ARMEN • NAZARYAN, SEDA • ROSTOMYAN, SAMVEL • SARGSYAN, ARMEN • SHAHINYAN, ARMAN • SIMONYAN, ARTAK • STEPANYAN, EDGAR • TADEVOSYAN, GAGIK • TER-HOVHANNISYAN, HRANT • TER-MARTIROSYAN, VAHAN • VARDANYAN, NAIRA • **AUSTRALIA:** ADAMS, ASHLEY • ADAMS, JULIANNE • ANDREWS, TROY • APPS, ROBERT • BANKS, JENNI • BARKER, PETREA • BEER, NORMA • BENNETT, EVAN • BIDDLE, ANTHONY • BIGNALL, KRIS • BIGNALL, PATRICIA • BIRD, PAUL • BLACKMAN, DONALD • BLAGOEV, BLAGOI • BLATTMAN, FABIAN • BLYTHE, SANDY • BOCK, RAELENE • BONSACK, ROD • BOS, WIM • BOYLAN, BRETT • BREMNER, KEITH • BROCKENSHIRE, SCOTT • BROWN, MATTHEW • BRUMMELL, RAY • BUCHANAN, MEREDITH • BURROUGHS, DAMIEN • CAHILL, PAULINE • CARLTON, MELISSA • CARTER, AMANDA • CASEY, SHONA • CECCONATO, ORFEO • CLARK, GRAEME • CLARK, JUNE • CLARKE, GEOFF • CLARKE, TONY • CLOHESSY, PAUL • COLEMAN, LYNETTE • COLLINS, DOMINIC • CONNELL, MICHAEL • COOPER, PRIYA • CORR, PETER • COURT, LEROI • COX, BEN • COX, HELEN • CRESTANI, ROB • CROKER, GARRY • CROSS, PAUL • CROSS, TRACEY • CRUMP, GREG • DASHWOOD, GEMMA • DAVIES, MARK • DAVIES, MARK • DE BURGH, CAMERON • DE LEEDE, ANTHONY • DENSON, BARBARA • DOWLING, MICK • EATON, STEPHEN • EDEN, JOHN • ELGIN, DONNIE • ELSWORTH, SCOTT • EVANS, DAVID • EWIN, PAULA • EWIN, STUART • FALZON, JANELLE • FARRELL, MICHAEL • FERRETT, MELISSA • FISCHER, IAIN • FISCHER, PATRICIA • FITZPATRICK, GRANT • FORSBERG, JOHN • FRANCIS, SALLY • FREW, KEVIN • FULLER, NEIL • GEORGE, COLIN • GIDDY, TERRY • GIVENS, FIONA • GOCKEL, PAUL • GODDARD, TREVOR • GODFREY-ROBERTS, MICHAEL • GOLDING, KERRY • GOODMAN, DAVID • GOODMAN, SCOTT • GOSENS, GERRARD • GOSENS, HEATHER • GOULD, DAVID • GOULD, GRAHAM • GRANT, RICKY • GRAY, MATTHEW • GRAY, STEVEN • GREEN, MARSHA • GREENAWAY, ANDREW • GROGAN, ADRIAN • HADLEY, ALEX • HALL, DAVID • HAMILTON, ROD • HARDY, JEFF • HARE, JO-ANNE • HARRISON, SEAN • HARVEY, BRIAN • HAYDON, SUE • HEWSON, GERARD • HILL, YVONNE • HINSON, RANDA • HOLLANDS, EDDY • HOMANN, PETER • HUYNH, TU • JACKA, DAVID • JARVIS, CRAIG • JENKINS, ALICIA • JONES, LACHLAN • JURICICH, ANDREA • KELLY, PETER • KENAGHAN, TERRY • KENNEDY, SARAH • KONEMANN, SHARON • KOSMALA, LIBBY • KSCHAMMER, TREVOR • LAHL, RACHEL • LAKE, PAUL • LAMOND, PAUL • LAWTON, WARREN • LEE, KATHY • LEE, SUE-ELLEN • LEPORE, LYN • LIDDELL, KARNI • LINDSAY, JOHN • LLORENS, LISA • LOCK, PETER • LONGDEN, MARY • MACDONALD, HAMISH • MACHEN, VICKY • MADSON, GREG • MALONEY, TIM • MATHEW, SUSAN • MATTHEWS, TIM • MCGREGOR, KERROD • MCNICHOLL, BRIAN • MILLINGTON, NEVILLE • MILLS, MARILYN • MODRA, KIERAN • MORRIS, NICK • MOSELY, ALISON • NICHOLSON, RICHARD • NOMARHAS, JIM • NORRIS, KEN • NOWITZKI, TAMARA • NUNN, CHRIS • NUNNARI, PAUL • O'NION, LISA • OLIVER, RICHARD • OLIVER, TRACEY • ORGAN, THOMAS • PAGE, LESLY • PERRIMAN, DONALD • PHILP, DONNA • POOLE, TERRI • PORTER, STEVEN • QUINN, ALISON • RACKHAM, SHARON • REID, BRETT • REYNOLDS, MARGARET • RICHARDSON, JOHN • RICKARD, SAM • RITCHIE, DONNA • ROGERS, KATHY • ROMAGUERA, JAIME • ROSE, AMANDA • SACHS, TROY • SAUVAGE, LOUISE • SAXBERG, JENETTE • SAYERS, JOANNE • SCARR, BRETT • SCHULZE, SARAH-JANE • SCOTT, CHRIS • SELBY, DAVID • SHERWELL, JOHN • SHORT, RUSSELL • SHUTTLEWORTH, BRIAN • SIMMONS, ANDREW • SIMPSON, JOHN • SLATTERY, PETER • SMITH, DARREN • STANLEY, FRANCES • STEPHENS, ROBYN • STEVENS, JOAN • STUBBS, ROD • SULLIVAN, CARLA • TESCH, LIESL • THEODORE, SAM • THOMAS, ALAN • THOMAS, BRAD • THRUPP, DARREN • TINKER, BOB • TITTERTON, JOANNE • TORO, DANIELA • UNGERER, GREG • VAN ELDIK, CORNELIS • VAN ELDIK, MATTHEW • VIERO, LEANA • WAALWYK, MANDY • WALKER, MARK • WALLROOT, BRUCE • WARRY, LYNDALL • WEBB, JANE • WEBB, KATRINA • WHITE, SUSAN • WHITEHEAD, BADEN • WIGGINS, PAUL • WILLIS-ROBERTS, JODI • WINGARD, DARRYL • WINTERS, AMY • WOODHOUSE, DAVID • WORRALL, JODIE • WORSLEY, PETER • WRIGHT, ELIZABETH • YORK, TRACY • YOUNG, JUDY • **AUSTRIA:** ADLER, ELISABETH • AIGNER, FRANZ • ALTENDORFER, FRITZ • AMANN, KONRAD • AUER, JOHANN • AUFSCHNAITER, HUBERT • BIEMBACHER, KARL • BINTER, DANIEL • BUCINA, GERHARD • CHOULI, SOFIA • DIBONA, PETER • DOLLMANN, MANFRED • DUBIN, WOLFGANG • EIBECK, WOLFGANG • ER, MURAT • ETZLSTORFER, CHRISTOPH • FAHRNGRUBER, JOHANN • FELSER, KLAUS • FINK, MARGRIT • FISCHER, RONALD • FRACZYK, STANISLAW • GANGER, THOMAS • GEILING, MICHAEL • GOELLER, THOMAS • GROSSEK, ANDREAS • GRUENDL, MARIO • HAJEK, RUDOLF • HAHN, EWALD • HALTER, HARTL, MANFRED • HIERZER, JOHANN • HONISCH, GUENTER • JONAS, HANS • KAIBLINGER, ALFRED • KRAMER, ANDREAS • KREUZER, OSKAR • KUEHNE, BRUNO • KUSIAN, ILSE • LARCH, GUENTHER • LEGNER, MARTIN • LOISINGER, JOSEF • MACALA, INGRID • MANDL, FRANZ • MAYR, KARL • MECL, ERICH • MEINDLHUMER, GUENTHER • MOESSENBOECK, BETTINA • MONSCHEIN, WILLIBOLD • PEISKAR, WERNER • PFALLER, WALTER • PICHLER, GREGOR • PRESSL, ERIKA • RAAB, FRANZ • RAMSAUER, ERNST • REITER, JOHANN • REISER, ERICH • REISINGER, KARL • ROMAN, ROLAND • SAILER, ALFRED • SALZMANN, KLAUS • SCHAFF, GERHARD • SCHERNEY, ANDREA • SCHEUTZ, ROLAND • SCHMEE, DIETMAR • SCHRANZ, GERALD • SCHWEITNECKER, GEORG • SCHWENDTNER, JOACHIM • SCHWENDTNER, SUSANNE • SEIDL, JOHANN • SIEGL, ANDREAS • STARL, PETER • STEINLECHNER, MONIKA • STEINER, ROBERT • STOTTER, SUSANNE • TAUPE-LEHNER, ANNA • ZETTLER, NORBERT • ZSIFKOVITS, PETER • **AZERBAIJAN:** ABDULLAYEV, ZAKHIR • ANTOFII, ALEKSANDR • GAMZAYEV, GUNDUZ • ISMAILOV, GUSEIN • MOUSADIG, VAGIF • **BAHRAIN:** AL-HIDDY, AYMAN • AL-MARZOOQ, REYADH • AL-MUTAWA, ADEL • AL-SAQER, KHALED • AL-SHAIKH, NADER • AL-THAWADI, SUBAH • AL-WADAEI, SAYED • JALLAQ, SALMAN • **BELARUS:** BOUBEN, VLADIMIR • BOUGAITCHOUK, STEPAN • BOURANOV, IOURI • CHELEG, GUEORGUI • CHEPEL, OLEG • DENISSEVITCH, NIKOLAI • FORTOUNOV, IGOR • GRICHKO, TATIANA • GROUDKO, VLADIMIR • JOUKOV, KI, VICTOR • KHRAMTSOV, MIKHAIL • KRAVTSEVITCH, DMITRI • LEONTIOUK, IRINA • LITVINENKO, ALEXANDRE • MATSKEVITCH, VALERI • NETYLKIN, ANATOLI • NETYLKINA, IRINA • NOVIKOV, IGOR • PLACHTCHINSKI, SERGEI • POTAPENKO, VLADIMIR • PROSKOURIN, IGOR • RYJKOVSKI, ALEXANDRE • SIVAKOVA, TAMARA • SKOROBOGATAIA, IADVIGA • YOUREVITCH, TADEUCH • **BELGIUM:** APPERMONT, STANNY • BELLAVIA, SABRINA

BOONEN, JAN • BORRE, INGRID • BOSMANS, ANNIK • CEULEMANS, LUC • CLEUREN, RITA • CULOT, GUY • DAUBRESSE, THIERRY • DE CRAEMER, GEERT • DE KEERSMAEKER, GINO • DE MEYER, MARK • DE VLIET, PETER • DEHANTSCHUTTER, STEF • DELAUNOY, FREDERIC • DELWASSE, YVES • DEPREUX, ROLAND • DESSART, LUC • DESWERT, LOUIS • DOUX, ALAIN • DRIESEN, PAUL • FACHE, PATRICK • FESTEN, LUC • GHION, DIMITRI •
GIRASA, PIETRO • GOSSELIN, JAN • GOVAERTS, BENNY • HARDY, JOHAN • HERMANS, ALEX • HOFFMANN, GEORGES • JAEKEN, DENIS • KLOMP, THEO • LEYS, JOS • LINSEN, PAUL • LIVENS, PHILIP • LORENT, ROBERT • MAESEN, LUDO • MERTENS, DIRK • MUYLLE, CARL • ORENS, STEVE • PLETINCKX, JEAN-MARC • POLLET, MARIE-LINE • SEYEN, CHRISTEL • STAMPER, HANS • TIMMERMANS, EMIEL • TORFS, KURT • TROKAY, PHILLIPPE •
VAN BRUSSEL, MARIANNE • VAN DAMME, GEORGES • VAN ENGELAND, JOS • VAN LANGENDONCK, RONNY • VAN PUYVELDE, CARINE • VAN RAEFELGHEM, KURT • VANDERHEYDEN, PIERRE • VERDICKT, HUGO • VERGEYLEN, NICO • VERSPEELT, NICO • VERSTRAETE, UGO • XHROUET, SEBASTIAN • ZOLTAN, YVAN • **BERMUDA:** ANDERSON, KIRSTY • HARSHAW, PHYLLIS • LEIGHTON, SUSAN • LINDROTH, ANN • SOUTHERN, JENI • **BOSNIA**
AND HERZEGOVINA: DIVCIC, ZORAN • GUHDIJA, MUSTAFA • OSMANOVIC, ALMEDIN • ZAIMOVIC, ENES • **BRAZIL:** ALVES, MARIA • ALVES, MARIA • AMADOR, DOUGLAS • ANDRADE, GENEZI • ARAUJO, HELDER • AZEVEDO, SEBASTIAO • BARBOSA, RICARDO • BASTOS, ROSANA • BOONE, JR • BORGES, ROGERIO • CARMO, ODIR • COSTA, ADRIANO • CRUZ, FERNANDO • D'AMARAL, TERESA • DA ROSA, FOGACA • DA SILVA, LUIZ • DA
SILVA, NILTON • DA SILVA, OSMAR • DA SILVA, RIVALDO • DA SILVA, TENORIO • DE LIMA, MAURICIO • DE OLIVEIRA, ALESSANDRO • DE SOUZA, RAMON • DIZ, ADEMIR • FERNANDES, GILMAR • FERREIRA, MARCOS • FILHO, JOAO • FILHO, OZIEL • FORTUNATO, LUCIANA • FREIRE, GILBERTO • GOMES, JULIO • GONCALVES, JEFFERSON • GUIMARAES, SUELY • JESUS, CONCEICAO • JUNIOR, FRANCISCO • KIENEN, CINARA • KNITTELL, GER-
SON • LAURO, FLAVIO • LAZZARETTI, ROMOLO • LIMA, ADRIANO • LIMA, ARILDO • LIMA, JOSIAS • MARTINS, RIVALDO • MATIAS, FRANCISCO • MEDEIROS, JOSE • MELO, ANDREA • MELO, ZAIRA • MIRANDA, VILMA • MORAIS, JOSE • MOREIRA, MARCIO • MOTTA, MARCELO • NETO, SEBASTIAO • OLIVEIRA, ADRIANA • OLIVEIRA, BENEDITO • OLIVEIRA, ELESSANDRA • OLIVEIRA, ELIANE • OLIVEIRA, IOLANDA • OLIVEIRA, SERGIO • PANOEIRO,
CLAUDIO • PASSOS, MARIA • PEREIRA, ADRIANO • PEREIRA, DENILSON • QUEIROZ, JOSE • REGIS, CHRISTINE • RIBEIRO, CINTIA • RODRIGUES, TANIA • SALES, FRANCISCO • SANTOS, ADRIA • SANTOS, ANDERSON • SANTOS, AURELIO • SANTOS, GILSON • SANTOS, LUZIMAR • SANTOS, MARCO • SANTOS, MARCUS • SANTOS, SOCORRO • SEO, JOON • SILVA, ANTONIO • SILVA, IRANILSON • SILVA, LUZIA • SOARES, GLEDSON • SUGIMORE,
FABIANA • TINOCO, ARLINDO • VASCONCELOS, IVANILDO • VERISSIMO, AMAURY • VERISSIMO, KLEBER • VIEIRA, BRANDAO • VITAL, ROBERTO • WATANABE, CLAUDIA • **BULGARIA:** ANGUELOV, DONKO • BOYTCHEV, PAVEL • DJOUROVA, POLINA • GERGANSKI, HRISTO • KOLEVA, IVANKA • LALOV, ILIA • NIKOLOV, NIKOLAY • SAKELAROV, GUEORGI • STEFANOV, STEFAN • ZAHARIEV, ZAHARI • **BURKINA:** FASO BORO, GAOUSSOU • FASO
KABORE, ISSIAKA • FASO OUEDRAOGO, IDRISS • FASO THIOMBIANO, DIEDAMBA • **CANADA:** ABBOTT, MARNI • ADAMS, JEFF • AHERN, SHIRLEY • ALDER, DON • ALEXANDER, TONY • ALLARD, RAY • ANDERSEN, ROB • BALES, ROSS • BEAUDOIN, ANDRE • BELANGER, DANY • BENOIT, CHANTAL • BERGERON, DEAN • BERKELEY, VIVIAN • BILOTTA, JIM • BLACKWOOD, FAYE • BONNEAU, PATRICE • BORISOFF, JAIMIE • BORNEMANN, BECKY
• BOUCHARD, JACQUES • BOULAY, JOHN • BOURBONNIERE, FRANCOIS • BOURGONJE, COLETTE • BOUW, JOANNE • BOWES, PAUL • BRINTON, DAN • BROWN, PETER • BRUCE, BARRY • BRUNO, FRANK • BUNZ, JOHN • CARON, MARIO • CASEY, PEGGY • CHRISTY, JEFF • CHURCH, EARL • CLEGG, ANTHONY • CLOUTIER, ALEXANDRE • COLLINS, WAYNE • COOK, DAVID • CORDICK, HOWARD • CORSAUT, ERICK • COTE, STEPHANE •
COURNOYER, JULIE • CREPAULT, JEAN • CUBITT, CECE • CUNNINGHAM, NICK • CURRIE, OLLIE • DECSI, LASZLO • DELESALLE, JASON • DENYS, ALEC • DESCHENES, ROBERT • DITTMER, DOUGLAS • DOUCETTE, CLARENCE • DOYLE, KEN • DROUIN, JANE • DUNLOP, BOB • DUREPOS, DAVE • ELLEFSON, STEPHEN • ENRIGHT, JIM • ERIKSSON, PETER • EYNDE, ERIC • FERGUSON, ERIC • FERGUSON, TRACEY • FORTIN, RAYMONDE • FREER,
DOUG • FRICK, TIM • FROGLEY, MIKE • GAGNE, FRANCE • GALATI, BENNY • GAUNT, ROB • GAUTHIER, PAUL • GEREIN, CLAYTON • GERVAN, JEREMY • GIESBRECHT, BARB • GIESBRECHT, BOB • GREENLAW, BILL • GRIFFIN, BARB • GRIFFIN, PAT • GRONMAN, RICK • GUPTILL, NOREEN • HALEY, ANDREW • HALL, KEN • HAMILTON, LINDA • HAMPSON, WENDY • HANET, AL • HANET, VI • HARRIS, GARTH • HAYES, PATRICIA • HEIDT, BRUCE
• HENDERSON, ROY • HEYDON, PAT • HICKLING, GARETT • HIGGINS, JOE • HOBBS, KEITH • HODGINS, KRIS • HONOUR, GREG • HOULE, ERIC • HOWE, DAVID • IYIDOGAN, SAVAS • JAMES, JANE • JARVIS, PAT • JOHNSON, JOE • JOHNSON, PAUL • JOHNSON, TRISTAN • JOHNSTON, JAMIE • KELLY, KEN • KIERSTEAD, BOB • KING, MARY • KNIGHT, COURTNEY • KOZAK, DEAN • KRANABETTER, KIRBY • KREMPIEN, JENNIFER • KRYWA, KELLY
• KUTROWSKI, LINDA • LABRECQUE, SUSAN • LACHANCE, JASON • LAFRENIERE, ALINE • LAROCHE, JEAN • LAROCHELLE, MIKE • LAROUCHE, GUYLAINE • LARSEN, JENNIFER • LEDREW, RENEE • LIZOTTE, RAYMOND • LJUBISIC, LILO • LONGHI, GARY • LUCAS, KRISTINE • MADORE, LORETTE • MAILLET, MARK • MARIASH, GLENN • MARQUIS, CARL • MARTIN, JACQUES • MATHIESON, COLIN • MAYNE, DON • MCCLELLAN, FLO • MCDON-
ALD, LANCE • MCGREGOR, STUART • MCKEOWN, STEWART • MCMAHON, BRENT • MCMILLAN, ED • MCPHATE, BRIAN • MCROBERTS, JOHN • MEADOR, KARINE • MELESKO, TRACEY • MENARD, NATALIE • MERRILL, HAL • MORTEN, PIER • MORTEN, SHELLEY • NAULT, ARTHUR • NORMANDINE, DANIEL • O'NEILL, KAREN • OHAMA, KENDRA • PAUL, MARTIN • PAYNE, MARNIE • PEEL, ANN • PELLETIER, RON • PENNER, BOB • PERIARD, PIERRE
• PERRON, MARIO • PETER, RICHARD • PETITCLERC, CHANTAL • PETTINICCHI, SABRINA • PUNZALAN, ALBERT • PURDY, ADAM • PUTNAM, STEFAN • QUALTROUGH, CARLA • QUESSY, MARC • QUINN, FRANK • QUINN, NANCY • RADKE, LORI • RADMORE, JOE • RAMSEY, JACK • REELIE, RICK • REILLY, JAMES • RIVARD, JOELLE • ROBERTS, WENDY • ROBINSON, LYN • ROBINSON, TERRY • ROSS, MARIE • ROWELL, JONATHAN • ROY, DIANE
• RUST, MARDY • SADD, LESLIE • SADD, ROY • SANDRIN, TONY • SCHRADER, BOB • SCOTT, JANE • SCOTT, LAUNEL • SEMENIUK, ALLAN • SHAND, CHARMAINE • SHAW, JAMES • SHEIKH, JEAN • SHEIKH, ZAK • SHEPPARD, CINDY • SHERRY, DONN • SHOPKA, WALTER • SIMPSON, MARIA • SKINNER, BRIAN • SMITHIES, MARNEY • SMITHSON, ELAINE • SNOEK, ROB • ST CROIX, SHARRON • STEEN, DON • STEVENS, LISA • STEWART, STEVE •
STUBEL, DARYL • SUAREZ-JORDAN, NORMA • TAPLEY, NANCY • THOMPSON, RON • TONELLO, JERRY • TREMBLAY, DOMINIQUE • TREUER, JAMES • TRIFONIDIS, CHRIS • TWEED, DAVID • VIGER, ANDRE • WALKER, ELIZABETH • WATSON, GORD • WESTERGAARD, KIRK • WILTON, DOUG • WRZESZCZ, ANDREW • WU, WALTER • WYSE, DEREK • YUSTAK, CARLA • ZACHAU, PAUL • **CHILE:** CONTRERAS, GABRIEL • LOPEZ, AMANCIO • O'KU-
INGHTTONS, GLORIA • REBOLLEDO, VICTOR • **CHINA:** CUI, BAOJI • DING, BOTAN • DONG, QIMING • GONG, BAOREN • GUO, JIANMO • GUO, YONGZHONG • HA, SILAO • HE, CHUNGUANG • HOU, BIN • HUANG, PEIXIAN • HUANG, WENTAO • JIA, YONG • LI, KEQIANG • LI, SHIWEI • LI, WEIPU • LI, XIUQING • LIU, HONGRU • LIU, JIARONG • LUO, FUQUN • LUO, ZHIQIANG • MAO, ABAO • MAO, QIWEN • MEN, RUNMING • NIU, SHUNLIN • SHI,
TIEYIN • SUN, CHANGTING • SUN, HAITAO • WANG, JIAN • WANG, SEN • WEI, MENGXIN • WU, HONGPING • WU, YANJIAN • XIA, KAI • XU, HONGYAN • YAN, WEN • ZENG, HUABIN • ZENG, JIAN • ZHANG, ANLIANG • ZHANG, GUO • ZHANG, HAIDONG • ZHANG, JUNMING • ZHANG, NAN • ZHANG, XIAOLING • ZHANG, YUAN • ZHAO, BIN • ZHAO, HONGBO • ZHAO, SU • ZHAO, XUEEN • ZHOU, JIAHUA • ZHOU, XIANGRONG • ZHU, WEIMING •
CHINESE TAIPEI :AU, MAN-KUAN • CHEN, CHI-CHING • CHEN, LUNG-CHUNG • CHEN, SEN-CHI • CHENG, SHOU-CHI • CHIEN, HSIN-YU • CHOU, CHANG-SHEN • HSIAO, HUANG-CHI • HSU, CHIN-SHAN • HU, MING-FU • HUANG, CHEN-HUA • KAO, JIUN-SHAN • LEE, CHING-CHUNG • LI, WEN-HAN • LIN, CHAU-MOU • LIN, SHU-CHUAN • ONG, YU-YU • TSAI, SHAN-CHING • TSAI, TSUNG-TA • WANG, CHUNG-FU • WANG, JU-KEN • YANG, JONG-
GUAN • YU, CHEN-HSIUNG • **COLOMBIA:** BAUTISTA, JOSE • CORTES, ORLANDO • LONDONO, OCTAVIO • MONTANEZ, ARMANDO • MOZO, MARTIN • TRONCOSO, HERNAN • **COTE D'IVOIRE:** AGBO, FLORENCE • KOUASSI, ALAIN • OUMAR, BASAKOULBA • YACE, FELICIEN • YALY, GASTON • **CROATIA:** BOONE, LIBBY • MIKELIN-OPARA, ROKO • MILINKOVIC, MILKA • OMAZIC, BRANKO • PEHAR, ANTE • RUZNJAK, MIRJANA • SRSEN, ANA
• STOJANOVIC, ZORAN • CUBA BELISER, LIUDYS • **CUBA:** CABALLERO, CEPEDA • CORTINA, PUPO • FROMETA, PABLO • GARRIDO, • GONZALEX, ULISES • GONZALEZ, DIOSMANY • LANDA, AMADO • LEON, BENITO • MILIAN, CHANG • MOYA, OMAR • NEIRA, CARLOS • PEREZ, GUILLERMO • RODRIGUEZ, PEDRO • ZALDIVAR, AMBROSIO • **CYPRUS:** ANTONIOU, CHRISTAKIS • FLOURENTZOU, SOTERAKIS • GAVRIEL, YIANNAKIS • KAFOURIS,
MARTIS • MICHAELIDES, KYRIAKOS • PRATSIS, CHARALAMBOS • SAVVA, SAVVAS • STAVRIDES, IACOVOS • **CZECH REPUBLIC:** BAJGAR, MILAN • BALAK, PAVEL • BEHALOVA, MILOSLAVA • BILOVA, TATANA • BUDIL, IVO • CECH, PAVEL • COUFALOVA, KATERINA • DANEK, JIRI • DANKO, STEFAN • DAVIDKOVA, JOLANA • DUCHACEK, VLADIMIR • DUNAJSKY, MIROSLAV • FOTKO, JOSEF • HOLUBCOVA, JITKA • HYBNER, JAROSLAV • JAN-
CUROVA, ALENA • JANECEK, MIROSLAV • JANOUCH, VACLAV • JIRASKOVA, VERA • KALINACOVA, ALENKA • KARABEC, IVAN • KOCOVSKA, DANIELA • KOLEK, ROMAN • KOVAR, MARTIN • KRECEK, JAROSLAV • KUBALA, MILAN • MASEK, LUBOMIR • MATOUSEK, MILAN • MOJOVA, JANA • MOURECEK, JAROMIR • NEHUDEK, KAREL • NETKOVA, ZUZANA • NEVRKLA, JAN • NOVAK, PETR • NOVAK, ZDENEK • NOVOTNY, KAREL • ONDRASIKO-
VA, LUCIE • OZANA, JIRI • PESTOVA, EVA • PINKAVA, JAROMI • POHLMANN, ROSTISLAV • PROCHAZKOVA, HELENA • ROUSKOVA, PETRA • SCHINDLER, RICHARD • SCHWEINER, MSTISLAV • SEBEK, ZDENEK • SEPS, VACLAV • SIBRAVA, PAVEL • SIMOVEC, LUBOMIR • SINDELAR, MIROSLAV • SINDELAR, RENE • SKORNIK, PETER • SLEGROVA, JITKA • SNAJDR, DANIEL • SNAJDR, DAVID • SNAJDR, LIBOR • SOUKUP, JIRI • STARK, MICHAL • STE-
FANU, MICHAL • STUDNICKA, PAVEL • SVOBODA, VACLAV • SVOBODA, ZDENEK • SYKORA, MILOSLAV • VAJGL, ZDENEK • VAPENKA, MICHAL • VASICEK, VOJTECH • VSOLAK, LADISLAV • VYBIRAL, TOMAS • VYTISK, LADISLAV • **DENMARK:** AGREN, CARSTEN • ANDERSEN, ANNE • ANDERSEN, BRITA • ANDERSEN, IDA • ANDERSEN, PETER • ANDERSEN, PETER • ANDERSEN, STEFFEN • BAK, ARVID • BAK-PEDERSEN, LONE • BARLUND, GRITT
• BERTHELSEN, FLEMMING • BONKE, LENA • BRADAL, THOMAS • BRAEUMSO, KAREN • BRONDUM, EMIL • BUNDGAARD, CHRISTIAN • CHRISTENSEN, JESPER • CHRISTENSEN, KARINA • CHRISTENSEN, NIKOLAJ • FISCHER, SOREN • FUDGE, JENS • GARST, POUL • GERLACH, THOMAS • GORMSEN, GORMSEN • HANSEN, ANNE • HANSEN, KASPER • HANSEN, MICHAEL • HAVE, SANNE • HEILMANN, FLEMMING • HINRICHSEN, PALLE • HOWALT,
ANN • JACOBSEN, MARTIN • JENSEN, CARSTEN • JENSEN, CHARLOTTE • JENSEN, LARS • JORGENSEN, HENRIK • JORGENSEN, JORGEN • JORGENSEN, PIA • KEHOE, INGER • LENTZ, KARIN • LIHME, LIS • LUNDSTEEN, KAI • MAGNUSSEN, EVEN • MATHIASEN, JAKOB • MECHULA, KAZIMIER • MOGENSEN, BIRTHE • MOINICHEN, PIA • MOLBO, HANNE • MORTENSEN, CARSTEN • MOSE-CHRISTENSEN, LARS • NAUERBY, JAN • NIELSEN, BRIAN
• NIELSEN, IVAN • NIELSEN, LISE • NIELSEN, MICHAEL • OLSEN, THOMAS • OVERBYE, LONE • PETERSSON, JOHN • RASMUSSEN, LINDA • SIDDIQI, MANSOOR • SONNICHSEN, BOGE • SORENSEN, BRITTA • SORENSEN, TORBEN • STENGER, RICKA • STOVRING, DORTE • STRETON, CHARLOTTE • THOMSEN, JANNIE • THOMSEN, PERNILLE • VAGNER, KIRSTEN • WAHREN, LISBETH • **DOMINICAN REPUBLIC:** JIMENEZ, ROBERT • PANIAGUA,
RAFAEL • VENTURA, CEFERINO • **ECUADOR:** CARDENAS, MANUEL • DE LACRUZ, WILSON • MARIN, MIGUEL • QUEVEDO, ANGEL • **EGYPT:** ABDIN, ZAKIA • AHMED, ABOU • AHMED, AHMED • ALY, WALID • AMRA, OMAR • ATTIA, ESSAM • BAKR, SHERIF • BARAKA, MOHAMED • DAHY, AHMED • DAWARA, SAID • ELATA, AYMAN • ELBEHIRY, HANY • ELGAWAD, AHMED • ELKOUMY, SOHIR • ELSADEK, TALAAT • ELSAFI, ASHRAF • ELSAMD,
HAMDY • ERAKI, MOSSAD • FARAG, ABD • FELEIFAL, KARIMA • GAWAD, MOHAMED • GERGES, SHERIF • GHARIB, TAREK • HAFEZ, WAGIH • HAMED, MOSTAFA • HASSAN, MOHAMED • HASSAN, MOHAMED • KASSEM, MOHAMED • KHATIB, SHAABAN • LATIF, HOSSAM • MADBOLI, EMAD • MAHMOUD, AHMED • MAKLAD, MOHAMED • MATHNA, METWALY • MOHAMED, EMAD • MOHAMED, EMAN • MOHAMED, GAMAL • NABIL, MAHMOUD •
OMAR, MERVAT • SADANY, ALY • **ESTONIA:** AIDLA, MARGIT • ARTAMONOV, VASSILI • JUHKAM, MALLE • KIIL, ALLAN • KOEL, MALLIKA • KOKK, EELA • KOLLOM, HELI • KORKJAS, MARGE • MAKSIMOVA, NADEZDA • MAND, HELMUT • OJASTU, ANNELY • POLDME, REIN • RAIDE, ANNIKA • SILM, HELENA • VALDRU, REIN • **FAROE ISLANDS:** HOJ, ESTER • JENSEN, TORILL • THOMSEN, RENE • **FIJI:** MAHARAJ, JAGDISH • SARISOSO, ELIA •
SIDAL, BISHWA • VEREVOU, JOSEVA • **FINLAND:** AHONEN, ARI • AIRAKSINEN, HANNU • ALASJARVI, MERJA • AROMAA, RAIMO • FINGERROOS, EEVA-RIITTA • GUSEV, JARI • HAMALAINEN, JUSSI • HANNINEN, KEIJO • HANSKI, MERJA • HEIKKINEN, RAIMO • HEIMONEN, MARKKU • HEINO, JARI • HULANMAKI, EERO • HUMPPI, MARTI • HUTTUNEN, TERO • HYTONEN, JOHANNA • JAUHOJARVI, TAHVO • JOENSUU, SEPPO • JOKINEN, KIMMO •
JUNTUNEN, JUSSI • KAIPAINEN, KALEVI • KALLUNKI, JANI • KANNISTO, MIKKO • KAPIAINEN, PETRI • KARI, JARMO • KARJALAINEN, ANTERO • KARKAINEN, PETRI • KAUPPILA, MARKO • KAUPPINEN, KATJA • KEITEL, IIRIS • KEMILAINEN, MIRJA • KEMPPAINEN, KATRI • KILPIA, NINA • KINNUNEN, ASKO • KIVIMAKI, HANNU • KIVINEN, JORMA • KOLKKA, TARJA • KOVANEN, PEKKA • KRISTOLA, RITVA • KURKINEN, JARI • LAASONEN, KYOSTI •
LAINE, JARI • LAINE, JUKKA • LAITINEN, JORMA • LAITINEN, TIMO • LANDSTEDT, REINO • LAUKKANEN, HEIKKI • LAUNONEN, MATTI • LEHTINEN, JAANA • LEHTOLA, JARMO • LEPPANEN, PAULA • LIIKANEN, PEKKA • LINDBLOM, HARRI • LINDELL, PAUL • LIUKKONEN, ESA • MAKINEN, ANTTI • MAKINEN, ARTTU • MARKKANEN, MIKA • MELANEN, LAURI • MIETTINEN, KIRSI • MIILUKANGAS, ESKO • MOJTAHEDI, MINA • MUINONEN, CARL •
MUSTIKKAMAA, TIMO • NIINIMAKI, MARKKU • NOROLA, PEKKA • OIKARAINEN, JUHA • PAASONEN, HANNA • PALONEN, TIMO • PEHKONEN, ARTO • PEKKALA, MARI • PEKKALA, PEKKA • PELKONEN, TARJA • PIIROINEN, MARJA-TERTTU • PULLI, MATTI • PURANEN, ERKKI • RANTAKOKKO, ARTO • RANTAVUORI, MARTTI • RISSANEN, PETRI • SALEVA, MIKAEL • SALONEN, REIJO • SAUNAVAARA, RAUNO • SIREN, SAMI • STENIUS, LEIF • TALA,
JUKKA • TASKILA, KYOSTI • TASKINEN, ILPO • TERVO, SAMI • TUOMINEN, VELI-MATTI • UKKOLA-ANTILLA, LAURA • VARE, MARJAANA • VARE, TIMO • VENALAINEN, OLAVI • VIHKO, MAURI • VILEN, KAI • VUORELA, TUULA • WONGPHUT, SAIJAN • **FRANCE:** ABELE, MARIE • ABOUKIR, JEAN-DENIS • AGUILLAUME, FREDERIC • ALBAJARA, BRUNO • ALBESPY, YVES • ALLARD, LAURENT • ALLO, OLIVIER • AMIEL, MICHELE • ARGELES, MICHEL •
BACHA, AMAR • BADID, MUSTAPHA • BADIE, CLAUDE • BAYLE, CHRISTIAN • BECHETOILLE, MARC • BELLANCE, ARTHUR • BELLOT, PIERRE • BENDERITTER, CLAUDE • BENEDETTI, BRUNO • BERTHEZENE, MICHEL • BERTOCHE, ALAIN • BERTRAND, JEAN-LOUIS • BESSEICHE, SERGE • BIDOIS, GILLES • BIZET, NATHALIE • BLANCHOT, GERARD • BLOM, CYRIL • BOURDONNAYE, GILLES • BOURGAIN, JOSETTE • BOURQUI, PASCAL • BOURY,
VINCENT • BOUSTILA, OUAHID • BOZZOLO, STEPHANE • BRAND, ERIC • BRET, DANIEL • BROCHIER, HERVE • BUART, JEAN-MARIE • CAILLET, STEPHANE • CARAYON, CHRISTOPHE • CENSIER, ERIC • CERIA, PATRICK • CHATEIGNER, OLIVIER • CHAVANNE, LIONEL • CITERNE, ROBERT • CLEMENT, JEAN-MARC • COGNE, MICHEL • COLLET, PAUL • COUPRIE, PHILIPPE • CRISTALLO, GUISLAINE • D'URZO, CORINE • DARRONDEAU, JEAN-LUC
• DARVAND, BERNADETTE • DE CAPPELLE, MURIELLE • DECHAMP, HERVE • DELAPIERRE, LUCIEN • DELASSUS, JEAN-LUC • DELAUNE, ANTOINE • DELBERT, JEROME • DELEPLANCQUE, AUGUSTIN-JEAN • DELPIERRE, CHRISTIAN • DELPY, FREDERIC • DENIAUD, OLIVIER • DEVOS, GUY • DRUVERT, JEAN-CLAUDE • DUPOYET, MARC • DURAND, CHRISTOPHE • DURAND, PASCAL • FAHRASMANE, MARIO • FARGEAU, DIDIER • FAVRE, JEAN-
MICHEL • FLAMENGO, JEAN-LOUIS • FLEURET, MARC • FOPPOLO, DAVID • FOURNET, HELENE • GABRIELI, ALAIN • GALL, GERARD • GARCIA, JEAN-FRANCOIS • GARNIER, JEROME • GAROFALO, THIERRY • GAUDEFROY, BRUNO • GAUDILLAT, PATRICE • GAUVIN, JEAN-MICHEL • GENETE, JEAN-LUC • GERGES, PATRICE • GIAMMARTINI, LAURENT • GIBELIN, ANNE-MARIE • GINTRAND, THIERRY • GIRARDET, ERIC • GOUBY, ANNIE • GREGORI,
PAUL • GUERCHOUCHE, HADDA • GUEZO, ERIC • GUILLAUME, DAVID • HADDAD, EDMOND • HAINAULT, DOMINIQUE • HALAGAHU, LUTOVICO • HANICOTTE, FRANCIS • HENNAERT, ANDRE • HERMSDORFF, ROBERT • HESS, BEATRICE • HYBOIS, MARIE-FRANCOISE • ISSORAT, CLAUDE • JACOBS, GREGORY • JEAMMIE, PHILIPPE • JEANNOT, JOEL • JOLI, PHILIPPE • KLEIN, DIDIER • LACHAUD, CHRISTIAN • LACROIX, EMMANUEL • LAFAYE,
ISABELLE • LARRIVIERE, JO • LARTIGUE, ALAIN • LAVAINNE, PASCAL • LEGRAS-LEMAIRE, MYRIAM • LETARTRE, JOSE • LEVESQUE, JEAN-LOUIS • LIBMAN, BERTRAND • LIEUTIER, JENNIFER • LINDMANN, ERIC • LOISEAU, LUDIVINE • MARTIN, THIERRY • MARX, ORISTELLE • MASSE, ERIC • MASSON, GERARD • MAUPILET, PASCAL • MENAGE, DIDIER • MERCIER, DAVID • MERY, DANIEL • MESSI, STEPHANE • MEURET, JACQUES • MICELI, YETI
• MICHOUX, NICOLE • MICHOUX, PHILIPPE • MIGNON, VINCENT • MINIER, JEAN • MIQUARD, FRANCK • MORE, CYRIL • MOREL, CYRIL • N'ZAHOU, GEORGES • NAILI, ABDE • NGO, MAI-ANH • NUTTIN, PHILIPPE • ODEIDE-SIMIAN, MARIE-CLAIRE • PACAULT, YVON • PAILLARD, CHRISTIAN • PAILLER, DOMINIQUE • PAILLET, HERVE • PARALITICI-BELGODERE, SOPHIE • PEETERS, MICHEL • PENAUD, BERNARD • PERIAC, FREDERIC • PEYRONNI,
BERNARD • PICHON, ALAIN • PICOT, PATRICIA • PINARD, PASCAL • PINNA, CHRISTOPHE • POITEVIN, JEAN-FRANCOIS • PRIEUR, JEAN-CLAUDE • PY, EMMANUEL • RACINEUX, ARLETTE • RAHMOUNI, LAMOURI • RANDAXHE, PIERRE • RAOUL, LUC • REGNAULT, JEAN-YVES • RENOUX, ALAIN • REZKI, BEL • RITTER, PATRICK • ROBERT, SERGE • ROCCA, HUBERT • ROINE, PHILIPPE • ROLLO, GERALD • RONDEAU, MARTHE • ROSIER, JEAN •
ROUCHOVZE, GUY • ROURE, RAYMOND • ROUZE, CHRISTIAN • SACHSE, AGNES • SACHSE, BERNARD • SALLEM, RYADH • SANRAME, ISABELLE • SARAMON, BERNARD • SCHALLER, MICHEL • SCHOENACKER, MAURICE • SCHRODER, JENS • SENMARTIN, PATRICE • SEVIN, MICHELLE • SIDOROWIEZ, MICHEL • SIMIAN-MERMIER, PIERRE • SIRY, DANIEL • SORIANO, JEAN-PAUL • STARCK, DANIEL • SUCHANECK, LEON • THEREZO, JOSE •
THIERRY, MARTINE • THISSE, MARIE-ODILE • THURIES, MICHEL • TISSERANT, GUY • TOLLE, CHARLES • TOLOUIE, GHAVAM • TOURET, THIERRY • TREMERIE, MICHEL • TRIPIER, VIRGINIE • TRUJILLO, FRANCISCO • TUIPOLOTO, PATITA • VERGER, PASCAL • VERGNAUD, ANNE • VERGUET, BERNARD • VOGEL, JOELLE • WALLON, LOIC • WESTELYNCF, JEAN-MICHAEL • ZAFRA, JEAN • **GERMANY:** ALTMANN, JENS • ANDERS, OLIVER • ANGGRENY,
LILLY • ANHALT, FRANK • BAERZ, TOM • BALICKI, JOZEF • BARSCH, STEFFEN • BARTHEIDEL, MONIKA • BARTMANN, UWE • BASSE, BERND • BATIZI, SANDOR • BAUTE, SUSANNE • BECKER, ARNO • BEEKER, BIRGIT • BEER, THOMY • BELITZ, GUNTHER • BERINGER, ALFRED • BERNER, REINHARD • BETHKE, ANDREAS • BETHKE, MARTINA • BETTINGER, CHRISTEL • BEYER, HORST • BITTERAUF, STEFAN • BLASE, CORNELIA • BLOMQWIST,
BIRGITTA • BOCK, HILDEGARD • BODEN, DANNY • BODMANN, CLAUDIA • BOEHL, FLORIAN • BOESCH, MARTIN • BOGNER, ALFRED • BOHLANDER, HEINZ • BOLTZ, SIMONE • BORIC, DRAZEN • BRAUN, HEINRICH • BRENNE, JOACHIM • BRINCK, ANNA • BROECKERHOFF, LIESEL • BROGLE, SABINE • BRUNOTTE, CLAIRE • BUDWILL, DIETMAR • BUGGENHAGEN, MARIANNE • BUSSE, INGO • BUSSEWITZ, MICHAEL • CAMPO-BITZER, DORIS •
CONRADI, ANNKE • DAENTLER, CHRISTINE • DAHMEN, THOMAS • DANNOWSKI, HARALD • DEMMELHUBER, GUNDI • DIESSL, CHRISTIAN • DIETZ, CONNY • DISTEL, BURKHARD • DOERR, WERNER • DREISZIS, BIRGIT • DROSTE, MARIA • DUNSTHEIMER, BIRGIT • DUSOLD, WALDEMAR • ECKERT, DETLEF • EGNER, URSULA • EICHBERGER, HANS • ERDMANN-FEIX, JUERGEN • ERTINGER, RUDI • ESPENHAYN, KAY • ESSBACH, DIETER • ESSER,
MICHAEL • EWERT, EDDA • FAEHNRICH, PETER • FAERBER, JENS • FALKE, FRANZ • FIGL, ROBERT • FLEISCHER, SILVIA • FOERDER, ISABELLE • FRANZKA, GERD • FREUND, SYLVIO • FRISCHMANN, JOERG • FRITSCHE, CHRISTIAN • GAEDICKE, KERSTIN • GAERTNER, CHARLY • GAETJE, JOERG • GEBHARDT, CHRISTA • GEFFERS, HOLGER • GEFFERS, INGO • GEILS, FRITZE • GEIST, ANDREAS • GEUER-WITT, RENATE • GIEBEL, JOSEF • GOTZE,
MARIA • GRABBE, RUDI • GRGIC, PAVO • GRIMM, THOMAS • GRYLAK, ROBERT • GUERTLER, JAN • HAASKEN, ELMAR • HABER, PETER • HAND-WIEDMANN, DODO • HAPPEL, ANJA • HARPERATH, RALF • HARTLEB, FRANK-THOMAS • HARTMANN, ROLAND • HAUCKE, RAYK • HAUSSIG, UWE • HEGEHOLZ, SIEGMUND • HEGEMANN, EBBA • HEGEMANN, ROLF • HEINRICH, PETRA • HEINZL, ANNA-MARIA • HELLENSCHMIDT, JENS • HELLMANN,
ROSITHA • HENGST, CLAUDIA • HENKE, DANIELA • HENKER, SIEGMAR • HERTRICH, MONIKA • HESSE, LOTHAR • HILLERS, ANDY • HOCH, HEIDEMARIE • HOEFLE, FRAENKY • HOEHNE, KLAUS • HOLZ, YASMIN • HOPF, YVONNE • HORN, MARTIN • HOWAH, DETLEF • HUBER, GEORG • ISECKE, REGINA • JACOB, JUTTA • JAEHRIG, GEERT • JAENICKE, BRITTA • JANKIW, AGNES • JARSZEWSKI, ANTJE • JASPER, BERT • JOHANN, ANDREAS •
JOSEFIAK, HANS • JOSWIG, DIETER • JUCHEM, THORSTEN • KADNER, ANNETT • KAISER, BARBARA • KAISER, ROLF • KAISER, STEFAN • KAMPRAD, VOLKER • KATZ, WERNER • KEGEL, SIMONA • KEMPF, JULIA • KEMPF, WOLFGANG • KERN, JUERGEN • KEUTHER, DIETER • KIMMIG, HOLGER • KIRSTE, HEIDI • KLEEKAMM, STEFAN • KLEINHANS, STEFAN • KLEPSCH, WINFRIED • KNAAK, WERNER • KNOELLER, HANS • KOCH, JOACHIM • KOE-
BERLE, HEINRICH • KOFLER, MARIO • KOHL, MANFRED • KOHLER, UWE • KOKOTT, CHRISTINE • KOSCHMIEDER, KARL-HEINZ • KOSEL, JURGEN • KRAUSE, CHRISTINE • KRAUSER, RAINER • KREIDEL, THOMAS • KRIESTEN, MICHAEL • KROMER, ADELBERT • KRUEGER, GUENTHER • KUCKUCK, RALF • KUHLMEY, MIRKO • KULLA, KLAUS • KURFESS, THOMAS • LEHMANN, STEFFEN • LIPINSKI, WILFRIED • LOBENSTEIN, BEATE • LOEFFLER, STE-
FAN • LUERIG, LARS • MAHLER, WOLFGANG • MAISSENBACHER, WERNER • MAYER, ANDY • MAZRI-ABES, NADIRA • MEIER, CLAUDIA • MERSDORF, THOMAS • MEYER, KLAUS • MICHAEL, WOLFGANG • MILLER, MAXIMILIAN • MIMBERG, DIRK • MUELLER, ANDREAS • MUELLER, BERND • MUELLER, GOTTY • MUELLER, OLIVER • MUELLER-WELLE, ADOLF • NEUMAIER, JOSEF • NGUYEN-THI, NU • NIEPOTH, ULRICH • NOLLAU, GRIT • NORT-
MANN, HERMANN • NOWOTTNY, ILKA • OEHME, MARIO • OSENBERG, ANGELIKA • OSEWALD, MARTIN • OTT, CAROLINE • OTT, CHRISTA • OTTO, RALF • OVERESCH, LOTHAR • OWEN, ED • PAPAGEORGIOU, ATHANASIOS • PAPE, CHRISTIANE • PAYSEN, FRITZ • PETERS, MARION • PETERSEN, WOLFGANG • PIERSON, ANGELIKA • PILZ, MARKUS • POHL, BIRGIT • POHL, DANIELA • POHLE, GISELA • POHLE, UDO • PRILL, SEBASTIAN • PURSCHKE,
TORSTEN • PUTZ, STEPHANIE • QUADE, KARL • RANZ, ELFRIEDE • REICHMANN, JOSCHI • RICHTER, MICHAEL • RICHTER, MICHAELA • RIEDE, ROLF • ROBITSCHKO, CORINA • RODE, BAERBEL • RODENBERG, DIRK • ROEHLE, DANIELA • ROOSEN, GISELA • RUEHL, CARL • RUNZ, GUDRUN • SACHSE, JESSICA • SCHALL, CORDULA • SCHALL, DOROTHEA • SCHERER, MARKUS • SCHEU, REGINE • SCHIEDEK, JOERG • SCHIPPMANN, BEATE •
SCHLUBECK, MATHIAS • SCHMANDT, ANDRE • SCHMID, JURGEN • SCHMIDL, BERNARD • SCHMIDT, DETLEF • SCHMIDT, RAINER • SCHMIDT, WERNER • SCHMIEDER, ULRIKE • SCHMITT, THOMAS • SCHNEIDER, KASPAR • SCHNEIDER, REINER • SCHOENFELDER, MARC • SCHRAMM, RENE • SCHRAPP, JUERGEN • SCHREIBER, PETER • SCHRETZMANN, BEATE • SCHULZ, LORAINE • SCHULZ, SVEN • SCHWANBECK, DIETER • SCHWARZ, ALEX
• SCHWARZ, SILKE • SCHWARZ, UDO • SCHWIETERING, RUDOLF • SEIDLER, ROSI • SEIFERT, NICOLE • SIALINO, ACHIM • SIEKMANN, MANFRED • SIGG, WINFRIED • SIKORA, MONIKA • SIMONAZZI, ROBERTO • SINSEL, FRANZ • SIRJEAN, AUBERT • SKRZOS, ALEXANDER • SOICKE, SIEGMUND • SOLBRIG, SVEN • SOMMER, ELMAR • SPIES, GUENTER • SPLETTSTOESSER, MEIKE • STELZNER, WINFRIED • STETTNER, FERENC • STOPPERICH, HER-
MANN • STORCH, CARMEN • STOSS, HELGA • STRASS, RENATE • STRASS, WALTER • STRIEGEL, ULRICH • STRIPPEL, THEODOR • STROHM, RITA • SZIBOR, DETLEF • TEUBNER, CORNELIA • THOMAS, ILONA • TRABERT, GELI • TRIPPEN-HILGERS, JOERG • TROTT, MICHAEL • TURTELTAUBE, SIEGMUND • VALIDIS, THOMAS • VAVALA, VINCENZO • VILSMEIER, OTTO • VOELPEL, JUERGEN • VOGEL, BERND • VOGEL, BIANCA • VON DER KUHLEN,
INGA • VON WELCK, FREIHERR • WEBER, MAX • WEBER-KRANZ, ESTHER • WEIBRING, ANGELIKA • WEINSHEIMER, THOMAS • WEISANG, RALPH • WEISSENFELS, KARL-JOSEF • WIEBKE, STEFFEN • WIEGMANN, JENS • WILLING, MARTINA • WIPPERN, WINFRIED • WITTMANN, CHRISTL • WODAK, REINHARD • WOISCHNIK, STEFFEN • WOLF, UDO • WOLLMERT, JOCHEN • WORTMANN, MAIK • WUENSTEL, PETER • ZANDER, GABRIELE • ZEHENT-
NER, KLAUS • ZEILERMEIER, CHRISTIAN • ZIELONKA, BERBEL • ZIMMER, MARKUS • ZIRKELBACH, BERND • ZIRKLEWSKI, INGO • **GREAT BRITAIN:** ADCOCK, CAROL • AITKEN, NEIL • AITKEN, SHELIA • ALLEN, MARGARET • ALLEN, ROBERT • ALLEN, VALERIE • ANDERSON, JIM • ARBUTHNOTT, KIRSTY • ARNOTT, PETER • ASH, ALAN • BAILEY, GORDON • BAILEY, SARAH • BAILLIE, SARAH • BAKER, KEVAN • BARELLA, JANE • BARRETT, ELAINE
• BASFORD, ALICE • BAULF, TINA • BAYLIS, ANDY • BENNETT, PAT • BENSON, LIZ • BERRY, BILL • BETTERIDGE, PAULINE • BIDWELL, EMMA • BINGHAM, ANN • BISHOP, CLARE • BLACK, GORDON • BLACK, JUDY • BLEAKLEY, LAURA • BOOKER, EMMA • BOOTH, JENNY • BOURNE, NIGEL • BRADLEY, JACK • BRAMLEY, DAVID • BRENTON, FRANK • BRENTON, KEITH • BROADRIBB, VICKY • BROADWAY-PARKINSON, ANDREA • BROWN, ELSPETH
• BROWN, MARK • BRUNT, STEPHEN • BUCHANAN, JIM • BULLOCK, MARK • BURTON, JANICE • BUTLER, KAREN • BUXTON, WAYNE • CAINE, STEVAN • CAIRNS, KENNY • CAPEWELL, NIGEL • CARLE, JOYCE • CARSCADDEN, CRAIG • CASSELL, ANDREW • CHAN, ARNIE • CHAPMAN, ANITA • CHEANEY, MARK • CHEER, IRENE • CHESTNEY, BERNARD • CHURCH, FRED • CHURCHILL, KENNY • CICHOCKYJ, JOSIE • CLARKE, DAVID • COATES,
DI • COLAINE, KENNY • COLEMAN, PATSY • COLLETT, RUTH • COLLINS, RICHARD • CONROY, SUSAN • COOPER, IAN • COOPER, ROBERT • COURT, PETER • CRAWFORD, LEE • CREAN, ROSA • CRUICE, ESTHER • CULLEN, ALLEN • CUNDY, JODY • CURRAN, BILL • CURTIS, ANDY • CURTIS, KEVIN • CUTCLIFFE, ANN • DALY, ANGELA • DART, FRANCIS • DAVEY, JEFF • DAVIES, KATHY • DAVIS, JUNE • DAVIS, MELANIE • DAWES, SONIA • DE
COURCY, JOHN • DERBYSHIRE, JOHN • DICKINSON, ZOE • DILLON, JERRY • DING, MARK • DINGWALL, MURRAY • DODDS, JACK • DOUGLAS, NANCY • DOWNS, TONY • DUCKERING, LORRAINE • DUDLEY, DAVE • DUNHAM, ANNE • DUNSON, BOB • EARLE, ALAN • EASTER, MELIANIE • ECCLESTON, MARK • EDGE, DILYS • EDGE, MICK • EDGE, ZOE • EDMANS, LEANNE • EDMUNDS, IVOR • ELIAS, MARY • ESLING, JEANETTE • EVANS, MARTIN
• EVANS, THOMAS • EYKYN, PETER • FARNELL, MARK • FAYERS, BRIAN • FELL, IAN • FELTHAM, STEPHEN • FERGUSON, LARA • FIRTH, FIONA • FOSBROOK, MARK • FOX, CHRIS • FOX, JILL • GALE, REBECCA • GARDNER, KEITH • GARMAN, PAULINE • GARNER, ROY • GEARY, FIONA • GILLESPIE, JAMIE • GITTENS, ERIC • GODDARD, CHARLI • GOLDSBROUGH, IAN • GOOSEY, VICKY • GORDON, CALUM • GOWANS, IAIN • GRATRIX, RYAN •
GREAVES, PAUL • GREEN, TIM • GREER, DOUGLAS • GREGORY, SANDY • GREY, TANNI • GRIFFITHS, STEPHANIE • GROVES, MALCOLM • GROVES, TINA • GUILD, ERNEST • GUTFLEISCH, OLIVER • HALL, PHIL • HALLAM, CHRIS • HARDIMAN, ROSALINDA • HARRIS, CHRIS • HARRIS, JOHN • HARRISON, IAN • HART, STEVIE • HEAPS, TIM • HEATON, DAVID • HEDDLE, DAVID • HEPTINSTALL, JOHN • HESLOP, KEVIN • HEWITT, DAVID • HILL, ROSE
• HINTON, TRACEY • HIRST, CLAIRE • HODGE, ANDY • HOGAN, JENAI • HOLDING, DAVID • HOLMES, CHRIS • HOLMES, MARGARET • HOLTON, SUSAN • HOOLE, BARBARA • HOPE, DAVID • HUDSON, PAUL • HUGHES, PAUL • HULME, JANE • HUMPHREYS, ROY • ILLINGWORTH, CHRIS • INNES, CAROLINE • JACKSON, JO • JACKSON, SIMON • JARVIS, NICOLA • JAYARATNE, JOE • JENKINS, PAUL • JENNINGS, EMILY • JOHNSON, CAROL •
JOHNSON, DAN • JOHNSON, NANETTE • JOHNSON, STEVEN • JOHNSTON, PAUL • JONES, KEITH • JONES, LES • JONES, MALCOLM • JUNIPER, MATTHEW • KEMP, HAZEL • KINDRED, SASCHA • KNIGHT, RAY • KONURALP, DERVIS • LANE, BARRIE • LATHAM, ROBERT • LAWTON, JANICE • LEWIS, JULIUS • LINDSEY, ANDREW • LISTER, MARK • LONG, GILES • LYNE, ALAN • LYNE, PETER • MARTIN, CHRIS • MARTIN, INA • MASON, DIANA •
MATTHEW, IAIN • MATTHEWS, BOB • MCCLUSKEY, EDDIE • MCCRAE, DAVID • MCELENY, MAGGIE • MCGLASHAN, MORAG • MCGREGOR, ALAN • MCKENNA, JACK • MCKENNA, JIM • MCMAHON, RICKY • MCMORRAN, JANET • MILES, KATHRYN • MILLER, STEPHEN • MISTRY, JAYANT • MITCHELL, MARK • MITTON, KEITH • MOORE, VERA • MORGAN, GARY • MORGAN, MADGE • MORGAN, MALCOLM • MORLEY, ADAM • MORLEY, HELEN • MOR-
RISS, KEITH • MULLETT, VIVIEN • MUNKLEY, JIM • MUNN, SIMON • MURLAND, JERRY • MURRAY, JOHN • NETHERCOTT, JOHN • NEWBERY, DAWN • NEWMAN, IVAN • NEWSTEAD, ISABEL • NEWSTEAD, JOHN • NEWTON, MARK • NICHOLLS, RON • NOBLE, PAUL • OSBORNE, GRAHAM • OULTON, KEITH • PADGEN, DAVID • PANTZER, PAUL • PARSONAGE, STEVE • PARSONS, MICK • PAWSON, SUSAN • PAYTON, STEPHEN • PEACHEY, RACHELLE
• PEARCY, ANDREW • PEAT, PHIL • PEDDLE, ANTHONY • PEEL, GARRY • PICKUP, JOHN • POTTER, RACHEL • POWELL, TERRY • PRICE, COLIN • PUDDEN, RO • PULLEN, STEVE • QUINTON, JENNY • RAFFERTY, STEVE • RANSOME, DARREN • RAWSON, JAMES • REDDIN, SALLY • REDDISH, TIM • REDDISH, TONY • REYNOLDS, JOHN • RICHARDSON, CARL • RICHARDSON, JIM • RICKETT, GAVIN • RICKETT, KIMIYO • RIDDELL, GEORGE • RIDING,
LYNNE • RISDON, JAMES • ROBERTSON, GORDON • ROBERTSON, JOHN • ROBINSON, NEIL • ROBINSON, STEVEN • ROCKETT, SUZANNAH • ROSE, IAN • ROWE, PAUL • RUSSELL, DAVID • RYDING, WAYNE • SAINSBURY, TONY • SALVARY, CHRIS • SCHABEL, RICHARD • SCOTT, PAT • SCOTT, THOM • SEARLE, CAROLINE • SHARPE, IAN • SHAW, NEIL • SHERRIFF, JOYCE • SHORRICK, SIMON • SIMPSON, MARGARET • SINKINSON, PHIL • SLATER,
NICK • SMITH, KATHY • SMITH, MARGARET • SMITH, NIGEL • STAINTON, JOHN • STANTON, NIKI • STEGGLES, JONATHAN • STIDEVER, JANE • STIRK, ANGIE • STODDART, LESLIE • STONE, LIZ • STONEHAM, KIRSTY • STRAUGHAN, PATRICIA • SWAN, JANE • TARKENTER, MALCOLM • TARR, ROB • TAYLOR, GRAHAM • THATCHER, NOEL • THOMAS, AUSTIN • THOMAS, DEAN • THOMPSON, IAN • THOMPSON, PETE • THOMSON, JIM • TILLOTSON,
DAVID • TIZZARD, ANNA • TOWNSEND, JOHN • TUBBS, DIANNE • TURNER, HOWARD • TYLER, PENNY • UREN, SHAUN • VICAREY, PETE • WALKER, YVONNE • WALSH, CATHY • WALSH, KEVIN • WALTON, CAZ • WARD, JONATHAN • WEBBORN, NICK • WEIR, DAVID • WEST, DANIEL • WHITELAW, JACKIE • WHITELEY, MARK • WILD, ANN • WILLAVOYS, MICHAEL • WILLEY, RUSSELL • WILLIAMS, PAUL • WILLIAMS, PAUL • WILLIAMS, TONY • WILLIS,
TONY • WISCOMBE, TRACY • WOFFINDEN, ANNE • WOOD, BEVERLEY • WOOD, MIKE • WOODS, MARC • WOODWARD, ROBERT • WOOLLARD, TONY • WORRALL, BRIAN • WRIGHT, GEORGE • YORKE, DAVID • YORKE, TONY • **GREECE:** ANARGYROY, STEFANOS • ANGOURAKIS, CHRISTOS • ANGOURAKIS, DIONYSIOS • CHATZIBEIS, IOANNIS • CHRONOPOULOS, POLYCHRUNIS • FYKAS, KONSTANTINOS • GIAPOUTZIS, ANTONIOS • GRIVEAS,
KYRIAKOS • KARAMINAS, GEORGIIS • KAZAKI, ARCHONTIA • KONSTANTANGAS, DIMITRIOS • KONSTANTOS, IOANNIS • KTENIDIS, EFTHYMIOS • PATATOUKAS, DIMITRIOS • PETROPOULOS, GEORGIOS • SEMERTZIDIS, PANAGIOTIS • SOTIRIADI, KONSTANTINIA • STAVRIDIS, KONSTANTINOS • TAMPAXIS, CHRISTOS • TOPTSIS, GEORGIOS • TSIVILIS, ATHANASIOS • VOVOS, STYLIANOS • VRYONIS, GERASIMOS • **HONDURAS:** GUIFARRO,
GUILLERMINA • HERNANDEZ, NARCISO • MARTINEZ, REINALDO • NUNEZ, MAILO • SIBERT, SONIA • **HONG KONG:** ANTUNES, CARLOS • CHAN, ALBERT • CHAN, RAYMOND • CHAN, SHING • CHAO, KWOK • CHEUNG, WAI • CHEUNG, YIU • CHIANG, SILAS • CHIU, JIMMY • CHUI, BEN • CHUNG, WAI • FUNG, YUET • HO, SUM • KWONG, ERIC • KWONG, SHING • LAM, JAMES • LAU, ANTHONY • LAU, SIK • LAW, ALICE • LEE, KWOK • LEE,
STEPHEN • LEUNG, APRIL • LI, TAK • LUI, PEGA • MAK, PATRICIA • NG, PATRICK • NG, WING • POON, KIN • SO, WA • TAI, NELSON • TANG, FIONA • TANG, FRANK • TANG, SUNNY • WANG, RUI • WONG, MAN • WONG, PUI • WONG, SUNNY • WONG, YIN • YEUNG, LENA • **HUNGARY:** BALINT, ANDRAS • BALLA, ENDRE • BALOGH, ISTVAN • BECSEY, JANOS • BELICZAY, SANDOR • DINYA, IMRE • DOMOKOS, ANDRAS • DOSEK, LAJOSNE •
ENGELHARDT, KATALIN • ERDEI, ILONA • ERDOS, LAJOS • FARKAS, LASZLO • GAAL, HEDVIG • GABRIS, LASZLO • GAL, JANOS • GRUIZ, KATALIN • HEGEDUS, BELA • HEGYSI, PETER • HORVATH, SANDOR • HUTTER, MARTA • JAROMI, MONIKA • KALLAY, KATALIN • KASZALA, FERENC • KENDERES, GABOR • KOVACS, ERVIN • KOVACS, GYOZO • KOVACS, LASZLO • KOVACS, ZSOLT • LALUJA, LASZLO • LEGEZA, GYORGY • MAJSAI, KAROLY
• MAKAROVSZKI, SANDOR • MANYAK, ATTILA • MAROSI, JOZSEF • MARTON, ANDREA • MENTES, EVA • NAGY, ISTVAN • NAVRATYIL, SANDOR • NEMETH, LASZLO • PAJER, JOZSEF • PALFI, JUDIT • PANCSA, JOZSEF • PANTO, TAMAS • PAPP, ANITA • PAZINCZAR, ATTILA • PERES, JANOS • PONYORI, SANDOR • RACZKO, GITTA • RAKHELY, BELA • SARNYAI, ILONA • SASVARINE, ILONA • STIRCZER, JOZSEF • SZABO, ENDRE • SZABO, LASZLO
• SZAVAI, CSABA • SZECSENYI, LAJOS • SZEKERES, PAL • SZEPESI, ATTILA • SZUCS, MIKLOS • TATAI, ZSOFIA • TOTH, ILDIKO • VERECZKEI, ZSOLT • ZAMBO, DIANA • **ICELAND:** EIRIKSSON, OLAFUR • ERLINGSDOTTIR, BARA • GUDMUNDSDOTTIR, KRISTIN • GUDMUNDSSON, PALMAR • GUDNASON, GEIR • GUNNARSSON, BIRKIR • GUNNARSSON, GUNNAR • GUNNARSSON, HAUKUR • HAKONARDOTTIR, KRISTIN • HRAFNSDOTTIR, SIGRUN
• JOHANNSSON, ERLINGUR • KRISTJANSDOTTIR, ANNA • LUDVIKSSON, SVEINN • MAGNUSSON, OLAFUR • SIGUROSSON, HAUKUR • SVERRISSON, GEIR • **INDIA:** BRAR, S • GAVIYAPPA, BETTAIAH • GIRISH, H • IYER, SHANKAR • KHAN, N • KRISHNAPPA, BHEEMANNA • MALLAIAH, MAHADEV • MUNISHWAR, V • PRABHU, H • RAMESH, H • SANTOSH, KUDALKAR • SHARMA, N • SHIVANANDA, GUNJAL • SINGH, M • VASHISHTA, Y • **INDONESIA:**
AK, BASRI • HIE, LANGGENG • NGADIYO, • PRIYONO, AGUS • SYAMSI, PURBADHI • **IRAN** AKBARI, ALLAH • AKRAMI, SHAHRAM • AMREI, SEYED • ASHOURI, FARSHID • AZGHANDI, ALI • BAGHERI, SEYED • BAGHESTANI, ABBAS • BARGHCHI, HOSSEIN • BEHTAJ, DAVOUD • BEIGI, ZAHRA • BOKHARAEI, ENAYATOLLAH • DEHGANIH, AMROLLAH • DEHGHAN, MOHAMMADRAHIM • EDRISI, KAZEM • EIMRI, JALIL • FAREI, BAHHMAN • FIROUZI,
PARVIZ • HAJMIRFATTAH, FATEMEH • HASSANI, MOHAMMAD • JABERI, MOHAMMAD • JAFARZADEH, MANOUCHEHR • JOKAR, ABDOLREZA • KARIMIPOUR, FERYDON • KASHFIA, ALI • KHALAFZADEH, JABER • KHARAZIAN, GHOLAMALI • KHILI, ALI • KHOSRAVIVAFA, MAHMOUD • MAHJORI, AHMAD • MEHRAEIN, MOHAMMAD • MEHRYAR, MOHAMMAD • MODABBERRAZ, GHADER • MOHAMMADI, MOHAMMAD • MOKHTARIAN, SAEID •
NEZAMOLESLAMI, MOHAMMAD • NOURAFSHAN, MOKHTAR • PAHLAVANI, MOHAMMAD • RAEF, FATEMEH • RASHED, KAZEM • RAVASI, ALI • REZAEIKARAKANI, HADI • SALAVATIAN, ALI • SHAHI, HASSAN • SIAVOSHANI, HOSSEIN • SOLEIMANIKHORAMDASHTI, MAJID • TOROGHI, MOHSEN • **IRELAND:** AHERN, JOHN • AHERN, JOHN • ALEXANDER, PETER • BAGNALL, BRIAN • BARRETT-CONDRON, GRAINNE • BEHAN, BILLY • BELL, FRANCIS
• BERRY, MAIREAD • BOYLE, EDWARD • BRIDGEMAN, JOHN • BUCKLEY, DONAL • BYRNE, JIMMY • CAREY, STEPHEN • CASSIN, PAUL • CLARKE, MICHAEL • CLEARE, EOIN • COFFEY, ANTHONY • COLGAN, COLIN • CONROY, PAULINE • CULHANE, TIM • CULLITON, GARRETT • CUNNINGHAM, MICHAEL • DELANEY, MICHAEL • DOCKERY, PATRICE • DORAN, STEPHEN • DOWNING, KEVIN • DUNNE, GERRY • DURAND, DERRY • EBBS, ANNE •
FARQUHARSON, MAIREAD • FULHAM, JOHN • FURLONG, PAT • FURLONG, TRICIA • GALLAGHER, LORRAINE • GAUGHAN, GRACE • GILMORE, MADELINE • GRANT, ROGER • GREEN, BRENDA • GREEN, TONY • GUERIN, ROY • GUEST, TONY • HARVEY, ANN • HENDRA, MIKE • HEWITT, WILLIE • JUDGE, PATRICK • KEARNEY, JASON • KEATING, ALMA • KEATING, CARL • LEAHY, TOM • LEISK, PAUL • LUCEY, MARY • LYNCH, BRIDIE • MALONE,
DAVID • MASSEY, GERALDINE • MASSEY, PADDY • MCBRIDE, JIM • MCCARTHY, BOB • MCCARTHY, JAMES • MCCONNELL, ROISIN • MCDERMOTT, STEPHEN • MCDONAGH, FRANCIS • MCDONAGH, MARTIN • MCDONAGH, THERESA • MCGRANE, JOEY • MCMACKEN, DENIS • MCNALLY, DAVID • MILLS, BRIAN • MURPHY, ANTHONY • MURRIHY, JAMES • NAZARALI, RAHIM • O'BRIEN, AOIFE • O'CONNELL, TREVOR • O'GRADY, CECILIA • O'GRADY,
SEAN • O'HARE, HEATHER • O'MAHONY, EILEEN • O'REILLY, COLETTE • O'RIORDAN, FINBARR • O'SULLIVAN, FRANK • O'SULLIVAN, JOHN • PHILLIPS, NATASHA • RICE, MARY • RICE, SHARON • ROCHE, JOHN • ROONEY, RONAN • SALMON, JOAN • SHELLEY, GAY • SMITH, BRENDAN • SMITH, MICHAEL • STYNES, ESTHER • SULLIVAN, JOHN • TWOMEY, JOHN • WALSH, BERNIE • WALSH, CATHERINE • WARD, DECLAN • **ISRAEL:** AHARONI,
SHOLMO • AHARONI, TIKI • ATIA, ELIYAHU • AVIVI, RONEN • AYGER, SHALOM • BAR-SHIRHA, ZIV • BARANES, ITZHAK • BASHA, URI • BELAR, AMITI • BEN-DOR, YAIR • BEN-HAIM, YORAM • BETTER, ZIV • BOLOTIN, RON • BRONER, AVRAHAM • BUDIN, HANOCH • CARMELI, TAMI • CHABRA, ELI • COHEN, IZHAR • DEKEL, MARIO • FARBER, AKIVA • FAYNTUCH, JAIME • FEIN, ALON • FRANKO, NISIM • FRIEDMANN, FRITZ • GLIKMAN, ZEEV •
GOLDSMITH, ALEX • HABA, GIL • HADASSI, ABRAHAM • HAHAMOV, MOSHE • HAREL, NISSIM • IVAN, • KALINA, ELIEZER • KARSH, ZVI • KASPI, YUVAL • KATAB, ITZHAK • KEDEM, DROR • KENZI, YOGEV • KLEIN, GYORA • LANZER, GAD • LEIBOWITZ, DAVID • MASAMI, BARUCH • MEISHAR, DOTAN • MOR, SIVAN • MOSES, URIEL • NAOR, GILL • PASMANICK, PHILLIP • PERLE, UZI • SAGIR, YAACOV • SHACHAR, SARA • SHAHAR, EYAL • SHAR-
TOV, EYAL • SHARF, YOAV • SHAZIRI, DORON • SHEMESH, ERAN • SHKEDI, ANITA • SHKEDI, GYORA • SHRIKAR, MAURICE • WALLACH, KINNERET • WOLF, NACHMAN • ZAMIR, HAGAI • ZHUR, CHEN • ZONNENFELD, MARGALITH • ZUCK, ITAY • ZUKERMAN, SAGI • **ITALY:** ADANI, RAFFAELLA • AGNESE, MANUELA • ALBERTI, MAURO • ALFIERI, GIUSEPPE • BAMBINI, DANIELA • BARBERA, VALENTINA • BARBISAN, PAOLO • BELTRAME, GIANNI
• BERNARDI, GERMANO • BERNARDONI, MASSIMO • BERTINI, MARIELLA • BERTINOTTI, GABRIELLA • BIANCHI, GIANFRANCO • BISLERI, SILVANO • BONATO, ARMANDO • BORELLO, ALBERTO • BOTTI, PAOLO • BREDA, REMO • BRUNO, GIANCARLO • CALEGARI, MARCO • CAMPEDELLI, PASQUALE • CAREDDA, MAURO • CARMENI, TULLIO • CARPIGNANO, MARCO • CASADEI, FAUSTO • CASSATA, CLAUDIO • CECCANTI, SORIANO • COSTA,
CLAUDIO • D'AGOSTINI, PAOLO • DE MEO, ANGELO • DE MICHIEL, DANIELE • DE MOLINER, RENATO • DE PELLEGRIN, OSCAR • DE VIDI, ALVISE • DURANTE, CARLO • ESPOSITO, MARIO • FANTATO, PAOLA • FARINAZZO, DINO • FERRO, MARTA • FILIPOZZI, SANDRO • FURLANETTO, PIERINA • GABELLI, GIUSEPPE • GALLI, GIANCARLO • GALLI, IVANA • GALLUCCI, ROBERTO • GILARDI, ORLANDO • GIONFRIDDO, MICHELE • GIUSSANI, ERNESTO
• GUALTIERI, CARMELA • GUSMEROLI, GIULIO • HELFER, RENATE • IOVINO, LETIZIA • KURIS, ALESSANDRO • LAMPACHER, JULIUS • LAZZARONI, ROBERTA • LEONORI, GIOVANNA • LERRE, ERNESTO • LIGORIO, MARIA • LION, GASTONE • LOA, CARLO • LOI, VITTORIO • LOTTI, MAURO • LUGARI, UBER • LUVISETTO, EZIO • MAFFIOLETTI, SANDRO • MAI, MARCO • MALOVINI, LUCIANO • MANCINI, MONICA • MANGANARO, ALDO • MANGANO,
SANTO • MARI, GERARDO • MARIANO, GIUSEPPE • MARINO, GIUSEPPE • MARTELLA, ANTONIO • MARTINI, PAOLO • MASIELLO, ENZO • MASTRODOMENICO, ANGELICA • MASTROFINI, UMBERTO • MENEGHELLI, SAMANTA • MILANI, MELISSA • MINI, PIERDOMENICO • MISTURINI, RENATO • NALIN, MAURIZIO • NARDELLI, MARIA • PACINI, FEDERICA • PANCALLI, LUCA • PEDRAZZI, MARCO • PELLEGRINI, ALBERTO • PEPE, ALESSANDRO •
PERASSO, FLAVIO • PERFLER, HUBERT • PERITORE, ANGELO • PISCITELLI, ROBERTO • PISCITELLO, GIANCARLO • PLONER, CHRISTINA • PODDA, CLARA • POLETTI, MARIO • PORCELLATO, FRANCESCA • PORCIANI, MASSIMO • PRESUTTO, LAURA • RABITO, MASSIMO • RICAGNI, ITALO • RIGOLO, CLAUDIO • ROSATO, BRUNO • ROSSO, MICHELE • RUGGIERO, GIANFRANCO • SACCONE, MONICA • SAINI, GIANLUCA • SCARSELLA, PIERINO •
SERAFINI, ALBERTO • SPADACCINI, PATRIZIA • TAFFONI, DEBORAH • TASSETTI, MATTEO • TAVECCHIO, ALESSIO • TORCOLACCI, FIORELLA • TOZZINI, MARINA • TRUCCOLO, SANDRA • VALORI, ROBERTO • VETTRAINO, ROSALBA • VITTORIOSO, ANTONELLA • ZANIN, MATTEO • ZANOTTI, DAMIANO • ZAPPULLA, LEONE • ZULLO, FORTUNATO • **JAMAICA:** BARNED, KAY • DAVIS, JEFF • GRANT, SYLVIA • MARTINEZ, JOHN • SINCLAIR, NEVILLE
• WILLIAMS, ERROL • **JAPAN:** AOKI, AKINOBU • ARAI, NORIKO • CHIBA, MASAAKI • CHINO, HIROAKI • FUJIGIWA, SHOZO • FUJII, HIROSHI • FUJIMOTO, SATOSHI • FUJIWARA, SHINICHIRO • FURUTA, KEISUKE • HASEGAWA, MASAO • HASHIMOTO, KAZUNORI • HASHITANI, TOSHITSUGU • HATAKEYAMA, KOSHIRO • HATANAKA, KAZU • HIROTA, HIROKO • HORIKAWA, SAYURI • ISHIDA, MITOYA • IWANO, HIROSHI • JIMBO, YASUHIRO • KAIDO,
OJI • KAJIWARA, NORIKO • KAKITANI, KIYOSHI • KAMON, TOMOKI • KANEDA, YASUMASA • KANKI, NOBUHIRO • KATO, HIROSHI • KAWAI, JUNICHI • KIMURA, HIROMITSU • KITAMOTO, KANAE • KITANI, MIKI • KOBAYASHI, JUNICHI • KORETOMO, KEISUKE • KOTAKI, OSAMU • KUBOTA, YASUMA • KUGE, KUNIHIRO • KURAMOCHI, HIROSHI • KUROGI, SHINGO • MAEBA, KAZUYA • MAEDA, SHOJIRO • MANABE, ATSUKI • MARUYAMA, HISAKO
• MASHIKO, MEGUMI • MATSUEDA, SHIGEKO • MATSUI, NAOKI • MATSUMOTO, TAKUYA • MATSUMURA, YUMEJI • MATSUNAGA, TAKEO • MIKAMI, SHINJI • MINAMI, KOICHI • MINAMI, MINOBU • MINAMI, TATSUYA • MINAMIKAWA, SACHIKO • MITSUI, TOSHIHITO • MIYAGAWA, HIROKO • MIYAHARA, JUNKO • MIYAKE, KATSUMI • MIYANO, MASAMI • MIYAOKA, YASUSHI • MIZUMOTO, EIKI • MIZUTA, KENJI • MORITA, TOSHIKO • MOTOHASHI,
AKIHITO • MUROZUKA, KAZUYA • NAGAO, YOSHIFUMI • NAKAGAWA, KAZUHIKO • NAKAJIMA, TAKENORI • NARITA, MAYUMI • NISHII, KENICHI • NURUKI, MICHIYO • OGAWA, MUTSUHIKO • OHARA, AKIKO • OKAMOTO, NAOKO • OKUHARA, AKIO • OMAE, CHIYOKO • OMORI, YASUKATSU • OSHIMA, TOMOHIKO • OSUGI, TAKASHI • OTSUKI, HIROYA • OZAKI, MINEHO • SAIDA, SATOSHI • SAIKI, SHUZO • SAKANO, YOSHIKI • SAKO, JUNKO •
SAKURAI, SEIICHI • SATO, MASAO • SHIBASAKI, KEIICHI • SHIMAUCHI, TAKAYUKI • SHIOTA, KIYOTAKA • SUGIMURA, MASAYO • SUGIYAMA, HIROSHI • SUTO, MASAKAZU • SUZUKI, HIFUMI • SUZUKI, KENICHI • TAKABAYASHI, MIKA • TAKAGAKI, OSAMU • TAKAHASHI, HIROSHI • TANAKA, HIDEO • TANAKA, TERUYO • TANAKA, TOSHIYUKI • TATSUMI, KOICHI • TSUKAMOTO, KYOKO • UEMURA, CHIKA • UNE, YASUHIRO • USHIKUBO, TAKIO •
ITAZU, KIYOFUMI • UWANO, YASUHIRO • WADA, YUTAKA • WAKANA, TSUNENOBU • WASHITAKE, YOSHIYUKI • YAMAGUCHI, MIKI • YAMAMOTO, MASAKO • YAMAMOTO, YUKIFUMI • YAMAURA, SATOSHI • YAMOTO, TOSHIMI • YANAGAWA, HARUMI • YANO, SHIGEKI • YANO, YOSUKE • YASOHAMA, SHIGETO • YASUDA, KYOHEI • YASUNISHI, KIYOMI • YONEZAWA, MASAKO • YOSHIHARA, SHIGEO • YOSHIMURA, TATSUHIKO • **JORDAN:**
BOUDI, ADNAN • AUDEH, MOHAMMAD • AWADHAT, ABDEL • GHARBAWI, IMAD • HUSSEIN, FIRAS • TARJALI, ADAM • ZARD, FAWZI • **KAZAKHSTAN:** ALPYSBAEV, MALIK • BUKATOV, NIKOLAI • FUX, ALEFTINA • KAMYSSOV, YRYSBEK • KHOKHLOV, SERGEY • KLYCHBAEV, OMAN • KOLODIOUK, ANATOLI • KONDRATENKO, NIKOLAY • KUKATOV, ALEXANDR • KULUSHOV, NURALY • NARBAEV, ORAZ • RYSBEKOVA, RITA • SAKBAYEV, BAKHIT
• SAURAMBAYEV, ZHANBEK • SUBBOTA, YORIY • TASHKUMBAEV, SHALKAR • TCHETVERIKOV, GEORGAI • **KENYA:** HELLEN, CHERONO • JAPHETH, MUSYOKI • JUMA, MARY • KIHUNGI, PATRICIA • LAGAT, JULIUS • LODOMO, JOHN • LOMONGO, JOSEPH • MAINA, SOSPETER • MATULAI, CHARLES • MOORI, CHRISTOPHER • MOSOTI, SAMSON • MUGA, DENIS • MUGAMBI, RACHEL • MURENYI, PASCAL • MUTETI, GRACE • MUTHAMA, PETER
• NAKHUMICHA, MARY • NDAMBUKI, DAVIS • NGANGA, RUTH • OLANG, ROSE • OMENDA, MILCAH • OTIENO, BARACK • THINDIU, ROBERT • VINCENT, KIMANTHI • WATSON, JEAN • **KOREA:** AHN, TAE • AN, JONG • AN, YOU • BONG, DOK • CHANG, CHOON • CHANG, MYOUNG • CHEON, HYE • CHO, HANG • CHO, HYEON • CHO, HYUN • CHO, SEUNG • CHOI, IL • CHOI, JONG • CHOI, JONG • CHOI, THOMAS • CHOI, WON • CHOI, YEON •
CHOI, YOUNG • CHON, JOONG • CHOO, SOON • HAN, MIN • HAN, TAE • HUH, DO • JEONG, CHOON • JEONG, EUN • JEONG, JIN • JEONG, KWANG • JIH, YOUNG • JOUNG, JAI • JUNG, KUM • JUNG, YOO • KANG, DAE • KANG, DAL • KANG, SUNG • KANG, YOUNG • KIM, DAE • KIM, DAE • KIM, DU • KIM, HAE • KIM, HEE • KIM, HWA • KIM, HYUN • KIM, IL • KIM, IM • KIM, JONG • KIM, JOON • KIM, KI • KIM, KYU • KIM, KYUNG • KIM, MI • KIM,
SO • KIM, SOO • KIM, SOON • KIM, SUNG • KIM, YOUNG • KIM, YOUNG • KO, HEE • KO, JOON • KOO, HEE • KWAK, JUNG • LEE, BONG • LEE, DONG • LEE, HAE • LEE, HONG • LEE, IL • LEE, JAE • LEE, KUN • LEE, KWAN • LEE, LEE • LEE, MIN • LEE, OUK • LEE, YOUNG • LEE, YOUNG • LIM, BYUNG • LIM, CHAN • LIM, CHANG • LIM, SOO • LIM, SU • OH, DOO • PARK, BUN • PARK, CHANG • PARK, EUN • PARK, HAUN • PARK, JONG • PARK,
TAE • PYUN, MOO • SEO, YOUNG • SHIM, MYUNG • SHIN, DAE • SONG, BANG • SONG, KI • SONG, SIN • UM, TAE • YONG, PIL • YOON, HEUNG • YOON, JOONG • YOON, SANG • YOON, SE • YOU, IN • YOU, WON • **KUWAIT:** ABDULLAH, MOHAMMAD • ABOU-EREJAIB, YOUSUF • ABUL, MAHMOUD • AGHA, YAKOUT • AHMAD, SALMAN • AL-ALI, AYAD • AL-ALI, MOHSEN • AL-AZMI, KHALED • AL-DOUSARI, ATEF • AL-ENEZI, HUSAIN • AL-ENEZI,
MUBARAK • AL-KHADHER, MESHARI • AL-KHELAIFI, ADNAN • AL-KOUT, FOUAD • AL-MUTAIRI, FAHED • AL-MUTAIRI, MAJED • AL-OTAIBI, MASHAL • AL-QALLAF, TARIQ • ALBAHRANI, ABDULHADI • BU-ABBAS, FADHEL • HABIB, AHMAD • MAKHSEED, AHMAD • MOHAMMAD, ALI • MUTAWA, ANWAR • SARKHOOK, ABDUL-RAZZAK • **KYRGYZSTAN:** CHALIEV, NIYAZBEK • EPELMAN, KLIMENTI • KACHALOV, ALEKSANDR • OMURBEKOV, ROMAN
• **LATVIA:** DUKALSKA, SANDRA • GRAUDINS, IVARS • GRAUDINS, VIESTURS • JANOVSKIS, JANIS • KAUSELIS, MARIS • LIETNIECE, SANITA • LIZBOVSKIS, ARMANDS • STILVE, VALDIS • SUPULNIEKS, ALDIS • **LIBYA:** ELMAGHRABI, ABDURRAZAG • GHRSA, ABDUSSALAM • HAMED, ABDELRAHIM • LASHEHAB, ABDELWAHAB • LASHEHAB, FATHI • SALEM, SALEM • **LITHUANIA:** BARTKENAS, KESTUTIS • BAUMGARTE, MALDA • CELIESIUS,
ANTANAS • GIRNIUS, VYTAUTAS • GRIGALIUNIENE, ALDONA • LEONAVICIUS, SAULIUS • MARKEVICIENE, SIGITA • RAKAUSKAITE, LINA • SAUSAITIS, ROMAS • SIMKUS, RAIMUNDAS • SOKOLOVAS, SERGEJUS • STANKEVICIUS, VIDAS • STOSKUS, JONAS • TATULIS, ALGIRDAS • URBONAS, ROLANDAS • **LUXEMBOURG:** GARDINI, FAUSTO • HEINRICY, MICHEL • MATHGEN, ROMAIN • SCHREINER, MARC • **MACAU:** BATALHA, CARLOS • DA
LUZ, JUNIOR • FERNANDES, ANTONIO • **MACEDONIA:** JOVANOVSKI, BRANIMIR • KRSTESKI, STEVAN • SAREVSKI, KIRIL • **MALAYSIA:** CHEOK, KON • JEMADI, PAIJO • LEE, SHENG • MUNIANDY, KUTTIAPAN • OTHMAN, KHASSERI • PERUMAL, MARIAPPAN • SINNATHAMBY, RADHA • SUPPAN, KARU • WONG, CHEN • WONG, PAK • ZARIN, ZAINAL • **MAURITIUS:** CUSTNEA, SARWAN • CYTHEREE, ENRICO • GOOLY, NAVIND • LUXIMON, JOSE
TANG, GEORGE • **MEXICO:** ALVA, RAFAEL • ARENALES, TERESA • ARREDONDO, PORFIRIO • AVILA, ROLANDO • BADILLO, GERARDO • BAZAN, SILVIA • BRAVO, FERNANDO • CASTANEDA, RICARDO • CASTRO, ARACELI • CASTRO, JOSE • DIAZ, SALVADOR • DOMINGUEZ, GUADALUPE • DURAN, MAURO • ESCALONA, HERIBERTO • ESPIRITU, MAGALI • FRANCO, ADRIAN • GALINDO, MOISES • GARCIA, DORA • GOMEZ, FELIPE • GORDIAN,
AARON • GUERRERO, ALEJANDRO • GUTIERREZ, FERNANDO • HERNANDEZ, GILBERTO • HERNANDEZ, SALVADOR • HERNANDEZ, VIRGINIA • HOFFMANN, CRISTINA • ISAIAS, MARTIN • LARRAGA, PABLO • LEDEZMA, NICOLAS • LUNA, JORGE • MACIEL, JOSE • MAGANA, RIGOBERTO • MATZUMURA, TAKASHI • MAXIMO, MAURO • MENDOZA, RAFAEL • MENDOZA, SAUL • MOLINA, CLAUDIA • MONSALVO, EDUARDO • NIEVES, RAMON •
NUNEZ, EDUARDO • OJEDA, MARCO • ORTEGA, RAUL • PAZ, ADRIAN • PAZARAN, MARIO • RENE, CORONA • RIOS, JOSE • RODARTE, GABRIEL • RODRIGUEZ, JESUS • RODRIGUEZ, MARIA • RODRIGUEZ, RODOLFO • ROSALES, CATALINA • ROSALES, MIGUEL • RUIZ, ARMANDO • SALAZAR, MARIO • SANCHEZ, JOSE • TABOADA, CLAUDIA • TERRANT, DANIEL • TORRES, LETICIA • VALLE, PATRICIA • VARGAS, ROBERTO • ZAVALA, SALVADOR
• **MOLDOVA:** BARBIEROU, NIKOLAI • DOVBANIOUK, ANATOLI • MARINENKOV, IOURI • POLKANOV, VLADIMIR • TCHOULAKOV, ALEXANDRE • TCHOUMAK, NIKOLAI • ZAIM, VALERI • **MOROCCO:** GARDA, KHALID • MARDI, MADANI • MESNED, EL • MOUTAOUI, ABDELLAH • OUAHBI, MOHAMED • TOUIL, SAID • **NETHERLANDS:** AMSING, MIRJAM • ASSENBERG, IRIS • BANFI, JOZE • BENNEKER, ERNA • BOEVINK, HENNY • BOLK, GERT • BOM-
MEL, JAN • BONHOF, BETSY • BOOM, BERT • BOSCH, MONIQUE • BOUWMAN, THEO • BRINK, ERIK • BROEK, EDWIN • BROERSE, YOLANDA • BROERTJES, GERARD • BUITENDIJK, WILLEM • BUURMAN, JORIEN • CAPPETIJN, WILBERT • DE BOER, JAN • DE GOEDE, FRANK • DE GRAAF, ARCO • DE GROOT, ALWIN • DE GROOT, INEKE • DE HAAN, JOUKE • DE HOOGH, JOOST • DE JONG, ARNO • DE KONING, ROB • DE PUNDER, INGE • DE
ROOY, ANTON • DE VRIES, JAAP • DE WIDT, CASPER • DE ZEEUW, JOKE • DENGERINK, CARLO • DETTMER, RUUD • DIEMEN, PAULIEN • DONNERS, OLAF • DOST, HENK • DRENTHE, SASKIA • DRIJVER, ARNICA • DROOG, PAUL • DURGE, RON • EGGERS, FRANCIENA • EILANDER, JEREMY • ENGEL, KASPER • ENGELSMAN, JURJEN • ENSER, PERCY • EVERS, JAN-HEIN • GELTINK, JESSICA • GESELL, RICHARD • GLIMMERVEEN, RENE • GUNTLIS-
BERGEN, PETER • HAEX, FRANCIEN • HARKEMA, FROUWKJE • HASSALL, CHRIS • HEERSINK, PAUL • HENDRIKS, DYANE • HENNINK, WILFRED • HESSELS, UDO • HOEK, ILONKA • HOORN, ABEL • HOUTSMA, ALWIN • HURK, MARIAN • IBRAHIMI, ASJOUSJA • JANSEN, JENNETTE • JANSENS, KOEN • JEBARI, MUSTAFA • K, SANDER • KALKMAN, MARC • KAMERLING, SERVAAS • KARSSEN, OLAF • KERSTEN, HAROLD • KONING, JOHN • KOOY,
MANFRED • KROON, GERARD • KRUIZENGA, JAAP • KUIJS, PIET • LAEMERS, TRUUS • LAMPERS, GERDA • LANGEN, TOM • LANTERMANS, KAREL • LEGERSTEE, PIET • LENTINK, JURGEN • MARKUS, SANDER • MARTENS, RENE • MOLIER, RICKY • MOS, JOSE • MULDER, JAN • NANNENBERG, JACQUELINE • NOORDEGRAAF, PAUL • NOORDUIN, WILLEM • NOOYEN, HENRI • OOMEN, HARRY • PAARDEKAM, JOLANDA • PARNIAN, TAQY • PEL-
EGROM, COR • PERNOT, DIA • PLOEG, MARIELLE • REEKERS, JOHAN • REMERY, GERARD • REUVEKAMP, PETRA • SCHOOTS, PASCAL • SIES, REGINE • SIJBESMA, KEES • SMIT, MAAIKE • SMIT, RIAN • SPREEUWENBERG, GER • STOKKEL, JOOP • STURKENBOOM, RUTGER • STUURMAN, ERIC • SWIENINK, BEN • TIGGELMAN, INGE • TOP, PIETER • TWARDY, FRANZ • UPPELSCHOTEN, MIRJAM • VAN AMELSVOORT, SYREETA • VAN ASTEN,
PIETER • VAN BAARS, HENNY • VAN BENTUM, TINEKE • VAN BREEMEN, IWAN • VAN BREEMEN, RUDY • VAN BUSSEL, IRMA • VAN DER LAAN, GUDA • VAN DER LINDEN, GERT • VAN DER SCHOUW, DENNIS • VAN DER WERF, KORNELIS • VAN DIJK, ED • VAN GEEL, RENE • VAN HOEVEN, FERROL • VAN HOEVEN, JOLANDA • VAN HOUT, HARRIE • VAN KEMENADE, ERIC • VAN KEMENADE, PAUL • VAN KEMENADE, RON • VAN LEEUWEN, EVE-
LYN • VAN LEEUWEN, MARJA • VAN LEEUWEN, PIET • VAN LOON, JEFFREY • VAN OMMEN, ASTRID • VAN RANGELROOIJ, GERTJAN • VAN REEDEN, RONALD • VAN TIL, MARIANNE • VAN UNEN, BJORN • VAN VEGGEL, JEANINE • VANDIERENDONCK, CHANTAL • VENDERBOSCH, ANDRE • VERVOORN, CEES • VERWIJ, GILBERT • VONHOF, HERMAN • VOORTHUIJZEN, JAN-WILLEM • WALSTRA, JACOB • WAQUE, FEIKE • WOLFS, TOINE • WOLF-
WINKEL, MARIJKE • **NEW ZEALAND:** ANDERSON, CHRIS • ANDERSON, JENNIFER • BIDOIS, AARON • BROWN, HADEN • CAMERON, REWITI • COFFEY, PAUL • COLLINS, HELEN • CONDON, KATHY • COURTIER, JACK • CRAIKE, JAYNE • DICKIE, ROB • DIJKSTRA, HENK • DOWALL, JOHN • FITZPATRICK, SANDY • GRIFFITHS, JASON • GUTHRIE, STEPHEN • HONEY, BELINDA • HORNE, PETER • HOWE, TONY • HUGHES, JOHN • KALE, DUANE •
KEEFE, PAUL • LINEHAM, CAREY • LOGAN, JANE • LUCAS, BEN • MACCALMAN, DAVE • MARTIN, PETER • MATHEWS, MERV • MAY, ANDREW • MCMURRAY, GARY • MURALT, JEFF • NEWSTEAD, JENNY • O'BRIEN, ERROL • PALMER, CURTIS • PEARSON, DAVID • PENNEY, KARYN • POWER, CLIVE • REDSHAW, SHAYNE • ROCHE, ANDY • SANDERSON, LUCY • SAVAGE, BEV • SAVAGE, DANNY • SAVAGE, TONY • SCOTT, CAMERON • SHARMAN,
GRANT • SHIELDS, JACK • SIMEON, TOM • SMITH, CRISTEEN • SOWDEN, KEN • STEWART, DEREK • STRATFORD, MARILYN • SUNDERLAND, LINDA • TAYLOR, SHOLTO • TINKER, GEREMY • TOCKER, BRUCE • WILLIS, COLIN • WORNALL, CHRIS • **NIGERIA:** AFOLABI, OLADAPO • AJIBOLA, ADEOYE • AKINLOTAN, OLUSEGUN • AKPOROWHO, MOSES • AKUTAEKWE, PATRICK • ARE, FEYISETAN • BAMGBOSE, ADEYEMI • BELLO, NOSIRU •
MOGHAVWE, MONDAY • OBARETIN, ABRAHAM • OBOT, JIM • SULE, NASIRU • SULOLA, OLATUBOSUN • **NORWAY:** AANDALEN, ROGER • ABRAHAMSEN, BJARNE • ANDERSEN, FINN • BERGERSEN, JAN • BJORNSTAD, HELGE • BRUNSTAD, TERJE • DOKKAN, JENS • EDVARDSEN, ROLF • EIDE, OLE • EKLUND, MORTEN • FRILUND, GEIR • GAASEMYR, JOERUND • GARTMANN, ANDREAS • GILLUND, SILJE • GRIGSON, HELLE • GYLAND, FRANK
• GYLAND, LENE • HALVORSEN, ERIK • HANSEN, WENCHE • HAUGSENG, EMIL • HELTZEN, MARIANNE • HESLE, JON • HJELLE, OLE • HODNEMYR, OLE • HOGNESTAD, AADNE • HORGEN, MARIT • HULTGREEN, WENCHE • INGDAL, ROGER • JENSEN, LARS • JEVNE, TORKJELD • JOENSBERG, AAGE • KARLSEN, KJELL • KIBUUKA, TOFIRI • KROGH, ROAR • LANNEM, ANNE • LILLEAAS, ROLF • LOEVAAS, TERJE • LYSE, KAARE • MOEN, RANDI •
OEN, TERJE • MORK, INGOLF • MOXNESS, HELGE • NESHEIM, NATE • NESHEIM, TOMAS • NOERSTERUD, JOHN • OLSEN, ALF • OLSEN, OEIVIND • ORE, ANNE • PEDERSEN, NOEL • PETERSEN, HEDI • RIMEJORDE, THOR • RODRIGUEZ, KRISTOFFER • RODRIGUEZ, RUDY • ROMSTAD, SVEIN • ROSTRUP, GAUTE • RUI, SIGRID • SANDVIK, STIG • SIQVELAND, JOHAN • SKYTTESAETER, JAN • SMITH, HELENE • SORLIE, SORLIE • STOKKE, TOR •
TORDAHL, JOSTEIN • STRAND, OEYVIND • TORKILDSRUD, HENNY • TORP, ERNST • ULVANG, RUNE • VENNESLAND, ANDREAS • VESTENGEN, SIW • **OMAN:** AL-BULUSHI, YAQOOB • AL-HARTHY, ISSA • AL-RAWAHI, MUKHTAR • AL-SAADI, IBRAHIM • AL-ZADJALI, FARID • SALEH, ALY • **PAKISTAN:** CHISHTI, ALI • KHEL, BAHADUR • SOOMRO, ASHIQUE • **PANAMA:** BATISTA, JOSE • GOMEZ, SAID • **PERU:** CHAVEZ, JUAN • EULERT, JIMMY •

GONZALES-MUGABURU, JOSE • HERNANDEZ, MARIA • VASQUEZ, AUGUSTO • **POLAND:** BOGUSZ, TADEUSZ • BORCZUCH, ADAM • BOSA, ANDZELIKA • CHMURZYNSKI, TOMASZ • CHRYCZYK, JAN • CIESLUK, MALGORZATA • CYBULSKI, MACIEJ • CZARNECKI, ZBIGNIEW • CZECHANIUK, BOZENA • DABROWSKI, JERZY • DANISZEWSKA, BARBARA • DLUZNIAK, WITOLD • DMENSKI, GRZEGORZ • FORNALCZYK, RYSZARD • GORA, ZYGMUNT • GREN, ANDRZEJ • GRZELAK, BOGUSLAW • GWARA, ADAM • HADY-BARTKOWIAK, KRYSTYNA • HALLMANN, LESZEK • HUMERSKI, CZESLAW • IWANIAK, ANDRZEJ • JABLONSKI, ARKADIUSZ • JAGODZINSKA, KRYSTYNA • JAKUBCZYK, MIROSLAW • JAROSZEWSKI, PIOTR • JONSKI, STANISLAW • JUREK, JANUSZ • KALETA, JAN • KARPINSKI, SLAWOMIR • KIKOLSKI, WALDEMAR • KLIMEK, EDMUND • KOHNKE, HENRYK • KOZLOWSKI, LUKASZ • KRAWCZYNSKI, ANDRZEJ • KROL, BOGDAN • KROL, WIESLAW • KRUSZELNICKI, JERZY • KRUSZELNICKI, TADEUSZ • KUBACKI, ZBIGNIEW • LAPINSKA, LUIZA • LEJA, STANISLAW • LEWICKI, ROMUALD • LEZANSKI, TOMASZ • LIS, BOGDAN • LUDZKOWSKI, ANDRZEJ • MALISZAK, JAN • MANIAK, MONIKA • MICHALCZYK, KATARZYNA • MICHEN, ZBIGNIEW • MIELECH, ZOFIA • MOSCZYNSKI, PIOTR • MOZDZYNSKI, KRZYSZTOF • MYSLAKOWSKI, JERZY • NOWICKI, TADEUSZ • OKOCZUK, EDYTA • OKUPNIAK, MALGORZATA • OLEJNIK, MALGORZATA • OLEJNIK, RYSZARD • OSADA, JACEK • OWSIANY, KRZYSZTOF • PALUBICKI, KRZYSZTOF • PAWLAK, WIESLAW • PAWLOWSKI, ARKADIUSZ • PIESAK, MIROSLAW • PIETRZAK, TADEUSZ • POLASIK, JADWIGA • POPLAWSKI, ALEKSANDER • PYCH, MIROSLAW • REBISZ, TOMASZ • ROZKRES, AGNIESZKA • SKUPNIEWSKI, MACIEJ • SLECZKA, KRZYSZTOF • SOCHACKI, JAN • SZYMUL, ANNA • TOMASZEWSKI, RYSZARD • UTECHT, WLODZIMIERZ • WANDACHOWICZ, KRYSTYNA • WANECKI, ROMAN • WARDA, MARIAN • WLOSTOWSKI, JAN • WOZNY, TOMASZ • WROBEL, ANDRZEJ • ZACMINSKI, RAFAL • ZAWISLAK, ADAM • **PORTUGAL:** ALPIARCA, NUNO • ALVES, JOAO • ARAUJO, ARLINDO • BACALHAU, EDUARDO • BARATA, FERNANDO • BARROSA, HENRIQUE • BARROSO, SUSANA • BASTOS, HELENA • BRUNO, HELDER • CARLOS, ALVES • CARRILHO, BRUNO • CARVALHO, FILINTO • CARVALHO, JOAQUIM • CARVALHO, JORGE • CARVALHO, ROSA • COELHO, PAULO • CONCEICAO, EMILIO • COSTA, ARMANDO • DA COSTA, ONOFRE • DA CRUZ, JOSE • DIAS, FRANCISCO • DURAES, ALVARO • ELDER, HENRIQUE • FERREIRA, CARLOS • FERREIRA, FERNANDO • FERREIRA, LUIS • FILIPE, VALTER • FIUZA, ODETE • GAMEIRO, JOSE • GERMANO, NUNO • GIRAO, BRUNO • LOPES, CARLOS • MACEDO, JOSE • MARQUES, ANTONIO • MARQUES, LEILA • MARQUES, VICTOR • MATOS, FATIMA • MENDES, JOSE • MOREIRA, ANA • MORGADO, GABRIEL • NOGUEIRA, TONY • OLIVEIRA, RUI • PACHECO, JOSE • PEDROSO, RUI • PEIXOTO, ALBERTO • PELICANO, LEONOR • PINTO, SUSANA • PROTASIO, FERNANDO • RAPOSO, ANTONIO • REIS, ORLANDO • RIBEIRO, AURELIO • SANTOS, JOSE • SILVA, LUIS • SILVA, PEDRO • VEGAS, JOAQUIM • VIEIRA, CESARIO • VILAR, CARLOS • **PUERTO RICO:** BATISTA-DELGADO, FERNANDO • CARTAGENA-RODRIGUEZ, GLADYS • GOMEZ-LOPEZ, NILDA • RAMOS-MILAN, LUIS • ROMAN-SANCHEZ, OSVALDO • TORRES, JAMES • VARGAS-OQUENDO, JOHNNY • VIGO-GARCIA, LUIS • **QATAR:** BOUCHAIB, HASSEN • MOTAWA, ABDULQADER • MULLA, SALAH • **ROMANIA:** BERBEC, AUREL • MILEA, MARIA • **RUSSIA:** ABAKAROV, GADJI • AVERINE, ALEXANDRE • BACHKIROV, VLADIMIR • BAKAEV, ALBERT • BARAMIDZE, AVTANDIL • BASHKIROVA, MAKINA • BATALOVA, RIMA • BELOKOBYLSKI, SERGUEI • BESTUCHEV, SERGEY • BOROVIKOV, ANDREI • BOUILOV, PETR • BOURENKIN, VLADIMIR • BYTCHKOV, VLADIMIR • CHABACHOV, OLEG • CHEMANINE, ALEXEI • CHEVELEVA, OLGA • CHEVTCHIK, LEONID • CHILOV, SERGUEI • CHNAIDER, VICTOR • DEMENKO, VIKTOR • DEMENTIEV, GUENNADI • EFIMENKO, ANATOLI • EMELIANOV, EVGUENI • ERCHOVA, TATIANA • FATIAKHDINOV, MARAT • FROLOVA, ELENA • GALEEV, INTAL • GAZEMAGOMEDOVA, ACHMED • GROMOVA, IRINA • GUERASSIMOV, GUENNADI • GUERTLEIN, ALLA • IACHKINE, VLADISLAV • IAKOVLEV, MIKHAIL • IVANOV, ALEXEI • IVANOV, MIKHAIL • JDANOVA, ELENA • KAPITONOV, KONSTANTIN • KAPURA, ALEXEI • KARTACHOV, SERGUEI • KHANOV, EUGUENI • KHODAKOV, SERGUEI • KHRIACHTHEV, SERGUEI • KLETSKOVA, NATALIA • KORENKOV, NIKOLAI • KOROL, IRINA • KOULAKOV, GVENNADI • KRONFELD, ELENA • KRYLOV, VITALI • LACHMANOV, ALEXEI • LOTAREV, VLADIMIR • LEBEDEV, ANATOLI • LEBEDINSKI, ANDREI • LEUTCHENKO, PAVEL • LOJETCHNIKOV, ANDREI • MALAKHOVA, LIOUBOV • MALTCHIKOV, DENIS • MALYCHEV, SERGUEI • MAMAYEV, RADJAB • MEZINOVA, TATIANA • MITCHOURINE, VENIAMIN • MOROZOV, VICTOR • NARTOV, PAVEL • NAZARENKO, YOURI • NEFEDOV, ANDREI • NIKACHINE, SERGUEI • ORECHKINE, MIKHAIL • OVRANOV, MIKHAIL • PATRIKEEV, VALERI • PEGOV, VALENTINE • POLOVKHINE, VLADIMIR • POMYKALOV, KLAUS • PONOMARENKO, VALERI • PROTASSOV, VLADIMIR • ROGODZIN, NIKOLAI • RYKOV, VALERI • SALAKHOV, ASGAT • SELEZNIV, LEV • SELIVERSTOV, ALEXEI • SELIVERSTOV, ANDREI • SEMIONOV, SERGUEI • SEVOSTIANOV, SERGUEI • SILATCHEV, ALEXEI • SIZOV, MAKSIM • SIZOV, PAVEL • SKOBELINE, SERGUEI • SOUKHOV, ANDREI • SOULIMTSEV, TIKHON • STARYKH, IOURI • TATAEV, GVENNADI • TCHAOUNE, EDOUARD • TCHESNOV, VLADIMIR • TCHKONIA, IZOLDA • TCHOURKINA, OLGA • TELIAK, LIOUDMILA • VAVILINE, VLADIMIR • VCHIVTSEV, VLADIMIR • VINOGRADOV, PETR • VOLKOV, VLADIMIR • VORONINE, GUENNADI • ZYKOV, MIKHAIL • **SAUDI ARABIA:** AL-DUGAISH, FAHAD • ALMOHANNA, MDAHER • JANDAL, HAMED • SUNBO, ALI • **SIERRA LEONE:** BECKLEY, PAMELA • MARAH, KELLEY • MOORE, VICTORIA • RICH, SARAH • **SINGAPORE:** CHUA, TINA • KUA, CHENG • LIM, POH • SCHMIDT, ADRIENNE • TAN, JU • WEE, AI • **SLOVAKIA:** BERDY, JAN • BETIN, PAVOL • BEZECNY, JAN • BRANDOBUROVA, KATARINA • BUCEK, PETER • CAPLA, MICHAL • CHOVAN, JAN • CSADER, MICHAL • DEDECEK, DUSAN • DOVALOVSZKI, EMIL • DUBOVY, PAVOL • GASPAR, LADISLAV • GODRI, FRANTISEK • GRICH, RICHARD • HANKOVA, HELENA • HOTOVA, IVANA • HUSAROVA, RUDOLF • JAMBOR, MIROSLAV • KOSCO, JAN • KOVAC, RICHARD • KUCHTA, RASTISLAV • LIBA, JOZEF • MAKOVNIK, JAROSLAV • MARCIN, ANDREJ • MATIASKO, PETER • MIHAL, JAN • MIHALCO, JOZEF • MISUNOVA, MARCELA • MORAVCIK, PETER • NESTORIK, MICHAL • NOVOSAD, LUBOMIR • PILLAROVA, MARIA • PROKEINOVA, MARGITA • RIAPOS, JAN • SEDLAK, PAVOL • SIPOSOVA, DANIELA • SLUKA, ANTON • STEFAK, JURAJ • STRAKA, PAVOL • STUDENA, DANA • TAKAC, PAVEL • TOMSIK, MAREK • ZATKO, ANDREJ • **SLOVENIA:** BURGER, HELENA • FERFOLJA, SVITAN • GORJANC, BORIS • HUDEJ, JANEZ • IZLAKAR, FRANJO • JAZBINSEK, ERNEST • KABIC, GORAN • KLUN, BRANKO • KREJAC, EDVARD • LAPORNIK, DRAGA • LOBE, LOU • MAJCENOVIC, SRECKO • MORE, ERLEND • NIMAC, M • PAVLINEC, DANIJEL • PINTER, FRANCI • POTOCNIK, DRAGO • RIBIC, PAVEL • ROSKAR, JANEZ • SLADIC, POLONCA • VEST, ALES • VINKLER, IVAN • VOGRINCIC, BOSTJAN • **SOUTH AFRICA:** BADENHORST, PETER • BEETON, HILLARY • BULLER, DAVE • BULLER, DEIRDRE • COETZEE, DANIE • COLEMAN, STEPHEN • CROUS, ALTA • FERREIRA, SCRAPYARD • FIELD, RORY • FIRER, PONKY • FITZGERALD, GLYNIS • GROENEWALD, CRAIG • HARRIMAN, MARGARET • HUMPHRIES, STEYN • IRVING, GWEN • JONKER, KOBUS • KLEYNHANS, EBERT • LABUSCHAGNE, LEON • LOMBAARD, FANIE • LOUWRENS, MICHAEL • MANDEAN, SCOTT, ANDY • SHUTTLEWORTH, PHYLLIS • SINGH, PAUL • SLATTERY, TADHG • SMITH, RUTHMAREE • SNEAG, BRIAN • SOMTSWAYI, NTOMBO • STADLER, WILLIAM • SWART, ELROY • TERBLANCHE, JAN-JACQUE • THEART, NAKKIE • THOMPSON, GLYN • VAN DER MERWE, GERT • VAN DYK, ERNST • VAN ROOYEN, BILL • VAN VUUREN, JACO • VENTER, JOHAN • **SPAIN:** ABAL, JOSE • ABENIA, ROBERTO • AGUDO, ADOLFO • AGUDO, ENRIQUE • ALONSO, JAVIER • ALOS, SERGIO • ALVAREZ, JOSE • ALVAREZ, MARIA • ALVAREZ, NEVS • ALVAREZ, RUBEN • AMADOR, LUIS • AMO, MAGDALENA • ANTOLIN, LUIS • ANTOLINOS, JORGE • ANTON, ELEUTERIO • ARENAS, VICENTA • ARMAS, CARLOS • AROLAS, VICENTE • ARRIBAS, JOSE • ARROYO, M • ARTERO, JUAN • ARZALLUS, AITZOL • BACK, CARLOS • BARBER, MARIA • BARREIRO, DANIEL • BAZALO, FRANCISCA • BERNARDO, ANA • BERZAL, MANUEL • BLANCO, ANTONIO • BLANCO, BEGONA • BOEDO, FRANCISCO • BULLIDO, LUIS • CABALLERO, JORDI • CALDERON, LUIS • CALVEROL, TERESA • CAMPINA, CINTA • CAMPO, MARIA • CAMPOS, FERMIN • CANALS, MONTSERRAT • CANDELA, MANUEL • CANO, LUIS • CAPA, MERCEDES • CARDONA, CHRISTIAN • CARLAVILLA, CESAR • CAROL, NEUS • CARRACELAS, SARA • CARRERO, MIGUEL • CASAS, MANUEL • CASTELLO, ANDRES • CASTILLA, JOSE • CAUS, NURIA • CERDA, TANIA • CHAVARREN, CARLOS • CHAVES, MARIA • CID, ANTONIO • CIEZA, MANUEL • COBOS, JOSE • CONDE, JAVIER • CORCUERA, JULIAN • CORRAL, PABLO • CORRAL, ROSARIO • CUBERO, ANTONIO • CUENDA, LAURA • CUESTA, ASUNCION • CUEVA, IRMA • DE ANTONA, ANA • DE PAZ, DIEGO • DELGADO, ANTONIO • DELGADO, PEDRO • DELGADO, RUBEN • DENIZ, MIGUEL • DIAZ, FLORENCIO • DIAZ, MANUEL • DIAZ, RAQUEL • DORTA, DARIO • DUCE, RAMIRO • DUENAS, MARCOS • EMETERIO, ENRIQUE • ESCRIBANO, FUENCISLA • ESMERALDA, MOISES • ESPARZA, TOMAS • ESPINOSA, MAITE • FERNANDEZ, CARLOS • FERNANDEZ, JOSE • FERNANDEZ, JOSE • FERNANDEZ, MARIA • FERNANDEZ, RAUL • FERNANDEZ, RICARDO • FIDALGO, ALFONSO • FLORES, SANTIAGO • FONTANET, JUAN • FRAILE, JESUS • FUERTES, JUAN • FUGUET, DAVID • GALILEA, JULIAN • GALLARDO, CRISTOBAL • GANDIA, ABELARDO • GARCIA, ALFREDO • GARCIA, ANAIS • GARCIA, ANGEL • GARCIA, ANTONIO • GARCIA, CANDIDO • GARCIA, INIGO • GARCIA, JOSE • GARCIA, JOSE • GARCIA, MIGUEL • GARCIA, PEDRO • GARCIA-ARCICOLLAR, ANA • GARRACHON, SINESIO • GASPAR, JOSE • GIL, JUAN • GIL, LAUREANO • GIMENO, SARA • GINARD, AINA • GOMEZ, FERNANDO • GOMEZ, MIGUEL • GONZALEZ, ARANZAZU • GONZALEZ, EMILIO • GONZALEZ, HIPOLITO • GONZALEZ, JESUS • GONZALEZ, JOSE • GONZALEZ-ESTEFANI, MANUELA • GORDILLO, FRANCISCO • GUIRADO, SONIA • GUTIERREZ, FELIPE • GUTIERREZ, JUAN • HASSEN-BEY, GEMMA • HENARES, ANTONIO • HERNANDEZ, CONCHI • HERNANDEZ, JUAN • HERVAS, IBAI • HEVIA, ROBERTO • HUGUET, DAVID • HURTADO, JOSE • IBARRA, ZURINE • IGLESIAS, JESUS • JIMENEZ, ANTONIO • JIMENEZ, DAVID • JIMENEZ, JUAN • JOFRE, ALBERTO • KELLER, STEPHANIE • LANAU, PEDRO • LARA, FRANCISCO • LARA, JOSE • LARRINGA, JOSEBA-JON • LASTRA, JOSE • LAZARO, ROSALIA • LEBRERO, JUAN • LLAMBRICH, DANIEL • LLORENTE, SANTIAGO • LLOVERAS, PERE • LOPEZ, EDUARDO • LOPEZ, SANTIAGO • LUNA, SARA • MALAGON, JESUS • MAROTO, PEDRO • MARTIN, ANTONIO • MARTIN, PABLO • MARTIN, YOLANDA • MARTINEZ, ALICIA • MARTINEZ, ANDRES • MARTINEZ, CESAR • MARTINEZ, FRANCISCO • MARTINEZ, JUSEP • MARTINEZ, SERGIO • MARTORELL, ANTONIO • MARZAL, ANTONIO • MATOS, JUAN • MENDEZ, FRANCISCO • MENDOZA, BEATRIZ • MENDOZA, JORDI • MENOR, JUAN • MESSA, MONICA • MIRA, EUSTAQUIO • MOLINA, CARLOS • MONREAL, FRANCISCO • MONTALVO, BEGONA • MONTALVOS, JUAN • MONTILLA, JUAN • MORA, MARGARITA • MORATE, PACO • MORCILLO, FLORENCIO • MORENO, RAFAEL • MORENO, SOLEDAD • MUNOZ, PACO • MUNOZ, PAU • MURILLO, BENITO • NUNEZ, JORGE • OLMO, JOSE • ORIBE, RICARDO • OROBITG, ANTONIO • OROBITG, MIGUEL • ORTEGA, VANESA • ORTIZ, LUIS • ORTIZ, PURIFICACION • PADRONES, ELENA • PALOMO, FRANCISCO • PARDO, BORJA • PARDO, PATRICIO • PEDRAJAS, JOSE • PEDROSA, JOSE • PELAEZ, BENITO • PELETEIRO, JORGE • PEREZ, ARTURO • PEREZ, BELEN • PEREZ, CRISTINA • PEREZ, FERNANDO • PEREZ, JAVIER • PEREZ, MANUEL • PEREZ, MANUEL • PEREZ, MARIOLA • PEREZ, MIGUEL • PEREZ, MIGUEL • PEREZ, YOLANDA • PESQUERA, SANTIAGO • POYAN, GUILLERMO • PRIETO, JUAN • RAMOS, JUAN • REDAL, BEGONA • REQUENA, JULIO • RICO, RAQUEL • RIERA, MIREIA • RIVERO, JOSE • ROBLES, MANUEL • RODRIGUEZ, EMILIO • RODRIGUEZ, HILDA • RODRIGUEZ, MANNY • RODRIGUEZ, MANUEL • RODRIGUEZ, PABLO • ROVIRA, DANIEL • RUBIO, BELINDA • RUFO, MANUEL • RUFO, MONTSERRAT • RUIZ, JOSE • RUIZ, MARIANO • RUIZ-COTORRO, J • RUPEREZ, FAUSTINO • SAAVEDRA, MARCELINO • SAAVEDRA, PABLO • SAAVEDRA, RAQUEL • SACEDA, CARLOS • SAGARRA, MIGUEL • SALGADO, LUIS • SANCHEZ, ANTONIO • SANCHEZ, ANTONIO • SANCHEZ, SERGIO • SANCHEZ-GUIJO, ENRIQUE • SANDEZ, M • SANTAMARTA, PURI • SANTANA, ANDRES • SANTIAGO, JOSE • SANZ, DAVID • SANZ, JOSE • SARDINA, FERNANDO • SAURA, BENITO • SEGARRA, FRANCISCO • SIERRA, MONICA • SIRERA, JOSE • SOLE, JOSE • SOLER, CARLOS • SORIANO, FRANCISCO • SUAREZ, MIGUEL • TAIBO, JUAN • TALAVERA, MARIO • TEN, RICARDO • TORNERO, ENRIQUE • TORRALBA, MIGUEL • TORRES, JAVIER • TORRES, JESUS • TOVAR, JOSE • TRAMUNS, LAURA • TRINIDAD, MARTA • TURATTI, RAFAEL • UBEDA, PEDRO • VAQUERO, JOSE • VAZQUEZ, IVAN • VAZQUEZ, JUAN • VAZQUEZ, JUAN • VELEZ, JOSE • VIDAL, JUAN • VIEDMA, JUAN • VILLAR, ANA • VISITACION, JESUS • VIVES, SILVIA • YRIZAR, JOSE • ZAJAC, SOFIA • ZARCOS, CESAR • **SRI LANKA:** DASSANAYAKE, JAYANTHA • PATHIRANA, KALIKA • **SWEDEN:** (INGVARSSON), GORAN • ABLORH, ENOCH • ABRAHAMSSON, JOSEFIN • AHLANDER, SUNE • AHLSTAD, SIMON • AKERBERG, TOMAS • AKESSON, KENNET • ANDERSSON, JORGEN • ANDERSSON, LISA • ANDERSSON, PETER • ANDERSSON, ROBERT • ANDREE, MAGNUS • APPELQVIST, MATTIAS • ARONSSON, AGNETA • AXELSSON, THOMAS • BADER, ROBERT • BAGGE, LASSE • BERGGREN, PETER • BERGLUND, GUNNAR • BERGSTROM, DANIEL • BERGSTROM, JENNY • BERGSTROM, JOHN • BJORKLUND, MARTIN • BJORE, CARIN • BLOCK, ERNST • BORG, HILDE • BORG, MIKAEL • BRANDHILD, TOMAS • BROKHOLC, KRISTINA • CARLSTEDT, JANNE • CELIN, JONAS • DETTMAN, SOFIA • EDSTROM, PETTER • ENGBLOM, TOMAS • ENGLUND, KERSTIN • ERICSON, STIG • ERIKSSON, BERNDT • ERIKSSON, HAKAN • ERIKSSON, JOHNNY • ERIKSSON, ROGER • ERIKSSON, STEN • ERIKSSON, THOMAS • FRESK, CARL-GUSTAF • FROJD, KENNET • GIEBNER, STEFAN • GORTZ, THOMAS • GOTSTAV, BO • GUSTAFSSON, ANNELI • GUSTAVSSON, JAN-KRISTER • GUSTAVSSON, JOACHIM • GUSTAVSSON, MALIN • HAGBERG, HELENA • HAGLUND, JOHAN • HAGSTROM, PATRIK • HAIDARI, HUSSEIN • HALL, PATRIK • HANSSON, ANDERS • HANSSON, HILLEVI • HANSSON, INGRID • HEDMAN, BJORN • HELSINGER, LOTTA • HJALMARSSON, LARS • HOGBOM, BERNDT • HOGSTEDT, PATRIK • HUSSON, EDRIS • ISAKSSON, JOHAN • JACOBSSON, SARA • JAKOBSSON, JONAS • JANSSON, LILLMOR • JOHANSSON, ASA • JOHANSSON, ASA • JOHANSSON, JORGEN • JOHANSSON, KATARINA • JOHANSSON, MARIA • JOHANSSON, PONTUS • JOHANSSON, THOMAS • JOHANSSON, TIM • JONASSON, ANNA • JONSSON, JOHN-AKE • JONSSON, PER-OLA • JOSEFSSON, BIRGIT • JOSEFSSON, ULF • JUNGNELL, JARL-OLOF • KARLSSON, KJELL • KARLSSON, MATTIAS • KASK, JENS • KJALLSTROM, MATHIAS • KJALLSTROM, PER • KJELLQVIST, TOMAS • KRANTZ, GUNNAR • LANDAHL, IDA • LARSSON, JOAKIM • LARSSON, THOMAS • LEGA, DAVID • LEHTONEN, ASA • LEHTONEN, THERESE • LEHTONEN, REINO • LEONARDSSON, MATS • LINDBERG, BENGT • LINDEBERG, LARS • LINDGREN, CHRISTER • LINDQVIST, BIRGIT • LLINARES, ASA • LOFSTROM, LARS • LUNDGREN, ANDREAS • LUNDGREN, BJORN • LUNDVALL, ANDERS • MATTSSON, JAN-OWE • MOLLERSTEN, LENA • NASMAN, FREDRIK • NILSSON, EILA • NILSSON, GERT • NILSSON, JESPER • NILSSON, KJELL • NILSSON, MARIA • NITTFORS, HELENA • NORDLINDER, KASPER • NORDMARK, LEIF • NORDSTROM, MATTIAS • NUHANOVIC, SEFKO • NYBERG, MIZE • NYLANDER, MARIE • OLOFSSON, BENGT • OLOFSSON, SARA • OLSSON, ANBRITT • OTTOSSON, JIMMY • PALM, CATARINA • PETTERSSON, MICHAEL • REINEBO, PETER • RYD, SAHRA • SAMUELSSON, BJORN • SJOBERG, JANNE • SKOGH, ROLF • SOHLMAN, HENRIK • SONDHI, ARUN • SORENSEN, KENNETH • STARK, PETER • STEFORS, EDDIE • STJERNVALL, MIKAEL • SUNDMAGNUS • SUNDELIN, JERKER • SUNDELL, ANDERS • SUNDELL, HENRIK • SYREN, MATTIAS • TALLEN, BJORN • TEMRIN, MATS • THULIN, JAN • THULIN, SIV • TYREN, MARITA • UHLEN, PER • UNDEMAR, LOTTA • VESTERLUND, PER • VESTLING, MIKAEL • VIKGREN, MARIA • WALLIN, PETER • WAPNER, CHRISTIAN • WEDIN, VIKTORIA • WEGEBORN, STEFAN • WIKSTROM, LINDA • WIREN, HANS • **SWITZERLAND:** ANDEREGG, RUEDI • BARTLOME, PETER • BERGER, HANS-PETER • BERSET, EMMANUEL • BERSET, JEAN-MARC • BLANC, JACQUELINE • BLANC, LOUIS • BOGLI, DANIEL • BRUNNER, CHRISTIAN • BURCH, HEINZ • CAVICCHIA, VINCE • CHRISTEN, LUKAS • DE BIASI, TONI • EGLI, CHRISTIAN • EGLI, MARKUS • EMMENEGGER, ANDREA • ERNI, MARTIN • ESSER, JAN • FORNI, GIUSEPPE • FORNI, THERESIA • FREI, HEINZ • GILGEN, LUCA • GREUTER, URSINA • GUNDEN, LENE • HEGI, EVELINE • HEULE, MARTINE • HILLMANN, DANIEL • KOLLY, URS • KUNZI, DANIEL • KURZ, KATRIN • LEUCH, CAROLINE • LEUENBERGER, ULRICH • LOHR, CHRISTIAN • MABILLARD, OLIVIER • MACCAFERRI, KURT • MARTI, WILLY • MEILI, BENJAMIN • MERKT, REGULA • METROZ, GERALD • MICHEL, ADRIAN • MOERCH, PHILIPPE • MULLER, GUIDO • MURSET, PETER • NIETLISPACH, FRANZ • PLATTNER, RATT, ALICE • ROSSIER, JEAN-LUC • SCHERLER, GEORGES • SCHMID, PIA • SCHNEEBELI, PAUL • SCHORNO, WERNER • SCHWARZENBACH, BEAT • SCHWEINGRUBER, URS • SETZ, ALOIS • STOLL, PATRICK • TAKACS, PETER • TARONI, HANNELORE • UTTINGER, DIETER • WEBER, FRANZ • WEBER, GERHARD • WEBER, JURG • WEHRLI, PETER • WIDMER, FREDY • WYSS, AUGUST • ZUMKEHR, ROLF • **SYRIA:** ALTRABOULSI, NOUR • HAJRA, BASSAM • ROUMANI, M • YOUNES, YOUSSEF • **THAILAND:** DEANGNUI, SOMPORN • JIRAYUKUL, CHAWALIT • LUANGAMORNLERT, CHAIYAPORN • LUCHSHAPHON, VEERA • LAGSANAPRIM, PANOM • RATTANASANG, SOMPONG • SAIKESENG, CAP • SUALUANG, AMPAI • THONGCHUEN, PRASIT • YODYANGDANG, JESADA • **TUNISIA:** BAHRI, WISSEM • BAROUDI, ALI • DHIFALLAH, ABDELJABBAR • HARZALLAH, ALI • MECHKANE, NEJIB • THABTIA, MESSAOUDA • **UGANDA:** BOGERE, RICHARD • **UKRAINE:** AFANASYK, MARIYA • AKOPYAN, OLENA • ANDRIYASHCHENKO, OLEXANDER • ANDRUSSENKO, ANATOLIY • ANDRYUSHYN, YURIY • ARBYTMAN, STANISLAV • BAIEVA, HANNA • BALANCHUK, MYKHAYLO • BARYBIN, ANDRIY • BAZYLYEV, STANISLAV • BONDAR, IHOR • DANYLOV, ANDRIY • DASHYVETS, VICTOR • DAVYDKOV, KOSTIANTYN • DVOSKINA, IRYNA • HOLOVKO, VALENTYN • HONCHARENKO, OLEXANDER • HORBENKO, IHOR • HOROVY, VASYL • HOVORUN, OLEKSIY • HURSKY, IHOR • HUTNYK, ROMAN • ILIASHENKO, OLEH • IVANOV, DMYTRO • KORNYEYEV, DMYTRO • KOVACH, ANATOLIY • KYRIT, ANATOLIY • LISHCHYNSKY, VASYL • LUKYANOV, SERHIY • LUTSYK, MAKSYM • MYRONENKO, SERHIY • NOSSENKO, OLEXANDER • NOSSYKOVYCH, BOHDAN • NOVIKOV, GENNADIY • OSTRYNSKY, PETRO • PASYUTA, VOLODYMYR • RIZNYCHENKO, VALENTYNA • SALINA, NATALIIA • SHCHYHOLEV, YURIY • SHOSTAK, MYKOLA • SKORIN, YEVHEN • SYZONENKO, VIKTOR • TAHILTSEV, BORYS • TRYFONOVA, SVITLANA • VDOVYCHENKO, YURIY • VYNOHRADOV, OLEXANDER • **UNITED ARAB EMIRATES:** ABDERRAHMANE, KIHAL • BOUALEM, BOUZAR • DALAM, HASSAN • GHARBI, OBAID • IBRAHIM, KHAMIS • RASHDI, ALI • ROOMI, AHMAD • SABAIT, NASEIB • SOLEH, HALIM • **UNITED STATES OF AMERICA:** ABARBANEL-WOLFF, ELI • AGUILAR, ADOLFO • AKINS, DEBBIE • ALBRYCHT, DANA • ALCALA, JOSE • ALLEN, MAC • ANDERSON, MARK • ARIAS, AL • ARMBRUSTER, JENI • ARMBRUSTER, KENNETH • ASBURY, ANDRE • ASHLEY, JOHN • ASTRADA, ARNOLD • ATWELL, JULIE • AUKWARD, STEPHEN • BABINEC, TIM • BACHER, ERIC • BACHRACH, LLOYD • BAKER, CRAIG • BAKER, DAVID • BALK, ROBERT • BALSLEY, DAVID • BARR, STEPHANIE • BARRACLOUGH, GARY • BARRETT, JENNIFER • BARROWS, DAVID • BAUER, KAREN • BAYON, CAROLINA • BECERRA, CHERI • BECKE, TOM • BECKFORD, JIM • BELL, COREY • BELL, DOUG • BELTRAM, PIER • BLACK, ANTHONY • BLACK, JIM • BLACKMON, WALTER • BLANKENSHIP, RYAN • BLANKS, GARY • BOURGEOIS, THOMAS • BRADY, WILLIAM • BRASILE, FRANK • BRAUGHTON, MICHAEL • BROOKS, KEN • BROOKS, STEPHANIE • BROWN, JANET • BROWN, SHAWN • BROWNFIELD, KIM • BRUDER, AIMEE • BUENDORF, LARRY • BULLOCK, DAVID • BULOW, MATTHEW • BURNS, GREGORY • BURRESS, GARLAND • BUTLER, DAN • BUTTREY, MICHAEL • CABLE, CANDACE • CAHILL, DIANE • CALOMERIS, THOMAS • CALVARIO, JONATHAN • CAMPBELL, MARVIN • CARLTON, LYNNE • CASTLE, MICHAEL • CECIL-RAMSEY, TERRI • CERUTI, DAVE • CHAFEE, ELLA • CHARTER, ROGER • CHRISTMAS, JOSEPH • CHUNN, CLIFF • CLARK, WILEY • CLAWSON, TICO • CLEMENT-ATKINSON, GAY • COLLIER, KURT • COLLINS, DAVID • COLLINS, RAYMOND • COLTON, REGGIE • COMBS, GREG • CONDRON, ROBERT • COOK, STEVE • COOPER, PERNELL • COTTINI, PATRICK • COUNCIL, WADE • COVINGTON, WILLIAM • COWAN, KELLY • CROSS, AARON • SHAWN • DOUDT, STEVE • DOUGHERTY, COLLEEN • DOUGLAS, SCOTT • DOYLE, MICHAEL • DRISCOLL, JEAN • DUCRET, WALTER • DUFFY, DAWN • DUGAN, JIM • DUNMEYER, RAY • DUNNE, CARA • EDGAR, KATIE • EDWARDS, SUE • EGENSTEINER-ASBURY, PATTI • ELLER, SHELLY • EMENER, BARBARA • ESPARZA, WALDO • ESPOSITO, MAUREEN • EVANS, SCOTT • FAGAN, WENDY • FARRELL, DOUGLAS • FENN, MARC • FERNANDES, PAMALA • FINGER, KELLY • FONTAINE, PAM • FOOTE, ARTHUR • FOPPIANO, DANIEL • FRANKLIN, JENNIFER • FRASURE, BRIAN • FROMMATER, RANDY • FROVIK, SUE • GADSON, WARDELL • GAILEY, ROBERT • GALLAGHER, JOFA • GARNER-SWEIGART, VICKI • GARRISON, DAVID • GATTI, LISA • GILL, CHUCK • GNEITING, PEDRO • GOITZ, HENRY • GOLDENBERG, LORI • GOLDSTEIN, ALAN • GONSALVES, NANCY • GORDON, SHERRY • GOULD, DAVID • GRESHAM, BARBARA • GREVEMBERG, DAVID • GRIMES, SUE • HACKER, DAVID • HAFT, JULIA • HAGEL, SUSAN • HALE, ROBERT • HALL, JAMES • HAMBLIN, GLORIA • HAMMER, BARRY • HAMMOND, DARREN • HANEBRINK, SANDY • HANSEN, CONNIE • HANSEN, KEVIN • HANSON, AUSTIN • HARMAN, SPENCER • HARNEY, GREG • HARPER, KATHY • HARRISON, ED • HATFIELD, TODD • HAYNES, WINFORD • HAZEN, JENN • HEDRICK, BRAD • HEILVEIL, JACOB • HEIR, DOUGLAS • HENDRICKS, PERRY • HENRY, DOUGLAS • HENRY, SAMMY • HENS, WILLIAM • HERBST, SHARON • HERMAN, ANNE • HERMANSON, STEVE • HILBORN, JASON • HOFF, GERALD • HOGANS, KELVIN • HOJNACKI, TONY • HOLLONBECK, SCOT • HOPPER, MICHAEL • HORTON, JASON • HUGHES, LARRY • HULETT, MICHAEL • HUNTLEY, COREY • HYMAN, ELLEN • III, LARRY • III, LUIS • INGRAM, DOUG • IRVINE, RONNIE • ISON, SCOTT • IV, FREEMAN • JAMES, ANGEL • JAMES, JAMES • JARVIS, RONDA • JELINEK, ELLEN • JOHNSON, DENTON • JOHNSON, JENNIFER • JOHNSON, JOSIE • JOHNSON, KENNETH • JOHNSON, TROOPER • JORGENSEN, SERGE • JR, ALBERT • JR, LARRY • JR, PAUL • JR, WILLARD • JUETTE, MELVIN • KARPUK, JOAN • KARRIS, NICK • KATZ, SUSAN • KAVANAGH, KIM • KAZEE, TIMOTHY • KELLIHER, ANDREA • KELLOGG, LILI • KELLY, DAN • KELLY, TRISH • KEOHANE, MICHAEL • KERNAN, JOHN • KERR, ROGER • KESSLER, JIM • KING, MATTHEW • KINNIER, NANCY • KISTNER, TIM • KLEMENTICH, JAKE • KNARR, JOHN • KNIGHT, ROB • KRAMER, PAUL • KRYCH, DAN • LANGE, JOHN • LAPICOLA, MARY • LARSON, DAVID • LARSON, TAMMY • LASSAHN, STEVE • LAUFENBERG, CRAIG • LAVIN, MATT • LAWRENCE, DAVID • LAWRENCE, WALTER • LEATHERMAN, JAMES • LEAVITT, WAYNE • LEE, DENNIS • LEE, LARRY • LEHMAN, CHRISTOPHER • LEHMAN, MISSY • LEHMAN, RENEE • LEIBOVITZ, TAHL • LESTER, THOMAS • LEVY, BRENDA • LEWELLEN, HOPE • LEWIS, BRETT • LEWIS, III • LEWIS, KAREN • LILLIEROOS, RONG • LINDSEY, MARK • LITTLE, AARON • LOCKE, WILLIAM • LOECHLE, JOHN • LOLL, ROBERT • LOPEZ, MARLON • LOWE, RICHARD • LUCAS, MARK • LUNA, JAMES • LUNCHER, JOYCE • LYDUCH, NORMAN • MAIR, DAVID • MALLINCKRODT, CRAIG • MANNING, LYNN • MARTIN, KIM • MARTIN, PEGGY • MARTIN, VINCE • MARTINSON, JIM • MASTANDREA, LINDA • MASTRO, JIM • MAUSSER, MAUREEN • MAXWELL, MARK • MCALLISTER, CHRISTY • MCCULLOUGH, JON • MCDANIEL, NANCY • MCDEVITT, LAUREN • MCDEVITT, MICHAEL • MCELHINEY, JIM • MCGONIGLE, PAM • MCINNIS, EDWARD • MCKINNEY, JOSH • MCKINNEY, MARTIE • MCMILLAN, MARK • MENDIETA, TINA • MEREDITH, SHAWN • MEZNARICH, PAUL • MILKOVICH, PATRICE • MILLAR, MARCY • MILLER, JIM • MILLER, TRACY • MILLHOUSE, GERRY • MITCHELL, ROBERT • MOHR, TRAVIS • MOLINATTI, ROBERT • MOORE, SCOTT • MORAN, PAUL • MORRIS, GEORGE • MOTT, DON • MOULTON, SUSAN • MUELLER, JOSEPH • MULLINS, AIMEE • MUNN, JEFFREY • MUNRO, EDWARD • MURPHY, MURPHY, KEVIN • MURRET, LAINE • NAREWSKI, STANLEY • NEAL, TOM • NEITZEL, ERIC • NELLIGAN, KATHLEEN • NELSON, JILL • NEWKIRK, DAVID • NICHOLSON, DAN • NILSSON, BJORN • NITZ, PAUL • NOBBE, CAROLYN • NORRIS, KAREN • NORVELLE, ROBERT • NUNEZ, RUTH • NYLAND, JOHN • O'NEIL, SHEILA • OEHLER, DENNIS • OLIVER, PAT • OLSON, NANCY • OSBAHR, ROBERT • OUTTROWSKI, MAGGI • OUELLETTE, LAUREEN • PACE, GAIL • PALUTSIS, GREGORY • PARKER, JOEY • PARKER, MARTIN • PARMELLY, CHIP • PARRIGIN, THOMAS • PARRY, MATT • PATRICK, REX • PATTERSON, ROB • PAULDING, PETER • PAULSON, AARON • PAYNE, JACQUE • PERKINS, NATHAN • PETERS, MIKE • PFIESTER, JUDITH • PIRRALLO, MARY • PITTMAN, ALLISON • PITTMAN, KIM • PONCE, BARBARO • PRIEST, BILL • PYRKOSZ, CHRISTOPHER • QUINTANILLA, ANDREW • RAFFERTY, SANDY • RAGLAND, GARY • RAGSDALE, RAY • RAMAGE, BRAD • REDDING, PAM • REEVES, BRIAN • REGISTER, JOHN • RENJE, BILL • RICHMOND, BRENNA • RICHNER, REGGIE • RIDGWAY, CHRIS • ROBERTS, PHILIP • ROBERTSON, II • RODRIGUEZ, BRIAN • RODRIGUEZ, MARIO • ROSENBAUM, RUTH • ROSENBERG, MICHAEL • ROSS-DUGGAN, JOHN • RUBY, JIM • RUFFALO, RICH • RUNKLE, DEB • RUNYAN, MARLA • RUSSO, TINA • SCHAFFHAUSER, TODD • SCHLAPPI, MIKE • SCHULTZ, LAWRENCE • SCHULZ, NORMA • SCHWANGER, LAURA • SCOTT, ANDRE • SCOTT, ELIZABETH • SCOTT, LINCOLN • SEGHI, GARY • SEIDENFELD, MITCH • SEILKOP, CHRIS • SELINGER, DORY • SELLERS, THOMAS • SENN, CARYL • SESTANOVICH, THOMAS • SHANAHAN, WARREN • SHANNON, LEANN • SHAO, ZHEN • SHAVER, LEW • SHEPHERD, MARK • SHEWMAKE, CRAIG • SHIELDS, BOB • SICILIANO, JOHN • SIEGLE, JUDY • SKINNER, JENNY • SMITH, ALEX • SMITH, JARONNIE • SMITH, KURT • SMITH, MICHAEL • SNOUSE, SUE • SNOW, RANDY • SOARES, JOE • SODOMA, DEANNA • SOMMER, MANDY • SPEER, KIM • STAHL, RONALD • STANAGE, FREDERICK • STAWICKI, LESLAW • STENBACK, ERIC • STERLING, JAMES • STEWART, TROY • STINEMAN, LEE • STORER, HUGO • STOVALL, MIKE • STRAN, MARGARET • STRAUB, DIANE • STRICKLAND, MITCH • STUMP, JANA • STYPERK, JAY • SULLIVAN, JOE • SUNDERMAN, DEBRA • SUTTON, KELLY • SWAUGER, RICK • SZOTT, KEVIN • SZYMANSKI, ROBERT • TABER, MICHAEL • TAYLOR, GREG • TERCEY, JASON • TERPENNING, JAMES • TERRANOVA, TERESE • TETREAULT, PAUL • THEOBALD, JOHN • THOMPSON, JIM • THOMPSON, MARY • THOMPSON, STEVE • THOMSON, JIM • THOMSON, TIMOTHY • TOWNSEND, SCHOENA • TOZER, TIANA • TRETSCHOK, TIFFANY • TURNER, PEGGY • TUTHILL, EDWARD • TYREE-GROSS, RENEE • UPDEGROVE, BRAD • URSCHEL, KATHLEEN • VAN TASSELL, DWIGHT • VARGO, JAMES • VINYARD, TERRY • VOLPENTEST, TONY • WACHTELL, LYNN • WACKETT, KIRK • WADDELL, CAMILLE • WADDELL, CHRISTOPHER • WALLER, DARRYL • WALTERS, ANN • WALTERS, MIKE • WARD, RANDY • WATERS, JEAN • WEGEHAUPT, BILL • WEIDNER, JIMMY • WELCH, STEVE • WELLENREUTHER, SASCHA • WENING, JASON • WERNER, JEFF • WHITFORD, BOB • WILLIAMS, SID • WILLIS, TIM • WILLS, ROB • WINAND, ROSE • WINTER, KATHLEEN • WOLFE, JULIE • WOLFF, RICK • WYATT, MIKE • WYETH, DUNCAN • YATES, SPENCER • YOUNG, ALISTAIR • ZIMMERMAN, DANA • ZORN, TRISCHA • ZUKAS, JANE • **URUGUAY:** BERRUETA, FABIAN • HERRERO, JUAN • LLERENA, JORGE • ORTIZ, JORGE • ROLAN, ROLAN • **VENEZUELA:** DIAZ, LUIS • GARCIA, RAFAEL • NARANJO, JOSE • NEIRA, CESAR • SUAREZ, CARLOS • TORRES, LUIS • URDANETA, YOLMER • **YUGOSLAVIA:** ADZIC, SLOBODAN • ALEKSOV, RUZICA • CVETKOVIC, PREDRAG • DJURASINOVIC, ILIJA • KECMAN, SIMO • KESLER, ZLATKO • KRISANOVIC, NENAD • MIJATOVIC, MILAN • MLADENOVIC, DANIJELA • NIKOLIC, SLOBODAN • RAKONJAC, RADOMIR • SOBOT, DRAGO • STANKOVIC, VELIN • VUKSANOVIC, NADA • **ZAMBIA:** CHISAMBI, KESHI • GONDWE, GEORGE • SINKAMBA, LANGO • **ZIMBABWE:** GRIFFIN, JOE • MAKATHA, EDMOND • MASABEYA, MOFFAT • SWEETS, FRED • WICKHAM, ROBERT •

LEGACY SUPPORTERS

WENDI LEA LAWSON • WILLIAM H. HALKER IV • STELLA IRVING • DOUG CARTWRIGHT • LISA HANSON • JEAN-MARC CHAPUIS • EUGENIA SCOTT • MARCIA VAUGHN • MARK E. SHEPHERD • JUDY ASKINS • FRANK RODRIGUEZ • SUSAN KLEINE • ANN KARWATKA • WILLIAM B. MARIANES • ELLEN F. CAMPBELL • JEAN K. CAMPBELL • FEDERATION FRANCAISE HANDISPORT • DR. HORST STROHKENDL • JACK DIAMOND • RON LYKINS • DIANE PRI NOLE • TAKAO HAYASHI - GLORIA TOURIST INC • MARTY OWENS • BARBARA MULVANERTY • TOM FLEMING • JUDITH H. ANDERSON • GREGG PLATIS • JAN ORLOVSKY • ORLY ASHAIR - NORA BEVERAGES INC. • MARALYN WEST • ERIC BROWN • IVAR SISNIEGA CAMPBELL - COMISION NACIONAL DEL DEPORTE • BARRY KING - U.S. OLYMPIC COMMITTEE • RICARDO FERNANDEZ • TERRIE PURVIS • NANCY DRAHEIM • LAURA STANG • RAY CORMIER • JUDITH RINGI • TRISH TILLMAN • LINDA J. HENSON • SANDY WEAVER • SANDRA LANGFORD • ANKE BROK • JARED CROWDER • TERESA BRUNSON • FRANCES NEWTON • CINDI PICKETT • BARRY C. RAY • DR. BILLY JACK TALTON • CARLOS RODRIGUEZ • DIANE R. HOLCOMBE • CAROLYN GEIS, M.D. • JAHANNA JOYCE KNASIAK • DR. WILLIAM G. STOUT • ALEXANDRA MATHIESON • ILLINOIS DEPARTMENT OF REHABILITATION SERVICES RESOURCE CENTER LIBRARY • KEVIN KANESHIRO • S.W.A.A. • DON PAYNE - LIVING EARTH CRAFTS • VANITTA F. OLINGER • NORIO HEYA • NANCY HENDERSON • CHRIS COHEN • BILLY BEHLER • DR. R. FRANZ • BARBARA LEGG • DAVID LEGG • FRANCISCO PELAEZ DEL ESPINO • NANCY LEHRER • GLENN KRIEGER, M.D. • LADSON B. CHANDLER • VALERIE RUNYAN • ALICE ARMITAGE • ROBERT BLADWIN E.S. • ANNETTE T. QUINN • CONNIE CLEMANS • RODNEY E. BOLIN • ROBERT PRATHER • JOHN LONG • BETTY MCCURDY • MICHAEL BURDEN • JOHN CUNARD • LAWREN THOMAS • BETTY SHAW • JESSICA KAPPLER • ETHEL WITTER • TERRY MCGOVERN • DEREK MIKITA • JOHN MCCULLOUGH • BILLIE MITCHELL • BEN COOK • JENNIFER LAMAR • THERY WIDMER • KEVIN LEWIS • BETH L. DIETER • KRISTI KING • TIMOTHY P. LACY • ROGER SULLIVAN • HOFF • DR. MUSTAPHA DUROJAIYE • IZUMI TANAKA • WAYLAND MADDEN • CHRIS GREENE • JILL HOUK • PHILIP CRAVEN • CATHY KUEPPER • LORETTA SNOWDEN • JIM BACHTELER • ELIZABETH JACKSON • SUSIE CARR • EDDY N. PHILLIPS • RUDI CHAPPEL • KIRBY PLANEBETTER • DWIGHT B. COCHRAN • PAULO FERNANDO CRUZ • MOHAMED SHTEAWI • PAT FETTIG • LAURA WILT • JOHN MONTGOMERY • ANN MILLER • SALLY HARDIN • BELGIAN OLYMPIC COMMITTEE • FEDERATION SPORTIVE BELGE POUR HANDICAPES - LIGUE FRANCOPHONE • GLYNDA WOODARD • DESIREE BAIRD • LAURIE DUPONT • J. LASATER • GLEN HARRIS • KIM CRISP • VICTORIA E. WINTERS • LINDSAY IRVIN • FERNANDA ESPARZA • MARNIE PAYNE • ENRIQUE SANZ • SUSAN FOWLER • NEW SOUTH WALES SPORTS COUNCIL FOR THE DISABLED INC. • LAURA TRAPPITT • LISA CAPPS • SUE RABSON • STEVE WALTON • MICHAEL J. BROWN • VANESSA CREECH • KATHLEEN ROSS • TOM MILLER • ALBERT THOMAS BAUGH SR. • ALVIN WEAVER • YAGESH BHAM BHANI • NICK BRIGHAM • ROSS DAVID • DAVIDA SHENSKY • MICHAEL PERRY • GUNTER SCHUMANN • JAYNE JOHNSTON • CHRIS HODGINS • KAREN LAUFER • UZI PERLE • SPORT CENTER ILAN FOR DISABLED (ISRAEL) • JULIO RAMOS • DEBORAH TEMPLE • & BARB LITTLESTONE • ARCHIE ALLISON • BRETT NAGATA • JOYCE KOPETSKI • CHARLES MILLER • PARKE RUBLEE • CHANTAL BENOIT • WALTER R. THOMPSON • GEORGIA STATE UNIVERSITY CENTER FOR SPORTS MEDICINE • DONNA HOWARTH • R. GLENN MOSCOSO • WANDA E. GUY • RHONWYN FULCHER • CAROL EVANS • JULIE L. HERHOLZ • HOLLY J. POLLAK • CINDY LEIPOLD • JAKE RINGER • C. HERBERT STAHL • DEBORAH BUSWELL • MOLLY TAYLOR • JACQUELINE L. MACOMBER • RUSSEL LAUB • PATRICK JARVIS • KIYOSHI OKADA • J. CUBITT • PIEBEN RASMUSSEN - BIBLIOTEKET DANMARKS HOJSKOLE FOR LEGEMSOVELSER • OLAF BLANKENBURG • HANDICAPIDRAETTENS VIDENSCENTER • F.J. KLEIN • ADRIANE LEROY • RON LUXEMBURG • ANN E. LARY • CHARLENE WICKS • C. RAY MCCULLY • MARK MOON • NEW KEY RODGERS • MARY THOMAS F. HOGAN III • DOUG CONYERS • DONALD S. PETERS • JIM ADAMS • DAVID AVERY • DENNIS J. WEBB • ANN WEBB • DOUG KEIM • ANNETTE CHAMBERLIN • GRACE YANG • FRED IFFLAND • BOB GUBAR • DONNA CHARETTE • EDWARD L. SCHROEDER • PATTI SMITH • SHARON L. PLANT • INGA FAGRELL • BARB KING • PABLO MURPHY • ELNETTA MITCHELL • PAT ANGELELLI • GREGG LAUER • KEN WILLIS • PAM SANGUINETTI • SOUVONG • PEGGY D. HINES • GEORGE KOLOMBATOVICH • GEORGE MCKNIGHT • ERNEST KEY • LORNA MARTIN • CLAUDINE SHERRILL • JOHN MICHAEL • LISA CAROLLO • PATTI HOGLE • MARIANNE HANSEN • CINDY MCKNIGHT • CHUCK SCHADL • PRISCILLA RIKE • ALAN PERRY • RACHEL VINCENT • JOSH DEISENROTH • ARIC FINE • TASHA KAPLAN • BECKY AZLEE • JESSIE M. HILL • LYN ROURKE • G. BARTH • JAY LINDSEY • GEORGE LEPORTE • ERIC W. O'BRIEN • DONALD W. MATHIS • AUSTIN NOBLINAGA • KATHY ALGER • JOHN DESIMINI • ANNE ALLEN • GLENDA G. ORTH • JOHN M. SIKORA - HEALTHSOUTH HARMARVILLE REHABILITATION HOSPITAL • DOUG FREER • THOMAS DREISEIS • MAXAM BOELY • LINDA KUTROWSKI • KATHRYN SCHRADER • LORNA SNOW • NATHALIE MINARD • TERESA A. WRIGHT • VIRGINIA VAZIN • ADRIENNE S. WIGGIN • SUSAN L. REDDAWAY • TATTERED COVER BOOK STORE • CLAUDIA GROSS • SHANNON WILKINSON • DIANE MATHEWS • COREY ELIZABETH BROWN • DEBRA WITHERSPOON • CHARLES J. EBERWINE • ALLISON GATES • MARK SHUTTLEWORTH • GEORGE FEINBERG • BILL PASCHKE • WINN CARROLL • KRISTIN KRASSEN • KELLY WINTER • LORETTA ROBITALLE • LAURA S. TIMPERIO • STEPHEN FARKUS • DANNY BROWN • TAKANORI TSURUHARA - JAPANESE SPORTS ASSOCIATION FOR THE DISABLED • TOM & JEANE KNICK • PEGGY POLAND • MICHELLE LANGLEY • BARBARA ROACH • NANCY ORNSTEIN • GIGI WINGATE • BARBARA YOSS • KELLY CARSON • JACK TODD • BRAND • DEREK COTTON • MARTIN AGUILERA • CAMILLA FABRITIUS • BRYAN MASI • SHIRLEY LOCKMAN • STACEY MCPHERSON-RICE • DICK ARNOLD • MEREDITH J. MCKIM • JOE CLARK • J. MERCER • SIBYL LANGLEY • DEBORAH DAVIS • E. JEHEE - MINISTRY OF HEALTH, WELFARE AND SPORTS • JOELLE RIVARD • ELLEN DE LANGE • NIKOLAI ZAITCHKOV - PARALYMPIC COMMITTEE (BELARUS) • ROBERT SCARFF • LAUNEL J. SCOTT • WILLIAM CHEUNG • SHARON M ULLINS • WILL VAN DE KIMMENADE • LOUIS LOBE • BRET BOUDA • DAVID EULITT - THE TOPEKA CAPITAL-JOURNAL • ALICE BRUTSCHER • FRANK SMITH • TRAVIS C. MALOY • PETE KAMMER • SUZY KLING • RICHARD CHISHOLM • CHARLY SCHWARTZ - DONNA BUSH - STEPHANIE BUCKLEY • DR. STUART SANDERS • MIKE WILLIAMS • VERONICA BURGESS • DONNA ARMITAGE • CATCH CATCHINGS • CHRIS SPARKS • HERB MORRIS • ANDREA JOHNSON • CYNTHIA WILSON • ED HARRIS - NATIONAL SPORTS FOUNDATION (U.S.) • MARJORIE STANSEL • DUSTIN LONG • THEODORA GORDON • GEORGE BAKER • BUTCH STANPHILL • STEVE MCKANNA • SANDY EMERSON • TOM MCWHORTER • JEAN SORENSON • DENISE BONENBERGER • STACEY PARSONS • JEANE WHITTENBURG • LYMAN JOHNSON • LISA WITHAM • RACHEL GOTT • ROSE MARY WEAVER • KATHY LAPORTE • MELL ROBINSON • FRITZ ELLMANN • MARCELLE C. WATKINS • PAUL JONES • KAMAL FARAH • BALFOURA LEVINE • WILLIAM CONLEY • SAULO KATCHER • SARAH DOMBY • BETH HEFFERNAN • HENRY M. ENTERLINE, JR. • MICHAEL ATKINSON • CHRISTINE PETERS • HJUDIY ARONSMEIER - OREGON GAMES DISABILITY SPORTS • CAROLY RICH • LOUVENIA WHITAKER • DANIELLE BLANKENSHIP • WILMA ARRINGTON • KAREN CASERTA • F.A. CAVATAIO • BRUCE CALDWELL • MICHAEL BICKMAN • JOAN MATTHEWS • GERHARD MUELLER • JANALEE REINEKE LYTH • MARILYN KEY • SUE E. FELDKAMP • ED POOLE • A.L. HOAGLAND, SR. • BARB DESHETLER • CATHRYN DUBOW • MARCI J. DESART • RUTHANN MOLLOY • RON KAGAN • BARBARA BARER • MONIKA BAUER • RICK CONYERS • SARAH WOELZ • SUSAN KLEINE • TRACI LEWALLEN • TRENT TRUMP • ELLEN NOWICKI • ANNETTE GORTNEY • MR. & MRS. D. HOUGH • BARBARA ANN CHAMBERS • JILL D. GROEZINGER • JENNIFER MCCLEARY • MO TADAYON • THELMA ROBERTS • NEIL FOSTER • RACHEL SMITH • RONNIE MOON • CHERRYMAE A. AROMAS • DEBORAH DAVIS • STEVE OWEN • BILL TEAGUE • LARRY MCDANIEL • GENE WATKINS, JR. • CHRISTINE BARRETT • PATRICIA B. FORTE • JANET HARRIS • JONATHAN REESER • JESSICA SHERRY • J. ADAM BECKMAN • DENISE SETTLE • JACK & TERESA HUGHES • TAMMY G. LAPREAD • DEBORAH DAWSON • SUSAN FELDMAN • JOANN BOHAM • NANCY GROVES • EVETTE M. WILLIAMS • ED CRAVER • AMIE NILSEN • NANCY LOU SEIFERT • DETLEV VON NOTTBECK • DORRIT DE DEMETER • TRISH BOLTON - ALBERT DOEVE • DONNA C. WEIDLER • CHUCK EDWARDS • RENEE VAUGHN • GERD FREUND - GERMAN CONSULATE GENERAL ATLANTA • HOLLY DEWITT • LINDSAY R. FOLEY • SONIA KUNIANSKY • JANE A. BOYD • DANA FIELDS • GREG FLINDERS • JANICE TETREAULT • PAULA BROWN • SANDRA JUSTICE • REBECCA PEDRICK • JON NIEMEYER • MICHAEL A. JOYCE • RICK FORTINI • DEBORAH TEMPLE • LEITA COWART • LYNETTE BLACK • PAT ALMY • ANGELA PAGE • EILEEN TURKO • DUNCAN SEYMOUR • DAWNENE GILNER • ROBERT WELLS • RITSY SMITH • MICHAEL WATSON • HENRY MCLAFTY • ROGERIA THOMAS • DONALD MCFARLANE • LORA BETH SATTERLY • HEATHER LOVELESS • FRANCES CURTISS • PAMELA OLIVER • STEPHANIE MARCHANT • MARIE JOHNSON • JOHN BEAUBE - BEAUBE-DAVIS INTERNATIONAL • MARY TILGHMAN • LAWRENCE WEBB • TOM MONIE • PHIL THOMPSON • ANN EZZELL • JULIANNE RIVERA • TONY CALENDER • THERESA WAGONER • TRACY VIDEON • JIM DUNCAN • BERT MACWILLIAMS • DON O'NEILL • SARAH S. ANDREWS • JOE LEWIS • EVE JONES • ANN DENNISON • MARGARET KLEIMAN • TAWNI MCBEE • STEPHEN KEARNEY • KAREN FOSTER • JIM HITE • EMI VISHOOT • KATHLENE FARNSWORTH • SHERON M. MEYERS • KIBBIE RICHARDSON • ROSALBA GIORCELLI • JOELLE RIVARD • FRIEDHELM JULIUS BEUCHER • ANTONIO PEREZ-HERRERO • HELMI L. WAITS - MSL SOFTWARE • PATSY A. GETZ • L.D. BLEDSOE • ALISON BURCHELL • JOHN TINETTI • COMITE PARALIMPICO BRASILEIRO • J. STEVE HILL • KAZUO SHIMIZU - THE PHOTO SERVICE ONE • FREDRIK KVELL • JOHN S. (JOCK) MURRAY • HANS LINDSTROM • CATHI MCMAHAN • JILL WHALEN • IRENE RAMOS • HILYARD COMMUNITY CENTRE (OREGON) • PAUL RITTLER • JAYNE CRESCIMBENI • JAMES K. SMITH • WAYNE GULLETT • PIERRE PINELLI • BECKY BROWN • LOUIS BROWN • ELIZABETH WILLIAMS • CANDICE BRUECK • ROBERT MARCUS • RICHELLE BENJAMIN • JOSHUA SACCA • ROBERT WOODS • MARY ANN SORICE • MARK PONZILLO • CHRISTIAN CHARLOTTE • RICKY SOSEBEE • ROBERT ITO • DAVID LEE • KATHY ZOLAD • MARC NADEL • BOB MCLENDON • KRISTIN KANY • VIRGINIA STANTON • DUANE & MARILYN ELDREDGE • NEIL FRITSCH • DEBORAH P. HIGHTOWER • JOHN A. MORGAN, II • MYRNA BESCHER • WALTER MASON • SANDY DYAR • APRIL C. SIMS • FAE GOLDSMITH • SANDY HOLLAK • SUSAN GREENWALD • PATRICIA HALL • JEFFY M. RAGSDALE • EVERLY LEWIS • SONJA TAYLOR • LIEVE VAN KERKHOVE • KELLY JOHNSON - SHEPHERD CENTER • WILLIAM ACORN • JERRY CLARKE • JAMES RONAI • JAMES H. SHEPHERD, JR. • DAVE DOOLITTLE • ROSEMARY GALE • LJILJANA LJUBISIC • JEFF MILLER • RUSSELL A. KO • REIKO YOSHIDA • IAN G. WING • LINDA VOYLES • THE LENYK FAMILY • STEPHANIE BEACH • KIRK BAUER • CAROLYN KOCH • DANNY SMITH • RICHARD MANN • T.E. DRYGAS • NANCY LAFONTAINE • MARK MURRAY • KRISTI M. BAER • REBECCA J. CLIFTON • ROBERT PATTON • RON SPENLAU • VIRGINIA M. HASKINS • INGRID M. KANICS • ELLEN SMITH • RICHARD T. BEOHM • KATHY CURTIS • SHELDON BURNS • GEORGE BABCOCK • ERIC FORSYTHE • BILL TAYLOR • KARINE MEADOR • JO-ELLEN ROSS • JOAN SAVOLT • MICKIE CHRONISTER • LENAUSTO AMAMAGAS • COLETTE BOURGONJE • RUSCONI GIUSEPPE • KAREN LEINAAR • LISA CAPE • ALOYZE SHAW • THE FARRELL FAMILY • JULIE & DAN CLARK • THE KELLEY FAMILY • DREW HITTENBERGER - DREW HITTENBERGER & ASSOCIATES • JOSEPH D. MELLON • MARCEE HOPPER • TANNI GREY • HIROMI KATAYANAGI - JAPAN WELFARE TIMES • PATRICK JARVIS • JACQUELINE L. MACOMBER • DAVIDA SHENSKY • JOYCE TROUT • JOSEPH TERPENNING • AIMEE BRUDER • JIM HARRISON • SANDY SCOGGINS • RODGER M. ROBERTS • RICARDO OLIVER • BARB MONTEMURRO • KATHERINE CARTER • DR. HOWARD C. PETERSON, JR. • MARALYN WEST • KIYOSHI OKADA • J. CUBITT • GAY KOOPMAN • WANDA E. GUY • RHONWYN FULCHER • CAROL EVANS • JULIE L. HERHOLZ • ANGELIQUE C. MIZERA • HOLLY J. POLLAK • JOYCE RINGER • C. HERBERT STAHL • DEBORAH BUSWELL • MOLLY TAYLOR • RUSSEL LAUB • MARTY OWENS • CATHRYN DUBOW • DARLENE BOYES - CALGARY PARKS & RECREATION • DORTE STOEURING • BETH WATKINS • W.S. POTTER • CHAD DEAL • KENDRA OHAMA • A. BENJAMIN • JOHN J. PESCE • UNITED CEREBRAL PALSY OF MINNESOTA • CYNTHIA BURKHOUR • MARGARET SANDERSON • JERRY MCCOLE • U.S. ORGANIZATION FOR DISABLED ATHLETES • UNITED CEREBRAL PALSY (OAKLAND) • CHRISTOPHER HILL • MARCIA J. DECAMP • JESSE DIODATI - LANGSTAFF SECONDARY SCHOOL • ELIZABETH COLE • F.H. (SAM) FROES - INSTITUTE FOR MEDICINE AND ADVANCED TECHNOLOGIES (BRITISH COLUMBIA) • STEVE VONWORDEHEIM • JOHN A. IREY • MARGARET BARLOW • WENDY RHODES • ERICH MENGER III • HOLVIN A. BALTODAURO • ANA SRSEN • STEVE HINSON • JOSEPH TERPENNING • RODGER M. ROBERTS • DAVID J. PIRES, JR. • KELLY O'NIEL • GARY ALPART • STIDEVER • KELLY STERLING • DEBORAH DAVIS • ANNE KILPATRICK • DAVID EWING • G.M. LOWE • R.A. MORGAN • KEN SOWDEN • ALAN B. GOLDBERG • C.M.A. SIMON • CANADIAN PARALYMPIC COMMITTEE • BILL & BETTY LOUSHIN • KATHI THOMPSON • HEATHER LESCH • JOHN JOHNSON • BERNIE FISTE • BRIAN NORDEN • LAUREN ROSEN • DR. LORRAINE BLOOMQUIST - DEPARTMENT OF PHYSICAL EDUCATION & EXERCISE SCIENCE • CONSTANCE HEAD • ELLEN BRIGGS • ROSANNA ROWELL-UNSWORTH • BARBARA LEGG • DAVID LEGG • TONY PHARR • MIKE SCHMIDT • JENE STARNER • PASCALE BELANGER • PETER BURNETT • DAVID A. SAMPSON • CONNIE CROSS • DAVID J. PIRES, JR. • LISA BOEVERS • SUSAN B. GREEN • DON CARROLL • LINDA NETHERTON • ROD MYERS • N. DIANNE GARTON • HELEN C. BRANSON • CARL STIFEL • LEE WOLF • STEPHANI VICTOR • JIM ROGERS - ORTHOTIC & PROSTHETIC ASSOCIATION • K. TANTIVEJKUL • III • DAVID L. THURBER • SUSAN R. BARTON • RENEE LEHMAN • NANCY BLAKE • JACKIE MACOMBER • SPINA BIFIDA & HYDROCEPHALUS ASSOCIATION OF ONTARIO • GAIL M. DRUMMER • DARREN HAMMOND • CONNY DIETZ • SUSAN SHARP • DEBORAH DAVIS • S. MCALLISTER • BRENDA F. LOWE • THOMAS L. ABRAHAMS • KATHLEEN KENNEDY • GRANT A. PEACOCK • ROD MYERS • MARY POWELL • NELSON B. MCDONALD • ORTHOTIC-PROSTHETIC DESIGN INC. • TOM STOKES • DIRECT CENTER FOR INDEPENDENCE, INC. • PROSTHETIC CARE INC. • THOMAS SHELTON • ROSLYN SKELTON • CHRISTIE SKELTON • ROBERT STOREY • PAMELA THOMPSON • WALTER & ELIZABETH THURING • SHERRI TROXCLAIR • HERMAN VAN COPPENHOLLE • MARK WARNER • CYNTHIA G. WEAVER • MARK WELLMAN • CAROL PRAXMARER • BARB WILHITE & LORI GOLDENBERG • PAWEL ZBIERANOWSKI • SANDY SCOGGINS • THOMAS FAMILY CHIROPRACTIC • NANCY STANGE • HANDI HOTLINE • KHALID JLIDAT • RICHARD S. MORETON, JR. • A.J. JONES • MELODY COLEMAN & BUDDY COLEMAN • MICHAEL & SHANNON DEMPSEY • NAOMI DEMPSEY • LORRAINE DOLL-TEPPER • PETER EDSTROM • STEVEN FARROW • J.S. FREEBODY • CHARLES C. GRAHAM • JUDITH D. HOOK • MAUREEN FRANCIS HOPKINS • JONATHON W. HUFF • ALICE HUGHES • CHRISTINE S. JOHNSON • PAMELA & FRANK JOHNSON • SUE KAYE • KELSEY & BARBARA KIRK • TIMOTHY KISTNER • SUSAN COOPER LABHARD • TERRY HENDERSON • JOYCE & ROBERT JANTZI • JEFF UNDERWOOD - LAKESHORE FOUNDATION • THE LAKESHORE FOUNDATION • WILLIAM P. ACKER, III • TOM ANGELILLO • WALTER M. BEAUFORT, JR. - WILLIAM J. BILLINGSLEY - JON J. BLANKENSHIP, PH.D. - MRS. F. DIXON BROOKE, JR. - ROBERT O. BURTON - VINCENT C. CAPONI - JENNIFER CHANDLER-JONES - ROBERT M. COUCH - MRS. LUTHER E. CRANFORD, JR. - BILL CRAWFORD - STEWART M. DANSBY - DERROL DAWKINS, M.D. - JAMES H. EMACK, SR. - ANTOINETTE SMITH EPPS - JOHN M. FORNEY - JAMES P. HAYES, JR. - DANIEL C. LANGFORD - FRANK M. LEE - CHARLES E. MCCRARY - HONORABLE BARRY R. MCCULLEY - MRS. JESSE E. MILLER - W.T. GOODLOE RUTLAND - FRED SINGTON - MICHAEL E. STEPHENS - LARRY D. STRIPLIN, JR. - ROBERT A. WASON, IV - THOMAS K. YARDLEY • SARA T. EVANS • SONIA MARIA RIBEIRO - THOR E. KLEPPE - THOMAS C. STRICKLAND • BRIAN A. PEACEMAN • ANA MARIA FONSECA TEIXEIRA • PHILIP GARDNER • ANN, JERRY & BRYAN LAM • STEPHEN LEVINE • LARRY STROM • BOB LOPEZ • DUNCAN MCCLUSKEY • MILLEDGEVILLE ORTHOTICS • CINDY MILLER & MARION BLAKELEY • PARSONS & ASSOCIATES - JESSICA PRESPERIN PEDERSEN • KATHLEEN M. PEEK • ROBERTO PENA • RACHEL POTTER • ED MARKSON • MARIS PARMARTER • VALLEY BAPTIST MEDICAL CENTER • SANDY ABERCROMBIE • JILL FARMER • LISA GREEN • SHRINERS HOSPITALS - GREENVILLE UNIT • TOM HENLEY • T.E. DRYGAS • IAN C. CHAFEE • JIM BURKE • STEVE BECKETT • JUDY AUKWARD • STEPHANIE VICTOR • BARB TRADER • DALTON M. STEELE • MARISA D. CHERMAN • HELEN C. BRANSON - HAJIME MORITA - BIBAI ROSAI HOSPITAL • DAVY LIN • JACKIE QUESENBERRY • KEN GINHAM - NEW SOUTH WALES SPORTS COUNCIL FOR THE DISABLED • ELLA KARRIS • VANESSA SIEGEL • CHRISTOPHER HOOD • E.J. SCHIPPER • MICHAEL A. WITT, M.D. • KATHLEEN KENNEDY • HANS-PETER ZIEGLER • JUDI MCCOY • ICHIRO MOMURA • RUSCONI GIUSEPPE • ED LAKOWSKI • DAVID LEGA • MARIO ANTONIO ORTIZ GARCIA • BETH MOORE • ROSIE O'NEILL • MARK T. RAVENSCRAFT • THE REFERT FAMILY • DORTE STOEVRING • BRAD WEICHERT • MARJORIE BOESHANS • MARTIN KUDLACEK • ELISABETH DE MATTOS • DR. A. AL-MATAR • JOAN FINCH • KAZUHIKO NAKAGAWA • MICHAEL HEINRICH • KAZU IMAI • TERESA BAKER • THOMAS & SUSAN BECKE - CALUMET REHABILITATION SERVICES INC. • KATHY MCLAUGHLIN • JACK W. DEMPSEY • CATHY DARGUE • COZY DORTON • JIM HARRISON • LISA YAMASAKI • PATTY KING • DEBBI GOLDEN • JERRY BAYLOCK, JR. • DON GREENBLATT • SUSAN R. BARTON • GINA RAIN • MARY ANN DOBUCKI • NANCY LAUREN • RON BIELECKI, JR. • BETH SIMMONS • GEORGE STEVENS • THOMAS L. ABRAMS • HOBBY NEWS NOTE • EDMUND O. NOSEGBE • DONNA NIETHE • RHONDA BROWNING • DOUGLAS MINERL • PETER BURNETT • DAVID EULITT • AUSTIN BAKER • FREDERICK T. KLINGBEIL, M.D. • K. TANTIVEJKUL • TONY CINQUE - SYDNEY 200 PARALYMPIC GAMES • A. BERYL BRICKMAN • GEORGIA CHAMPION • MICHAEL MOLLGAARD NIELSEN - DANISH SPORTS ORGANISATION FOR DISABLED • KATHERINE CARTER • THOMAS INE GEDDES • RONALD LUBLINK • BEN T. JORDAN, III • NANCY KLEMENTICH • ROBERT D. SCHRADEL • TONY VAN DER WAARDE • GRANT A. PEACOCK, III • MARTIN MILLER • CHRISTY MCALLISTER • JON DECKER • BEN VAUGHN • JAPAN SUN INDUSTRIES • NINA MARITA WIKEN GRANAAS • CONNIE CROSS • JEAN STONE - BWSF GUTTMANN SPORTS CENTRE • DANIEL WOLFF • MARALYN WEST • THOMAS E. CROSS • GERALD R. METRO • VALERIE ALLEN • CLAUDIO ARRIGONIS • ASOCIACION MEXICANA DE MEDALLISTAS PARALYMPICOS • ATLANTA PROSTHETICS, INC. • BIANCA BRETE • OSTR PROF. HASLINGER FRANZ - BUNDES-BLINDENERZ. INST. • CARL STIFEL • BORIS GORJANC • KARIN LENTZ • KARL VILHELM NIELSEN • JEAN STONE - BWSF GUTTMANN SPORTS CENTRE • DANIEL WOLFF • MARALYN WEST • THOMAS E. CROSS • GERALD R. METRO • VOGT FAMILY • JERRY L. RICHARDSON • KATSUKO SUZUKI • KATIE WENKMAN • NEIL R. FOSTER • FRANKLIN A. AGUILO • FALLER PHOTOGRAPHICS • T.L. WOOD • JODI LITTLESTONE • JOSEPH D. MELLON • FAYE BLACKWOOD • ALEXANDRA MATHIESON • UZI PERLE • PATRICE THOMPSON • NEWTON M. GALLOWAY • SANDEE ROGERS • BILL CARNEY • DEBRA R. RUNKLE • SARA M. WERNER • JEFF ARDIS • JOHAN HAGLUND • DONNA WEIDLER • DAVID A. SAMPSON • RENEE LEHMAN • VALERIE WAYDA • N. DIANNE GARTON • KATHRYN M. REICH • RACHEL J. GOTT • EILEEN M. TURKO • SCOTT N. SHELAR • MARTIN AGUILERA • KATHLEEN ROSS • CENTER FOR INDEPENDENT LIVING - SW PENNSYLVANIA • W. HERB STEET • SEMO ALLIANCE FOR DISABILITY INDEPENDENCE • NANCY FORD • CHAIR GINGER - AREA CHILD AMPUTEE CENTER • KURT SMITH • MILLER-DWAN MEDICAL CENTER • RIKKI S. EPSTEIN - NATIONAL THERAPEUTIC RECREATION SOCIETY • CHANNEL ISLAND PROSTHETICS INC. • ROY BROSWELL - WARM SPRINGS REHABILITATION HOSPITAL • CAROL SAXTON • GUS SORENSON • JUDY STANTON - SHEPHERD CENTER • SANFORD S. GLASSNER • W. DAVID LUIKAART • STEVEN BUDRICK • JOEL HIRSCHFELD • KRISTINA M. DANCHETZ • F.T. LEHMAN • MAURICE LAPLANTE • SZILVIA PIEREN • JACKIE MACOMBER • CINDI PICKETT • LEE WOLF • FRED KOCH • ELIZABETH TURNER • BRENDA F. LOWE • ROBIN WENNEKER • ROSEMARY GALE • JOACHIM SCHWENDTNER • LISA BOEVERS • DR. CRISTINA RIERA • SUSAN FELDMAN • BRADLEY A. BEARD • JO ANN M. RUF • RICHARD R. THOMPSON • PETER J. MILNE • PROS-TECH, INC. • MICHAEL GOLDSTEIN • DR. HOWARD C. PETERSON, JR. • GAIL DUMMER • MARY LE BLANC • FRANK MATSON • PATRICIA SCHELL • JENNY ECKHARDT • JACK R. WALTER • LINDA MEYERS • ALAN TOMASKO • SPINA BIFIDA AND HYDROCEPHALUS ASSOCIATION OF ONTARIO • GABRIELLA NEGY • KURT FARNINGTON • RON DAVID • GREG MEDARA • JAMES THOMPSON • BREAKING DOWN BARRIERS AN INDEPENDENT LIVING CENTER • BARBARA DOWNIE • D. FRANK • KIMBERLEY SMITH • LIZ WILSON • JOYCE KOPETSKI • JOAN LANGLEY • INDEPENDENT LIVING RESOURCE CENTRE • WENDY WORSFORD - THAMES VALLEY CHILDREN'S CENTRE • LINDA HAMILTON • DEBRA HESSE - COLORADO EASTER SEALS • NIAGARA FRONTIER CENTER FOR INDEPENDENT LIVING • LAVERNE ALLEN-BARKER • ALLEN ORTHOTICS & PROSTHETICS, INC. • LYLIAN MELENDEZ - UNITED CEREBRAL PALSY RECREATION • LIVING INDEPENDENCE FOR EVERYONE, INC. • LEIMKUEHLER INC. • ROBERT LEIMKUEHLER • JOE KSIASKIEWICZ • JANET A. SEAMAN • UNITED CEREBRAL PALSY S. CENTRAL WISCONSIN • OPPORTUNITIES FOR ACCESS "A CENTER FOR INDEPENDENT LIVING" • CENTER FOR INDEPENDENT LIVING OF CENTRAL PENNSYLVANIA • SUSAN MULVEY - THE EASTER SEAL SOCIETY OF VIRGINIA • DOUG MAYES • ANDY CHASANOFF - CHILDREN'S SPECIALIZED HOSPITAL • MR. R. KONING • DEENA SCORETZ • EXOR INTERNATIONAL INC. • JEFFREY JONES - RIC • RANDALL L. BRADDOMMA • PAUL DIBELLO - NATIONAL SPORTS CENTER FOR DISABLED • THOMAS RICHEY • TOM GRAZIANI • CARMENIA E. MAY • TAKAO HAYASHI - GLORIA TOURIST INC. • SUSAN B. GREENFIELD • DEBRA SANDERS - NOVACARE SABOLICH • BETTY OKAMURA - US DEPARTMENT OF VETERAN'S AFFAIRS • SHELLEY WILLIAMS • CHRISTIAN SAQUES • EDWIN COLE • MINDY ELLIS • BOB BAYLEY • CHRIS SIMON - BRITISH PARALYMPIC ASSOCIATION • KELLY ASMUSSEN • BOB FIERMAN • HOWARD & MARY PHILLIPS • CAROLE NICHOLSON • JANET KLION • KAREN JOHNSON • WAYLAND R. MADDEN • DANIEL SULLIVAN • BARRY BRASS • ROBERT BINDER • TIM CLARK • NANCY MCMILLAN • DR. RONALD HONEYCUTT • ANNE LEOTA HART • BRUCE TEFFETELLER • ROBERT MONASTER • MARC ANDERSON • MARY-JO CORBETT • ANN SFEN • JAI K. RANJAFFA • LINDA MAIER • BRAD FULLERTON • GUAN ABREGO • KARIN SEGAL • PETRA SLIEGER - DOMINO